PELICAN BOOKS

T. S. ELIOT

Allen Tate, who was born in 1899, is Regents'
Professor Emeritus at the University of Minnesota. He was educated at Vanderbilt University,
where he gained a B.A. in 1922. He won the Bollingen Prize for Poetry in 1956 and the Gold
Medal of the Dante Society of Florence in 1962,
and in 1963 he was the recipient of a $5,000
Fellowship of the Academy of American Poets.
In 1958–9 he was Fulbright Professor at Oxford
University. He is a member of the American
Academy of Arts and Letters. The nineteen
volumes of which he is author include *The Fathers*,
a novel, (1938, published in Penguins 1969), *On
the Limits of Poetry* (1948), *Poems* (1960), *Essays
of Four Decades* (1969) and *The Swimmers and
Other Selected Poems* (1970).

T. S. ELIOT

THE MAN AND HIS WORK

~~~~~~~~~~

Edited by Allen Tate

PENGUIN BOOKS
IN ASSOCIATION WITH
CHATTO & WINDUS

Penguin Books Ltd, Harmondsworth, Middlesex, England
Penguin Books Australia Ltd, Ringwood, Victoria, Australia

—

First published in the U.S.A. 1966
Published in Great Britain by Chatto & Windus 1967
Published in Penguin Books 1971

—

Made and printed in Great Britain
by Richard Clay (The Chaucer Press), Ltd,
Bungay, Suffolk
Set in Linotype Plantin

CONTENTS

CONTENTS

ON T.S.E.

Notes for a talk at the Institute of Contemporary Arts,
London, 29 June 1965

By I. A. Richards

IN talking of a writer we have known – and to those to whom
he has mattered – how can we speak without feeling that he
himself is by far the most important part of the audience? As
indeed he is, not in any supernatural or transcendent sense, but
as represented here, now, in minds which are in a measure
what they are through him, so that in their judgement and
reflection he is active. Of no one is this more true than of
T.S.E. In one degree or another we are all products of his
work.

My College, Magdalene College, Cambridge, has been
happy through the last half-century in a succession of poets as
honorary fellows: Thomas Hardy, Rudyard Kipling, T.S.E.
I have felt this sense of presence most *dauntingly* with Kipling, remembering 'The Appeal' which T.S.E. put at the end
of his *A Choice of Kipling's Verse*.

> If I have given you delight
>   By aught that I have done
> Let me lie quiet in that night
>   Which shall be yours anon:
> And for the little, little span
>   The dead are borne in mind,
> Seek not to question other than
>   The books I leave behind.

T.S.E.'s is a more benign, a more placable, but not a less controlling presence.

Would it not be an excellent thing if this sense of presence,
impelling one to speak only as though the author were here at
one's side listening to one's every inflection, could become a

universal rule in criticism? How it would help with the two main occupational diseases of what is too often a belittling trade: I mean our impudence and our vanity. But I rebuke myself for even referring to that unhappy side of criticism in talking of one who was so much the reverse of petty: generous and forbearing beyond easy belief.

This is a commemorative occasion. Recollections will be in place. So will a few examples of those of T.S.E.'s critical observations which seem to help most towards ... well, what? *Toward* or *towards*? Should it be *to'ard* or *towards*? I remember consulting T.S.E. about these two words. It was this sort of point which brought out the wide range of considerations (all the night sky seeming to bear upon it) and the free swing of the deliberation by which he guided his preferences. Just what would the word be trying to do in the place where it would be used and how would its sound most help *that*? Maybe, when it knows what it is pointing to, it can best be *to'ard*; and when it doesn't, *towards*?

Few minds have more enjoyed the process of pondering a discrimination: pondering it rather than formulating it or maintaining it, though he could be reckless in formulation as well as stubborn. And with a formidable air of authority, a deep firmness in the utterance, even in those early days. The sense of that goes back to my first meetings with him in 1920 in Cambridge. There were two concerns behind those meetings. The poetry: *Ara Vos Prec*. I remember sunlight on those large, fine pages and a breathless exhilaration as I came away with it – unable NOT to read it in the Market Place after happening on it in Galloway & Porter's bookshop – spreading the resplendent thing open: lost in wonder and strangeness and delight. I suppose somebody must have talked to me of him and told me he was in a bank and about his critical writings. But I don't recall being, in those early days, much concerned with his criticism – no, only with the poetry and almost at once with the idea that he would be *the one hope* for the then brand-new English Tripos. I was just beginning to lecture for it. And I was soon full of dreams of somehow winkling Eliot out of his bank and annexing him to Cambridge.

From the English Tripos angle I still believe *that* was the best idea there ever was. But how dangerous ideas are! Cambridge might have prevented there being any more poetry! I think something of this may have been in T.S.E.'s own head, when, the second time I saw him, I 'sounded him out'. What a phrase! I expect I did it as delicately as any bulldozer. We had perhaps had twenty minutes' conversation: 'conversation' is the word – he being utterly and perfectly bank-like, as composed and cautious as a cat, and I, perhaps, like some sort of enthusiastic dog. 'No, he wasn't at all sure that an academic life would be what he would choose.' How strange that this lapsed academic should have provided so much fodder for academics! We of the young English Tripos in our benevolent excitement thought of teaching English literature as very Heaven. So this quiet, cool, and cagey stance impressed me then beyond all words. We none of us had the least notion of the Harvard opening he had in its department of philosophy. Indeed we knew fantastically little about him. What occupied most of our mental vision of him was the fact that this great new poet (*O poor, poor man!*) was stuck in a bank: forced to placate Coleridge's 'two giants leagued together ... whose names are BREAD & CHEESE' – forced to stave off C. K. Ogden's 'hand-to-mouth disease' – by adding up figures all day.

In spite of his disappointingly detached attitude to the English Tripos, it was not long before I was with him in his bank. All very surprising. I was not a bit sure how you called on a junior member of a banking staff in Queen Henrietta Street, I think it was. But T.S.E. was reassuring: 'Just ask for me and they will show you.' What they showed me was a figure stooping, very like a dark bird in a feeder, over a big table covered with all sorts and sizes of foreign correspondence. The big table almost entirely filled a little room under the street. Within a foot of our heads when we stood were the thick, green glass squares of the pavement on which hammered all but incessantly the heels of the passers-by. There was just room for two perches beside the table.

Perhaps it was those heels striking – they didn't use rubber so much in those days – above our heads. Anyhow, this was the time, I think, that I learned that T.S.E. had done a good deal of extension lecturing before joining the bank. Lecturing among other things on poetry. The most successful poem to give an audience, he told me, was T. E. Hulme's 'Fantasia of a Fallen Gentleman on the Embankment'.

> Once, in finesse of fiddles found I ecstasy,
> In a flash of gold heels on the hard pavement.
> Now see I
> That warmth's very stuff of poesy.
> Oh, God, make small
> The old star-eaten blanket of the sky,
> That I may fold it round me and in comfort lie.

Not only good for an audience, but a very good poem, he told me. I agreed and I agree. Don't you think so, too?

What was he doing there under the pavement? Setting in order the affairs of the late Houston Stewart Chamberlain, one of the philosophic fathers of fascism. A multi-lingual correspondence of the utmost complication, I gathered. Not the adding up of figures but a big, long headache of sorting out a highly tangled story.

By accident shortly afterwards I got the bank's view (or at least one of the bank's views) on 'our young Mr Eliot'. I came across a shrewd, kindly, and charming man (up at Arolla in the Swiss Alps, it was) who turned out to be a high senior official in that very Queen Henrietta Street focus of the great bank's far-flung activities. When he learned that I knew T.S.E., I could see that he was getting ready at once to shape a question. Something in his hesitant approach made me a little wary in my turn.

MR W.: You know him, I suppose, as a literary man, as a writer and ... er ... and ... er ... as a poet?

I.A.R.: Yes, he's very well known, you know, as a critic, and as a poet.

MR W.: Tell me, if you will – you won't mind my asking, will you? Tell me, is he, in your judgement, would you say, would you call him, a good poet?

I.A.R.: Well, in my judgement – not everyone would agree, of course, far from it – he *is* a good poet?

MR W.: You know, I myself am really very glad indeed to hear you say that. Many of my colleagues wouldn't agree at all. They think a banker has no business whatever to be a poet. They don't think the two things can combine. But I believe that anything a man does, whatever his *hobby* may be, it's all the better if he is really keen on it and does it well. I think it helps him with his work. If you see our young friend, you might tell him that we think he's doing quite well at the Bank. In fact, if he goes on as he has been doing, I don't see why – in time, of course, in time – he mightn't even become a Branch Manager.

I relayed the conversation, of course, to T.S.E. without delay. 'Most gratifying' he found it. A little later, after my marriage, he got into the way of coming fairly often to stay with us in Cambridge, at first on King's Parade directly opposite the gate of King's. He used to arrive wearing a little rucksack which protected him, he felt, from molestation by porters. It contained night things and a large, new, and to us awe-inspiring prayer book: a thing which in my innocent mind hardly chimed with, say, 'The Hippopotamus'. This, in those days, with 'Mr Eliot's Sunday Morning Service', represented for us what we took to be his position on the Church. I suppose a more experienced reader would have felt the Catholic trend in them. But we were listening to other things. I lent my copy of *Ara Vos Prec* to A. C. Benson, whose comment was: 'Watch out! I hear the beat of the capripede hoof!' We were suddenly made aware of our total inability to advise on (or even discuss) the character of the various services available on Sunday mornings. We didn't even seem to know – such was the deplorable nature of our Cambridge circle in the mid-twenties – any person to consult. What struck us too, against the casualness of Cambridge, was a formality, a precision, a concern for standards in dress and deportment, a kind of consciousness of conduct which was individual and *not*, we felt, merely the outcome of studying the ways of several countries other than his own. It went along with delighted and highly critical immersion in records of 'The Two Black Crows', especially of a record involving 'All aboard for St Louis'. I don't know how often we were patiently taught how to say this right. I do know very well that I have never got it right.

In between his visits we used to call upon him in London – once on Good Friday, when his precision occupied itself much with the exactly right temperature at which hot cross buns should be served. What was peculiar to T.S.E. in this sort was the delicately perceptible trace, the ghostly flavour of irony which hung about his manner as though he were preparing a parody. For example, when we went to Peking in 1929, we wrote pressing him to come to stay with us in that enchanting scene. His reply: 'I do not care to visit any country which has no native cheese.' Not too much, I think, should be made of these 'deliberate disguises', but he did have a repertory of more or less confessed poses which his friends were not debarred from seeing through. 'Sometimes I pose and sometimes I pose that I pose' – as Stella Benson beautifully put it. What this did was to add perspective to the intimacy and the affection he was so richly adept in.

Of course it made monkeys of a lot of critics. I forget who denounced him as far too young a man to call himself an 'aged eagle': a sort of attack that T.S.E. deeply relished.

The 'aged eagle' *persona* was dear to him. I tested this on the last occasion on which I talked in public about him. It was a rather special occasion, a celebration in his honour at Eliot House, Harvard, and I had T.S.E. himself right at my elbow as I talked about him. Rather hard, you may think, on him and for me. But no. It was not in the least a constraining occasion. True, it needed control. But Valerie Eliot was not far away and Dorothea Richards was in view, and control was no problem. What I tried out was a passage from Browning's 'How It Strikes a Contemporary'. Its focus was a most notable feature of my old friend's countenance – then a yard at most from me – his nose.

> ... there wanted not a touch
> A tang of ... well, it was not wholly ease
> As back into your mind the man's look came –
> Stricken in years a little, such a brow
> His eyes had to live under! – clear as flint
> On either side the formidable nose
> Curved, cut and coloured like an eagle's claw.

While the audience verified the accuracy of Browning, I too looked at my subject. Our eyes met. All was well!

Now for the few examples of those of T.S.E.'s utterances which may help us towards or toward ... better reading. For me these are liberating utterances, as when in 'The Frontiers of Criticism', his great 1956 Minnesota lecture, he remarks that

the only obvious common characteristic of *The Road to Xanadu* and *Finnegans Wake* is that we may say of each: one book like this is enough.

This should of course be taken in its context, in which he says such gentle and grateful things both of John Livingston Lowes and of Joyce. Gentleness and justness, these are the marks of his later criticism, with its elaborate measures taken to repair any injustices – to Milton, to Shelley, to Coleridge, or to *meaning* or to *interpretation* or even to *education* – that his earlier pronouncements seemed to him to have committed. The only writer he is rough with in these later pages is himself. How gladly he takes occasion to deprecate the 'assurance and considerable warmth' of his early statements, or their overconfidence and intemperance. I doubt if another critic can be found so ready to amend what he had come to consider his own former aberrations. There was more to this, I think, than just getting tired of long-occupied positions. These reversals and recantations strike me as springing from an ever-deepening scepticism, a questioning of the very roots of critical pretensions. It is as though, in the course of acquiring the tremendous authority that the editor of *The Criterion* came to enjoy, T.S.E. had learned too much about the game of opinion-forming and had become alarmed and indeed irked by the weight his judgements were being accorded. He was no longer amused by the reverence with which they were received.

I revert to the Minnesota lecture, 'The Frontiers of Criticism', his most sustained attempt to redress imbalances and warn against their dangers: source-chasing, formula-mongering – e.g., dissociation of sensibility, objective correlative, 'a few notorious phrases which have had a truly embarrassing success in the world' – riddle concoction, the mistaking of explanation for understanding, and what he happily labels 'the lemon-squeezer school of criticism'. This last warning culminates in a truly subversive suspicion:

... after reading the analyses I found I was slow to recover my previous feeling about the poems. It was as if someone had taken a machine to pieces and left me with the task of reassembling the parts. I suspect, in fact, that a good deal of the value of an interpretation is – that it should be my own interpretation.

Where does that leave us – forty-five years on from the founding of, say, the English Tripos? In an excellent position, I would say myself, a position from which we may – well warned by these youthful diseases – usefully take up again the old endeavour, to quote from the same lecture:

We should endeavour to grasp what the poetry is aiming to be; one might say – though it is long since I have employed such terms with any assurance – endeavouring to grasp its entelechy.

With that in mind let me conclude with two extracts from T.S.E.'s broadcast on 'Virgil and the Christian World', which I

14

hope and believe will say for us far better than I can what may well remain in our minds in thinking of the mystery of this great poet. One is on inspiration:

... if the word 'inspiration' is to have any meaning, it must mean just this, that the speaker or writer is uttering something which he does not wholly understand – or which he may even misinterpret when the inspiration has departed from him. This is certainly true of poetic inspiration: and there is more obvious reason for admiring Isaiah as a poet than for claiming Virgil as a prophet. A poet may believe that he is expressing only his private experience; his lines may be for him only a means of talking about himself without giving himself away; yet for his readers what he has written may come to be the expression both of their own secret feelings and of the exultation or despair of a generation.

'Only a means of talking about himself without giving himself away'; 'the expression of their own secret feelings and of the exultation or despair of a generation'.

The other extract is discussing destiny. If the first passage was about the source of poetry, this is about its ultimate aim, what it is *for*.

Destiny is not necessitarianism, and it is not caprice: it is something essentially meaningful. Each man has his destiny, though some men are undoubtedly 'men of destiny' in a sense in which most men are not; and Aeneas is egregiously a man of destiny, since upon him the future of the Western World depends. But this is an election which cannot be explained, a burden and responsibility rather than a reason for self-glorification. It merely happens to one man and not to others, to have the gifts necessary in some profound crisis, but he can take no credit to himself for the gifts and the responsibility assigned to him .... The concept of destiny leaves us with a mystery, but it is a mystery not contrary to reason, for it implies that the world, and the course of human history, have meaning.

T. S. E. – A MEMOIR

By Sir Herbert Read

In England, July 1917 was the deepest and most despairful trough of the Great World War, but that was the moment chosen to launch a new illustrated magazine of the arts. An editorial in the first issue of *Art and Letters* tried to justify this act of defiance.

Objections on the score of scarcity of paper and shortage of labour may surely be overruled when we remember the reams of of paper wasted weekly and the hundreds of compositors daily misemployed on periodicals which give vulgar and illiterate expression to the most vile and debasing sentiments.

The self-appointed editor of this periodical, Frank Rutter, had planned such a venture before the war, when he was director of the City Art Gallery in Leeds, and it was then and there, as a student in the University of that same city, that I had met this now forgotten art critic. He was too old or too unfit to serve in the Army, but when I went to the Front we kept in touch by correspondence and together continued to discuss the project.

A modest paperback volume of poems was published in that same year 1917 by *The Egoist*, a periodical to which I subscribed. I immediately acquired *Prufrock and Other Observations* and suggested that its author should be enlisted as a contributor to the new magazine. In the autumn of that same year I came to London on brief leave from the Front, and during these few days Rutter made contact with the confidential clerk in Lloyds Bank and we dined together at a restaurant in Piccadilly Circus called The Monico – it has since disappeared.

The author of *Prufrock* at this time was a very modest

young man of twenty-nine, dressed correctly in a dark city suit. The attitude he adopted towards the two people who had been mad enough to launch a new periodical at that particular time was understandably cautious. He himself had recently been appointed literary editor of the other periodical I have mentioned, *The Egoist*, and it may have been in its pages, before the publication of *Prufrock*, that I had first met his name. But I was devouring every available avant-garde review at that time, so it is equally possible that I may have seen it elsewhere – perhaps in *The New Age*, to which Ezra Pound had been contributing for some years.

I still have a distinct image of Eliot as he sat between us, his back to the wall. The restaurant had a faded pseudo-rococo elegance, but what war-time fare we were offered I cannot remember. I was excited and indifferent to food. I had been that very day to Buckingham Palace to receive a medal (the justification of my leave from the Front), and I was exhilarated, not so much by that honour, which I affected to despise, as by the feeling of escape from the horrors of the trenches, by the unaccustomed warmth and luxury, by the sudden plunge into an atmosphere of art and letters. Eliot was no doubt a little abashed by the apparition of one who, like Stefan George's young captain, had come

> *aus dem zerstampften Gefild*
> *Heil aus dem prasselnden Guss....*

He seemed anxious to make excuses for his own civilian status – he had, he explained, made an application for a commission in the Naval Reserve, but had waited in vain for his call-up. I remember being indifferent to his scruples – I was already a pacifist in spirit and my only wish was to see the end of the war and the beginning of a new life devoted to literature.

A promise of collaboration was given, with perhaps a slight reserve that might have been critical of enthusiasm of any kind or, as my subsequent knowledge of his personality would rather indicate, with some cautious strategy. In the years to come, when we had become close friends, he would often recommend caution – caution in showing one's hand too soon, caution in speech and correspondence, caution in the small exchanges of literary life. 'Always', he would say, 'acknowledge the gift of a book before there had been time to read it: if you wait you have to commit yourself to an opinion.' Another of his rules was: 'Never contribute to the first number of a new periodical – wait to see what company you are going to keep.'

There was nothing from Eliot in the first two or three issues of *Art and Letters*. The war dragged on and publication became more difficult. It was not until the spring issue of 1919 that his first contribution appeared, an essay on Marivaux. In the next number (summer 1919) 'Burbank with a Baedeker' and 'Sweeney Erect' were printed, and this number also includes an essay by Ezra Pound on De Bosschère. To the autumn issue of that same year Eliot contributed 'Notes on the Blank Verse of Christopher Marlowe'; to the next number, '*The Duchess of Malfi* and Poetic Drama'; and finally, to the spring number of 1920, 'Euripides and Gilbert Murray'.

Art and Letters did not survive beyond the year 1920. In its later stages my anonymous part in the editing of the magazine had been taken over by Osbert Sitwell – still in association with Frank Rutter. It had been a brave effort – it published articles, stories, and poems by all the Sitwells, by Richard Aldington, Wyndham Lewis, Ford Madox Hueffer, Aldous Huxley, Ronald Firbank, Katherine Mansfield, and Wilfred Owen. It reproduced drawings and paintings by Picasso, Matisse, Modigliani, Gaudier-Brzeska, and Wyndham Lewis. But it lost money and went the way of all such idealistic enterprises in a philistine world. Its significance is that it was in some sense a forerunner of *The Criterion*.

My acquaintance with Eliot, in the years immediately after the war, ripened to friendship slowly but surely. Eliot married and brought his pretty vivacious wife to the Saturday afternoon tea-parties given by Helen Rootham and Edith Sitwell in their Bayswater apartment. The euphoria of our first meeting had faded : the soldier had become a civil servant, but one who was still busy with literary projects. It was Osbert Sitwell, who was free and comparatively wealthy, who assumed the leadership, and it was the Sitwells, as a trio, who for a time made the pace for us all. Pound disappeared towards the end of 1920, ostensibly disgusted with British philistinism but really because there was no place for him in post-war England. It may be doubted if he ever understood the English – certainly not typical eccentrics like the Sitwells. But the Sitwells were genuinely English; their rejection of British philistinism was as absolute as Ezra's, but they wished to concentrate their forces on the home front – they were indifferent to Ezra's troubadours and symbolists. And Ezra was committed in the first place to American editors such as Harriet Monroe and later to Margaret Anderson and Scofield Thayer. He was exporting what little talent he could find to America, and that helped no one in England. If he had any local allegiance it was to that oddity *The Egoist*, and it was he who in 1917 had persuaded its owners, Harriet Weaver and Dora Marsden, to appoint Eliot as literary editor. Not that the post gave him much scope, for the primary object of the journal was to publish Dora Marsden's own esoteric philosophy, and though space was found for the serial publication of Joyce's *Portrait of the Artist as a Young Man* (1914–15), the literary contents were usually limited to a short poem or two, an article on music, and two or three reviews of books.

The Sitwells were apt to make fun of Ezra – indeed, it was very difficult for anyone to take him seriously in person (and it was his *persona* that he used to project). Apart from his exotic appearance, he rattled off his elliptic sentences with a harsh nasal twang, twitched incessantly, and prowled round the room like a caged panther. He was not made for compromise or cooperation, two qualities essential for any literary or artistic 'movement'. He disappeared, first to Paris and then to Rapallo, and the place he might have occupied in the post-war literary scene in London was quietly assumed by Eliot.

It was quietly assumed by a man who had lost all superficial

19

trace of his American origin and who had already decided that his spiritual home was in England. The complexities involved in this decision were not to be appreciated by a true-born Englishman, but I was aware of the struggle that was going on in Eliot's mind. 'Some day,' he wrote to me on St George's Day, 1928 (his own inscription),

I want to write an essay about the point of view of an American who wasn't an American, because he was born in the South and went to school in New England as a small boy with a nigger drawl, but who wasn't a southerner in the South because his people were northerners in a border state and looked down on all southerners and Virginians, and who so was never anything anywhere and who therefore felt himself to be more a Frenchman than an American and more an Englishman than a Frenchmen and yet felt that the U.S.A. up to a hundred years ago was a family extension. It is almost too difficult even for H. J. who for that matter wasn't an American at all, in that sense.

By this time Eliot had become an Englishman in legal fact, and apart from the occasion of our first meeting in 1917, when the war situation was compelling him to acknowledge his nationality, or on one or two later occasions when in a mood of solemn gaiety he would sing a ballad like 'The Reconstructed Rebel', I was never conscious that he was in any way less English than myself. From the first he fitted naturally into English clothes and English clubs, into English habits generally. In fact, if anything gave him away it was an Englishness that was a shade too correct to be natural.

It is difficult, at this distance of time, to reconstruct the events between the end of the war and the foundation, in 1923, of *The Criterion*. From that year Eliot was our undisputed leader. I imply the formation of a party, of a 'new front', and that was indeed the intention, as the 'commentaries' in *The Criterion* soon made clear. *Art and Letters* had come to an end mainly for financial reasons, and from that moment (the summer of 1920) the foundation of a new and better magazine was constantly discussed whenever we forgathered. There were by then three centres of intellectual ferment in London: the so-called Bloomsbury Group; the poets associated with Harold Monro and his review, *Poetry and Drama*; and the Sitwells, who still carried on a campaign against the literary establishment (the Squirearchy, as it was sometimes called, for its most prominent member was J. C. Squire). Middleton Murry should perhaps be mentioned; as founder and editor of *The Adelphi* he had gathered round him a distinct group, disciples for the most part of D. H. Lawrence, but he never came to terms with Eliot (though he greatly respected him as a critic) nor with modern poetry (his own conventional verse is the best evidence of that). He was also of an older generation and, brilliant as he was as a literary critic, never had any real understanding of the poetic revolution that began with *Prufrock*.

Nor did Harold Monro, for all his eager devotion to poetry as a cause and to Eliot as a friend. It is a melancholy fact that as owner of The Poetry Bookshop he had rejected 'Prufrock' when it was offered to him for publication in 1917. As the years passed and Eliot's prestige grew he became somewhat embittered, and though we all attended the parties he gave at the bookshop, we knew that in any vital sense he was not with us.

Nor, of course, was the Bloomsbury Group. Leonard and Virginia Woolf, who were the real heart of that group, were very devoted to Eliot, and it was they who, as the Hogarth Press, published not only the *Poems* of 1920, but the first edition of *The Waste Land* in 1922. But the publications of the Hogarth Press, which were at that time actually composed and printed by the Woolfs in the cellar of their house in Richmond, were in no sense representative of the Bloomsbury Group, and whatever the possessive attitude of Bloomsburyites such as Clive Bell may have been, the truth is that Eliot carefully kept his distance. The obituary of Virginia which he wrote for *The Criterion* shocked us all by its chilly detachment.

There was no other group that mattered. There was Orage,

in some respects the most effective catalyst of the period, but *The New Age*, which for several years provided Pound with an outlet, was now given over to Social Credit (with Pound as a convert) and to the doctrines of Guardjieff (which were too esoteric even for Pound). There were anonymous institutions like *The Times Literary Supplement*, and its editor, Bruce Richmond, deserves to be remembered as one who quickly appreciated the new talents that were forming around Eliot and gave them substantial encouragement in his columns (the early reviews of *Prufrock* and *Poems* (1920) should not be remembered against him; no one, in the years to come, regretted them more than Richmond).

Such was the literary situation in 1923 when Eliot, aided by a subsidy from Lady Rothermere, decided that the time was ripe to launch a new review. He slowly surveyed the scanty field and chose his team with great deliberation. The group that rallied round him was unique in that it never questioned his leadership – but there were two that held back: Richard Aldington, who had developed an intense jealousy of Eliot, and Wyndham Lewis, who, though pressed by Eliot to collaborate, preferred as always to cut his own lonely and aggressive swathe. For myself it soon became a question of deep personal devotion, and Eliot responded with a confidence which I have valued more than anything else in my life.

*

I will now try to describe the personal relationship that developed between Eliot and myself over a period of nearly fifty years. It will not be easy and it will involve some confessions that are not altogether creditable to myself.

When I first met Eliot I was, from an intellectual point of view, both ignorant and *naïf*. I had not had the advantage of his orderly education and philosophical training. The only credit I might claim was the experience of war, and, though Eliot respected this, I was in the process of disowning it. The pacifism that had become a deep conviction for me was to be one of the few areas of mutual misunderstanding. The reasons which led Eliot to reject pacifism were perfectly logical, whereas it was war itself that had given me the right to be illogical and angry. But neither this issue, nor the many issues bound up with it (the whole complex of humanism and romanticism), ever threatened our devotion to each other. I do not know what he found to like or respect in someone so fundamentally different in background and temperament, but first my Englishness, I suppose. My naïvety, even after the experience of war, was still that of a country boy, uncorrupted by society or learned sophistication. The literary enthusiasm that had survived a war was but another aspect of this same naïvety, and Eliot must have been aware that it embraced him with an intuitive sympathy and understanding. This poet, in spite of his reserve, was not indifferent to devotion, and he felt the need for one or two disciples.

The illusion that I might become one of these disciples was fostered for a time by my editing of the posthumous papers of T. E. Hulme. I do not think that Hulme's *Speculations*, when they were published in 1924, made any difference to Eliot's political idealism or philosophical faith, but his convictions were immensely strengthened. As the man who had rescued Hulme from a probable oblivion I had earned Eliot's deep gratitude. At first he must have assumed that I could have undertaken such an unremunerative task only from some sense of intellectual affinity, whereas in fact I had done the work to oblige Orage, who had been entrusted with the task by Hulme's executors. Orage had been very kind to me as a young aspiring writer, and when he suggested (perhaps a little disingenuously) that the editing of Hulme's papers would be an educative experience for me, I agreed, not realizing (though I had often read Hulme's contributions to *The New Age*) what a bombshell I was innocently manufacturing.

From 1919 to 1922 I was an assistant principal in the Treasury, a position that meant I could not publicly take part in activities, such as journalism, that might be held to compromise my official duties. For this reason, though I was in effect an editor of *Art and Letters*, my name never appeared on the title-page. But in 1922 I left the Treasury for a more congenial post in the Victoria and Albert Museum. I was still a civil servant, but provided I was discreet no one would object to my literary activities. The transfer coincided more or less with the foundation of *The Criterion* and with Eliot's resignation from the City bank. Since Eliot's time was now more elastic than mine, and in order to preserve a regular contact, it was agreed that we should meet for lunch one day every week in South Kensington, and for the next seven years we forgathered at a pub called The Grove in Beauchamp Place. The Grove became a Mermaid Tavern to which, week by week (I think it was every Thursday), came not only some of the regular contributors to *The Criterion*, but also any sympathizing critics or poets from abroad who might be visiting London. The 'regulars', apart from Eliot and myself, were F. S. Flint, Frank Morley, Bonamy Dobrée (absent in Egypt part of the time), and one or more of my museum colleagues.

But these lunches were not the *Criterion* meetings. These took place in the evening, about once a month, and usually in a small private room at the Ristorante Commercio in Soho. Their purpose was not so much to discuss business as to introduce contributors to one another, to exchange ideas, and to build up some kind of 'phalanx' whose unity would be reflected in the pages of the magazine. I doubt if they achieved this purpose, but they were enjoyable and intellectually stimulating. They were in no way dominated by the editor; they were not very serious. On such occasions Eliot often revealed a gay and even hilarious spirit far different from his normal demeanour.

'My conception of leader or "organizer" ' (he wrote to me in a letter which is undated but apparently of October 1924) 'is simply of a necessary organ in a body, which has no superiority at all, but simply exercises a particular function, and makes it possible for others to do their best work.' This is the 'conception' he maintained during all the years of his editorship of *The Criterion*. The letter is a long one, and includes an apologia which perhaps I should quote, because it shows how early Eliot had formulated certain principles of personal conduct which he was to maintain for the next forty years:

The ideal which you propose in your letter is very near to that which I proposed to myself when I undertook the review, and which I have kept in mind ever since. The ideal which was present to the mind of Lady Rothermere at the beginning was that of a more chic and brilliant Art and Letters, which might have a fashionable vogue among a wealthy few. I had and have no resentment against her for this, as I have no criticism to make of her conduct throughout: she has given me a pretty free hand, has been quite as appreciative as one could expect a person of her antecedents and connexions to be, and the game between us has been a fair one. I have I think given her as much as possible of what she wants, and she has given me the possibility of an organ. It is true that I have laid myself open to the censure both of persons who assumed that I was making money out of the work, and of those who knew that I was taking nothing for it – and who consequently believe that I am running the paper for other discreditable reasons – which latter group of persons, by the way, includes my relatives in America. One does not like to explain oneself only to arouse the accusation of hypocrisy, to be associated with the other causes of impeachment, and one learns to keep silence. I have another reason for keeping silence, and that is that I sometimes give people an impression of arrogance and intolerant self-conceit. If I say generally that I wish to form a 'phalanx', a hundred voices will forthwith declare that I wish to be a leader, and that my vanity will not allow me to serve, or even to exist on terms of equality with others. If one maintains a cause, one is either a fanatic or a hypocrite: and if one has any definite dogmas, then one is imposing those dogmas upon those who cooperate with one.

I wish, certainly, to get as homogeneous a group as possible: but I find that homogeneity is in the end indefinable: for the purposes of the Criterion, it cannot be reduced to a creed of numbered capitals. I do *not* expect everyone to subscribe to all the articles of my own faith, or to read Arnold, Newman, Bradley, or Maurras with my eyes. It seems to me that at the present time we need more dogma, and that one ought to have as precise and clear a creed as possible, when one thinks at all: but a creed is always in one sense smaller than the man, and in another sense larger; one's formulations never fully explain one, although it is necessary to formulate: I do not, for myself, bother about the apparent inconsistency – which has been made the most of – between my prose and my verse. Why then should I bother about particular differences of formulation between myself and those whom I should like to find working with me?

This is to make a little clearer my notion of a phalanx. When I *write*, I must write to the limit of my own convictions and aspirations: but I don't want to impose these on others, any more than I should be willing to reduce myself to the common denominator of my colleagues. What is essential is to find those persons who have an impersonal loyalty to some faith not antagonistic to my own.

Here we have the demand for 'an impersonal loyalty' – loyalty not to an individual, not even to a political or critical programme, but to 'some faith not antagonistic to my own'. Eliot in this letter went on to discuss persons, possible contributors, and they range from conservatives such as Charles Whibley to 'modernists' such as Edwin Muir. Always there is the assumption that I am by his side, an *aide-de-camp* in 'what might easily become a heart-breaking struggle'. My own faith was judged as certainly not antagonistic to his own. But what was my own faith?

It was to be defined, tentatively, in the volume of essays which Eliot asked me to prepare for the first list of the re-organized firm of Faber & Gwyer (later Faber & Faber), which he had joined as an editorial director. This book, *Reason and Romanticism*, was published in 1926, and though the Reason of it owes something to Hulme and even more to Eliot, the Romanticism was my own. It was already my declared purpose to seek some reconciliation or 'synthesis' of these opposed faiths. If Eliot had any desire to check me at that time it was all done with a very gentle rein, and our intimacy became closer week by week. At this period, 1926–31, we were seeing each other so frequently that the correspondence is sparse, and I am thrown back on my imperfect memory to recover the immediacy of the events. All those years I commuted to a suburb of London and in 1926 built myself a house near Beaconsfield, about twenty-five miles to the west of the City. The station for Beaconsfield in London is Marylebone, and Clarence Gate Gardens, the block of flats which Eliot had lived in earlier and to which he returned about 1927 or 1928 was a few hundred yards from this terminus. It became convenient to dine with the Eliots occasionally before catching a train to the country.

Before this, however, Eliot and Vivienne had lived for a number of years in a small house at 57 Chester Terrace, in that part of London that hesitates between Belgravia and Chelsea. After the *Criterion* dinners, which generally lasted too long for me to catch my last train home, I would sometimes spend the night at Chester Terrace. I remember how on one such occasion I woke early and presently became conscious that the door of my room, which was on the ground floor, was slowly and silently being opened. I lay still and saw first a hand and then an arm reach round the door and lift from a hook the bowler hat that was hanging there. It was a little before seven o'clock and Mr Eliot was on his way to an early communion service. It was the first intimation I had had of his conversion to the Christian faith.

This reticence was maintained in all his private affairs. I was a close witness of the tragic progress of his first marriage. Vivienne was a frail creature and had not been married long before she began to suffer from serious internal ailments. These exasperated an already nervous temperament and she slowly but surely developed the hysterical psychosis to which she finally succumbed. Eliot's sufferings in these years were acute, but only once did he unburden himself to me. This was in a letter which I received while I was on a short holiday in Sussex, but this particular letter has disappeared – it is possible that I was asked to destroy it. Posterity will probably judge Vivienne harshly, but I remember her in moments when she was sweet and vivacious; later her hysteria became embarrassing. My own first marriage was to break up under very similar circumstances and that too, as time passed, increased our mutual sympathy. Eliot, however, could not accept my drastic solution of the problem, which was the dissolution of the marriage. Though eventually legally separated, he remained single so long as his first wife was alive.

His moral rectitude, though explicit, was never unctuous. In conversation he would freely express his disapproval of the conduct of his friends, but I do not remember that he ever brought a friendship to an end on such grounds. He would often 'demur' to some line of action (a letter to the press, for example, on some political issue) but I was reproved only once with something like sternness. This was ten years ago. Wyndham Lewis had published a pamphlet called 'The Demon of Progress in the Arts', which contained a malicious and I thought at the time a treacherous attack on me. It came as a surprise because I had known Lewis since 1917, and though I had never felt quite at ease with him (who ever did?) I admired him both as a painter and as a writer. In the year in question, 1949, the Institute of Contemporary Arts, of which I was president, had organized an exhibition called 'Forty Thousand Years of Modern Art', and the selection committee, of which I was not a member, had chosen two early abstract paintings by Lewis, belonging to private collectors. Lewis heard of this and I immediately received from him telegrams and registered letters protesting against what he considered a deliberate misrepresentation of his status as an artist. Very reluctantly, on my request, the committee agreed to withdraw the pictures, but the incident continued to rankle in Lewis's schizophrenic mind (I use a clinical expression, but it had for long been obvious that Lewis suffered from what, in less clinical language, we call a persecution complex).

My answer to this attack was a lecture delivered at the Institute of Contemporary Arts which I called 'The Psychology of Reaction in the Arts'. I did not wish to indulge in personal polemics so I carefully avoided any mention of Lewis's name, discussing in general terms the 'case' of the artist who renounces his early revolutionary fervour to become a reactionary in later life – I gave Wordsworth as a typical example.

My subtlety misfired – practically nobody identified my remarks with Lewis; so when *The Sewanee Review* published the lecture in the fall of 1955 I added a footnote which was meant to be ironical but would reveal my target to anyone who had read Lewis's pamphlet. I should add that before this, on the basis of the script of my lecture, Eliot had made some objections which were fair enough and meant to safeguard his own position. In a letter of 16 September 1955 he had written:

I still do not think, however, that you have made clear enough the distinction between your *general* use of 'reactionary' in contrast to 'conservative' (a distinction which has only to be drawn to be accepted). In the former sense, the term applied to Charles Maurras, for example. In the latter sense it is either your own invention, or is perhaps borrowed from psychologists: in either case, it seems to me to need more explicit definition for the general reader. And of course I am still very doubtful about the propriety of the psychological approach in such a controversy.—, of course, is in his own way as much a 'case' as Lewis; but wouldn't it be better to ignore what they say than to rebut them on that ground? A man's mental kinks may very well account for his being wrong; but should not one first meet him on his own ground and prove that he is wrong, before explaining how he came to be wrong?

I thought that that was exactly what I had done. In any case it was too late to withdraw (my lecture had meanwhile been issued as a pamphlet by the I. C. A.). But this first rebuke was mild compared with the sternness that followed the publication of the lecture in *The Sewanee Review*. The ironical footnote caused Eliot 'a fresh shock', as he says in a letter of

14 November, and 'I shall have to take a little time to perpend and decide what, if anything, I have to say further'. I waited like a condemned criminal for my sentence and it came five days later in the following letter:

Dear Herbert,

I have no desire to prolong our recent correspondence, and I should like to be able, after writing this letter, to close the subject altogether. But your letter of the 12th made me realise that I could not have made my position clear, and I want to do so, defining the issue with which I have been concerned.

My interest in this discussion has not been in Wyndham Lewis personally, or in his personal disagreement with you, or in opposed views of modern art. In such matters, I should certainly not intervene: I would not enter the lists with artists and art critics. What first interested me was a question arising out of Wyndham Lewis's book and your pamphlet: the question of the wisdom (two distinct but related questions) of the use of psychological artillery in a battle of this kind. This is a fascinating question, which I should like to take up some day, in a cooler atmosphere; but it is not germane to my recent perplexity. This arose solely from the fact that our conversation on the subject, and the content of your letter of the 18th September, gave me reason to suppose that the origin of your pamphlet was the need which you felt to reply to Lewis, that a direct rebuttal would be futile, and that the form of reply you had adopted was an analysis of a psychological type, as instances of which you told me you had Lewis and Chirico in mind. You will therefore judge of my surprise on reading, in the Sewanee Review, the explicit statement that your article – to which you had given the new title of 'The Lost Leader' – had no application to Lewis. And your letter of November 12 didn't succeed in clearing away my bewilderment.

That's all there is to it. And I hope, after so many years' friendship, that you will always be equally frank with me when you find my published words unsatisfying.

Yours ever
Tom

I defended myself to the best of my ability and ten years later I still think that the most effective reply to a malicious attack is a cool analysis of the state of mind that occasions it. But the footnote was a mistake: if I had wanted to implicate Lewis in my argument I should have done so openly. It was naïve to imagine that the public would join in a game of blind man's buff.

Eliot was to add his own ironic footnote. On one of the last occasions that I lunched with him alone at the Garrick Club, he confessed that in his life there had been few people whom he had found it impossible to like, but Lewis was one of them. What should be realized, by anyone who wishes to understand the complexity of Eliot's moral conscience, is that he could be fiercely loyal to people whose 'faith' he respected but whom he could not love.

Perhaps he could be equally loyal to people he loved but did not respect, and I may have come into this category as time passed and our opinions continued to diverge. When he announced in the preface to *For Lancelot Andrewes* (1928) that he was a classicist in literature, a royalist in politics, and an Anglo-Catholic in religion, I could only retort that I was a romanticist in literature, an anarchist in politics, and an agnostic in religion. But such a statement of differences he could respect; what he could not tolerate was any false interpretation of the position he himself held. I remember one occasion of this kind. In the first edition of my autobiography, *Annals of Innocence and Experience* (1940), there was a sentence, or part of one, to which he took strong exception: '... it is a genuine puzzle to me how anyone with a knowledge of the comparative history of religions can retain an exclusive belief in the tenets of his particular sect'. This led to some earnest discussion, but I see that the only correction I made in subsequent editions was to italicize the word 'exclusive', with an intention that now escapes me. It may be, however, that the original objection was to the sentence as it appeared in the typescript or proofs of the book, which Eliot would have seen as a director of Faber & Faber.

*

I now want to get a little closer to the nature of this poet I knew so well for so many years, but I begin with an overwhelming sense of the complexity of the subject, and of my inadequacy to deal with it perceptively. One's first fear is that one may be reading an intellectual refinement, a subtlety of mind and thought, into the personality of a man who was fundamentally simple. There is no necessary correspondence between thought and personality: a man of very simple habits, such as Kant, can be master of a very complex philosophy. But Eliot was certainly not a Kant. It is true that he led a comparatively sedate life: he too was regular in his habits and punctilious in his manners – he even held that regular habits were conducive to poetic creation, in this, as in so much else, agreeing with Coleridge, 'the sad ghost' that beckoned him from the shades. He loved his office-work at Faber's, and kept up his duties there long after there was any need to do so – though by nature he was apt to be cautious in financial matters. He was never mean, but he was not extravagant – he would take a bus or a tube in preference to a taxi if the cheaper service were easily available. He lived comfortably in town apartments and would never have indulged in that last infirmity of a romantic temperament, a country house. He was, in fact, a townsman by preference and never at ease in the country. He might enjoy a holiday in the south of France or, in his later years, in the West Indies, but he was not a traveller by choice and often reproved me for my cultural peregrinations. (He thought that activities like lecturing and reviewing should be kept within strict bounds. A poet, he said, should not write reviews after the age of thirty-five – indeed, he did not approve of reviewing at any time as distinct from the writing of critical essays.) He had a positive distaste for the weekly critical journals and boasted that he had never contributed to *The New Statesman*.

He had been, as is well known, a serious student of philosophy, but he did not parade his knowledge of the subject. He would occasionally refer to Bradley, and more often, in an anecdotic fashion, to his Oxford tutor in philosophy, Harold Joachim. But mainly, if we were in a literary mood, our talk would be quite general, concerned with our work, our friends, and the gossip of the day. As the years passed he became just a little pontifical, and would refer to his own writings in a tone of voice that was a shade too solemn. He would use expressions like 'Valéry, Yeats and I' – with perfect justice, but one was rather checked by the calm acceptance of a status that one felt should be left to others to confer.

Of classical authors he undoubtedly felt most affinity for Dante; his appreciation of Shakespeare and all the Romantic poets was subject to his moral or religious scruples. He knew perfectly well that a good poet is not necessarily a good Christian; nevertheless, he maintained that the poet, as a member of a Christian community, must be judged by the moral standards of that community. This brought him nearer to a man whom I believe he honoured above all other English writers – Samuel Johnson, with whom he shared a faith in God and the fear of death. Johnson, both as a poet and as a critic, was constantly in his mind, and he had a factual knowledge of Boswell's *Life* that enabled him to play a game of quiz with fellow Johnsonians like Frank Morley – a game that could become rather tedious to the uninitiated. The same game, on a somewhat more frivolous level, was played with the complete works of Conan Doyle and (more arcanely) with the complete works of Wilkie Collins. I once earned his surprised admiration by answering some ploy of this kind with a quotation from *Poor Miss Finch*, a novel by Collins which my wife had picked up at a country auction. I had opened it idly and read with amusement that the heroine's father, a politician from South America, had 'succumbed to his seventeenth revolution', a beautiful phrase that had stuck in my mind.

His admiration for his contemporaries was limited and uncertain. I have mentioned his loyalty to Lewis. Eliot once publicly committed himself to the opinion that Lewis wrote the best prose style of our time, the truth being that there was nothing to recommend it except a forcefulness that occasionally degenerated into brutality. To James Joyce he was completely devoted, both to the writer and to the man. He helped him in many practical ways, and even remitted in his case his moral sanctions. His relations with Pound are clear from the published correspondence. Again Eliot was always solicitous for the personal welfare of a friend to whom he felt he owed a great debt. But to appreciate how clinically cool Eliot could be even to the best of his friends, one he had called 'probably the most important living poet in our language', we have only to read the two pages devoted to Pound in *After Strange Gods*. If Shakespeare and Shelley are not to be spared the moral criterion, there was no reason to spare 'poor Ezra'.

This firm assertion of a moral criterion (the criterion of *The Criterion*) has to be accepted as the key to Eliot's character (his *character* and not his personality, but that distinction of mine was precisely the one he could not accept). Once the finality of that criterion was accepted it could be ignored – it never stood in the way of the most affectionate relationships with heretics or pagans like Pound and myself. And yet one always had a slight uneasiness in his presence, fearing that he might at any moment assume the judicial robes. If Shelley's ideas could be dismissed as 'shabby' and most of his verse as 'bad jingling', where, in Mr Eliot's final judgement, did we stand?

It has been said that this moralistic attitude, which was extended to all forms of liberalism, must necessarily have put Eliot on the side of autocracy and, not to evade the word that has been used, fascism. This is not true. In all the years I knew him I never heard him express any sympathy for either Mussolini or Hitler – from his point of view they were godless men. 'The fundamental objection to fascist doctrine,' he once wrote, 'the one that we conceal from ourselves because it might condemn ourselves, is that it is pagan.' He did not believe in democracy, and who can blame him? He believed in 'a community of Christians', and when it came to a close discussion of what he meant by this ideal, it seemed to have more in common with my anarchism than with any form of autocracy. He believed in 'roots' (see his Introduction to Simone Weil's *The Need for Roots*, which he wrote at my suggestion), and above all he believed in tradition. He knew that the values he cherished could not exist in the modern state, democratic or totalitarian.

He has been accused of anti-Semitism, but again I never heard such sentiments from his own lips. I know that there are one or two phrases in his writings that lend some substance to this accusation, but all of us, if we are honest with ourselves, must confess to a certain spontaneous xenophobia. It is an instinct that the educated man controls or eradicates, and in this respect Eliot was as controlled as the best of us.

Perhaps too controlled for general converse. From the beginning there was a withholding of emotion, a refusal to reveal the inner man. I always felt that I was in the presence of a remorseful man, of one who had some secret sorrow or guilt. What I took for remorse may not have had its origins in personal experience; a feeling of guilt may be caused by a realization of 'the all-consuming power of original sin'. This Eliot, like Kierkegaard, certainly possessed.

His emotional reserve may have had a remoter cause – after all, he had had a puritanical background in his childhood. I know that my own reserved nature, which I inherit from my Yorkshire ancestry, is often mistaken for an absence of feeling or sympathy; whereas, to paraphrase one of Eliot's own well-known aphorisms, only the man who feels deeply experiences the need to hide his feelings. So long as she was alive Eliot must have felt very close to his mother, but he never talked about her, and when he published her 'dramatic poem' *Savonarola* (the volume is not dated, but I think it was about 1925–6), he handed a copy to me with a deprecatory gesture. The Introduction he wrote for this volume is again an impersonal document, devoted to 'History and Truth' and 'Of Dramatic Form' and telling us nothing directly about the authoress. Indirectly we may gather that she was a disciple of

Schleiermacher, Emerson, Channing, and Herbert Spencer; that she was (or might have been) a contributor to the *Hibbert Journal*; and that she was opposed to ecclesiasticism. All this, we are told, can be deduced from the text of the play, which renders 'a state of mind contemporary with the author'. The condemned Savonarola in his cell utters these words:

> This is the Hall that grew with my desire
> And quick-winged words that flew like shafts of fire.

Change 'Hall' (the Hall of the Grand Council) to 'Hell' and we have words that strangely anticipate the 'flame of incandescent terror' in 'Little Gidding':

> We only live, only suspire
> Consumed by either fire or fire.

*

I must now draw this brief memoir to an end, with the realization that I have completely failed to convey the nature and the presence of this great man. I have said that he was inaccessible, but perhaps some other friends were luckier than I and found intimacy as well as loyalty and affection. I shall probably wait in vain for such revelations, and, to tell the truth, they would not make any difference to my knowledge of the man. The man I knew, in all his reserve, was the man he wished to be: a serious but not necessarily a solemn man, a severe man never lacking in kindness and sympathy, a *profound* man (profoundly learned, profoundly poetic, profoundly spiritual). And yet to outward appearance a correct man, a conventional man, an infinitely polite man – in brief, a gentleman. He not only was not capable of a mean deed; I would also say that he never had a mean thought. He could mock folly and be severe with sin, and there were people he simply did not wish to know. But his circle of friends, though never very large, was very diverse, and he could relax with great charm in the presence of women. He had moods of gaiety and moods of great depression – I have known occasions when I left him feeling that my spirit had been utterly depleted. Often he was witty (in a somewhat solemn voice); his anecdotes were related with great deliberation. He did not hesitate to discuss policies or personalities, but he condemned idle gossip (of the kind typical of the Bloomsbury set). In personal habits he was scrupulously correct and clean, never a Bohemian in thought or appearance; but he had a streak of hypochondria, and was addicted to pills and potions. He had good reason for taking care of himself, for he easily took a chill and often suffered from a distressing cough. I never saw him indulge in any sport. One weekend he spent with me early in our friendship (it was 1927 or 1928) he came clad in a most curious pair of chequered breeches, neither riding-breeches nor 'plus-fours', but some hybrid which was certainly not from Savile Row. He made a fetish of umbrellas, as is perhaps well known. He had them specially made with enormous handles, with the excuse that no one would take such an umbrella from a cloakroom by mistake. He relished good food and beer and wine, but his speciality was cheese, of which he had tasted a great many varieties. I think I gained a point in his esteem because I came from a region responsible for Wensleydale, 'the Mozart of cheeses'. At his club the cheeseboard would be produced with great solemnity and the quality or maturity of the cheeses tested before being offered to his guests.

In all affairs he was a man of taste, but taste, like tradition, is acquired. I do not think he had any direct sensuous appreciation of the visual arts. After our lunch at The Grove he would sometimes return to the Museum with me to see some particular treasure I had mentioned, but he did not respond to such things with more than a respectful curiosity. I rarely discussed contemporary art with him, and though I once or twice tried to establish some personal contact between him and artists like Henry Moore and Ben Nicholson, my efforts came to little or nothing. If pressed he would no doubt have admitted that the tradition that led from Poe and Baudelaire to Laforgue and Rimbaud and his own poetry could not be entirely divorced from the tradition that led from Delacroix and Cézanne to Matisse and Picasso, but he would not himself have made much of the comparison.

Finally it might be asked whether such a great poet ever discussed poetry, and the answer is No if we mean poetry in general (that he reserved for his books). He would often consult me about particular poets who wished to be published by Faber's, and we freely discussed the relative merits of our contemporaries, English and American. In the early years he would sometimes show me the draft or proofs of one of his own poems and invite my criticism, but this less and less as the years went by. He sometimes commented on poems I had written and his criticism was always practical and acute, concerned with the meaning of words or some infelicity of phrase. He never expressed any general opinion about my poetry, though he often blamed me for neglecting poetry for art criticism and other non-poetic activities. I knew, however, that I had some measure of his esteem – after all, he sponsored the publication of my poems with Faber's. I have mentioned his self-esteem, without questioning his perfect right to it; but this was an attitude to which, as a poet, I could only oppose a self-effacing modesty. I once wrote a poem which, after I had written it, I realized had perfectly described our relationship as poets – a poem in the Chinese manner called 'Lu Yün's Lament'; but neither Eliot nor, as far as I know, anyone else ever saw its application. Like my footnote on Wyndham Lewis, it was ironic to the point of irrelevance.

*

The most significant of all Eliot's poems, from a confessional point of view, is 'The Hollow Men'. It was written in 1925, the year of religious crisis, and apart from some minor poems, it is the last example of what I would call his *pure* poetry. *Ash-Wednesday*, which followed in 1930, is already a moralistic poem, especially in the last two sections. All the poetry that follows, including the *Four Quartets*, is, in spite of flashes of the old fire, moralistic poetry.

There are no strict rules for the creation of poetry, but nevertheless a poem is neither an arbitrary nor a deliberate event. As critics we must act on the assumption that a correspondence exists between the shifting levels of consciousness and what we call moments of vision or flashes of inspiration. One of the critic's tasks is to survey the devious intercommunications between these various levels of consciousness. So long as the lines of communication are open, inspiration, as we say, *flows*. For a time, for a year or perhaps five years, rarely more than ten, the divine madness, as Plato called it, descends on a mortal and then burns out. 'The Hollow Men' is a celebration of this incineration. 'Mistah Kurtz – he dead. A penny for the Old Guy.' But Mistah Kurtz, though he may have been a bad man, a corrupt man, a suffering man, saw visions that were splendid. Even when, as in this poem, he is evoking 'death's other Kingdom', he does so in bright images, 'Sunlight on a broken column', 'a tree swinging'; but then, alas, 'Between the emotion/And the response/Falls the Shadow'. What Eliot meant by the Shadow is clear enough and it is not a Shadow that we encounter in his poetry without sorrow.

Ash-Wednesday should be read with a poem of the same year, 'Marina', where the new resolution is made clear in these lines:

> This form, this face, this life
> Living to live in a world of time beyond me; let me
> Resign my life for this life, my speech for that unspoken,
> The awakened, lips parted, the hope, the new ships.

The problem of poetry and belief was endlessly discussed in these years 1925–30, in conversation and in print. But though it was always posed as a problem of poetry and belief, what Eliot and Richards and the rest of us were discussing was poetry and beliefs – there is a difference between a belief which is a belief in God, or in the Incarnation, and the beliefs which are formulated as the Thirty-Nine Articles of the Church of England or the Constitutions of the Society of Jesus. It is perhaps the same kind of distinction that Eliot himself made between poetic assent and philosophical belief, and I am only suggesting (following Kierkegaard) that we must distinguish between Christianity and Christendom. Eliot wrote (in his essay on Dante) that the advantage of a coherent traditional system of dogma and morals was that 'it stands apart, for understanding and assent *even without belief*, from the single individual who propounds it'. This distinction between dogma and belief would allow us to assume that belief is a process of psychic integration, precariously maintained. As such it need not conflict with poetic intuition, which is also a delicate process of psychic integration. In this both belief and poetry differ from those inflexible moral commands to which a man must, if he resigns his life and would have peace, assent. This was made clear by Pascal, and by Unamuno in *The Agony of Christianity*. The Jesuits, we are told, do not ask for faith but for obedience; and Unamuno suggests that it was such a demand that led Pascal, in a moment of fear, to cry: *It will stultify you. (Cela vous abêtira.)* The fragmented conclusion of 'The Hollow Men' is the same cry of despair, the same broken utterance:

> For Thine is
> Life is
> For Thine is the

Perhaps the key to Eliot's agony lies in this essay on Pascal; his was the same agony as Pascal's, but I think that in the end Eliot resigned his life for that life, *stultified his speech* for that unspoken law. Pascal, he said, was to be commended

to those who doubt, but who have the mind to conceive, and the sensibility to feel, the disorder, the futility, the meaninglessness, the mystery of life and suffering, and who can only find peace through a satisfaction of the whole being.

Eliot himself, I believe, was not of those who doubt, but rather one of those great mystics who, in his own words, 'like St John of the Cross, are primarily for readers with a special determination of purpose'.

I am not trying to suggest that there is any incompatibility between the religious *belief* of a man like Eliot and his poetic *practice* — how could I with the examples of George Herbert and the later Donne to prove the contrary, not to mention Dante? But a problem does exist for the poet who has 'a special determination of purpose'; such a phrase implies a process of rationalization, by which we mean a conscious justification of dogma and morals as distinct from beliefs that are essentially irrational or instinctive. The habit of rationalization sustains the mystic, but it is a deadly habit in the poet.

I do not presume to judge Eliot; I even tremble as I attempt to reveal some of the dimensions of his agony. But if in this context I am to give my first allegiance to poetry (and I do not for a moment question the allegiance that a Christian poet must give to one whom Kierkegaard called 'the unique person'), it is not honest to pretend that the poet can have any other life or kingdom but poetry. The Shadow that falls between the emotion and the response is the shadow of the moral judgement, the Tables of the Law, the Commandments. For a year or two the old images will haunt the mind —

> Distraction, music of the flute, stops and steps of the mind
> over the third stair,
> Fading, fading. . . .

But eventually

> We must be still and still moving
> Into another intensity
> For further union, a deeper communion. . . .

'In my end is my beginning' — yes, but it is the end of the earthly poet and the beginning of the redeemed sinner, 'The awakened, lips parted, the hope, the new ships'. The old ships are left burning on the waters

> Burning burning burning bunrning

REMEMBERING ELIOT[1]

By Stephen Spender

IN *World within World* I wrote that I first met Eliot in 1930 when he invited me to lunch at a London restaurant. I had forgotten that the first meeting must have been at University College, Oxford, when he addressed an undergraduate club, the Martlets, on Wednesday, 16 May 1928. There was a dinner, at the end of which the menu was passed round and signed by all present. I still have this menu, with Eliot's autograph; that I should have kept it bears witness to the aura Eliot's name already had for undergraduate poets. Eliot attended the meeting of the Martlets, on the condition that he should not give an address, but would answer questions only. Inevitably, the club being half literary, half philosophical, the discussion turned to the problem, 'How can we *prove* that a work of art is beautiful? . . .'

One generation's taste is another generation's vomit. How, then, can a work of art stand outside the changing value which it has in the mind of human generations? . . . How can we be sure that there is a consciousness in which *Hamlet* and the Acropolis forever remain the same constant in their truth and and beauty?

T., an undergraduate who was reading philosophy and who grew tenser and tenser in his cups, and more and more voluble about Santayana, said that he did not believe there could be any absolute aesthetic criterion unless there was God. Eliot bowed his head in that almost praying attitude which I came to know well, and murmured something to the effect of: 'That is what I have come to believe.'

1. Reprinted from *Encounter*, March 1965, by permission of the editor, Stephen Spender.

Already in 1928 T. S. Eliot was a legend to the young poets. Now, when his poems seem almost inseparable from the explanations of them, may be a good time to recall the attitude of young writers to him a few years after the publication of *The Waste Land*.

The notices that appeared after his death show that there is a danger of two opposing attitudes towards him becoming crystallized. The one, that he was the Grand Master of the academy of allusiveness and strategy in deploying influences in modern poetry, and that his attitudes and beliefs do little more than provide occasion for him to push forward the 'frontiers of language'. The other view is that he was a once-revolutionary poet turned reactionary in politics, narrow-minded (and anti-Semitic) in his culture, and obscurantist in religion. In case this second view seems overstated, the reader can consult the correspondence columns of *The New Statesman* a week after Eliot's death. And I may add that when I said recently to a well-known Oxbridge don that I thought it strange that no member of the cultural branch of the British Labour government – neither Miss Jennie Lee nor Lord Snow – had attended the Westminster Abbey memorial service to Eliot, he replied that it was entirely appropriate that a man with the liberal views of C. P. Snow should have abstained from paying homage to the author of the unfortunate 'Burbank with a Baedeker: Bleistein with a Cigar'.

I think there is a danger of people interpreting the whole of Eliot's development as the unfolding of a predetermined pattern. Philip Toynbee (in *The Observer*) seemed to suggest that Eliot conformed to the pattern of Wordsworth: the revolutionary who becomes a reactionary, disappointing his followers. Most recent critics seem to read Eliot's conversion of 1927 into *The Waste Land* which was published in 1922. They do not seem to reflect that if Joyce had, like Graham Greene, written novels of wry Catholic orthodoxy, instead of *Finnegans Wake*, they would have been reading his reversion into *Ulysses* (which has already been interpreted by an American critic as a hymn to the sacrament of marriage, as perhaps it may be).

With all its virtues, the danger of critical analysis is that in tracing the graph of a writer's development it arrives at a pattern which looks like a rigid plan. Eliot lends himself particularly to this kind of treatment on account of declarations like the famous one about his being royalist and Catholic, and the still more famous one about the 'progress of an artist' being 'a continual self-sacrifice, a continual extinction of personality'. Yet the position of an artist is decided not just by himself but by an interaction between his work and his readers at various times. Part of the effect which a poem or a painting has is not what people think about it forty years later, but what they thought and felt about it when it was painted or written. In deciding, for example, whether *The Waste Land* adumbrates a Christian orthodoxy which became clarified in the *Four Quartets*, I. A. Richards's view (put forward in 1926) that it was a poetry 'severed from all beliefs' should be taken into account just as much as the view of someone today who using hindsight sees *The Waste Land* almost as a Christian poem. A different evolution of Eliot's ideas was possible, and if it had happened, would have made Richards right. Incidentally, if Eliot's own views are to be considered, I once heard him say to the Chilean poet Gabriela Mistral that at the time when he was writing *The Waste Land*, he seriously considered becoming a Buddhist. A Buddhist is as immanent as a Christian in *The Waste Land*.

In 1927 and 1928 writers like Eliot and D. H. Lawrence had not undergone any rigorous process of critical evaluation. They had their supporters and detractors, that was about all – except that the supporters seemed on the side of 'the future' and the detractors against it. One effect of the comparative lack of analytic discussion of contemporary writers was that we tended to relate poetry and fiction by living writers directly to the world around us, and to our own behaviour. We did not ask ourselves whether a work was in line with the Great Tradition.

We felt drawn to it if it was about the world we knew we lived in, the things that deeply concerned us, and – if we wanted to write – written in a way that seemed to help us to do so.

For example, it never occurred to us that Lawrence was a novelist in the Great Tradition, in direct line with the Organic Community by way of a puritan chapel-going culture, which was a hotter line connecting with the past than T. S. Eliot's one of the Anglican communion.

This lack of critical evaluation prevented us perhaps from understanding the wealth of reference, the allusiveness of contemporary writing. But the fact that, if a poem or novel seemed living, we felt the presence of a force challenging us, made discussion lively. We were divided in our views about Lawrence, because although we were agreed that he was one of those very rare writers who can make the reader feel alive beyond the surroundings of his room and his armchair – we also were agreed that Lawrence's main purpose in writing was to recommend behaving in a Lawrentian way. While I, for one, felt romantically drawn by this, most of my friends felt differently. Alec Grant – one of those whose autograph is on the menu of that Martlets meeting – said, after reading *The Plumed Serpent*, that after all what Lawrence stood for was 'a dervish dance'.

Lawrence, indeed, did seem to be addressing us forthrightly, sometimes too much so. He wrote poems sneering at our 'superior Oxford' voices. And in 'Sea-Bathers' he slammed the whole younger generation:

> Oh, the handsome bluey-brown bodies, they might
>   just as well be gutta percha,
> and the reddened limbs red india rubber tubing,
>   inflated,
> and the half-hidden private parts just a little
>   brass tap, rubinetto,
> turned on for different purposes.

This would seem hitting below the belt anyone determined on cool detached critical appraisal. Perhaps this is why – apart from the frenetic trial of *Lady Chatterley* – there has been no sustained attempt to fit the later Lawrence into the approved Lawrence canon.

Even Eliot could be less than helpful if one tried to 'explicate' him. In 1929 there was a meeting of the Oxford Poetry Club at which he was the guest of honour. Before it some of us arranged a separate meeting with Father M. C. D'Arcy, with whom we studied the text of *Ash-Wednesday*, just published. Some points were not cleared up, and at the later meeting an undergraduate asked Eliot: 'Please, sir, what do you mean by the line: "*Lady, three white leopards sat under a juniper tree*"?' Eliot looked at him and said: 'I mean, "*Lady, three white leopards sat under a juniper tree.*" . . .'

This was not altogether a fair reply, indeed it was flirtatious, considering that Eliot had surely opened himself to this kind of question about his poetry with the notes to *The Waste Land*. Yet later he gave as his reason for adding those notes that Leonard and Virginia Woolf considered the poem rather short for the volume they were printing, so he added them; much as he explained to me once that some of the poems in his first volume were only there because the book seemed so short. In the notes to *The Waste Land*, there is a good example of the kind of interpretation leading away from the poetic image to the literary reference, which Eliot seemed to be taking exception to when he mildly snubbed the undergraduate at the Poetry Club. One note tells us: '. . . the one-eyed merchant, seller of currants, melts into the Phoenician Sailor, and the latter is not wholly distinct from Ferdinand Prince of Naples. . . .'

Now this all too easily might cause the student who reads the explanation first (and the trouble now is that nearly everyone reads about the poem before he reads the poem) to write in his note-book: 'One-eyed merchant = Phoenician Sailor = Ferdinand Prince of Naples.' But it is far more important to see the Phoenician Sailor as a white, new-drowned corpse, devoured by fishes, than to see him as a symbol equated with other symbols. The fact that this section of the poem is a translation of an earlier poem of Eliot, written in French, confirms the suspicion that the linking-up is an arbitrary cinematic effect like a 'fade-in'. We saw the Phoenician Sailor as the Phoenician Sailor.

Thirty-five years ago sensitive undergraduates worried a lot about what was 'real'. It would take too long to analyse all we meant by this. But looking back I can see that the concern with being 'real' or 'unreal' arose because we felt ourselves to be living in a contemporary reality from which we were somehow shut out by circumstances. One aspect of this reality was the events which had produced the war and the general strike, and were later to produce the slump and fascism, leading into yet another world war. The sense of *entre deux guerres* was pervasive, though not fully conscious, and this contributed to the sense of unreality. The other aspect was the feeling that we were prevented in some way from becoming, intellectually and physically, ourselves. We were encouraged by the writings of D. H. Lawrence and vague intimations of psychoanalysis, to think that we might discover our real instinctual selves through sex.

When we looked at what was being written, we instantly felt that some writers were concerned with the problem of 'reality' and that others were not. From our undergraduate viewpoint writers fell roughly into three groups.

(1) The generally approved Book-Society-Chosen novelists and political poets who were names to us, mostly respected, not thought about critically, but who, though we thought of their work as literature, did not seem to touch our lives at any point.

(2) Writers who were experimental, concerned with being new at all costs, and whom we connected in our minds with new painting, new sculpture, new music, new art movements in Paris and Berlin.

(3) Writers who were directly or indirectly concerned with our own problem of living in a history which though real was

extremely difficult to apprehend, and with the problems of living real lives.

The first group included Georgian poets and the novelists praised week after week by Gerald Gould, J. C. Squire, Frank Swinnerton, *et al.* in *The Observer* and *Sunday Times*. The second group included Gertrude Stein, Edith Sitwell, E. E. Cummings, and experimental writers in the little, mostly Paris-published, magazines. Also, the occasionally published fragments of James Joyce's Work in Progress, and puzzling cantos of Ezra Pound which were beginning to appear in rare editions.

The third group included the James Joyce of *Ulysses*, D. H. Lawrence, E. M. Forster, W. B. Yeats (when *The Tower* appeared), and T. S. Eliot. So *The Waste Land* was exciting in the first place because it was concerned with the life which we felt to be real. It carried the equipment of the world beyond the screen, a landscape across which armies and refugees moved.

To us, in 1928, it very definitely made a pronouncement. It pronounced doom. The poet also had the sense of our problems. For him sex seemed to be rather sordid, involving 'Stockings, slippers, camisoles, and stays'. 'The young man carbuncular' who assaulted 'The typist home at teatime' had a great deal in common with any undergraduate who went down to London and had a whore in a bed-sitting room, returning, in time to climb into college, by the train called 'the fornicator'.

We connected *The Waste Land* in our minds with other great modern works of destruction and evil: Proust's volume *Sodome et Gomorrhe*; various German novels appearing about this time, notably Hermann Broch's *The Sleepwalkers*; and current philosophies of doom – the most famous of which was Spengler's now rather discredited *Decline of the West*.

Read together with *The Sacred Wood*, Eliot's poetry combined plunging into a world of chaos and absurdity with a '*rappel à l'ordre*'.

Apart from the concern with 'reality', various catchwords

of the time are revealing: for instance, 'symptomatic', by which was meant that writing must not only be technically interesting but also be significant in relation to the time; and, a bit later, catching on, I think, from Leavis's *New Bearings in English Poetry*, 'contemporary sensibility'.[2] There was a great deal of discussion about the concept of a 'new synthesis'. In the Auden–Day Lewis Introduction to *Oxford Poetry 1927*, the editors allot to poets a role in achieving a new synthesis.

Emotion is no longer necessarily to be analysed by 'recollection in tranquility': it is to be prehended emotionally and intellectually at once. And this is of most importance to the poet: for it is his mind that must bear the brunt of the conflict and may be the first to realise the new harmony.

In 1927 Eliot was the poet who seemed, in *The Waste Land*, to be fulfilling this role.

The charge of 'intellectualization' was at the centre of the subsequent battle round Eliot. That he was an intellectual was precisely the complaint of his opponents, who felt that poetry should not be intellectual.

In June 1945 *New Verse* cited some opinions of contemporaries about poets, collected by a New Zealand journalist, Ian Donnelly, and published in a book called *The Joyous Pilgrimage*. A foremost novelist is quoted as saying:

The trouble is that all these people (i.e. Day Lewis, Auden, Spender and the rest) have been influenced by T. S. Eliot, and Eliot is definitely a bad influence. He is donnish, pedantic, cold. He is an example of the over-educated American, and Henry James was another. It would have been better for contemporary English literature if Eliot had stayed in Louisville, or wherever he came from.

2. Incidentally, I refute absolutely the legend that our generation had not discovered Eliot, Lawrence, or Gerard Manley Hopkins until the publication of this book. Already in 1928 the work of many young writers showed the influence of all three.

Humbert Wolfe:

Eliot is a poet who cannot write poetry. He has a great mind, but, spiritually and intellectually, he is muscle-bound.

Blunden:

I don't know why Eliot should feel so badly about things. There is no reason why he should have to write in that 'I-cannot-be-gay' manner. He did not have to go through the war.

These quotations sum up pretty well the literary establishment's dislike for Eliot even as late as 1935.

Today one can feel envious of a poet who is attacked by adversaries whose function seems to be to define only their own incomprehension, making themselves the foil to his intelligence.

Their mistake was to think that the intellect is necessarily cold. If Eliot had been cold we would not have been drawn to him. The fact is, of course, that his intellect burned white-hot. What attracted the young poets to *The Waste Land* was that rhythmically the language was so exciting. To say this is to say a great deal, for rhythmic excitement of the order of *The Waste Land* is rare in poetry, and not necessary to it. What is necessary is that rhythm should be interesting, unique to the poet, the handwriting of his sensibility, even of something beyond sensibility, the indefinable quality of his being. All Eliot's poetry has uniqueness and interest, but *The Waste Land* does more than hold the reader's interest and admiration, it makes the poetry become a passion to the reader. When this happens with a poet, his readers take up an entirely new attitude to him. Of modern poets, one could see it happen to Yeats when he published *The Tower*, which has rhythmic excitement. Although what is now perhaps Yeats's most famous poem, 'The Second Coming', was written as early as 1922, it was not until *The Tower* that readers really woke up to the fact that Yeats had emerged completely from the Celtic Twilight, and from being a minor had become a major poet of the present century.

One learned from *The Sacred Wood* of Eliot's views about tradition. But I myself enjoyed reading *The Sacred Wood* as I might any excellent critical essay, relishing particularly the quotations from the Elizabethans. It was not *The Sacred Wood* so much as the rhythmic excitement of *The Waste Land* and *The Tower* which really gave me an appetite to look for the same excitement in past poetry. It is a quality so present in the Elizabethans that when one is young one can be deluded for a time into thinking Webster and Tourneur almost as great as Shakespeare. I found it in Donne's epistles, in *Samson Agonistes*, and in passages of *The Prelude*. It occurs in one poem of Dylan Thomas ('In Memory of Anne Jones'). It is the lack of it in Pound that caused Yeats to say to me once that he considered his poetry 'static'.

Apart from *The Waste Land*, Eliot's only poem which has this quality is 'Gerontion', which after *The Waste Land* is his poem the most Elizabethan in feeling. One might say that intellect in Eliot is Dantesque, but up to the *Four Quartets*, the passion is Elizabethan.

We formed a mental picture of Eliot. He was the poet/anti-poet – if long hair, long country walks, shaggy tweeds, beer, and bread and cheese made a poet, as one gathered they did from the Georgians. For us, his private life was summed up in the line 'the awful daring of a moment's surrender'; and apart from his pin-stripe suits, rolled umbrella, short hair, and ordinary man's job in a bank, his poetry had a good many stage properties, of a slightly music-hall kind: the boarding house, Doris padding with bare feet down the corridor, the seaside, and the beach.

The bank-clerk image was superseded by that of the editor of *The Criterion*. The loss of romantic appeal was compensated for by the possibility of being published by Eliot, of meeting him.

The secret of Eliot's influence over the young lay in a paradox of his personality. With a gesture of reversing current theories about the self-expressing poet, he dramatized a necessary shift in sensibility, from a subjective concern with the poet's self to an objective one with the values of a civilization endlessly created in men's minds. He wrote a new, a really new poetry, which set up connexions with the old, the really old. He was more inimitable than any other modern poet (as would-be imitators find to their cost) yet more could be learned from his theory and practice than from any other writer. This man who seemed so unapproachable was the most approached by younger poets – and the most helpful to them – of any poet of his generation. Whoever had the will and intelligence to do so could grasp the principles by which he worked and lived, could read what he had read, could understand what he believed. All this was far more important than whether one agreed with all his opinions. One could see the relevance of his relation to the time in which he lived, and to the past. Religiously, poetically, and intellectually, this very private man kept open house. And all the rooms, and the garden, made clear sense. Yet in spite of all this he was sly, ironic, a bit cagey, a bit calculating perhaps, the Eliot whom Ezra Pound called 'Old Possum'.

At the Martlets we glimpsed the Eliot of whom it was rumoured that he was being converted to Christianity. But at this time the unredeemed Eliot whom we got from the early poetry seemed more real to us. And there was some evidence in his lesser works for the existence of a street-haunting dandified nightbird Eliot. Undergraduates who went to Paris came back with copies of Charles-Louis Philippe's *Bubu of Montparnasse*, with an Introduction by T. S. Eliot. Then, later, there was the Eliot who advocated Djuna Barnes's *Nightwood*, and who admired the *Tropic of Cancer* of Henry Miller. Of course, these were literary judgements, but they also contained an obscure element of empathy.

Our next meeting was the one I have described in the restaurant, which took place in 1930. Eliot inquired rather searchingly about my attitude towards my work. I said I wanted to be a poet, adding also that I wanted to write stories and novels. He said that if one wanted to write poetry one could not write anything else creative. I said: 'What about Hardy?' He said he thought that Hardy's poems were amateur. 'Then what about Goethe?' 'I have always considered Goethe rather an extreme case of Hardy.' This was not meant altogether seriously, for later (in March 1932) he wrote to me that he liked Goethe's poetry but was bored by most of his prose, with the exception of one magnificent book, 'the invaluable *Conversations with Eckermann*'. This was the year of Goethe's centenary. And he went on: 'What I chiefly dislike about Goethe is the fact that he is having a centenary. I always dislike everybody at the centenary moment ...'

When Eliot talked about poetry it was as the one wholly serious activity to which a poet should devote his life. He didn't speak of it as though it were a kind of by-product of being born with a poetic gift. The phrase so often heard from the mouths of Georgian poets, 'in these lines there is a true poet', would have meant nothing to him. The question would be – 'are the lines poetry?' Poetry required concentration, dedication, and work. There was also a place for magic and inspiration, but I think one of the things that marked the difference of Eliot from the Georgian poets was that they thought that inspiration and magic preceded work, he thought that work preceded magic and inspiration. He once mentioned in a letter that he found he began a poem 'with a rhythm'. This being so, it is evident that a part of writing poetry is a kind of perpetual listening, waiting for the rhythm. One of the things that may prevent one's writing poetry or that may coarsen one's writing is filling one's mind with the rhythms of prose fiction.

The other thing I remember from that first luncheon is his answer when I asked him what future he foresaw for our civilization. 'Internecine fighting. ... People killing one another in the streets. ...'

At this point I should emphasize that although I knew him for a long time, I did not know Eliot well. A few times when he was sharing a flat with his devoted friend and adviser John Hayward, my wife and I dined with him and Hayward, and after his very happy second marriage we dined two or three times with him and his wife. But between 1930 and the outbreak of war I never went to see him at any rooms where he was living. He was rather hierarchical by temperament, and in the hierarchy of his friends I was certainly in an outer circle. On the other hand, he was consistently kind and even affectionate with me. Also – and I expect that others who knew him as much or as little as I did, will understand what I mean – although at the time when one spoke with him or even received a letter from him he never seemed to reveal anything of his feelings and personality, when one added up a sum of impressions got from being with him, they were very revealing of his attitudes, if never of his personal life.

His conversation could be dry and factual, and if early on one got onto some unpropitious subject – the weather or the sales of poetry – he might pursue it remorselessly, like a tram going through a slum. Rather drab yet not unmusical dialogue which occasionally breaks into shrewd observation or characterization, or irony – a bit sententious in tone – characterizes some passages of the plays. And his conversation was often like this. Some people were disappointed or bored, but to me his conversation always seemed music. His talk had a subdued metric quality which held my attention, as in the line once made at tea I have quoted elsewhere 'I daren't take cake, and jam's too much trouble.' He made shrewd observations in his manner of gravely considering the problem: 'I've often noticed that it isn't what's said in a review that matters, but the length of the review.' When he laughed he bent his head forward and looked down at the table or floor and seemed to chuckle inwardly. He had a peculiar brand of sharp comment, without malice, almost affectionate, and yet to the point. Of that first conversation with me, Allen Tate has reported his saying: 'I noticed that Spender spoke of wanting to be a poet, not of writing poems.' Of all my generation, he most admired

Auden, but once when we were praising Auden's criticism, he said 'All the same, he's not a scholar.' 'Why?' 'I was reading an Introduction by him to a selection of Tennyson's poems, in which he says that Tennyson is the stupidest poet in the language. Now if Auden had been a scholar he'd have been able to think of some stupider poets...' And of the anarchism of his friend Herbert Read, whom he loved and esteemed very highly: 'Sometimes when I read Herbert's inflammatory anarchist pamphlets I have the impression that I am reading the pronouncements of an old-fashioned nineteenth-century liberal.' He said that James Joyce was the man most completely centred on his own inner world he had ever known. We were talking about a book which had just appeared on his *Four Quartets*, and he said slyly: 'Sometimes it occurs to me that people when they think that they are writing about my poetry, are really writing about the kind of poetry they would have wished to write.'

He was very deeply concerned for others. He once told me that he had always felt disturbed and unhappy that a contemporary of his at Harvard, Conrad Aiken, had had so little success as a poet. 'I've always thought that he and I were equally gifted, but I've received a large amount of appreciation, and he has been rather neglected. I can't understand it. It seems unjust. It always worries me.'

The very elusiveness of Eliot's poetry and character – of which one occasionally caught glimpses like the vivid blue flash of a kingfisher's wing – fascinated, so that younger poets when they met him gathered up Eliotana like crumbs that fell from the table. Auden, who was staying with me in Hampstead in 1929, went to see Eliot about the publication of his verse play *Paid on Both Sides* and waited an hour in a waiting-room at Faber & Faber. In 1930 Wynyard Browne when he was an undergraduate had the temerity to call at the Eliots' home. A lady opened the front door, asked him what he wanted, and on hearing 'Mr Eliot' wailed, 'Why, oh why, do they all want to see my husband!' and slammed the door in his face.

During the war, at Eliot's request, I gave a lecture about Yeats to something called The Tomorrow Club at which Eliot took the chair for me (I have a vague impression that he did this as the price for avoiding giving a lecture himself). It was terribly embarrassing to stand there talking with Eliot sitting a yard behind me, to the side. I wrote out the whole lecture, as though it were an essay for a tutor. Before going to the hall where I had to speak, Eliot took me to dinner at his club. Sherry, wine, and brandy with the meal. I was so overcome by the liquor and my awe that whenever in the course of my lecture I came across the name W. B. Yeats, I said, 'T. S. Eliot', and then turned to the chairman and said, 'Sorry, I meant W. B. Yeats.'

Among the few notes I made of Eliot's conversation, the only ones I can find are about the first meeting of Eliot with Igor Stravinsky, which Nicolas Nabokov asked me to arrange. In them Stravinsky steals the show, but that he should have done so is also characteristic of Eliot:

I drove Eliot to the Savoy. He was in a good humour. The conversation was carried on mostly in English, though some of it was in French, which Eliot talks slowly and meticulously. Stravinsky started talking about his health. He complained that all the doctors told him to do different, sometimes quite opposite, things. He suffered from an excessive thickness of the blood. Moving his hands as though moulding an extremely rich substance, he said: 'They say my blood is so thick, so rich, so very rich, it might turn into crystals, like rubies, if I didn't drink beer, plenty of beer, and occasionally whisky, all the time.' Eliot said that a pint of beer did him less harm in the middle of the day than two glasses of red wine. Stravinsky returned to the subject of the thickness of his blood.

Eliot said meditatively: 'I remember that in Heidelberg when I was young I went to a doctor and was examined, and the doctor said: "Mr Eliot, you have the thinnest blood I've ever tested." '

Stravinsky talked about Auden writing the libretto of *The Rake's Progress*. He said it went marvellously. Auden arrived at the Stravinskys' house in Hollywood, ate an enormous dinner and drank much wine, went to bed at exactly half past ten, and then was up at 8 the next morning ready to listen to Stravinsky's ideas. No sooner were these divulged than he started writing the libretto. He would think of something, write it, then ask himself where it could be fitted in, pulling out lines and phrases, and finding places in which to insert them, as though he were fitting the pieces into a puzzle. After consulting with Chester Kallman, within a few days Auden returned the libretto, neatly typed out. Only minor alterations had to be made, and Stravinsky only had to suggest that there was some difficulty somewhere and the solution to the problem would arrive by return of post.

Stravinsky started talking about the annoyance of publicity. A reporter had rung up and suggested coming to his hotel to take down notes of his reaction to the performance of one of his works on the B.B.C. Vera Stravinsky chipped in here and said: 'We explained that we never listen to the radio.' Stravinsky added a terse comment on the British conductor.

Eliot asked him what he did when people wrote asking for photographs.

Stravinsky said he did not send them, because they cost money. He said that when he was in Venice, where a choral work of his was performed in St Mark's, *Time* had created a link between him and T. S. Eliot by captioning their review of it: 'Murder in the Cathedral'. He said that after this performance, he waited 25 minutes so that the crowds might disperse, and then, accompanied by friends, walked out into the piazza. There were very few people by this time, but as he walked across the square, a few people seated at tables saw him and started clapping. He said he was extremely touched. The performance had been broadcast through amplifiers into the square, and these people, most of them young, had waited in order to applaud.

I asked Eliot how it felt to address 14,000 people at a meeting in Minneapolis. He said: 'Not 14,000 – 13,523. As I walked onto the platform, which was in the largest sports stadium there, I felt like a very small bull walking into an enormous arena. As soon as I had started talking, I found it much easier to address several thousand people than a very small audience. One has not the slightest idea what they are thinking, one sees no features of any face, and one feels exactly as if one were speaking to an anonymous unseen audience through a broadcast system. They all seemed very quiet, but I could not tell how they reacted....'

After our first two or three meetings in the early thirties, I was abroad in Germany and Austria for a good deal and we corresponded by mail. When one received a letter from Eliot, often it seemed flat and impersonal (and indeed most of these letters are purely about business) but on re-reading them a good deal stands out that is revealing both of his own work and of his wish to help and advise a young man. 'I confess that personally I take so little interest in novels that I am inclined to deplore your devoting so much time to prose, instead of poetry' – this is a theme he returns to several times. His criticism of my writing is thoughtful, sympathetic, encouraging. There are flashes of self-revelation. He writes that he is very glad I am listening to the posthumous Quartets of Beethoven.

I have the A minor Quartet on the gramophone, and find it quite inexhaustible to study. There is a sort of heavenly or at least more than human gaiety about some of his later things which one imagines might come to oneself as the fruit of reconciliation and relief after immense suffering; I should like to get something of that into verse before I die. (28 March 1931)

I have written above that I could never seriously disapprove of Eliot as a 'reactionary'. But in the spring of 1932 I seem to have written him a letter attacking the Church, calling religion an 'escape' from social struggle. He quoted this letter in a broadcast (which I did not hear) and writes excusing himself for doing so without my permission. In his letter he answers some of the points I had raised. He points out that religion is a less effective escape than that used by thousands who 'escape by reading novels, by looking at films, or best of all, by driving very fast on land or in air, which makes even dreams unnecessary'. He asks me whether I mean what I say when I write associating 'chastity, humility, austerity, and discipline' with school-room chapels. 'If people really knew what the words mean, they would lock up or deport anyone who pronounced them.' Events of coming years in Germany (and those today in South Africa) prove that there was some truth in this.

In 1933 I published a review attacking some of his views in *The Use of Poetry and the Use of Criticism*. I felt miserable at doing so, and wrote to him apologizing. He replied: 'Your criticisms are much milder than my own; in fact you give me the impression of having gone as far as possible to be generous; perhaps too far.' He then goes on to point out that some of my attack is based on my not understanding when he is being ironic. 'In short, your only weakness consists in taking the lectures too seriously.'

In a letter (9 May 1935) about my critical volume *The Destructive Element*, he is severe with me whilst also being severe with his own *After Strange Gods* (though he also writes that he thinks his criticism in that volume is more interesting than his early work; later he came to dislike it more than any other book he had published). He says the danger of this kind of criticism is that one reads in order to prove one's point. 'I was not guiltless of that', and he insists that it is necessary to 'know one's authors from cover to cover – and I didn't', adding with courteous irony, 'I am not quite sure that you did either.' 'You ought to have read every scrap of James before trying to fit him into any social theory . . . you don't really criticise any author to whom you have never surrendered yourself.' And: 'Even just the bewildering minute counts; you have to give yourself up, and then recover yourself, and the third moment is having something to say, before you have wholly forgotten both surrender and recovery. Of course the self recovered is never the same as the self before it was given.'

Applying these principles to his own work, he thinks his essays on Jonson, Tourneur, and Bradley good, that on Machiavelli 'rubbish'. He thinks that a study of Henry James's story 'The Friends of the Friends' would make 'otiose and irrelevant your questions about James's virility'. Rather astonishingly he pronounces that 'James wasn't an American' because, although he had an acute sense of contemporary America, he had 'no American Sense of the Past'. Eliot adds about his own America that '*our* America came to an end in 1829, when Andrew Jackson was elected president', and he qualifies what he has said about James by adding that James had unconsciously '*acquired,* though not inherited, something of the American tradition. He was not a descendant of the witch-hangers.'

Looking back, I see that in my twenties I was too much in awe of Eliot to realize how much trouble he was taking in seeing me and writing to me. Being over-impressed by others makes one fail to take seriously what they have to give, because one cannot really believe they take one seriously. It is almost a form of ingratitude.

Eliot was a man with the highest standards, in his poetry, his criticism, and his behaviour to others. I think it is worthwhile to draw a contrast between his attitude towards young writers and that of the magazine *Scrutiny*, which also maintained and presented high standards. Eliot encouraged, talked with, wrote to young poets. He may have been too kind, too generous, he may have made mistakes, and one (I deliberately choose the impersonal pronoun) may not have deserved his charity and trust. *Scrutiny* took none of the risks involved in charitable judgement; which did not prevent them in the exceptional cases, where they went all out to use one or two reputations as sticks with which to beat others, from making glaring mistakes. Their frequent policy with young writers was to destroy a reputation before it was made. It was bad enough that a young poet had been published at all, but at least they could do their best to prevent their readers liking him. Moreover, the publication of their literary periodical was also bound up with theories of education. Young men reviewing were given editorial instruction as to the lines on which they should attack other young writers.

In pointing out how immensely concerned Eliot was, I want to emphasize that there are ways of encouraging literature other than being intolerant to beginners. The reason why this may be a good occasion to do so is that the English schools in the new universities are likely to play an extremely influential role in criticism of contemporary writing during the next few years. The power of English teachers will extend beyond the universities to the B.B.C., the British Council, and to literary periodicals. They really have to choose between the methods of *The Criterion* and those of *Scrutiny*. Not that *Scrutiny* was not admirable in criticizing and drawing attention to works which the editors liked. Referring to Eliot's letter about my early essays on James, one might say that *Scrutiny* performed the greatest services in appreciating and criticizing some dead and a very few living writers when its critics had accepted and read them in their entirety.

So to our generation, Eliot was the poet of poets, closer to us than Yeats though Yeats might be 'greater'. We looked to the poetry, and all disagreements about the opinions seemed superficial and could be shrugged off. As a man we thought of him as sophisticated, ironic, erudite, serious, but approachable and friendly, though keeping one at a distance. On account of his seriousness, his lack of emphasis on cleverness, he seemed less alarming than, for example, Lytton Strachey, who could soar far above one with his wit and then follow this up with the depth-charge of one of his famous prolonged silences. Other than Eliot the only two older writers who made themselves *present* to contemporaries twenty years younger were E. M. Forster and Virginia Woolf.

It was astonishing to discover that to his immediate contemporaries Eliot was a subject for endless anecdotes, in which he appeared extraordinary (that was the Bloomsbury word – '*extraordinary*') for his naïvety. It was not at all that they did not appreciate his genius, nor feel, indeed, extremely fond of him. But they doubted whether he put 'personal relations' as high in the scale of values as they did, and they disapproved of his being religious.

Recently I questioned a lady who knew Eliot well from 1913 onwards. The first time she met him was at Bosham in Sussex. She described him as wearing white flannels, standing by the shore looking out at the waves. Her family and the Eliots went on picnics together. What struck her about the young Mr Eliot was his inability to express himself conversationally, to enter into personal relationships. She thought he knew little about other people. His first wife, who had been a dancer (she was called by someone the 'river girl'), was gay, talkative, a chatterbox. She wanted to enjoy life, found Eliot inhibiting and inhibited, yet worshipped him. (One knows tragedies of the too-lighthearted tied to the too-serious.) There was a time when the Eliots separated, and Eliot lived by himself, wore a monocle, and was known to the neighbours as 'Captain Eliot'.

I asked her whether she thought that Prufrock and the other 'I' characters of the early poems were self-portraits. 'Oh, no,' she said, 'they weren't him. They were characters in a scene which he thought represented what life was like. Prufrock and "the young man carbuncular" who seduces the typist, with "her drying combinations touched by the sun's last rays", were vignettes of what he thought real people to be. They weren't his own life, not at all.'

Aldous Huxley used to describe Eliot taking dancing lessons, rolling back the carpet of his flat and seriously fox-trotting with his wife. He went to dances at the Hammersmith Palais de Danse. 'When I visited him at his bank,' said Aldous Huxley, 'he was the most bank-clerky of all bank clerks. He was not on the ground nor even on the floor under that, but in a sub-sub-basement sitting at a desk which was in a row of desks with other bank clerks.'

Eliot and Virginia Woolf understood each other very well on the level of their poetry. (It is unfashionable to say so but I think she had a poetic gift comparable with Eliot's.) An extremely complex game of serious-nonseriousness was being played when one day at tea in Tavistock Square, Virginia Woolf needled Eliot about his religion. Did he go to church? Yes. Did he hand round the plate for the collection? Yes. Oh, really! Then what did he experience when he prayed? Eliot leaned forward, bowing his head in that attitude which was itself one of prayer ('Why should the agèd eagle stretch his wings?'), and described the attempt to concentrate, to forget self, to attain union with God.

There are many other anecdotes, probably most of them exaggerated and some invented. My reason for referring to them is that they do lead back into the atmosphere of Eliot's poems up to and including *Sweeney Agonistes*. The anecdotes are, as it were, the masks or *personae* created in other people's minds by Eliot the bank clerk, with his bowler hat, carrying his umbrella. After 1930 or so – that is, after the break-up of his first marriage, and after his conversion – this Eliot disappears, and that is why the early legendary Eliot seemed strange to us. But hearing such reminiscences of the early Eliot we rediscovered the poet of the 'awful daring of a moment's surrender' whose character we had vaguely intuited when we first read *The Waste Land*.

I did not realize when I met him in 1928 that Eliot was just traversing a period of great unhappiness, when he was separating from his first wife, who was on the verge of insanity and who later did become insane. It is true that in conversation with outsiders Eliot gave no indication of this, and with his closest friends, I am sure, he never showed any sign of pitying himself. But I do not think it is correct to say (as some writers have done) that he never spoke to anyone about his private affairs. I suppose that he confided in Geoffrey Faber, Frank Morley, Herbert Read, and, later, John Hayward, whose advice he sought in his writing. I suspect that in the late twenties and early thirties, some of the heads of the firm of Faber & Faber were a kind of committee, advising and helping Eliot. Not only was his office a home from home, but during the most agonized years of the break-up of his first marriage Geoffrey Faber and his family provided Eliot with their own home.

In the last ten years or so of his life, after his second marriage, Eliot achieved with his radiant wife the happiness which had been denied him during most of his maturity, a happiness of which one guesses he had glimpses as a child. There are indications of a great personal assuagement in his published poetry, for example in the references in *The Elder Statesman* to the bliss of Oedipus at Colonus, and in the dedicatory lines of that volume to his wife.

These late works are not Eliot at his best and strongest. They suggest a return to the personal, as though towards the end Eliot felt that the aim of a complete objectivity and impersonality in poetry had in it an element of pride, like that of James Joyce's Stephen Dedalus.

Eliot's last poetry does not quite round off his life-work, but it suggests how it might have been rounded off, with a return to human affection, acceptance of sensual experience, and perhaps even a less catastrophic attitude towards society. In America, shortly after the war, I once brashly said to him that in his early poetry there was a feeling of despair about this world and the next, and the imprisonment of each individual in his separateness; in *Four Quartets* and the plays, he had expressed his belief in a metaphysical world, and hope for the redemption of each individual; but he still offered no hope for civilization. My thought was that at some point he would envision people as citizens in the human city (of course, in *The Idea of a Christian Society* he did this, but he had never done so in his poetry). He smiled and said: 'Now you have put that thought into my mind, I shall instantly forget about it. But perhaps one day it will bear fruit.'

Probably I was merely being foolish, and he was being ironic. What I am trying to suggest though is that if one regards Eliot's development not as a kind of logic of the mind and imagination which developed a pattern inevitable from the start, but as architecture, then it suggests a structure planned as a whole, but which has gaps, unfinished fragments, and only indications of a crowning tower. The underlying logic of the design is everywhere felt, but the whole has not been realized in the concrete imagination.

Moreover, although Eliot gives hints and indications of consistency, unity, wholeness, yet when one comes to examine the separate parts of the poetry, one has a Wyndham-Lewis-like picture of a man who for the purposes of making each poem has separated part of himself from the whole. Thus in 'Prufrock' and the early poems, despite the elaborate self-mockery, the point of view is essentially aesthetic. The artist, too sophisticated to be a Ruskin, a Pater, or a Wilde, nevertheless has a deep nostalgia for a past – almost any past – in which men lived by their visions. In the poetry after *The Waste Land* the poet seeks to free himself of the love of creatures, particularly human ones, and to penetrate moments outside time, moments in which the temporal intersects with eternity. The rejection of ordinary values of living, and of the animal side of human nature, is absolute. But the poetry even when it is very beautiful runs the risk of simplist generalizations, which many people might feel to belie human experience:

> Those who sharpen the tooth of the dog, meaning
> Death
> Those who glitter with the glory of the humming-
>   bird, meaning
> Death
> Those who sit in the sty of contentment, meaning
> Death
> Those who suffer the ecstasy of the animals, meaning
> Death

Reading these lines and reading in all the plays, until the very last, the poet's doctrine of renunciation of life and of attachment to other human beings, I am struck by the fact that he has renounced so much, that the poetry, beautiful as it is, is forced into very narrow channels of vivid spiritual experience. This narrow and concentrated poetry is intensely beautiful, intensely expressive, with a command of language that is absolute:

> It is possible that sin may strain and struggle
> In its dark instinctive birth, to come to consciousness
> And so find expurgation. It is possible
> You are the consciousness of your unhappy family,
> Its bird sent flying through the purgatorial flame.
> Indeed it is possible. You may learn hereafter,
> Moving alone through flames of ice, chosen
> To resolve the enchantment under which we suffer.

In its expression in controlled language with a rhythm inseparable from a translucent imagery to which it adds force, this is great poetry. A question arises, though, of how much experience the poet can imagine and express in poetry of this quality. What I think one finds in Eliot is that in different periods his imagination dwells on different phases of experience, but in each work the view of life is partial. In the early poetry life is seen exclusively as hell, in the middle poetry it is rejected too easily – everything (like marriage and work) to do with actual living is reduced to the same grey dull average. The temptations of Thomas à Becket in *Murder in the Cathedral* are not tempting, and the knights who assassinate the martyr are figures out of Bernard Shaw. In spite of this, *Murder in the Cathedral* is a masterpiece because it is conceived of as a great processional scene of sacrifice rather than as a tragedy in which there are temptations which tempt and a conflict between good and bad forces which are fairly equal.

I cannot go further here than to suggest that Eliot's work points towards a synthesis in which opposing worlds are reconciled – not, of course, in the sense of good coming to terms with evil, but in the sense of the body and the soul, the reality of time as well as of timelessness, being imagined with equal intensity. But the synthesis is never fully complete. The two great works in which he comes nearest to a marriage of heaven and hell are *The Waste Land* and the *Four Quartets*. And both those poems have public and social aspects: *The Waste*

Land having deep roots in the First World War, and the last three of the *Four Quartets* in the Second World War. It seems that the objectivization of his poetry towards which Eliot strove came nearest to realization when the poetry was concerned with an actual crisis of civilization: the phase of disillusion and despair against a background of revolution and collapse after the first war, the air-raids and the cause of Britain during the second.

At the same time, when he turned outwards in his poetry towards society, it reflected the fragmentation of his own soul. So he was driven back onto the position that in times of the breakdown of civilization the individual becomes peculiarly responsible to himself, has to remember that he lives not just in this time of collapse, these disrupted cities, but also in eternity, and in the city of God.

Possibly, then, the centre of Eliot's work is its exploration of the truth that there cannot in our time be a synthesis between the modern city of the industrial world – bound entirely to the temporal and gambling at every moment with destruction – and the eternal city with aims of civilization outside the temporal. And therefore true art has to be, for us, fragmented art. Perhaps the force of his attack against Lawrence is not that of the puritan against the sensualist, but of this truth – that there can be no synthesis – against the false idea of Lawrence that the modern world can be saved by the sexual relation of the human pair.

This brings me back at the end to considering again Eliot's idea that the progress of an artist is 'continual self-sacrifice, a continual extinction of personality', with its rider that 'to escape from these things' one must 'have personality and emotions'. On one level all he is doing here is opposing the kind of self-expression found in the poetry of Rupert Brooke, and upon which Owen's poetry is dependent, with the truism that the artist has to draw upon techniques and traditions which are objective and greater than himself, to surrender himself to the past. But there is also a hint of something else:

STEPHEN SPENDER

that the artist has to fight against attitudes in his personality
which distort his vision, with hatred, with unhappiness even.
These attitudes of intense personal feeling we find in writers
who agreed with Eliot's kind of classicism: in Ezra Pound and
Wyndham Lewis, for instance. The problem of objectivization
now becomes more complex and difficult. A programme of
extinguishing the personality seems inadequate. For to achieve
the kind of objectivity where the writer's view is not distorted
by his personal emotions of suffering, rejection, and so on,
means that he must develop as it were a personality beyond
even the impersonality. And here by tracing the progression of
the sensibility which calls itself 'I' in Eliot's poetry one is able
to follow the development from the projected *personae* – the
mask of Prufrock and the other 'I' characters in the early
poetry – to the 'Issues from the hand of God, the simple soul',
'I' thrown back upon itself, seeking redemption, of the *Ariel
Poems* and of *Ash-Wednesday*; to the impersonal representative war-time air-raid warden and church-warden 'I' of the
Four Quartets; and finally to the Oedipus-at-Colonus 'I' in
whom there is a hint of the reconciliation of body and soul, of
the marriage of heaven and hell in a person beyond both personality and impersonality.

In Eliot's personal life, one can rejoice that during the last
ten years the synthesis was achieved, the reconciliation was
complete. This fulfilment was hinted at but not realized in his
poetry. Somehow one knew all along that it could not be, that
he would hymn no Yeatsian triumph of old age.

T. S. ELIOT

A PERSONAL REMINISCENCE

By Bonamy Dobrée

IT isn't easy to write a 'personal reminiscence' of someone known over a number of years (if one has ever 'known' him); to recapture the significance of that particular glance at that particular moment, the pressure of the handshake just then. It all amounts in the end to a very individual sense of a presence, which it is impossible to communicate. But perhaps one can give some sort of idea of how this sense came into being, and gradually established itself.

My first awareness of Tom Eliot's existence came to me, in 1917 I think it was, when I was on leave in Alexandria from the Palestine Front, and E. M. Forster, whose acquaintance I had just made, put into my hand a small pamphlet, saying, 'I don't know if you care for this sort of thing?' It was 'The Love Song of J. Alfred Prufrock'. Care for it! It excited me. I had depended latterly on Palgrave's good old *Golden Treasury*, as being of convenient size to carry about in one's haversack, and the fresh attack enchanted me. The actuality of the whole thing, yet all expressed with considerable musical quality, struck me as belonging to life. Then there were such vivid analogies:

The yellow fog that rubs its back upon the window-panes,
The yellow smoke that rubs its muzzle on the window-panes . . .

and the normally 'poetic' conclusion, enlarging, rather than making precise, the imagination.

After coming back to England in 1919, I heard vaguely about 'Eliot', but nothing came clearly to my mind until in 1921 John Rodker gave me a copy of *Ara Vos Prec*, of his own

69

printing. This fascinated me, though I daresay for the wrong reasons:

> Polyphiloprogenitive
> The sapient sutlers of the Lord. . . .

(had anyone before made a single word the first line of a poem? and such a witty addition to our vocabulary?), and I rejoiced in 'The broad-backed hippopotamus', not seeing the implications of the last lines of either of these poems. And then there was the more solemn music of 'Gerontion' and of 'Portrait of a Lady', with phrases that linger in the memory as do those that really matter. Here, I felt, was a poet who meant something in terms of today. I was becoming aware of a personality.

In early 1924 (I think it was), when I was living in the Basque country, I wrote a review for Leonard Woolf, then editing *The Nation*, having been recommended to Woolf by Francis Birrell, for whom Eliot had great regard. On a visit to England I went to *The Nation* office to introduce myself to Woolf, who then invited me to dinner. In due course I went out to Richmond, where the Hogarth Press was coming into being, to join in the evening meal in the kitchen with Leonard and Virginia, whom I was meeting, all agog to do so, for the first time. There was another guest there – T. S. Eliot. I was naturally intrigued by this quiet person, not at all 'poetic' in appearance, who had written the astonishing *The Waste Land*, which I had read, being a subscriber to *The Criterion*, the first number of which had contained it. I had not then grasped *The Waste Land* fully (perhaps I have not yet done so), by which, after an initial rebellion, I had been enormously impressed, especially by the bold mixture of the low colloquial and superb music (e.g., such a haunting line as 'Filled all the desert with inviolable voice'), the wonderful marriage of tradition and individual talent, and the sense of its 'mattering' here and now.

I wasn't exactly shy – one isn't in one's early thirties – but as a new entrant in the literary field I didn't know where I stood. From the first everything was easy and friendly; I didn't for a moment feel that I was, so to speak, under examination for fitness of inclusion in their company. I don't remember much of the conversation, except that at one moment Eliot asked me, 'Do you read *all The Criterion*?', and I answered, 'Not *all*: do you?' Eliot was amused at this rather pert remark (but still, Aldington was then part editor); he laughed, but he remembered the remark, for some four years later he wrote to me: 'As you know, I never read *The Criterion*.' He was kind on that evening, but did not seem much interested in anything I had to say until, after dinner, Virginia Woolf asked me what I was then doing. I said I was trying to write a play, but wasn't certain whether to do it in prose or some kind of verse. This at once interested Eliot – the 'how' of a thing, the technique – and a good discussion followed. I believe that it was largely the encouragement I got from him then that made me write *Histriophone*, a dialogue on stage speech, later published by the Hogarth Press.

He accepted the idea of lunching together; so a few days later I descended into the bowels of Lloyds Bank in the City, and we went off to some restaurant. Soon after we sat down he went out to buy cigarettes, and was away an unconscionable time, so that I uncomfortably wondered if he were coming back. He did, and we talked desultorily. But as I was going along with him after lunch, I said that one of the things I most liked about *The Waste Land* was its dramatic movement. Eliot at once warmed. Here was something very close to one of his deep desires, and it seems that I was the first person to have noticed this about the poem.

So began my acquaintance with Eliot, which in due course ripened into friendship. I found him reserved, but not standoffish, ready to talk on equal terms about matters of common interest. I was from the first taken by his kind, encouraging, and helpful attitude. When I first sent him an article for *The*

Criterion, on Laforgue, nothing could have been more comfortingly phrased than his rejection of it. And when a year or so later we came to live in London, and he met my wife, she too was impressed, not only by his look and talk, and the distinctive quality of his voice, now familiar to everyone, but also by his unusual courtesy, a really natural courtesy which in most other people would have seemed affected. Later again, when we were in Paris with him, she noted the grace with which he conformed to the manners of the country, kissing her hand when we met there in the summer of 1926. Knowing we were going to Paris, he sent us an invitation to a concert to be given by Ezra Pound of his own music – a unique experience. We travelled over together. I got his ticket for him, and he implored me 'for Heaven's sake' not to forget it, and to be sure 'to reserve seats in the 2nd-Class *Pullman* where the dinner is, according to English railway standards, extremely good. And the distance from London to Newhaven allows just enough time to dine without haste.'

By that time I had had a good many discussions with him about various literary schemes; he had been kind enough to get Richard Aldington to review my works in *The Criterion*, and had there published my first biographical dialogue. On this particular Paris excursion he asked me to go and see Cocteau's *Orphée*, and write an article on him as a dramatist, or rather, as he stressed, a man of the theatre. This I did, and on re-reading my effusion it seems to me generous and fairly understanding: Eliot evidently thought so too, because it appeared in October 1926. One person, however, was not pleased, namely Jean Cocteau.

Mon cher Eliot [he wrote in November]. De mon immense effort, de cette longue agonie, de cette opération chirurgicale qu'est mon œuvre, *rien n'est vu ni même entrevu*. Mais chez vous, cela me peine plus que partout. Je vous embrasse. Jean Cocteau. [P.S.] Il n'y a pas [un] symbole dans Orphée. C'est 12 ans de drame jetés là.

cachés

72

In sending me this letter Eliot wrote to me, 'Don't worry over Cocteau! There is no pleasing people like that, & I have too much experience of offending people to care. I shall write and rebuke him and point out the English view of such matters.' Beautifully reassuring. (A few years later he wrote to me, 'to hearken to criticism is to invite paralysis'.) From that time he allowed me to be a constant reviewer in *The Criterion*, which I shall shortly talk of.

Before doing so, there is one 'episode', to give it that name worth retaining in the memory, since it throws a light on Eliot's attitude towards the Church. In the summer of 1926 the City churches were largely threatened with destruction, as the Church wished to raise funds for better-attended places of worship. Eliot was deeply opposed to this, as indeed I was, though not altogether for the same reasons. At all events I agreed to write a broadsheet for sale or distribution in the City (I have lost all trace of this, and even the memory of it), of which Eliot approved. I extract from three letters of August 1926.

Your broadsheet seems to me admirable. . . . As for borrowing from my paragraph, you have borrowed only the one thing in it worth borrowing, i.e. the contrast of visible and invisible church, which I think is a good one and you must keep it. The only disadvantage that I can see is that just this point might make some reader of both think that the broadside was written by me, and the only disadvantage of that is that the authority of 'Some Men of London' (a good signature) might be diminished if it were thought that this imposing menace concealed merely T. S. Eliot. (11 August)

I quite agree about the distinction between the picturesque and the monument of a civilisation. And I make the further point that to destroy these churches is to accelerate the decay of the Church – it is not party funds that makes a church prosperous. Though it seems almost inevitable that Canterbury should eventually be superseded by Rome in any case. It is their own fault. (15 August)

I do not expect that Canterbury will EVER embrace Rome, or vice versa. What I meant was that after Disestablishment the Church of England will lose its whole reason for existence; and that its more serious members will gradually go over to Rome. Some will fall into nonconformity; the majority will content itself with civil marriages and individual Gods (my God for my dog, my pipe, my golf-tools and my allotment garden, your god for yours) but Rome will very slowly become stronger. (21 August)

So one Saturday afternoon my wife and I accompanied Eliot at the head of a protest procession through the City, at intervals chanting 'Onward, Christian Soldiers' and other hymns. The churches were saved.

In a memoir of this sort it is impossible – and luckily it is unnecessary – to adhere to subject or follow chronology. In the interests of the latter, however, and as illustration of how he would enter into the ideas as well as lives of other people, and take trouble over their activities, even though the prospect did not attract him, I would quote from two letters written at a time when he was being most encouraging to myself, bringing me, as far as possible, into the literary circles he inspired. When my wife sent him her first book, *Your Cuckoo Sings by Kind,* he wrote, after a little delay, on 25 March 1927:

Dear Mrs Dobrée

I admit that I postponed reading your novel as long as possible. I have had enough experience in reading books, when I know the author to [word indecipherable – dread?] it. But now I have read it, and can, to my great relief, say that I like yours *immensely.* I feel quite incompetent to judge novels, and I confess a complete ignorance of human 'psychology'. Outside of detective stories, I regard 'fiction' simply from the point of view of a verse maker. That is, what impresses me is something I call 'tone' or atmosphere. I find it in the novelists I like – Turgenev, & Tolstoi, & Flaubert, & Dickens. I think your novel has this 'tone' – I get a feeling about Christina from the beginning, which belongs to her and to no one else whom I have known

– and that is the main thing. And it seems to me one of the saddest books I have read. I should like to forget it, but can't.

> Yours very sincerely,
> T. S. Eliot.

And in a letter to me mainly about *The Criterion* (11 April), he ends:

I finally found time to read 'Your Cuckoo', and wrote to your wife about it. I think she got my letter just before leaving England. [I had taken up a post in Egypt.] I may not have expressed myself very well, but I was much impressed and moved by the book, and I look forward to her next work. . . . One of the things I especially liked about your wife's book was a certain objectivity; I mean an interest in the way things look, and a cutting out of superfluous detail about the way they feel. Mr and Mrs Harris had a kind of reality which has been disappearing from English fiction within the last fifty years. This leads me to think she could invent and imagine objectively outside of what might be called her own experience. This sticking to one's own experience by novelists seems to me to narrow the field of experience itself.

To go back to subject matter, not for the moment too much outraging chronology. Eliot's letters to me about the City churches illustrate another point about him; he did not expect his friends to share his opinions. He could sympathize with your views, even though he disagreed with them, so long as he felt that your attitude towards his was at any rate to some degree understanding. That is why conversation with him was so easy. You could state your views about literature or anything: he would listen and accept, and state his own. He never attempted to argue, or to convert you. You felt all the time that he respected your personality, and that any person was entitled to his views so long as they were honestly held, and not produced for the sake of controversy. He was quiet and deliberate, never impetuous, in his discussions. That is one of the reasons why it was so pleasant to meet Mr Eliot, with

his conversation, so nicely
Restricted to What Precisely
And If and Perhaps and But,

because it made you think, and be on your toes.

Nor was there anything rigid or intolerant in his views of other people's opinions. Early in 1929, after I had written to him from Cairo about his latest book, which I had just acquired, he wrote:

I am glad you can speak so favourably of Andrewes, beyond my hopes. Your criticism is useful, because it makes me see I have probably given a wrong impression of my attitude towards Babbitt. My point is: I don't object in the least to the position of Babbitt for Babbitts. It is a perfectly possible position for an individual. I only say: this is not a doctrine which can help the world in general. The individual can certainly love order without loving God. The people cannot. And when I say people, don't think I mean any slum or suburb or Belgravian square; I mean any number that can be addressed in print. I should say of humanism as many say of mysticism: it is unutterable and incommunicable. It is for each humanist alone. It is not only silly, but damnable, to say that Christianity is necessary for the people, until one feels that it is necessary for oneself. I'm not attacking humanism: I should be more hostile to a catholicism without humanism; I only mean that humanism is an ingredient, indeed a necessary one, in any proper catholicism; and I want to point out the danger of Babbitt's leading some of his followers to a kind of catholicism which I should dislike as much as he does.

A little later, in a further letter, picking up some other point, and evidently some remarks I had made:

All Babbitt has to offer positively, I'm afraid, is Babbitt's idea of what is proper, and that is pretty vague. I hate mixing things up and at the same time I find it more impossible to isolate any purely 'literary' etc. problem, but am forced to a 'synthesis'. A 'passionate activity' is good until it is self-conscious, i.e. so long as it is a passionate activity TOWARDS something else, but when it comes to the conclusion that its own passionateness is what is admirable then the passion cools into sentiment etc. do I make myself clear I do not. QUESTIONS TO ANSWER. What makes the World go Round? Why did they wear Bowler Hats? Why did their Chariots have square Wheels?

The last two sentences need explaining.

They are part of an elaborated joke, nurtured through years. It is about some primitive people called the Bolovians, who wore bowler hats, and had square wheels to their chariots. This invention he apparently began to toy with when he was at Harvard, there figuring King Bolo and his Queen. He did not tell me much about those characters – though he sent me a drawing of them – but I was given portions of a Bolovian Epic (not always very decorous) and something about their religion. This latter was in part an amiable satire on the way people, anthropologists especially, talk about the religion of others. One piece of sheer fantasy concerned the name of their two gods, both called Wux, and how to pronounce the name. I give extracts.

First, the W. The w is halfway between the WH as pronounced in the Gateshead & Newcastle district ... and the HW of Danish (not the corrupt Danish of Jutland and West Friesland, which are affected by High and Low Dutch respectively, but the pure Danish of East Friesland) as in *hwilken.* ...

Second, the U. The u is very long, and might be rendered OOUHOUHUH. There is a slight, a very slight, Caesura in the middle of the u, which is expressed, in Pure Bolovian, by a slight Belch, but no European can render this, so do not try.

Third, the X. This is a combination of the Greek Ksi and the German schch. If you attentively Cough and Sniff at the same time you will get nearer to it.

A letter of a little later (12 November 1927) shows his extraordinary capacity for leaping from one thing to another. The first part, mixed with jokes about my life in Egypt, is mainly about *The Criterion*; follows a little about the Bolovians, and then:

I am very busy writing a Poem about a Sole. That is, about a Channel Swimmer who has a Sole as a mascot; you see it is allegorical, and everything can be taken in an allegorical, analogical, and a bolovian sense. So it is giving me much trouble. There is also a Dove that comes in, but I don't understand how

> The Dove dove down an oyster Dive
>> As the Diver dove from Dover....
> Then the sole

>> was solely sole
> Or solely sold as sole at Dover ...

You get the drift of it, but it is Difficult. When he reaches the other side

> 'He's saved his sole whole!' Cry'd the Priest
> 'Whose Sole?' 'OUR Sole!' the folk replied....

> This Sole, which had been Dover bred,
>> Was shortly cooked with chips in Greece....

It is very difficult to put all this together; it is called How we Brought the Dover Sole to Calais.

DONT try to Pronounce Wux. I cautioned you. Else you will suffer the same fate as dear old Profer. Krapp of Koenigsberg, who died a martyr to the cause of Bolovian Phonetics. He lived for 3 months on Beans, then on Asparagus, then on Chestnuts etc. trying to get the right accent. And then he got acute dyspepsia and colic, which spoilt his temper, so that he swallowed his front Teeth and so died in a Phrensy.

Then, astonishingly, with a complete change of mood and subject:

I think there is some misprision on your Part about my Truth. I would not wish to make truth a function of the will. On the contrary. I mean that if there is no fixed truth, there is no fixed object for the will to tend to. If truth is always changing, then there is nothing to do but to sit down and watch the pictures. Any distinctions one makes are more or less arbitrary. I should say that it was at any rate essential for Religion that we should have the conception of an immutable object or Reality the knowledge of which shall be the final object of that will; and there can be no permanent reality if there is no permanent truth. I am of course quite ready to admit that human apprehension of truth varies, changes and perhaps develops, but that is a property of human imperfection rather than of truth. You cannot conceive of truth at all, the word has no meaning, except by conceiving of it as something permanent. And that is really assumed even by those who deny it. For you cannot even say it changes except in reference to something which does not change; the idea of change is impossible without the idea of permanence. E. and O.E., and without prejudice.

A change now, evidently in reference to some earlier talk:

Oh I suppose the only thing to be done about W. Civilisation is to think as clearly as one can. The first thing is to understand the disease, if there is a disease. Benda is rather sound this way.

A few words of good wishes for my family, and then, as a postscript, as though, perhaps, he feared any sense of pomposity in his words about truth:

The Sole –

> Although it hung about the Plaice
> 'Twas solely sold as Sole at Dover....

Now to *The Criterion*, sustained over some seventeen years, passing through various stages – *The New Criterion, The Monthly Criterion*, and back to *The Criterion* – the changes marking various crises. From the beginning it was very distinguished, so that I felt it an honour to contribute, its outstanding virtue being its wielding together of so many kinds of contributor, from Wyndham Lewis, F. M. Ford, Virginia Woolf, to lesser lights and beginners. Above all it was the seeing of all European literature as one, whence the frequent contributions by foreigners, and reviews of European and

American literature, including journals. Although, after the withdrawal of Richard Aldington, Eliot ran it himself, there were constant parties where contributors gathered to discuss, and if possible supply, ideas. I remember one or two formal gatherings at Faber's, but more clearly the dinners which used to take place in a reserved room in a Soho restaurant. These were by no means cold or highbrow gatherings. We naturally discussed literature more than anything else, but the atmosphere was entirely gay. There were Herbert Read, Harold Monro, J. G. Fletcher, F. S. Flint, T. O Beachcroft, Frank Morley, Montgomery Belgion, and J. B. Trend, among the twenty or so people gathered there. One night, I remember, we sang a catch, written (words and music) by Orlo Williams, for three voices.

> FIRST VOICE: Sweeney said to Misses Porter
>   Pretty bit of po'try about you and me.
> SECOND VOICE: Who's this Eliot any way?
>   Well, from all I hear, he's a personal sort of beggar.
> THIRD VOICE: I like young Eliot, he's got style
>   But, I ask you, is it po'try?

This went well. Eliot was hugely amused. When he liked he could be the soul of gaiety. Very little of the conversations at these dinners remains in mind, but I remember one little interchange. Someone – let us call him X – mentioned the *Bhagavad Gità*, to which Eliot, with great interest: 'Oh, have you read the *Bhagavad Gità*?' 'Er, well,' X answered, 'I can't say I have in the original – but in translation I've studied it, and though of course in translation. . . .' Then Morley broke in: 'It's all right, X. You're among gentlemen here.'

Eliot looked forward to these dinners with pleasure, as occasions where people would not only be themselves, but, so to speak, play their special parts in a show. He more than once sketched out to me an entertaining travesty of the sort of thing that lay at the back of his mind, and I quote the shortest, inviting me to a dinner on 3 May 1932.

The Characters in their Order of Appearance.

F. V. Morley – An honest downright farmer.

T. S. Eliot – A student.

F. S. Flint – A roaring boy.

O. Williams – An Italianate gallant, newly returned from his travels.

J. B. Trend – A phantastical master of Arts.

B. Dobrée – A needy half-pay captain in the train bands.

In one of these casts he billed himself as 'the bellowing baritone'.

The dinners were enormously stimulating, but more so were the small evening gatherings which dovetailed with and eventually took the place of the dinners, at Harold Monro's above his bookshop opposite the British Museum. These consisted of Monro himself, of course, Frank Flint, Herbert Read, Morley – and later Belgion. The conversations there were equally gay, but more useful. There we really did discuss policy and contributions. Sometimes the conversation tended to the deeply serious, but Eliot did not like too ready a mixture of the serious and the convivial. ('I hate mixing things' – in a letter they were separated.) On one occasion, when someone began to intrude a religious issue, Eliot put a stop to it by saying, 'The only two things I care for are dancing and brandy.' Monro was horrified. 'O Tom! You mustn't say things like that!'

Eliot enjoyed these gatherings, but it is doubtful if he got much help from them. In a letter he wrote me on 31 November 1936, on *Criterion* note-paper, where *The Criterion* is described as 'Edited by T. S. Eliot', he inserted after 'Edited': 'without any help from his "friends"'. The letter is worth printing in full, running as it does into so many fields, and exhibiting a pervading sense of humour overcoming worry:

Dear BONAMY,

You are a nice kind of Friend, to take no notice of any body all this time: here I've been back since Oct. 12th and plunged into Arrears and then caught cold and have been having Injections which they say had proved useless in the Post Office, and my doctor has made me promise to address the League of Mercy at Lady Cynthia Crinkley's in Hyde Park Sq. and I have had to talk in Cambridge twice, last week and aiagain [*sic*] tomorrow, which they don't even pay one's fare for, so why does one do it I should like to know, and I addressed the 6th Forms on the Wireless yesterday, and no end of practical problems to solve before I can get to work on trying to write a play. So you might have enquired after me I do Think. And next Sunday evening I have to read poetry to some students to please Canon Tissington Tatlow D.D., why does one do it. With all this how can I be expected to attend to Christmas Cards? Well what about it. Leeds, I mean, and Boston Spa. And the History – and what's this queer 6 volume work of yours announced by the Cresset Press? [*Introductions to English Literature*, ed. by me] – and that volume I worked so hard for [*From Anne to Victoria: an essay on Byron*], when it it to appear? John Hayward and I want our 15 guineas we do, and what with the doctor and the dentist I think I am going to lose another Tooth. And where is your Soul? at present. Would Georgina [our daughter, *aet.* 6] whom God preserve be interested in my two latest poems or not? I mean *Growltiger's Last Stand* (picaresque) and *The Old Gumbie Cat* (domestic) or not? And may I hear from you, or not? Now, would you be coming up to London before Xmas if we had a Criterion Yuletide Revel? and when? Not worth while unless you could spend two nights, so that we could have a QUiet Evening as well, with some decent vintage instead of the vile sherry and hock which is all the Criterion minions deserve. And seriously, now that you are a Perfesser, may I put you up for the O. & C. Club, which you ought to join, and can join at the moment because the entrance fee is temporarily abrogated. Seriously, I am quite in the dumps about the European Situation, so I need your cheering company. With love to Valentine and Respects to the General will close.

T. S. E.

Such letters were a relief from tension, as were, occasionally, light verses. In July 1934 he wrote to me:

I don't think my poetry is any good: not The Rock anyway, it isn't; nothing but a brilliant future behind me. What is one to do?

I was lunching one day in the Princess Louise
  When I passed a remark to a man in white spats
Who was eating a plate of fried gammon and peas;
    So we soon fell to talking of thisses and thats –
    Such as Pollicle Dogs and Jellicle Cats.

I have teeth, which are False and quite Beautiful,
    And a Wigg with an Elegant Queue;
And in closing I send my most dutiful
    Respects to your Lady and You.

Evidently *Practical Cats* was already in his mind; and it will be remembered that one of the people to whom Old Possum dedicated this work, with thanks for help, was 'the Man in White Spats'.

Varied matters, and especially the elaborated jokes, were more for long letters when I was in Egypt, about which he continually craved information, e.g. 'If you can, find out about the Ostridge (does he run backward to keep the sand out of his eyes, & has he hemorrhoids in consequence?)'. His letters when we were living in the country in England were more about what we discussed on the many occasions when we met. These are usually about literary questions, and in September 1930 we had evidently been discussing somebody's book of criticism, and he wrote on the 13th:

The book is excellent, the views just; but I did not feel that he was deeply enough moved by the subject to justify it. His remark that criticism should be written like philosophy does not worry me, because it does not seem to me to mean much; there are many ways in which *good* philosophical works have been written. The danger is chiefly in writing criticism like second rate philosophy. I doubt myself whether good philosophy any more than good criticism or any more than good poetry can be written without strong feeling. But one only argues from oneself; I am sure that any prose I have written that is good prose, is good because I have strong feelings (more than adequate knowledge) – my essay on Machiavelli for instance, is not good, not because I didn't know enough (which I didn't) but because I had not soaked deep enough in Machiavelli to feel intensely – therefore, in so far as there is any good in it, that is because it is not about Machiavelli at all.

He was always extremely patient, ready to answer questions, and illuminate a blunter understanding. I had long been revolted by the quotation that he placed as epigraph to *Sweeney Agonistes*: 'Hence the soul cannot be possessed of the divine union, until it has divested itself of the love of created beings.' In 1936 I told him that I regarded this with horror, and he wrote:

The doctrine that in order to arrive at the love of God one must divest oneself of the love of created beings was thus expressed by St John of the Cross, you know: i.e. a man who was writing primarily not for you and me, but for people seriously engaged in pursuing the Way of Contemplation. It is only to be read in relation to that Way: i.e. merely to kill one's human affections will get one nowhere, it would be only to become rather more a completely living corpse than most people are. But the doctrine is fundamentally true, I believe. Or to put your belief in your own way, that only through the love of created beings can we approach the love of God, that I believe to be UNTRUE. Whether we mean by that domestic and friendly affections, or a more comprehensive love of the 'neighbour', of humanity in general. I don't think that ordinary human affections are capable of leading us to the love of God, but rather that the love of God is capable of informing, intensifying and elevating our human affections, which otherwise have little to distinguish them from the 'natural' affections of animals. Try looking at it from that end of the glass!

And here I could note that allied with Eliot's sense of religion was his sense of the necessity for order. Writing to me in November 1930, after some discussion about Christianity, he went on:

I think we are in agreement that 'Order' and 'Authority' are more dangerous catchwords now, than 'Liberty' and 'Reform' were fifty or seventy-five years ago. Order and Authority may point more directly to the yellow press and the crook capitalists than Liberty and Reform pointed to Socialism. I am terrified of the modern contempt of 'democracy' ... I am as scary of Order as of Disorder.

He put this succinctly, in a different context, in one of his essays on education: 'The danger of freedom is deliquescence; the danger of strict order is petrifaction.' I remember once meeting him accidentally in Piccadilly during the coming into prominence of Hitler, and saying, 'I suppose one must have order', and his answering: 'Yes, but there are different kinds of order.'

This naturally links up with his views on politics, of which he did not pretend to understand the intricacies. But in February 1931 he wrote:

The only other notions in my mind are Garvin's clamour for a Coalition (thinly disguised under the more grandiose title of a National Party) than which I should prefer a *coup de force* (with of course ourselves, Mosley and O. Stanley posing on the balcony). Nothing to my mind could be worse for the country than the present shuffling of Old Gangs, than a Union of all the Old Gangs, with L. George, Snowden, Churchill, Ramsay, Stanley and Jix hanging round each other's necks. That wd be the last straw.

What interested him at one time was the *New English Weekly* movement, if it can be so called, run by A. R. Orage, whose death he felt to be a great loss, and he was glad to find the paper being continued by Philip Mairet. This involved him in Social Credit, and it was through his encouragement that many of us including myself wrote pamphlets on the subject – Herbert Read, Edwin Muir, and Ezra Pound, the last writing two pamphlets, one in verse under the pseudonym of Alfred Venison. That was in 1934, and the idea, as we know, has fizzled out, though it still has small devoted centres. By the end of the decade he was in despair, writing to me at the beginning of 1939:

Yes, we are in a trough of decadence, in a manner of speaking. I don't know which alternative depresses me most, the continuation of soft decay, or galvanisation into artificial revival. Is the only remedy that people will now accept for plutocracy, political despotism?

Most of his letters, however, are about personal matters, or relating to his own work. In 1933 he began work on *The Rock*, and asked me to point out any errors in diction as regards the conversation between Wren, Pepys and Evelyn (a quite unnecessary safeguard), and put it into good period language. On 10 May he wrote:

The only really interesting thing about the 'Rock' (28th inst) will be to see how the public responds to the political allusions in it. But I fear a dull and lethargic audience for that sort of affair.

He need not have feared. The audience (which included my wife and myself) seemed far from lethargic. This was the beginning of his dramatic ventures (*Sweeney* was a sighting shot), which were eventually almost wholly to engage his literary activities. He was abandoning the writing of poems, because, he once told me, he did not want to repeat himself. His interest, naturally, was turned towards the kind of speech to be used on the stage, one he had exhibited at our first meeting. Writing to me in January 1938, after modestly scouting any idea that he knew anything about prosody, he went on:

I am inclined to think that the iambic pentameter business accounts for the inferiority of post-Miltonic blank verse, and for the puzzling difference between Shakespearean blank verse and later imitations. Why is it that the versification of *The Cenci* etc. ought to be as good as minor Jacobean tragedy and actually is as the worst margarine to bad butter?

The stress on stressing is I am sure right. The number of syllables doesn't matter.

Procrustes.

However, my own criticism (and its faults) will be apparent rather from my next play [*The Family Reunion*] when you see the text. It is in lines of mostly four stresses (irregularly placed) varied by lines of three and sometimes (for choral purposes) of two. Every now and then there is a line that could be scanned as a regular iambic pentameter. (It is interesting that when actors have to declaim real verse (Shakespeare) they try to turn it into prose, whereas when they have to declaim what is obviously bad verse (cf. Shaw: The Admirable Bashville) they do make it sound like verse). I have kept in mind two assumptions:

1. If you can't make the most commonplace remark and still make it sound manifestly VERSE and not prose,
2. If you can't utter the most exalted sentiments, express the most rarefied or intense emotions, without the audience thinking at once: 'this is poetry!'

then it isn't dramatic verse.

The audience ought not to be aware continuously that your characters are talking verse. It ought to be too interested to stop to notice that you are talking verse instead of prose.

When I read the first scene of 'Hamlet', or the Recognition scene in 'Pericles', I am too interested to worry about Poetry, Verse, and Prose.

'The Way of the World' isn't prose while it's going on: it's prose after it's over. 'Hamlet' isn't poetry while it's going on: it's poetry after it's over.

Writing a little later about some remarks of mine in an essay on English poetic drama, in which I had quoted some of *Murder in the Cathedral*, he says that he has found a better medium for dialogue than he had in *Murder*, and:

One reason why I am dissatisfied with MURDER is that there are too many bumps of poetry sticking up like outcrop, and the poetry is not sufficiently integrated into the drama. This was partly a weakness of the situation; the plot material is so scanty that I had rather to overweight the play with lyrical outbursts, and now I think I have got nearer this integration.

In April 1939, writing of *The Family Reunion*:

I think there is one fault in particular which I ought some-how to have avoided: the first scene of the second part is really

explicatory matter which should have come earlier; and coming
at that point, has the effect of interminable explanation with
nothing happening. I think that the play succeeds in scenes, but
not as a whole. There are some faults certainly militating against
popular success, which I still don't know how I could have
coped with in *this* play. I think one ought to have a satisfactory
explanation for what happens, on every plane. Not having been
able to prevent people from asking: why does Harry go away? I
ought at least to have had an answer for them on that plane. It is
a great mistake to allow people to raise questions for which there
is no answer. I am by no means sure about the chorus: I mean
whether I shall look upon it as a permanent element for the
future, or whether it is a vestige, something the employment of
which has been a help to *me* in finding the way from non-
dramatic to dramatic verse.

I would like at this point to say that I think Eliot's plays to
be grossly underestimated, certainly in England; in America
there has been the admirable study by Mr D. E. Jones. Their
linking of the modern world with Greek tragedy is in itself of
major importance – more than a mere matter of tradition. It is
part of the statement that Eliot was constantly making as to
the unchangeability of human nature and its problems. They
are universal. Again, they are extremely actable, holding audiences as being based on contemporary actuality. In the end
Eliot evolved a masterly model of stage speech, telling to the
hearers, and easy for actors to say.

Eliot was devoid of arrogance, and welcomed friendly criticism. In 1930 I was bold enough to query the punctuation in
the third stanza of 'Whispers of Immortality'. He wrote:

I am much obliged to you for calling my attention. It's ALL
wrong; please read COMMA after *sense*, SEMI-COLON after *penetrate*; and COMMA after *experience*. That's better. I shall expect
everyone but yourself to PURCHASE a new edition; as for you,
please paste this in your copy if you have one.

In 1941 he sent me a draft copy of *Little Gidding* which
differs considerably from the final version – asking for com-

ments and criticism. I fear I was of little help, except to say
that I thought it splendidly continued the line of the previous
Quartets and to point out that, as he then had it, 'summon the
ghost of a rose' seemed a reference to *Urn Burial*. He said that
John Hayward had already drawn attention to 'the Browne
pinch' of which he had been 'cheerfully unconscious': he
thought he would go the whole hog and say 'raise up' instead
of 'summon'. Eventually as we know, he printed 'summon the
spectre'. I had also asked him about the significance of the
rose, which occurs in many of his poems. He answered:

> There are really three roses in the set of poems; the sensuous
> rose, the socio-political Rose (always appearing with a capital
> letter) and the spiritual rose: and the three have got to be in
> some way identified as one.

I must confess that I was not much illuminated.

His reasons for inviting criticism are interesting, revealing
his manner of working, and his essential humility:

> I seem to need other people's opinions (or those of a small
> number of people) more than I once did: I suppose it comes
> partly from the different way of working appropriate to middle
> age, which becomes more deliberate and painstaking. And I feel
> the need for it especially just now, when I have been conscious of
> working, so to speak, against time. One sees certain things one
> wants to do, and everyone must have a feeling of precariousness
> of the future; and as my natural way of writing verse seems to
> require a long period of germination for each poem, before I
> address myself to the machine, I am afraid that I have been over-
> producing, and at last trying to make poetry out of unseasoned
> material.

He goes on to reprove me for not making more criticisms
(pointing out what he thinks to be weak spots in the poem), but
admits that this sort of criticism needs practice, 'and I therefore allow for the leniency of the beginner'.

I had met Eliot continuously since about 1926, first at regular lunches somewhere opposite the Victoria and Albert

Museum, so as to make it easy for Herbert Read (who had invited me to join them) and Christopher Codrington, both of them officials at the Museum. He would occasionally ask me to meet someone – Frederic Manning, or Ralph Hodgson complete with his bull-terrier Pickwick. Then there were the *Criterion* meetings, and later small dinners at E. C. Gregory's flat, to discuss together with Read and Henry Moore the allocation of the Gregory Fellowships in poetry, painting, sculpture, and music at the University of Leeds. Latterly there had been fortnightly lunches with him, Read, and Morley at each others' clubs. In the last few months these were confined to Eliot and myself. All this, of course, apart from visits to our house in Suffolk or Yorkshire (always a considerate as well as appreciative guest), to see my wife and daughter as well as myself, and the visits we paid to him and his wife in his last eight happy years. All the time my sense grew of his kindness as well as of his stature, of ease in his presence, and enjoyment of his active sense of humour.

So my image of Eliot is that of a great gentleman, after Newman's pattern as described in *Idea of a University* (Discourse VII. 10), a gentle man in the best sense of the term – which is not to say that he could not be angry against people whose behaviour he thought abominable or spiteful. Generous himself, he could not abide lack of generosity in others. A man of complete integrity, he was ever prepared to help people, often at great trouble to himself. He always had regard for those he was with, and would note their qualities. I give as an instance a letter he wrote to my wife on the death of her father, who used to take him to church on Sundays in a little car when he stayed with us in Suffolk:

Dear Valentine,

I was particularly sorry to learn your news from Bonamy, because I remember your father so well – I mean, more clearly & definitely than one usually remembers the relatives of one's friends, meeting them in that way – and I have a strong impression of the respect and regard in which he was evidently held

by the villagers of Mendham. You have my warm sympathy.
[And in the margin] He was so very nice to me, too.

For all the complexity of his mind, he was fundamentally
simple, with regard for his acquaintance and a deep affection
for his friends. It is difficult to pay tribute to a man so quiet
and yet of such force, with whom one never felt uncomfortable
because of his candour and forbearance, understanding one's
stupidities, and warm in his sentiments. By his being he com-
manded respect; by his response to one's own being he nurtured the profoundest and most lasting affection.

FOR T. S. E.

HIS was the true Dantescan voice – not honoured enough, and deserving more than I ever gave him.

I had hoped to see him in Venice this year for the Dante commemoration at the Giorgio Cini Foundation – instead: Westminster Abbey. But, later, on his own hearth, a flame tended, a presence felt.

Recollections? Let some thesis-writer have the satisfaction of 'discovering' whether it was in 1920 or 21 that I went from Excideuil to meet a rucksacked Eliot. Days of walking – conversation? literary? le papier Fayard was then the burning topic. Who is there now for me to share a joke with?

Am I to write 'about' the poet Thomas Stearns Eliot? or my friend 'the Possum'? Let him rest in peace. I can only repeat, but with the urgency of 50 years ago: READ HIM.

E. P.

A FEW RECOLLECTIONS OF ELIOT

By Frank Morley

FIFTEEN years or so ago I wrote a personal piece about Eliot for one of those *Festschriften* which are rather too easily cooked up, and did so only after strictly limiting the circle of discourse. In that conversation the scheme of reference was the canon of the Sherlock Holmes stories, for that was a canon familiar to Eliot and me, and it provided an appropriate puppet-stage setting within which to convey, with a trifle of *badinage*, something of the spirit of the first decade of Faber & Faber. The *Festschrift* was for Eliot's sixtieth birthday, and it was well to pretend (according to the Holmesian canon) that 'there was that in the cool, nonchalant air of my companion which made him the last man with whom one would care to take anything approaching to a liberty' – and then proceed to take the liberty. Now Eliot is dead, and gone are many of the old faces. Yet in again speaking familiarly about him as Tom Eliot in the middle of the road of life, and of such details as the husbandry of *The Criterion*, I shall not transgress another carefully selected scheme of reference: which shall be *Don Quixote*, 'The Donkey Book'. 'The Donkey Book' was as it was known to Henry Ware Eliot of 2,635 Locust Street, St Louis, and so known to Tom's older brother Henry Jr, and to the sisters, and to Tom himself. 'The Donkey Book' was the particular copy of the fat outsize London edition of *Don Quixote* illustrated by Gustave Doré, which had been purchased and inscribed with his name and address by H. W. Eliot. It was later inscribed again 'For Tom – from his brother Henry. 1930' and sent to Tom in London. Tom pasted in his bookplate with its elephant's head (the elephant never forgets) and lugged it with him through several changes of address. Then in 1936 he lugged it to Pikes Farm in Surrey and presented the volume, with a suitable inscription of his own, to my wife and me.

I shall return to 'The Donkey Book' because it meant something within the family of Henry Ware Eliot. I note in a letter from Henry Jr to me in 1946 that he mentions:

I am glad that you have the Donkey Book. The pictures were beloved by all us children, and all in turn, I am sure, sat on the book at Christmas and Thanksgiving dinners when we were allowed to eat with the big folks.

But apart from family significance I wish to use the text of *Don Quixote* as my reference scheme. Sitting here with big folks I claim no less and no more licence than that of Sancho Panza, who knew and who never said otherwise to Don Quixote's face or behind his back, either to other squire or to Duke or Duchess, than that his master 'has not one grain of knavery in him', that there were times when he could be 'as dull as an old cracked pitcher', and – ever that divine *and* – 'and he is so simple that I cannot help loving him, with all my heart and soul, and cannot leave him, in spite of all his follies'.

Oddly, I notice that in the more transportable Bohn Popular Library edition of *Don Quixote* to which I turn to verify my quotations there is a pencilled note within the back cover – 'T. S. Eliot, Imperial, 1.15'. No date. Probably a reminder scribbled from an office diary into the book I happened to be carrying. Other evidence suggests March 1925. Herbert Read had introduced me to Eliot at lunch at the Imperial Restaurant adjacent to South Kensington Station at, or certainly not much earlier than, the beginning of 1925, and lunches there for threes or twos or more on Thursdays became frequent; but it wasn't long before we took agin the Imperial, and Read's energy and ingenuity found other quarters for what became Thursday *Criterion* lunches for a fluctuating number (perhaps 5 or 6 to 12 or 15) of regulars and visitors. For some years we were all tolerated in a below-stairs room at The Grove in Beauchamp Place (the name seemed to tie in with *The Sacred*

Wood), where we could make as much noise as we liked, and
we did.

*

In a personal note about some aspects of Eliot as a man, in his
thirties in the 20s, in his forties in the 30s, I am not of the
slightest use unless I skip around and mention other remarkable men of the time – Read and Wheen, younger than Eliot,
Bruce Richmond, older – and even how I came to be sucked
into some of the adventures. If you should think that I am
suggesting anywhere *pars magna fui*, then I will say you
simply do not understand. You ought soberly to go away and
read Don Quixote's letter: 'I desire thee to observe, Sancho,
that it is many times very necessary and convenient to thwart
the humility of the heart, for the better support of the authority of a place.'

Arthur Wheen I had met at New College, Oxford. Wheen
was three years older than I was. He had been delayed that
length of time by active service at the Front: perhaps you
have read *Two Masters*, which he wrote in the Oxford period.
Of immense educative importance to me was Wheen's per-
ceptiveness, his built-in gold-leaf electrometer (such as Coleridge mentions). When we came down in 1923 we lived for half
a year or so in a garret (I mean garret) in Upper Bedford Place
and might have gone on longer in the garret if a friend had not
come with a placard which he nailed up for us to contemplate
– white placard with two menacing black words – STOP
DITHERING. That broke the garret period. Wheen was pitch-
forked into the job of a librarian at the Victoria and Albert
Museum. The combined fortunes now being more affluent we
took rooms and board at a farmhouse near Effingham in
Surrey, where at right moments there was wild parsley to look
at, sunlight on the lilac, thrush-song from the hedges, and a
big rubbish-pit with nightingales. There again in part-time
way we went on dithering.

What I am attempting to recapture is a receptive state of

dither to which the war had brought some people, making them try to look over the hills and find if there was any way across a Great Divide. Hints from any direction had value. I don't recall just when – it may have been after he met Read – Wheen found a book of poems called *Otherworld* by F. S. Flint. The effect upon Wheen's electrometer was most observable. Here was a poetry made new to Wheen, who all the while had been teaching me to see things in poetry that were new to me but old to him. I had no special instinct for poetry: I was made to be interested by very different people. I had been running around Fleet Street. At one end there was E. V. Lucas at Methuen: I met him, as I met many other writers, through my older brother Christopher who from the moment I reached England was continually prodding me from New York. Lucas enjoyed visits to Oxford – W. P. Ker or Raleigh would always put him up; it was on one of those visits, I think, that he gave me the copy of *Ulysses* which he had smuggled from Paris. I tried it first on Wheen. There was more to old Lucullus Lucas than met the eye or ear: he was more than a most generous host, or *diseur de bons mots* at the Garrick Club or elsewhere, though he was those things also. At the other end of Fleet Street there was Bruce Richmond. Richmond was a New College man, partial to New College men if only for that reason. In the garret period of 1923 I was for a short time regularly sitting in Richmond's office the while *The Times Lit. Sup.* was made up and put to bed. I think it was even then (it might have been later) that Richmond mentioned Read to me – 'He has such a beautiful *walk*,' he said – for Richmond had been an athlete, and was a Grecian, and looked at a man entire and whole. Wheen knew of Read by that time (*Naked Warriors*) and what Wheen kept telling me was 'Read has big bones – I feel he has big bones.' Richmond spoke of Eliot, and *The Sacred Wood*, which Methuen had published, and it was not immodest for me to mention that to Lucas. You had to be modest about what you mentioned to Lucas, for he would promptly give it to you. He gave me his copy: 'Here you are;

it may mean more to you than to me.' Wheen's electrometer pronounced *The Sacred Wood* as 'very competent'. We did not go in for encomiums within the garret. Then he or I happened to find the first issue of *The Criterion* with *The Waste Land*, and in the slang of these days, we'd had it.

I don't believe the war as such, or the aftermath as such, was a main cause of Eliot's poetry; but the war and aftermath certainly made some others who were trying to get their bearings discover their woe to be set by Eliot in wider context. I know that I, even I who knew so little – that's the whole point – even in the garret days of 1923 and with scads of 'work' to do, was forced by the explosion to shove everything else into the corners and take a sheaf of foolscap and write a title:

T. S. ELIOT AND HERBERT READ

I did not get far with that one. The attempt was absurd and it was not absurd. Wheen spoiled it by going away. When we resumed dithering at Effingham in 1924 the attempt was resumed. It was a private must. Christopher was keeping on at me from New York to write London Letters for *The Saturday Review of Literature* about 'literary' goings-on, but this was different. This (don't altogether laugh at me) was a secret effort of a young man (I was ten years younger than Eliot, five younger than Read) who had never studied anything except a few departments of geometry to find terms of reference for poetry. I did not find difficulty with Eliot's idiom. *The Waste Land* had instantaneous power of trespass. Read and some others were more difficult. But there was Wheen muttering at me in Mrs Saunders's farmhouse not about Read's neatness but about 'big bones' – or suddenly swivelling at me to say, 'When you are writing about Read, shove in the word *romanesque*.' 'I don't know what that means,' I said. 'Never mind,' said Wheen, 'shove it in somewhere, anywhere will do. If Read sees your piece, I want to see what he says.' 'This piece is not to be seen,' I said. 'This piece is for me.'

Wheen at the V & A in 1924 had met Read (not too much

flesh on him either) and they were quick at interlocking. I was mostly away on various adventures and in September was off to America to do a business job for *The Times* supplements and was engaged to return before the first of the year as London manager for The Century Company (publishers) of New York. Walter de la Mare was travelling at the same time to give the Turnbull Lectures at the Johns Hopkins, so naturally our home at Baltimore was to be home from home for him as his home at Anerley had been for me since 1920. At a last moment before our joint departure it occurred to me to pack my privy piece on Eliot and Read.

You see what I am trying to say? Simply that climates change. In 1923 and 24 to nearly all of my friends and companions it would have done less than no good to mention the name T. S. Eliot. The only people that I then knew (apart from Wheen) who volunteered a word about Eliot (except anathema) were Richmond (that noble Grecian) and Ralph Hodgson (who somehow turned up on a visit from Japan). In memory dates slip and slide, but I think it was at as early a period that I stood with Hodgson on the steps of St Paul's and received his remark: 'Don't sell short those compatriots of yours, Pound and Eliot.' Hodgson said it in the same tone with which he had been introducing me to a Worcestershire sauce much superior to Lea & Perrins – I wish I could recall *its* name – and talking of the points of the most splendid of bullterriers, Sam Lavender. In memory I put Hodgson's remark a good ten years before he brought the later bull-terrier which was his own true love, Pickwick, to Pikes Farm.

Nowadays my incoherent privy piece (if it were extant) might seem callow but scarcely subversive. In New York of 1924, since brother Kit had so often needled me, I showed it to him. As he skimmed through it he pulled at his upper lip and handed it back as if ('The Sign of Four') 'a child has done this horrid deed'. Be fair: it was Kit's part to know the New York climate for paid journalism, and it was the part of a kid brother to be corrected and to tag along to the Three Hours for

Lunch Club (we had not then invented The Baker Street Irregulars). Never was there a rift at any time in our devotion; but what interested me was that the quotations, the *Ding an sich*, seemed not to touch Kit. Those bullets found no billets at Haverford College or at the Tudor and Stuart Club at the Hopkins. Eight years later, after Eliot had been invited to Harvard (I believe that was engineered largely by John Livingston Lowes), he was invited to give the Turnbull Lectures at the Hopkins. As a Hopkins man I felt sore that the Hopkins had to wait upon Eliot's receiving an accolade from Harvard, but perhaps that was just as well. In 1924 an invitation from the Hopkins might have impeded Faber & Gwyer, might have impeded *The Criterion*.

*

I go on to the first meeting with Mr Eliot in person, arranged by Read at the Imperial Restaurant, South Ken, for that established the Quixote–Panza scheme of personal reference. I need say nothing about the physical appearance of these men, for surely that's unnecessary? Eliot's complexion struck me as a bit sallow, the pupils of his eyes rather small. Eliot brought along a letter which he had written overnight to Arnold Bennett, chastising him for some remark Bennett had printed about highbrow journals. After Read had read it and was silent, it was passed to me. It was Sancho Panza's part to say in effect: 'very good letter to no useful purpose'. Read called me later to suggest another lunch. I asked, 'What did Eliot do with that letter?' 'He thought your remarks were judicious,' said Read. 'He tore it up.' Don't be foolish if you are reading this – I said I would expose part of the nature of a relationship which grew tacitly – it was my *business* to know Fleet Street and a range of writers in their clubs and homes and in their cliques and gangs. No shikaree boasts that he knows all about the jungle, but that was my utility to the *Criterion* group, the utility of a shikaree. Read was the organizer of the at first sporadic, later fairly regular, *Criterion*

lunches at The Grove. There we had a dingy downstairs room
to ourselves, small, cluttered with disused furniture, three
mauve pots of aspidistras on a broken sideboard half-hiding an
undressed doll with a fuzz of black hair with faded ribbon.
Barely space to get round the central table. Food bad, slow in
coming; big communal glass jugs for beer. Men who came
regularly from the Museums were Read, Wheen, Codrington,
Thorpe, Tandy; Flint, Eliot, Hamish Miles, Beachcroft, and
I came from other directions. Flint and Codrington were the
irrepressible noise-makers. Eliot sat at an end of the table,
torpedoing the lot.

The Grove was of course only a part of the *Criterion* group.
Some of the stand-bys of the periodical – Alec Randall, Orlo
Williams, Trend – rarely, if ever, went there. The place was
inconvenient, the lunches were uncomfortable. Wheen said
nothing; Read not much; I felt like something sewn up in a
sack with a bunch of sharp knives. But it was a place to bring
occasional people to: I brought Laski – once – but the once
made Laski a subscriber to *The Criterion*. It was automatic to
pilot Allen Tate to The Grove for his first physical meeting
with Eliot and Read. Important to me was a quieter habit,
which persisted longer than The Grove, of meeting with just
Read and Wheen at The Hoop and Toy or one or other of the
tea-shops at the other side of South Ken Station, and of listening to them. Not so much quieter as you might think, for Read
and Wheen, reserved in any general gathering, were talkative
if there were only three present; *two* gold-leaf electrometers
can make continuous clatter, so that I could eat all of the toast
or crumpets unobserved. If in that time you had asked Read
why he took so much trouble about *The Criterion* and all, I
think you might have had an answer involving a sense of glory,
and, if you were not sure what that meant, next time he would
give you – mark you, give you – three volumes of Vauvenargues. Wheen, I don't know: he was shy on glory. Something or other in Eliot continued to knit something in our own
strands. Then and later we used to play tricks on Eliot. A later

instance will suffice, from Faber days. Somebody had proposed that F & F should do a series of short books of 'Poets on the Poets'. Eliot at the office book-committee had evinced no approval. At a South Ken tea-shop (I suspect The Sheilan) Read and Wheen were unexcited. 'I believe No. 1 is being commissioned,' I said. 'Eliot dislikes the whole idea. How about No. 2, by Eliot, then stop the series? Eliot, in words of two syllables, on Dante?' The electrometers clattered. 'Be good if he'd do it,' said Wheen. '*Challenge* him,' shouted Read. Oh yes, Read could shout, upon occasion. Eliot did his short book on Dante. Then we dropped the series.

To return to The Grove. I have no record of the date, but one Thursday in 1925 Eliot appeared in a costume more *sportif* than usual – he had been summoned to Switzerland. The lady who had been paying the bills for *The Criterion* was in Switzerland. At a meeting at The Grove after his return he reappeared with the announcement (to put it in Sherlock Holmes language): 'The Red-Headed League is Dissolved.' The bill for the previous issue of *The Criterion* had been paid. There would be no further payments. There would be no further issues.

In the language of 'The Donkey Book', what was this but Don Quixote saying: 'I have been somewhat out of order by a certain cat-encounter, which turned out not much to the advantage of my nose.' With some of the records in front of me I can give as much as need be of subsequent wheels within wheels. A few significant dates go back a little. On 25 January 1925 C. W. Stewart wrote to me; in April Stewart and I began to lunch regularly. Stewart was manager of The Scientific Press, a Gwyer interest. Before that Stewart had been with the O.U.P., and so had Geoffrey Faber. Faber was now returning from Strong's Romsey Ales to re-enter publishing; he and Gwyer changed The Scientific Press into Faber & Gwyer, general publishers. Eliot was joining them. Stewart presently asked, could I suggest a production manager. It was not difficult to suggest Dick de la Mare, who had been best man at my wedding. A jubilant card from Dick, 12 October 1925: 'To-day was my first at F & G's. All went well and it was a positive joy to be at work in an orderly office at a living wage. All thanks to you!' After that Faber and I were lunching pretty often, not so much in clubs as inconspicuously at the Connaught Grill in Great Queen Street, where there were the best prunes in London (I mean eatable prunes with cream). As yet this has nothing to do with *The Criterion*. But Stewart is the man to keep your eye on. Up to the time of the cat-encounter Don Quixote had kept everything to do with the publishing of *The Criterion* wholly and scrupulously apart from Faber & Gwyer. There he was, after the cat-encounter, sitting in an office at Faber & Gwyer, and the *Criterion* boys couldn't understand why he did not do the obvious, simply ask Faber & Gwyer to take on *The Criterion*. The boys raved: *The Criterion should not cease*. Eliot did nothing.

I think Eliot had been profoundly grateful to get out of Lloyds Bank and into the berth with Faber & Gwyer. It had become increasingly impossible for him to keep to banking hours in the City. I suspect Richmond had a hidden finger in that move; I never asked; Faber once told me Hugh Walpole had a finger in it; so, probably, had Whibley. And, in what Eliot conceived to be his responsibility to the new firm, I believe he felt Faber & Gwyer ought not to be persuaded to publish *The Criterion*. Consider: he would never contemplate editing it in order to make it pay its way. His friend Cobden Sanderson produced it expensively and was doing all right if *he* could find another patron. Eliot himself at F & G was stymied. He couldn't (at any rate didn't) ask an outside patron; he couldn't (at any rate didn't) ask a personal favour of Faber & Gwyer. Remember that for himself Eliot would ask no man for financial help; remember, he intended *The Criterion* not to make money. Do I in any way explain his situation? The boys couldn't see it. Eliot's inertia was letting them down. It was clear one issue would be lost. The electrometers flapped. Nobody got a response out of Eliot except a feeling of Doom.

Perhaps I had better try another language altogether (that of *The Jungle Books*, wherein you remember that Kaa was not accustomed to call for help). If Tom at times could be a pretty spry sort of a fellow, at times he could be as sleepy as the rock-python (and in forty years we watched him change some skins). Perhaps when the electrometers girded me to go to see him in his room (the room we were later to share, *Inferno* XXXII, 124–9) he was just sleepy. My strongest card was that I had nothing to gain from *The Criterion*. A strong card (not to be shown) was that I had had a talk with Stewart. His private opinion was that he could cope with the husbandry and Dick with the production if the bills were paid from outside; that probably Faber and possibly Gwyer would invite Tom to the F & G imprint for *The Criterion* if the bills were paid from outside. I used the first but not the second card to wake Tom up: to tell him (I hope boldly) that The Red-Headed League would not dissolve unless he did. He might have lost an issue of *The Criterion*, but if he did not dissolve he could spread the word the thing would go on, the bills would be met. Tom opened one eye. 'All right,' said Tom, 'I'm tough. Who pays the bills?' I don't believe I answered. I was already on the way to find Bruce Richmond.

Richmond was the Secret Agent in the whole thing. If you found Richmond at home he might be playing Chopin and you did not interrupt, but I found him before he left his office. Richmond permitted himself one chortle of amusement, then took about ten minutes to list a dozen names which were to be ever anonymous, and another twenty minutes to give me notes to some of them, making a memo that he would attack others. There was nothing for me to do but bank the fund in a separate account at the bank I used for The Century Company. Presently Stewart had done his work. Faber and Gwyer both invited Tom to use their imprint. I know none of the details of taking *The Criterion* over from Cobden Sanderson. I don't believe I ever mentioned the matter to Faber. I have a few of the formal little notes from Stewart presenting the *Criterion* accounts and acknowledging payments. After two or three issues I think that what Richmond predicted came true – that Faber became interested (the change had probably been noticed at All Souls) and Faber then reorganized *The Criterion* or *New Criterion* as a subsidiary company, and only once more, in 1928, did there have to be a whip round for another fund. Arnold Bennett, by the way, contributed to the second whip round. *Criterion* dinners began to be held first at The Commercio, then at The Swiss Hotel, Old Compton Street, Soho (upstairs). I enjoyed the name of The Swiss Hotel. Each member might bring one guest, 'but the guest should be a person who either has been, will be, or might be useful in one way or another to *The Criterion*'.

To complete the above half-quotation from 'The Donkey Book' about the encounter 'which turned out not much to the advantage of my nose', you remember that Don Quixote was enabled to continue: 'but that is nothing, for if there are necromancers that misuse me, there are some that defend me'.

*

During the next years the Fabers, the Eliots, my wife and I, became close friends. The London office of The Century Company was a convenient stance for me, but there were signs that the old company was slipping. Looking through old engagement diaries, I note that my wife and I were in America in the summer of 1927. There is a memo: 'Allen Tate? N. Y. wants to introduce Read's R & R for Boni's: WHO IS HE?' Presumably I found out. We did not manage to meet then, but there was pleasurable correspondence in 1928 and 29. In 29 there were real clouds over The Century Company. I went for '40 days in the U.S.' in January–March. There was a *Criterion* dinner on 9 January: memo for my trip 'Aiken re exchanging subscription lists Hound & Horn with Criterion'. In the *Aurania* I took with me the German text and Wheen's translation of *All Quiet on the Western Front*. The Century Company broke my heart by turning it down. My 40 days were puzzling. I still have Faber's letter to me from Faber &

Gwyer, written 15 February 1929. He had finally arranged to buy out Gwyer and form a new company under one of four names: 1. Geoffrey Faber Ltd, 2. Faber & Co. Ltd, 3. Faber & Faber Ltd, 4. Faber & Morley Ltd. 'Of these I prefer the last, and so does Stewart.' The offer was, could I then or later put up £2,500? It was a very generous offer: he was to put up ten times as much. I see that I totted up my available assets – $534. I added expectations: the sum was $798. Kit was in the money, but it was all locked up (and later went) in the Rialto Theatre in Hoboken. My shrewdest consultants in New York, Alfred Harcourt and Donald Brace, took me to lunch on the question, strongly advised me against. They would not put any of their money into it. They knew their London. 'Faber is a gambler,' said Don. 'A bunch of Oxford amateurs,' said Alfred; 'won't last.' (Alfred used to pronounce it 'wunt'.) I finally cabled Faber I could find no £2,500, but I would come into his new company by the end of March as an ordinary director, no name on the banner.

'A bunch of Oxford amateurs' was certainly what the London Book Trade thought of the new company of F & F (cables *Fabbaf*), and there was I in the same room with Tom Eliot. The reference above to the *Inferno* is not for the squeamish, but the operative phrase of being in the same hole with Tom is

> il sovran li denti all' altro pose
> là 've il cervel si giunge con la nuca.

Sharing a room with Eliot does not mean that I shared the *editing* of *The Criterion*. He did on occasion attempt to harry me to write for it, and handed me assignments, always much too difficult, and accused me of funk, and that was accurate. The only thing I did write for him was due to a suggestion of Ez P'o. There is a letter from Ezra (undated of course): 'why don't you WRITE a few geometric squibs fer N/E/W/, the wyper needs livenin' '. (Ezra meant the 'new' *Criterion*.) Tom challenged me, so I did a short piece of geometry as it were for the Sports Section, a redaction of a lecture of my father's. It had an awful effect on Flint. He had a mystical excitement – all you had to do was to write *e* to the minus iota theta and you had to spend hours at The Garrick (pub not club) to weather his explanation. Flint, in Lamb's phrase, was a rum genius. The Grove went on now and then, *Criterion* dinners now and then: one immortal occasion was Monty Belgion's story of 'The Man with the Silver Hip'; another often remembered was when we all sang 'Sweeney's Round' by Orlo Williams. Younger faces appeared: Auden, Spender. I don't recall that *The Criterion* was ever asked to, or ever did, show a profit. Indirectly, yes.

*

Pikes Farm, in the angle where Surrey, Kent, Sussex come together. First perhaps a note of fun? Tom was a visitor soon after we bought the place in 1930 (I could borrow money to do that). Tom was naturally Uncle Tom to the children: he was godfather to Susanna, born 1932. Tom and Vivien (she sometimes spelt it Vivienne) came from London for the christening in August. Tom drove his tiny Morris. Rendezvous Oxted, where I was to meet them in my second-hand American Ford V-8 and blaze the trail – not more than 20 m.p.h. – for the Morris to follow through the twisty narrow lanes. Wonderful hot summer day. We met on time, we started sedately. I had forgotten that in a lane half way there was a bend and a slight rise which the Ford had never noticed. Before the spot I tooted to give warning fore and aft, went around the twist and up the rise, and waited. Don Quixote – almost I hesitate to tell it – was not prepared, had trouble, missed his gear-change, pressed everything, pulled everything, stalled, began to roll back – I draw a veil. Another thing I had forgotten was that in the back of the Morris there would be the heaviest of suitcases – Tom never journeyed without the *heaviest* of suitcases. Another thing I remembered was that Tom would intensely dislike any notice taken, any assistance. I went on waiting. Unveil now, and listen: at a third attempt and with unexampled gallantry Tom with the heart of a lion did charge to the top of the mountain. Vivien's nerves withstood the strain better than mine. And at the top, and all in an instant, the perspiring Knight of the Doleful Countenance turned into the Knight of the Lions, conformable to the ancient custom of knights-errant. The (though still perspiring) Knight of the Lions was hilarious with laughter and success and a happy memorable day was had by all, with lunch *al fresco*, small children quick now, here now, in the garden.

I can neither conceal nor evade the fact that when Tom returned from Harvard at the end of June 1933, he did not return to Vivien but came to Pikes Farm. As regards the arrangements he might write in advance with superficial jocu-larity, giving us (3 May) 'carte blanche to commit me to any-thing' or (2 June) 'O Boy say that Good. I'll be seein' yuh.' That did not disguise his private turmoil. Into the depths of his feelings at that time it was not our part to peer. It was enough for us to know that it was for him a moment of crisis, and a turning-point. Look again at the 'conclusion' of *The Use of Poetry and the Use of Criticism*, significantly dated 31 March 1933, significantly ending with the sad ghost of Coler-idge beckoning to him from the shadows. You must turn to Herbert Read for a proper direct approach in these matters, which are beyond my scheme of reference. Domestic life has also to be coped with, somehow. It had seemed to Tom least worst to accept that Vivien's relations and Enid Faber would do what they could for Vivien in London, and that he should come to Pikes Farm if he had to know as Dante knew how salt is the taste of another's bread, how hard a path the going up and down another's stairs. The arrangements (if you wish to see Hamlet putting his hat on and off in the green-room, or Shelley plain, not tuppence-coloured) were simple enough. He was to have a bed and working-room and such meals as he might wish to have by himself at the house of Mrs Eames, wife of the foreman of the immediately adjacent brickworks. That was Uncle Tom's Cabin, a matter of thirty paces to the open doors (front or back) of the farmhouse, where he could have at any time company, or crossword games, or anything. He wirelessed from his ship; I met the train and took his heavy luggage to the country. He spent one night at his London club; we met him next morning at our local station with the dog-cart, which at once reminded him of Sherlock Holmes and appeared to please him very much.

At Pikes Farm there were no large animals – no cows, of which Tom was scary. Tom wrote about the many small animals and small doings to his brother and sisters in America, but he rightly never gave the idea that Pikes Farm was posh, or a dude-ranch. The battered seventeenth-century brick farmhouse, with a very wavy ancient red-tiled lichened roof which architects said would fall in, contained a thousand inconveniences. Lighting and cooking were done by petrol-gas; the rickety and dangerous machine in an outside shed was worked by compressed air which had to be pumped by a long lever, back and forward. Pumping was a chore Tom liked to do: he said it gave him more regular exercise than he had had since as an undergraduate at Harvard he and his classmate Peters had persuaded themselves to undertake Sandow's instructions. Emergency pumping was a frequent occupation. The life of Pikes Farm was a ramshackle life, many things homespun, homemade, improvised; not a neat and tidy life – most things ought to have been done the week before last. But Tom knew that beforehand. There were retainers inside the house and outside who knew Tom and he knew them. When he had been installed in Uncle Tom's Cabin, and knew the running of the whole caboodle, and knew that Cooper would harness Duppy and drive him to and from the station or when and where he wished, my wife and I just left him (nominally in charge) and went for three weeks to Norway. There we were up in the Arctic Circle, ungetatable.

Whether that is the right treatment for a man who is climbing his private mountain of Purgatory, I don't know – you never know. There are times when a man may feel as if he had come to pieces, and at the same time is standing in the road inspecting the parts, and wondering what sort of a machine it will make if he can put it together again. It was fourteen years later, and speaking of his own feelings, that Tom used that figure of speech, and I fancy there was a stress upon the pronoun; he had to draw upon *his* sources, for reconstruction, perhaps involving redirection, of the machine he knew about better than any outside mechanic. We were back from Norway, I see from the records, on 7 August. The estate was in good heart, and so was Tom. He was sunburnt, but, more important, he had been in touch with people he had thought of, and was planning to write *The Rock*. The table in Uncle Tom's Cabin was not sufficiently steady for his typewriter : we bought for him a small and steady kitchen table. Correspondence had been flowing; now people began to come down for days and nights, Geoffrey Faber, Donald Brace from New York, to see what he was doing. He was keeping up with business, he was also writing *The Rock*, he was also learning to bake bread. We did our own baking, and Tom was very proud of the first loaf he made – insisted on a photograph with him holding it well forward to make it appear bigger. In odd moments we invented various kinds of crossword games, in different languages. Before he left Harvard Tom had thought of spending three summer months at Pikes Farm, but he was still there for the fireworks on the Fourth of November – fireworks over the front pond, and a fireboat (reflection in a pond doubles the effect). On 10 November Tom and Donald Brace and I went off to Scotland – we were met by George Blake at Glasgow to drive over Rannoch Moor and to and from Inverness. He left Pikes Farm before Christmas, when his custom then was to go into retreat. When he returned to Town I see he went to Courtfield Road : he was disgusted that his landlady had given him moor hen to eat. He said he preferred to see moor hen swimming on the Pikes Farm pond, their small heads jigging to and fro, like the motion of petrol-gas pumping. He soon moved to Grenville Place, and to other places.

Tom's move to Town was partly to get into theatre. What

had begun with *Sweeney Agonistes*, or before that, was working strongly in him. Talk in that Pikes Farm period was, of course, as matters happened to come up. The forthcoming visit to Scotland put him in mind of Samuel Johnson: he was always ready to talk of Johnson, who meant much to him. I recall one crisp wintry night, hard white frost on the grass under a full moon which dimmed the stars but caused vivid black shadows, when, out of doors, we happened to be talking about George Herbert. It made me think, erroneously, he might be thinking of an essay, and I asked him. 'Not yet,' said Tom, or something to the effect that he had marked many passages in Herbert but, or so I gathered, had not felt ready to write about him. When was it – thirty or more years later? – Bonamy Dobrée was giving lunch to Read and me, and said that Tom had promised him an essay for the British Council pamphlets, but they had never agreed on a subject. I suggested, try him on George Herbert. Read's electrometer woke. 'Would he do it?' asked Bonamy. 'Try him,' suggested Read. Bonamy tried him, and by then Tom felt ready.

*

In recollections of continuous companionship there is always a danger, into which this Sancho may have fallen (though not so with the original Sancho Panza), that the amount of detail may obscure rather than illuminate the portrait. What I have been doing is to talk a little about Tom at a moment when he was surrounded by a domesticity reminiscent in some ways of his own childhood. He talked fairly often at Pikes Farm about childhood days in St Louis, with a fair amount of domestic detail. If he was at the time reviewing his life and his intentions, the setting in which to do so seemed appropriate. Pikes Farm certainly seemed an appropriate interlude to Tom's sisters and brother in America; he may have written to them with a view of giving that impression. When, in February and March of 1934, I was on a business trip to America, Tom's brother, Henry (then in New York), and his sisters, Ada and

Marian (she sometimes spelt it Marianne), in Cambridge were surprisingly knowledgeable about details of our country goings-on, and then and thereafter (our household moved to Connecticut in 1939) treated all of us as 'family'.

Henry liked very much to talk about childhood, and particularly Tom's childhood, in St Louis. He regarded that, I think, as 'roots that clutch'. Ada – I shall refer to Ada in a moment – was not at all so sure as Henry that St Louis was 'roots'. The sisters and brother talked more about their father than their mother, and the impressions naturally varied with each individual. They did not hesitate to correct one another, and to correct Tom, as is not unknown in other families, and is a warning to biographers not to accept 'facts' from one source only. All agreed that the father at St Louis was a Christian gentleman of charm and humour – he used to draw faces for the children on their boiled eggs – that he was extremely fond of what a later generation called 'a leg-pull', a term which I gathered would have shocked him. All agreed that Henry W. Eliot, the elder, would pronounce the flower-name 'nestertian' with the intent of teasing somebody to correct him, and so on. All agreed that H. W. E. was a man of sensibility who could erect defences and keep his thoughts to himself. He was the champion of the family at chess (not merely of the immediate family) and when I was impertinent enough to write a book which had 'chess' in the title, Henry Jr sent me to keep and cherish (as I do), the 'chess-book' of H. W. E., the elder. It is a folio account book (Shallcross Printing & Stationery Co. of St Louis) from which the first 66 and last 8 pages had been excised. Presumably those pages had been used for the family business, managed by H. W. E., in bricks and mules. The remaining pages 67–144 contain chess-problems neatly cut from several newspapers (mostly *The Globe-Democrat*) and neatly gummed in. The problems are usually two to a page, and H. W. E. first pencilled in his own solutions, and then the solutions from the newspapers: with his private annotations, usually 'O.K.', once 'G O O D', occasionally an indignant 'just as good' or 'something wrong'. The handwriting could easily be mistaken for that of his son Tom. I look at the significance of the 'chess-book', as I look at the family significance of 'The Donkey Book', which H. W. E. read aloud to each child in turn, while they followed the pictures.

It was Tom's oldest sister, Ada, for whose intelligence Tom always expressed the greatest respect – he often said that she was the Mycroft to his Sherlock Holmes – who contradicted Henry's hopes that Tom's childhood roots had struck very deeply. Ada's first remark to me is one that I remember. I had duly presented myself, by invitation, at her house at Cambridge (in Gray Gardens) for dinner on Friday, 2 March. She looked at me steadily over her glasses, and her first words were, 'I guessed right.' It was up to me to guess, although I had to wait until the guess was verified, that after giving the matter consideration in advance, she had decided it would not be necessary to provide me with fish to eat on a Friday. Her exclamation was not unlike her father's exclamations to himself when he had solved a chess-problem. Ada and Tom were the most intellectual of Henry Ware Eliot's children. Ada, when I knew her, was a formidable grey-haired lady with a wide experience of practical social work – she had done years of work with prisoners at The Tombs – and she had a capacity to express her thoughts in formulations. Her husband, Professor Sheffield ('Sheff' to his friends), was in physique small, quick, birdlike, and greatly interested in semantics, and would keep up a running translation into his own terms of whatever Ada was saying or you were saying, as fast as it might be said. Their talk was, though, high-powered rather than rapid, and in talking about Tom there was no less affection than that shown by all of the family, but there was a different perception. Perhaps it is often hard for a close-knit family to accept that its youngest member has really 'gone away'. I don't believe Henry ever relinquished the fantasy that Tom would somehow 'come back'. Ada's affection for Tom was more clinical. She was not possessive about Tom, but was concerned about his health: not so much his physical well-being as his psychic health. She was not an alarmist: she said in effect, 'Tom not only says he is tough, but is tough.' But she was both interested and concerned about Tom's 'Way of contemplation', which she was imagining might divorce him from 'human' relationships and drive him into a shadow-world of 'dramatism', into increasing tendencies of outward 'acting' and inward 'mysticism'. She saw two forces pulling apart, yet compensations of each other. I don't think she was disrespectful to the 'Way of contemplation', but she had, I think, something of a horror for 'theatre' as encouraging the dramatist to 'play-act', not on the boards but in an attitude to outward life.

I am not sure how accurate this reporting may be as to Ada's words, for I am compressing impressions of a decade of conversations with the formidable old lady, and Sheff, as I said, was often (though charmingly) confusing the talk by rapidly translating and interpreting whatever was said. As to family significance which Henry found in such items as 'The Donkey Book', or Eliotiana, Ada rather smiled. She thought, though, that 'family' could be something of a fantasy among grown men if the family name of a particular branch was not perpetuated. This may have come up in conversation about *East Coker*, for which in 1940 I was arranging American publication. Tom wished the poem to appear first in some unexpected place: I suggested *Partisan Review*. Tom cabled his approval and told me to keep his spelling of *aresse* for *arras* (line 13). The reason? The spelling *aresse* is out of *The Governour*, by Sir Thomas Elyot. T. Elyot was a grandson of Simon E. of East Coker. At Harcourt, Brace we had a standing order to follow, exactly, the Faber spelling. The Faber spelling, and therefore the 'H,B' spelling (in 1943), was *arras*. I gathered there had been a row about it. Geoffrey Faber wanted all old spelling modernized: Bruce Richmond, when consulted, didn't want that: Faber 'compromised' by chucking Sir Thomas Elyot out. Tom yielded, but it rankled. 'You may say all this doesn't matter; but it does to me. (ob. 1546 ... ob. 1946? beginning & end of A epoch).' Ada, I think, would have sided with Faber, and regarded the *aresse* as so much momie-cloth.

*

It is in Part II, Chapter LXVIII, of *Don Quixote*, the chapter in which the knight and squire talk about sleep and death and family inheritance, that Sancho asks the question which has been with me throughout this short memorial: 'what have the Panzas to do with the Quixotes?' The scheme of reference might be wider than I have made it, or talk go on for longer, for there is no dearth of episodes and escapades into which I was led by this outstanding man. The daily connexion ceased in 1939, and so I stop at the period of Pikes Farm. I see from my engagement-books that various Town-diversions ameliorated office-work. In 1934 it was a custom to weigh ourselves before and after lunch at the Oxford and Cambridge Club. On 29 June H.R. was raised from 11:3 to 11:6; T.S.E. stayed put at 12:4; F.V.M. lifted from 16:1½ to 16:3 (weights at the O & C were recorded in stones). 11 July, when we lunched, Force-Stead was worse. F.-S. was 10:5 before, 10:7 after; T. S. E. jumped incredibly from 11:13 to 12:2¼; and F.V.M. from 15:13 to 16:0. The guests gained more than the home-team, as is proper; but of the home-team, F.V.M. was the more consistent feeder. Oh well, Sancho was ever a cordial friend to a plentiful way of living. After such a lunch, Smith, the cheese-waiter, might detain me with a message: 'There's a Blue Cheshire I've been saving for Mr Eliot, sir – if you and Mr Eliot were to find it convenient to look in at half-past five, I judge that at half-past five it will be just rightly brown.' Cheese at its moment of perfection was of pleasure to Tom, and when there was a troublesome matter, such as finding a right title for *Murder in the Cathedral* (which, once found, sounds easy enough), a right dry sherry with a right cheese at the right minute might help. Different tipples were allocated to different places: there was a pub in Store Street to which we repaired for Russian Stout (which Richmond had taught us to drink), and seeing me off by my train at Victoria, the ration at The Shakespeare would be two large measures of gin and ginger. Adventures with Tom continued on his visits to Pikes Farm. One of those summers he took Uncle Wheen and my son Donald for a voyage on the big pond in the punt, the *Tarry Hind*, Tom paddling the other two all the way to Ultima Thule and back, and commenting on each strange port into which they called. A voyage like that was apt to be seen by Tom with the mind's eye: I don't believe he saw country things with direct sensuous appreciation. In his Town diversions his eye was perhaps quicker for the object: in the country he tended not to look. With the children at Pikes Farm he was never otherwise than kindly and avuncular, but I am not sure how clearly he *saw* them. Donald at the age of nine in 1935 had begun to edit *The Family News*, a monthly periodical hand-published once a year. Tom submitted poems, but not until 1938 was a poem of Tom's accepted by Donald. That was a poem on Cows. Poems on Cats had been rejected. Donald had his own cat, which he had named Saucerer. Perhaps Donald as editor felt there was a spoof, somewhere, about Tom's Cats. It did take a bit of knowing, always, to separate Tom's wit from his chaff.

*

I have dwelt upon younger days because spontaneous love for Tom was not then to be so easily understood by all of my sporting friends, journalist friends, business-like friends. I thought of his charm, which at tough times he never lost. At the well-attended service at Westminster Abbey on 4 February 1965, I was thinking, as were many others there and elsewhere, of Eliot as a man who had very unusual powers of trespass into different hearts. It was a moving, seemly service at the Abbey, in every way a meet and right memorial. You remember that the punctual and most sagacious Cid Hamet said to his pen: omit here the lamentations of Sancho. But I also mentioned Dante, and you recall the lines:

Risposemi; 'Così com' io t'amai
nel mortal corpo, così t'amo sciolta.'

AT EAST COKER

By C. Day Lewis

1

At the far end of a bemusing village
Which has kept losing finding and losing itself
Along the lane, as if to exercise a pilgrim's
Faith, you see it at last. Blocked by a hill
The traffic, if there was any, must swerve aside:
Riding the hilltop, confidently saddled,
A serviceable English church.

Climb on foot now, past white lilac and
The alms-house terrace; beneath yew and cedar
Screening the red-roof blur of Yeovil; through
The peaceable aroma of June grasses,
The churchyard where old Eliots lie. Enter.

A brass on the south wall commemorates
William Dampier, son of this unhorizoned village,
Who thrice circumnavigated the globe, was
First of all Englishmen to explore
The coast of Australia ... An exact observer
Of all things in Earth, Sea and Air.

                                       Another
Exploring man has joined his company.

In the north-west corner, sealed, his ashes are
(Remember him at a party, diffident,
Or masking his fire behind an affable mien):
Above them, today, paeonies glow like bowls of
Wine held up to the blessing light,
Where an inscription bids us *pray*
For the repose of the soul of T. S. Eliot, poet —

A small fee in return for the new worlds
He opened us. 'Where prayer is valid', yes,
Though mine beats vainly against death's stone front,
And all our temporal tributes only scratch
Graffiti on its monumental silence.

2

But soon obituary yields
To the real spirit, livelier and more true.
There breathes a sweetness from his honoured stone,
A discipline of long virtue,
As in that farmside chapel among fields
At Little Gidding. We rejoice for one
Whose heart a midsummer's long winter,
Though ashen-skied and droughtful, could not harden
Against the melting of midwinter spring,
When the gate into the rose garden
Opening at last permitted him to enter
Where wise man becomes child, child plays at king.

A presence, playful yet austere,
Courteously stooping, slips into my mind
Like a most elegant allusion clinching
An argument. Eyes attentive, lined
Forehead – 'Thus and thus runs,' he makes it clear,
'The poet's rule. No slackening, no infringing
'Must compromise it.' . . . Now, supplying
Our loss with words of comfort, his kind ghost
Says all that need be said about committedness:
Here in East Coker they have crossed
My heart again – *For us there is only the trying*
To learn to use words. The rest is not our business.

T. S. ELIOT IN THE THEATRE

THE DIRECTOR'S MEMORIES

By E. Martin Browne

BEFORE I left home for a children's party, my mother's last injunction, after she had straightened my tie and smoothed my hair to her satisfaction, would always be, 'Now dear, don't forget to say "Thank you".' – It would remain an insistent pressure in my mind; but if the party was not a good one, the pressure would be safely relieved by my insincerely pronouncing the dictated words. After a good party, however, I would as often as not forget, in the spate of enjoyment, to say anything.

Now that the thirty years during which I worked with T. S. Eliot are over, I wonder whether the biggest of all my thank-you's was adequately said. For such an association, including not only the direction of all the full-length plays but a considerable amount of consultation in the shaping of them, is very rare in the life of any director, and this one was unique because of the personality of this playwright and his approach to the work. That it was accompanied by an ever-growing friendship is an uncountable bonus.

The most constructive way to offer thanks would seem to be to recall memories for the benefit of those who come after. Of critical scholarship there is and will be an abundance. First-hand memories are rarer. Mine are fallible, of course, and supported by very little documentary evidence, since most of our commerce in the making of a play was by word of mouth. But to begin to put them in order seems to me the best tribute I can pay.

We met in December 1930, at the house of George Bell, since the previous year Bishop of Chichester. Bell, among his many achievements, was the pioneer of a *rapprochement* between the Church and the creative arts. In 1928, as Dean of Canterbury, he had invited Masefield and Gustav Holst to write the first original drama to be presented in an English cathedral since the Reformation. In 1930 he appointed me as the first to hold a dramatic post in the modern Church, 'Director of Religious Drama in the Diocese of Chichester'.

Mr Eliot had recently found his haven, after a stormy journey, in the 'higher' reaches of the Church of England. I had arrived, by a less rugged route, at much the same place. This may have made him feel somewhat at ease with me. So, perhaps, may the nature of my short experience in the theatre hitherto, very little of it spent in 'the profession', much more in the acting and direction of poetic drama, from the Oxford University Dramatic Society and Masefield's Boar's Hill Theatre onwards. Even though he wanted, in drama as in poetry, to see the shackles of dying conventions cut away, it was perhaps easier to see hope of useful assistance from one who had worked a little in the poet's medium.

This is speculation, however, based on hindsight; for 'at ease' is not a true description of any of us at Chichester that week-end. Mr Eliot was in his most silent period. He was always averse to using words which he had not carefully considered and exactly chosen; and since this was probably the loneliest period of his life, conversation was at a minimum. On the Sunday evening George Bell asked him to read *Ash-Wednesday*, which had been published in that year. At the end, a long silence, then hesitating attempts to talk about it, not at all assisted by the author who always deprecated this method of seeking understanding. I began to learn, what even in the different medium of drama I have always found true, that his writing has to be absorbed before it can be analysed.

We saw little of each other during the next two years, but the seeds of friendship sprouted; and the hope of offering him an opportunity for play-writing was always in my mind. Of what sort could it be? *Sweeney Agonistes* had been published some years before, but no one attempted to perform it until

Rupert Doone staged it for The Group Theatre in their own club-room in 1932. To the theatre-folk of the day, dominated by naturalism, such a work was incomprehensible; its verse was too off-beat for the playwriting poets; and for my church audiences, just emerging from a puritan night, it would have been an unbearable shock.

Looking back from the 1960s, I realize that if the path mapped out in the *Sweeney* fragments had been pursued, the Eliot canon of plays would seem more immediate today. But I doubt whether the author himself would have been in the vein for this: the climate of his poetry had changed so radically from *Sweeney* to *Ash-Wednesday*. He had not lost his fondness for music-hall as a dramatic medium; but the content of his drama, whatever the medium, was bound to be very different.

Such speculation is futile, because the opportunity that came next was different anyway. I was approached by the Forty-Five Churches Fund, established to build and endow new churches in the fast-growing outskirts of London, to produce a pageant. They had conceived it on the conventional pattern of Church history and had already allotted some scenes to groups of parishes. I persuaded them, not without much difficulty, that a fresh approach was needed and got them to invite T. S. Eliot to write a work – which they insisted must incorporate the scenes already allotted. It was not a pre-possessing proposition: some millstones round his neck, and no alternative form which could offer an adequate opportunity to a poet as yet devised. But to my joy, he accepted.

We used to meet for lunch, about once a month, usually at the Garrick Club, to search for a form in which to cast the show. It was to be given in Sadler's Wells Theatre. We talked round and round the problem each month, seeing no light until at last, the day before the deadline for a scenario, some broke upon me. We could model it upon the type of revue, bound together by a thin thread of plot, currently presented by C. B. Cochran. It would allow both for spectacular scenes acted to music and for a chorus, who instead of displaying their physical charms could use their speaking voices in delivering verse.

The Verse Chorus was at that period enjoying a vogue. Beginning, I suppose, from the choruses in Gilbert Murray's translations presented by Granville Barker and afterwards by Lewis Casson and Sybil Thorndike, it had been taken up by poets wanting to write for the stage, and teachers such as Elsie Fogerty, Marjorie Gullan, and Mona Swann had fashioned groups of their pupils into fine instruments. But their audiences were the devoted lovers of poetry, not the theatre public. Could choral verse win the attention of a general audience? This was the crucial question.

The scenario had been accepted at the last possible moment, and the author of 'the words' (as he correctly puts it) for *The Rock* had to work against time. When I began to receive the chorus speeches I experienced a great surge of exhilaration. Here was choral verse which combined the grandeur of prophetic with the directness of colloquial diction. The audiences we were gathering for the Sadler's Wells fortnight would not find themselves in a strange world but in their own. The prophet's voice whose rolling phrases were moulded on the Bible would suddenly sharpen to make the suburbanites laugh at themselves:

> 'Their only monument the asphalt road
> And a thousand lost golf balls.'

Marxists and Nazis would fight over the golden calf presented by the Profiteer. The builder's foreman and his wife would celebrate their wedding-day in a music-hall song. The unemployed in the docks and at the street-corners would speak out in reproach to our careless society:

> No man has hired us
> With pocketed hands
> And lowered faces
> We stand about in open places
> And shiver in unlit rooms.

All this was not achieved without much toil. It is typical of the author's humility, and his view of himself as a craftsman learning the playwright's trade, that he should say of me in his Foreword: 'submissive to whose expert criticism I re-wrote much of them'. In fact, we were searching together for the means of 'getting across' to large audiences at every level of education. Their overwhelming response showed that these choruses had opened a new era for the poet in the theatre.

The struggle against odds had produced a total result very far from ideal; the commission had been fulfilled by a piece for its occasion which the author afterwards deliberately allowed to go out of print. But the ground had been broken, ready for the plough: and the final chorus, for which more writing-time could be allowed while the earlier ones were rehearsed, showed what a fine crop could grow in it.

George Bell came to see *The Rock* and from his visit arose another invitation: would Mr Eliot write a play for the Canterbury Festival of 1935? Bell had founded, on the proceeds of Masefield's *Coming of Christ* (referred to above), an annual Festival of the Arts with a play as its centrepiece. Hitherto, it had relied on existing scripts: this was to be the first of a series of original plays. Once more, the cast would be mostly amateur: the chapter house where the show must be given was an uncomfortable auditorium with a narrow platform stage and no exit save through the audience; a week's run of a play, strictly limited in length to an hour and a half, was all that could be looked forward to. And yet, once more, Mr Eliot accepted.

During the ensuing winter, he spent a week-end with us in Sussex. My wife, Henzie Raeburn, became a partner in our discussions and rehearsals of the play about Thomas Becket and finally its godmother when his namesake accepted her suggestion of the title *Murder in the Cathedral*.

He was still a very silent guest. We took him on the Saturday to see a play by Mona Swann at her school in Eastbourne. She had made two or three plays out of the words of the

Authorized Version, using Psalms chorally spoken as a means of expression for the Israelites as a people. On the Sunday we ourselves put on a 'triple bill' in our village church at Rottingdean: the Annunciation from *Ludus Coventriae*, *The Liège Nativity* in Richard Aldington's translation, and a modern play which Mr Eliot understandably found to compare poorly with the medieval offerings. All this perhaps supplied a background for the conversation which finally flowed over the Sunday evening baked potatoes (with plenty of butter).

The first section of the script of *Fear in the Way* (as it was then provisionally titled) to reach me took the play as far as the scene of Becket's return from France. It was complete, establishing the style both for Chorus and for the individual characters, who up to that point are three Priests and the amusingly self-opinionated Messenger. With it came an outline of Part II; and the question, how was the gap between the Return (2 December 1170) and the Christmas Sermon to be filled. It was necessary that in this interval the background of Becket's return and approaching death be presented. Taking my cue from the style of the opening, I suggested that it was plausible to have certain visitors – a crony from Becket's youth, an 'unofficial' emissary from the King, a 'spokesman' for the dissident Barons – call upon Becket. A draft was actually written along these lines; but Becket's opening speech already indicated a deeper dimension of his spiritual conflict than could be dramatized in this realistically historical fashion, and neither of us was satisfied with it. Doone solved the problem with his idea of the Tempters. This opened the way also for the addition of the Fourth Tempter, one of the most original and successful creations in the play.

The presentation of drama is influenced, more than that of any other art, by the cultural conventions of the moment. You may acquiesce in them, you may flout them, but you cannot ignore them, or your play will simply flow by the first-night audience uncomprehended and evoking no response.

Murder, when completed, contained two passages which

seemed to me in different ways liable to this fate: the Temptations, written in a rather cryptic style and alluding to historical details which few of the audience could recall; and the Knights' apology, which used shock tactics comparable to those of Shaw's Epilogue to *Saint Joan* to leap the gulf of 765 years and make a direct contact with the modern audience. It seemed to me that they would be helped in grasping the themes of the two sets of speeches, and be released from troubling about the detail, if the parallels between the two groups, which were very close in every case save one (and that the least significant), could be suggested in production. I therefore adopted the device (which also made the best use of Canterbury's exiguous resources of acting strength) of 'doubling' the parts of Tempters and Knights. The author agreed, and made a few alterations to facilitate the plan; most of these had other reasons to commend them. Because the matter has been much discussed, however, it may be of interest to quote a letter in which, twenty-one years later (20 September 1956), he reviews the case and comes to the opposite conclusion:

I am by no means now sure that it is not better to have the knights played by different actors from the tempters. I like to leave questions for the audience to resolve for themselves, and one question which is left for them if the knights and tempters are different actors, is the question of whether the fourth tempter is an evil angel or possibly a good angel. After all, the fourth tempter is gradually leading Becket on to his sudden resolution and simplification of his difficulties.

The Chorus, as Helen Gardner has pointed out, is really the protagonist in the play. Here is the finest writing: here is the real development, for the core of the drama is not in Becket's struggle towards martyrdom (already near completion when the play begins) but in the progress of the Christian community, represented by the Women, from fear through sympathy and shared guilt to repentance and thanksgiving. This Chorus did not have its full dramatic value in the first production. One reason was that, the platform-stage being only nine feet deep, the actresses were perforce confined to a static position at the sides of the stage through most of the play: they had no room to move and no opportunity of getting on or off the stage. Another was that this group was not rehearsed with the rest of the show. Being teacher-students from Elsie Fogerty's school, they were trained (magnificently) by her in London and only brought down for the dress-rehearsal. So little integration was possible. The play has progressively gained in power as the Chorus has in my subsequent productions been developed as a group of women of varying ages and individualities, bound together by their common faith and their common love of Becket and, sharing fully in the whole of his experience, occupying the same stage with him throughout. The Christian group has no need for a special place of its own, such as the *orchestra* occupied by its Greek counterpart.

The production took seven weeks to make, since the amateurs were only available intermittently and some of them needed a lot of training. At this time we had two young children. I had no other work and we had to live carefully. We rented a tiny bungalow called 'Geralda' from a teacher who was on leave, in a dreary seaside town called Tankerton. The first weeks of rehearsal moved very slowly and we had misgivings; but with the arrival of Robert Speaight, who was to play Becket, and later of the Chorus, everything came together according to plan. The author said very little; he did not yet feel at home in the theatrical atmosphere, and his chief concern was that his lines should be spoken accurately. But his occasional observation was always significant and penetrating.

Despite its inevitable shortcomings, this was a historic production, because the play was recognized as a landmark in twentieth-century drama. Arrangements were at once made by Ashley Dukes to transfer it to the Mercury Theatre, London, in the fall. This of course involved a professional cast, but since the theatre seated only 136, salaries had to be nominal, ranging from £10 to 30s. a week. Under these conditions, the play ran for a year; then it was moved to the West End for six months, followed by two big provincial tours. It achieved the staggering feat of capturing large theatre audiences for a religious play written in an eclectic style; and this was the looked-for proof that the controversial poet of the twenties had displayed the gifts of a major dramatist in the thirties.

During the winter of *Murder*'s arrival in the London theatre, we saw a good deal of Tom (as he had now become to us); and naturally discussed what was to follow this success. He was quite determined in refusing invitations to undertake further work for the Church; once in the theatre, he wanted to stay there. He was equally set on attempting a contemporary subject: no more history or ritual! Any poet who wanted to speak to today's audience must speak in today's language of people like themselves: and he would try to do it.

The first draft of *The Family Reunion* reached us when we were, with Ashley Dukes, presenting the London production of *Murder* in New York. Tom had read portions of it to us before we left London. Once more, it needed absorbing; for once more he had, in teaching himself to write for the stage, broken much new ground. The success which was most immediately apprehensible was in the versification; the firm yet infinitely flexible rhythms of the verse, which allowed contemporary characters to speak with apparent naturalness yet to rise without a jolt into the higher reaches of poetry, were to be the medium of all his subsequent playwriting. As, in later plays, the naturalistic surface has occupied attention for more of the time, the poetry has been more severely 'rationed' (the poet's word) by the test of strict dramatic relevance, and the verse has, in the naturalistic passages, a somewhat looser form, with more run-on lines. I have regretted this because it deprives the poet of his peculiar power, and feel that of the modern plays *The Family Reunion* is the one which has most lasting value. And yet, in feeling so, I may be falling into the very trap from which its author was trying to free himself and the verse-play, the tendency to create a poetic world other than the real world of contemporary human beings.

Other aspects of the play, however, contradict this fear. For never, surely, has the depth of contemporary despair been plumbed so thoroughly as by Harry Monchensey. In the process of his suffering he speaks profoundly to our condition. It is significant, I think, that the clarifications I asked for as I studied the script were not concerned with that process but with its origins and its outcome : and the magnificent letter of exposition which is quoted at length by F. O. Matthieson[1] deals with such matters. This was written (19 March 1938) about the first draft of the play, when major questions such as the introduction of Arthur and John, the relationship between Harry and Mary, the truth about the death of Harry's wife, and the specific nature of Harry's own future were in discussion. It is a tribute to the author's sureness in planning that what resulted were mostly clarifications, rather than alterations, of the original.

For the first production, an alliance was made between Ashley Dukes and the London Mask Theatre management at the Westminster run by J. B. Priestley, Ronald Jeans, and Michael Macowan. They had a permanent nucleus of actors for the 1938–9 season, including Stephen Murray (who played Charles) and Ruth Lodge (Mary). The theatre is not in the Shaftesbury Avenue area, but with 600 seats it was able to offer adequate remuneration to actors who wanted to do interesting work, and we were blessed with Catherine Lacey as Agatha and Helen Haye as Amy. Henzie Raeburn was suggested by the author himself to play Ivy, the one of the four uncles and aunts whom he had based upon a relative of his own. Michael Redgrave, though he confessed himself rather out of his depth in the latter half of Harry's part, brought a great deal of sensitive understanding to him. Stella Mary Pearce's device, in designing the women's costumes, of making them all of one fabric and using the same dress for each

1. *The Achievements of T. S. Eliot*, Oxford University Press, 1947.

character (with the necessary changes of detail) throughout the play, had a valuable unifying effect.

The author didn't come much to rehearsals; besides being busy, he was perhaps still feeling the specialized world of actors a strange place. But when he did come, he was ready to be helpful to them. To the question 'What happens to Harry after he leaves?', which my wife and I had already asked and which Redgrave repeated, he replied with an addition of fifty lines to his scene with Amy and Agatha (Part II, Scene 2). Harry's description of the life that lies ahead of him owes something to the life in Algeria of Charles de Foucaud (already referred to in the final Chorus of *Murder*). But the definition of where he is going:

Somewhere on the other side of despair

and Agatha's comment:

In a world of fugitives
The person taking the opposite direction
Will appear to run away

get to the heart of the experience involved.

The play was received with incomprehension, exemplified in James Agate's silly-clever review in a parody of its verse. March 1939 was not the best moment for a work which pulls off blinkers: England was still trying too hard to keep them on. When I revived it at the Mercury in 1946, its purpose was instantly appreciated, and even though its faults were not glossed over it was recognized as a major play. Before this production, we corresponded about the possibility of a fairly considerable revision, and he was interested by some suggestions which I made. But 'as soon as I start thinking about the play, I have inklings of altering it still further'. And 'my goal has been to ... start a new play'. So 'I feel it would be healthier for *me* to leave it alone'. (27 August 1946) I do not, now, regret this decision: for the longer I live with *The Family Reunion* the more value I set on it, and, admitting its flaws as the author himself did (exaggeratedly, to my mind) in his lecture on *Poetry and Drama*, I believe the homogeneity of the original creation is of greater importance.

The start on a new play had been postponed *sine die* by the coming of war. For much of it, he lived with friends at Shamley Green, near Guildford in Surrey, going to London on publishing business and to do his turn of duty as fire-watcher at Faber & Faber during the blitz. I was running a travelling company, The Pilgrim Players, and when we came to Guildford with *Murder in the Cathedral* he attended a performance and we spent some time with him. He was interested in this work and when at the end of the war we settled at the Mercury for three years and produced plays by several of the Faber poets who were his protégés, I saw a good deal of him.

He did not begin work on the new play until he was established in Chelsea, sharing an apartment overlooking the river with John Hayward. By this time, the Mercury seasons were over and I was Director of the British Drama League. Our meetings were usually in Tom's quiet little study at the back of his apartment, in the evening after dinner. On 18 July 1948 he sent me the first draft of three acts; and on the title-page was the name *One-Eyed Riley*. But the alternative title was already in discussion, and soon *The Cocktail Party* was agreed upon, a decision never regretted.

This draft is a fascinating document; as one compares it with the final script, one can see the process by which the style of the post-war comedies was developed. In the draft there are a good number of those cryptic observations which characterize *The Family Reunion*, because the central experience of that play is on a subconscious plane. In the final version, these are almost eliminated in favour of direct statement. The verse likewise is shorn of imagery and evocative phrases, and the repetitions (a favourite technical means of recalling previous scenes) are made to appear natural.

In form, too, there is steady development towards comedy and towards a natural flow. The draft contains all the chief scenes of what are now Acts I and II. 'Each is of great interest in itself [I wrote on 31 July] but they do not seem to be sufficiently integrated into a pattern of action. The solution of this problem seems to lie in the use of Julia and Gibbs.' Plans for their interventions during the action were worked out, which had the further advantages of strengthening these characters and of increasing the comic element in the play.

Work went on through the autumn. Meanwhile the question arose – where and by whom should the play be presented? The author was much attracted by the Edinburgh Festival, which after two years had already the highest international reputation. Accordingly, I went to see Rudolf Bing, its begetter and manager. He was excited at the prospect of a new Eliot play, and urged me to approach the Old Vic, with whom he was in treaty to produce the dramatic offerings for the Lyceum Theatre, then the only house for 'straight' plays under the Festival Society.

I wrote to Hugh Hunt, the newly appointed Director, giving a synopsis of the play. He replied that no decision could be taken without a complete script, at least in draft, and that 'I cannot agree that the play be tied to a particular producer (i.e. director).' I understood his stand, in view of the fact that the Old Vic was a repertory company; but when I put it to the author I received one of the most moving letters of my life:

6th January 1949

My dear Martin,

I return herewith Hugh Hunt's letter to you of the 4th January. It has always been an understanding between ourselves that you should produce this play, and I should consider it turpitude to throw over my producer! I assure you also that from my point of view I think it might be grasping the shadow and dropping the substance since I should feel grave hesitation in putting it into other hands. I assure you that self-interest combines with loyalty to induce me to turn the proposal down without more ado.

Yours ever,
Tom.

Returning to Mr Bing, I found that, meanwhile, the nego-
tiations with the Old Vic had failed and he was entrusting the
Lyceum to Henry Sherek. To him, accordingly, I took the
three-quarters of the play which I had in first draft. The joints
had not yet been made between the scenes, and there was no
last act; but he had no hesitation in agreeing to do it at Edinburgh.

So began an association which lasted through the rest of
Tom Eliot's playwriting life. We invited author and manager
to meet for the first time at lunch in our apartment at Port-
land Court; this was an occasion of acute embarrassment for
all four of us, but from this unpromising beginning there developed increasing appreciation on both sides. At this stage,
Henry Sherek's shrewd theatrical judgement was of much
value to Tom, who from then on came more and more to
rehearsals and enjoyed the company of his actors. I feel that he
was very fortunate – and so was I – to work with an individual
manager, and such an individualist, with so personal a love for
the theatre.

By this time the last act was in draft.

On one of Tom's frequent visits to us, our question about
Harry was repeated about Celia. 'What exactly does happen to
her?' asked my wife. 'I want to know.' The reply was duly
written into the script: and everyone was horrified. The
crucifixion of Celia was made real – 'the lowest and most
indecent horror', as Charles Williams says of the crucifixion of
Christ. The gruesome details given in the first performances at
Edinburgh were reduced thereafter, since they produced so
much physical revulsion that they damaged the effect of the
last act as a whole. But the essential horror remained. Tom
was always determined on facing the truth. And this resulted
in joy as well as in pain. The play is a comedy, as all the later
plays are, and however disturbing it may be at some times, the
end, in its own terms of ultimate truth, is happy. As Reilly
says of Celia:

That way, which she accepted, led to this death.
And if that is not a happy death, what death is happy?

Sherek skilfully piloted the play from Edinburgh to New
York, where a brilliant cast led by Alec Guinness and Irene
Worth helped to make it a smash hit. Another cast had to be
assembled and directed for London; and Tom, who had
missed the New York opening, saw this one with Rex Harrison
as Reilly and Margaret Leighton as Celia. The play was now
doing big business on both sides of the Atlantic, and the
famous poet had become the famous dramatist as well.

Such plays as his take a lot of writing. He was always a
meticulous worker, hence a fairly slow one; he had many other
responsibilities; the rate at which plays came from his pen
could not be swift. It was in fact good going to write three
within a decade.

His growing mastery of the current theatre techniques, as
well as of dramatic poetry, was shown by the fact that, both
for *The Confidential Clerk* and for *The Elder Statesman*, I
received complete scripts. I do not mean, of course, unalter-
able scripts; no dramatist was ever more willing to attend to
critical questions and suggestions, especially from the one who
had to make the play work on the stage, and over both these
plays we had many conferences both in the months preceding
rehearsal and when the actors revealed, as they so often do to
the observant eye, weak points in the script. The bit which the
actor finds difficult, or misunderstands, is always worth re-
examining: of course he may be being obtuse or have some
private reason for his trouble, but it is just as likely that the
writing needs clarification. As Tom put it to me in an earlier
letter (19 March 1938): 'Where I think you may have mis-
understood me, that is significant too, as indicating that I have
not made the meaning transparent.'

The Clerk is the best constructed of all the modern plays: it
builds steadily (after a slow opening) to a last act which is taut
and full of good surprises, and in the theatre, with a very fine

team of actors, it got a warm response. Yet it has been almost forgotten in the last ten years. I think this is partly because of its very success in terms of the theatre it was written for. By 1953, the wind of change was blowing through our drama; the ferment that gave us our present crop of brilliant young dramatists was already breeding dissatisfaction with the conventions of the upper-middle-class play which had dominated our stage for so long. My first reaction to *The Clerk*, I remember, was a mixture of pleasure and dismay; the almost feudal attitude to one another of the rich business man and his old confidential clerk gave it the air of a period piece, and the tangled pattern of mistaken identities reminded me of Gilbert or Oscar Wilde. I was right here: the form of classic comedy had been used to say some profound things about human relationships; but it was only in the heart-rending scene between Colby and Lucasta that one saw clearly how completely relevant the play was to this era of broken homes and rootless young people.

The success of this play gave Tom great pleasure, in which we shared. Before the next one came his marriage in 1957 to Valerie Fletcher. We returned from New York a few weeks after it happened, to rejoice in the happiness which, after so hard a life's journey, had come to enrich his remaining years. *The Elder Statesman* was begun during 1957 and our work on the script was carried on at their Kensington apartment; here I found the glow that is reflected in the whole tone of the play, and gives it a mellow beauty unlike any previous work.

It is founded on *Oedipus at Colonus*, which Sophocles wrote when he was eighty years old. We celebrated Tom's seventieth birthday after the London first night. As with *The Clerk*, its style is minimally poetic; but it shares with Sophocles' play the underlying poetry of a life fully lived, fully suffered, and the end has a mystical character.

The love-scenes, which the author attempts here for the first time, have the same simple directness that Shakespeare, at the parallel time in his life, gives to Ferdinand and Miranda in

The Tempest – a treatment which poises them on a knife-edge between ecstasy and embarrassment. Vanessa Redgrave, in the television production, proved how finely these scenes could play. The comic gift is still as strong as ever: indeed, I would reckon Mrs Carghill's scene with Lord Claverton as Tom's best comic creation.

That was the last play. I think I always knew it was, and perhaps, though we talked hopefully of another, he knew it too. The closing days were very happy ones, thanks to his wife; and even though he realized that the fashion and mood of this moment were alien to some elements in his work, he knew also that it contained the seeds of its own permanence.

GERONTION

By John Crowe Ransom

WHEN Mr Eliot's death was announced, I think the news did not wholly discomfit us on his physical account. It was our understanding that he had been seriously ill, and suffering pain. How natural and merciful that his mortal turn had come; and we knew as well as he that his literary testament was finished and secure. Still we were greatly moved. We had now acquired a responsibility which it would be difficult to discharge. We must re-read him, and think a long time about his achievement, and about how the parts cumulated into a whole; thinking as precisely as we could possibly think about something intangible, in order to say what he had meant to English letters. His writings had already been committed to the public domain, but suddenly we had become the executors who must appraise the estate.

A special burden rested upon me, from which I am sure the other tributaries in this collection of essays have been exempted. Twice only have I written pieces about Eliot, and now I have to make two recantations. The first time I scolded him for *The Waste Land*, with what I took to be its academic trick of recondite allusions on the one hand, and on the other hand its want of a firm and consistent prosody, such as I seemed to require. I was mistaken about the allusions. It turned out quickly, and increasingly, that they meant a great deal to the members of a very important public. These were the remarkably bright young scholars and critics who aspired in that age to a complete learning, including the precise identification of original texts which might be referred to, even if ever so slightly. They were as tough-minded as they were competent, and when they succeeded they were elated like professional sportsmen over their triumphs. But they were most challenged when Eliot gave them sly literary allusions from which some religious or moral faith depended, and over which hovered the sense of a secret passage from Eliot's mind to theirs. Eliot was always a religious poet, though he never propounded the dogmas of his faith, which evidently was rather eclectic; it could be Hebraic, or Christian, or Greek, or even Oriental. But those sturdy people who studied his *Waste Land* felt the passion which he had put into the transaction. They must have had a feeling of having been starved of something or other in the poverty of their intellectual interests, and now of knowing that what they had missed was the religious sense in which they had been reared. (I am afraid it becomes less and less in the rearing of our successive modern generations.) Their vague uneasiness in their occupation became a good plain nostalgia when they saw what it had meant. Eliot gave back their old world to them. It was a beautiful predicament, and repeated many times.

As to the prosody, it took me rather longer to repent. But by the time when the *Four Quartets* was finished, I had come to think that, of all the pioneers who had looked for a suitable modern prosody, Eliot was the best. He favoured a profusion of new rhythms replacing the steady old rhythms, which seemed worn to death; or keeping more or less the iambic pentameters of the blank verse he needed by 'counterpointing' them with smaller cross-rhythms. Somebody, by precept and example, had to bring into the music of poetry the grace and freedom which had arrived in the art of pure music many years before. Eliot was the man.

My other unfortunate estimate of Eliot came when I wrote a harsh review of *Murder in the Cathedral*. I read the play at one sitting, and wrote my piece the next day at another sitting. The trouble was that in that period I was studying my Milton, and had a special liking for *Samson Agonistes* over all his other works. The *Murder* like the *Samson* was in the Greek form of drama, but it seemed to me that the *Murder* was always running wild, and rejecting its form. I disliked the

Interlude containing the Becket sermon, the language of the poor old women employed in the Chorus, and especially the speeches of the silly young royalists who tried to justify themselves for murdering an archbishop. But I was able after a little while to be reasonable, and to reflect that the form of drama is subject to changes as soon as a new and able dramatist wants it so, and that as a rule the new wine tastes better to his own public than the old.

I have chosen to write something about 'Gerontion', a very important poem in the Eliot canon; and besides that, the particular poem in which Eliot first worked out to his own satisfaction that brisk prosody which was to be his staple thereafter. Allen Tate wrote approving my choice, and saying that he liked this poem better than any of Eliot's except the *Quartets*. It is he that should be writing up my topic; but his job of collecting and editing all these essays was prior, and prohibitive.

The man of the poem in this dramatic monologue is in that final stage of human misery when there is nothing to do but brood over what little remains of a life that came rather early to have no principle of direction except its worldly interests; and to wish and wait for death, which is imminent, as its perfect ending. The poet does not name him as Geron, who is any old man, but as Gerontion, a little old man, shrunken in body and soul. But we must say emphatically, not in the force of his intellect. When characters are obliged by their poet to speak for themselves, they have to be supplied with a suitable poetry, and a great poet may bestow upon an important character a poetic immortality. Gerontion is still in complete possession of intelligence and wit, but the wit is as acrid as the substance, and the whole of the monologue is as magnificent as it is tragic.

But I must digress for a few minutes. Is there any critic who tries to see this poet whole, yet never looks away from the particular poem in question to the analogies and differences that exist in the other poems? Here we are reminded inevit-

ably of the poem about Prufrock, five years earlier. He and
Gerontion are two of the living dead who abound in Eliot's
verse, especially in *The Waste Land*. Prufrock is of middling
age, though grown too lean, and balding; perhaps a rather
charming man and still an eligible bachelor; but fatally divided between his amours and his morals. He is given to citing
Scripture, at least to his better self, his conscience or Super-
ego to whom his words are spoken; and surely is acquainted
with the letter of Paul to the Church at Corinth, where in the
seventh chapter Paul proposes a way of life whereby married
partners may keep their chastity, then adds a few words to
help the unmarried and the widows: 'But if they cannot contain, let them marry; for it is better to marry than to burn.'
And indeed it may seem that Prufrock has found his woman;
if it is really she who is twice referred to as 'one', among the
women in the drawing-room about whom with some contempt
he makes the refrain,

> In the room the women come and go
> Talking of Michelangelo.

How could they have had any inkling of that glory which
Michelangelo had put into his marbles and his paintings? And
a more pointed question: Was there in the special woman's
head any possible cranny into which the sense of divinity could
find an entry?

His name is Prufrock, and to the women that sounds like the
name of a man both 'prudish' and 'preachy'. He may have
looked the part, and perhaps he has incautiously spoken once
or twice in that character, this being the real reason they look
upon him as a laughing-stock. It makes him extremely self-
conscious in their presence. Perhaps Prufrock is the most
sensitive and self-depreciating of all dramatic heroes. He
cannot bring himself to speak up for Christ; so far from being
an intellectual that he does not know how, and so afraid that
he will not try. He says he is no prophet like John the Baptist,

Though I have seen my head (grown slightly bald) brought
in upon a platter.

It might have been easier to say he had walked the narrow
streets of the poor quarter,

> And watched the smoke that rises from the pipes
> Of lonely men in shirt-sleeves, leaning out of windows. . . .

which would have been a Christian's way of raising the social
issue. Here is the latest and longest of these key passages:

> And would it have been worth it, after all,
> After the cups, the marmalade, the tea,
> Among the porcelain, among some talk of you and me,
> Would it have been worth while,
> To have bitten off the matter with a smile,
> To have squeezed the universe into a ball
> To roll it towards some overwhelming question,
> To say: 'I am Lazarus, come from the dead,
> Come back to tell you all, I shall tell you all' –
> If one, settling a pillow by her head,
>> Should say: 'That is not what I meant at all.
>> That is not it, at all.'

I have belaboured the poem to this length because I think
too many critics who are generally admirable have not seen it
in a very clear perspective. They may have been deceived by
its full title: 'The Love Song of J. Alfred Prufrock'. And
Eliot may have gleefully expected them to be. At one period I
always knew a few of my students would write in their examination papers something like this: 'The poem therefore means
to say that Prufrock was too cowardly to pop the question to
his lady.' Critics whom they had read had said as much, with
more vocabulary and circumstance. And certainly that question is in Prufrock's mind. But another question has to come
first: How does she feel about religion? If he asked it, and she
was displeased with him for asking it, he would be displeased
with her for not answering it, and they could reject each other
simultaneously.

Prufrock's indecision is finally decisive; he returns to his mermaids, and that is the moral end of him. We are not obliged to see the physical end of him, but the moral crisis has been fully resolved, and it is downhill for him all the rest of his life. The pleasures of the body, however, have a high rating in most societies, as they should, and at the moment of his final surrender the actuaries could probably read off their tables for him a generous 'life-expectancy'. We must define the dramatic mode of this poem as tragi-comedy. But 'Gerontion' is pure tragedy.

We have been given to know that Eliot intended the 'Gerontion' of 1920 to be part of *The Waste Land* of 1922, which was already in preparation, and that Pound dissuaded him. But I cannot remember knowing Pound's objection. Eliot would have told him of his plan to write the book in the form of a poetic symphony having five movements; and Pound was by long odds the most knowledgeable adviser to poets that Eliot could have found. May not Pound have told him that 'Gerontion' was already a sort of symphony having five movements, or at least the perfect miniature of one; and that Eliot could not reduce a symphony of five movements to a single movement in another symphony? It happens that 'Gerontion' is about the length of the average of the five movements in *Waste Land*; and that the second of the movements of 'Gerontion' has three parts, though they are perfectly consecutive, and only the third part ends with a period stop. But all its five movements are as distinct from one another as the five in *Waste Land*, and the six movements in *Ash-Wednesday*, and the five movements in *Four Quartets*. I think it is generally agreed that in music proper the particular symphonic form is subject to the composer's will; and why may we not extend the same privilege to the poet? It is true that the movements in *Waste Land* and *Ash-Wednesday* and *Quartets* are announced by title at the top, or by Roman numerals, or by both. But to deny 'Gerontion' because it does not exercise that privilege would be pettifogging; we may insert our own numerals in our copies. If nevertheless 'Gerontion' is probably the littlest symphony ever published, in pure music or in poetry, it becomes all the more prodigious. It has everywhere in it all the wealth of detail and imagery that we could ask, but compacted; and I have come to think that nothing else in Eliot fills us with such an awe of his power.

*

[I]

Here I am, an old man in a dry month,
o -- o - - o o- - /

Being read to by a boy, waiting for rain.
o o - o o o- - o o - /

I was neither at the hot gates
o o - o o o - -

Nor fought in the warm rain
o - o o - - /

Nor knee deep in the salt marsh, heaving a cutlass,
o - - o o - - /- o o- o

Bitten by flies, fought.
- o o - /- /

My house is a decayed house,
- - o o o - - /

And the jew squats on the window sill, the owner,
o o - - o o - o - /o - o/

Spawned in some estaminet of Antwerp,
- o - o - o-/o - o /

Blistered in Brussels, patched and peeled in London.
- o o - o - - /o - o /

The goat coughs at night in the field overhead;
o - - o - /o o - oo - /

Rocks, moss, stonecrop, iron, merds.
- - - o - - /

The woman keeps the kitchen, makes tea,
o - o - o - o /- -

Sneezes at evening, poking the peevish gutter.
- o o- o - o o - o/- o /

                              I an old man,
                              o o - -

A dull head among windy spaces.
o - - oo - o- o/

142

This movement stands in sixteen lines, and is very slightly longer than the average of the five. Nine of the lines could be considered pentameters: Lines 1–2 and 8–14. But rarely does the old iambic rhythm hold up; that rule has been discarded, in the interest of fresher and more spontaneous rhythms for the modern ear. Can we imagine a symphonic poem whose rhythms are otherwise? The long lines mean mostly to be broken up into rhythms corresponding to their phrase-units. This movement starts by identifying the man, and the man's age and helplessness, then the man's house, and household, and landscape. The whole movement gives us Gerontion exactly as he is, and leaves it to the later movements to identify his intentions.

Let us look closely at a sufficient number of passages both as to their substance and as to their rhythms. Lines 1–2 are a model of introduction, brief without a wasted word or syllable. The rhythm which appears three times in line 1 ends with a spondee (containing two adjacent stresses) preceded by one or two unstressed syllables which I shall call unstresses. Line 2 has two rhythms which match sufficiently, each showing two stresses of which one is final, and a swarm of unstresses to be distributed. But in lines 3–6 the fireworks begin. Lines 3 and 4 are phrases in rhythms which match each other almost precisely; there are three stresses, of which the concluding two make a spondee, with unstresses preceding the first stress and the final spondee. In both lines the theme is the valour of soldiers in combat; it is repeated in line 5 by another pair of two-stress rhythms; and again, beginning towards the close of line 5 and continuing into line 6, by a still fiercer pair of two-stress rhythms in which the first word has one stress and the last word has the other. But it could hardly have been expected that Gerontion would take such an honest care as, at the very beginnings of the first three lines, to deny that such valour had ever been his own. The four lines end with the powerful monosyllable 'fought'. It stands independent of any rhythmic pattern, but is a heavy and important word that refers back to the whole passage about soldiery, like a final chord of music in the right key that is held for a moment after a rhythmic passage.

In line 7 we have another introduction which concerns Gerontion's house and uses a pair of rhythms which show again the spondaic structure. Then we pass to the household, and it appears that the owner of the house is himself a resident, like Gerontion who rents it. He is described by his tenant with lordly contempt in three lines which rival for poetic supremacy lines 4–6. But Gerontion is a lord of language, like Virgil in Tennyson's poem, and prepared to turn on his full power even when he speaks evil. The tone-quality is very crisp and beautiful, and the rhythms especially decisive. Without dwelling unnecessarily upon them – they are marked if the reader wants to consult my text – I wish to notice what happens rhythmically if my readers will agree with me about the status of those three phrases which stand at the ends of lines 8–10. They read respectively: 'the owner', 'of Antwerp', and 'in London'. The first of these phrases is isolated completely by the final punctuation mark and also the one which preceded it; the others have punctuation after them but not before. But why not treat them all as unnecessary excrescences upon the preceding rhythms, language-wise, perfectly agreeing with each other rhythmically? By these considerations I felt entitled to think of the three rhythms as echoing one another and composing a valid rhythm, though widely separated.

Two other remarks may be made about the prosody of Movement I. First, there is the memorable line 12, which we might have said was a pentameter making a single rhythm of five bare monosyllables. But I have taken the extra syllable of the third one as important because of its addition of an unstress, and as perhaps our cue to look closely and see if we may not suppose a strong caesura at that point, dividing the pentameter into a pretty trimeter and a crushing dimeter. The words 'Rocks, moss, stonecrop' make just such a series of detail as Wordsworth might have employed lovingly in one of his listings of the features of a fair landscape. But the landscape in question is only 'the field overhead', where the goat ranges; and the dimeter gives it quite another status. We may take the 'iron' to mean the scrap-iron of used-up metal gadgets tossed from the passing cars, and composing not a landscape but a litter; and merds are merds. There could not be terms terser and more euphemistic at the same time, but they have their savagery.

Finally we have to concern ourselves with that last sentence of the movement, lines 15–16. It is set away and Southeast from the body of the movement, but it recapitulates the theme in terms and rhythms somewhat like the first two lines. We may call it a coda, as according to the style of symphony.

But perhaps now we are entitled to a sort of inkling of what this symphonic poem is going to mean to our old castaway, whose power of poetry is his only possession.

The soft reader, because he is a sentimentalist, may not care much for this movement. It has a very homely theme, upon which it expends very little latinity, and has for its biggest word the French *estaminet*. But the poetry seems to be redeemed at least twice by gorgeous passages, in lines 3–6 and 8–10. How melancholy it may appear that the heroic martial strain of the first passage should be repudiated three times, and at the very beginning of the lines, as having nothing to do with his own history. And it must be equally sad that he should compose so grand a passage as the second one about an unsavoury person. But we must concede them, and be glad of them. Gerontion knows that valour always deserves the grand style though he has not personally experienced it; and as to the disreputable theme of the second passage he knows that in proportion to its own excess it too must be treated extravagantly.

Must we not subscribe to Kant's definition of the famous pleasure which is unique in poetry, and other arts? Aristotle must have been the first theorist who proposed this association, but apparently it is going to last for all the eternity which poetry may expect. Kant did not reject it, but he defined it, by means of certain exclusions which did not contain it; and his definition-by-exclusion satisfied Hegel, who commended it as the first rational word that had been spoken in aesthetics. Kant was bold enough to say that the pleasure of poetry (and of every other art) did not consist in the pleasures of the greedy body, nor the pleasure of the understanding (or science) when it succeeded in its purpose whether as theory or as utility, nor even in the noble pleasure of a good conscience; and capped all these exclusions by remarking that it did not matter to poetry whether the world it set up had real existence or was only imaginary. Let us keep Kant's doctrine in mind throughout 'Gerontion', to see what the outcome will be. But not without knowing well that Eliot was accomplished in philosophy, and would have agreed with this Kantianism.

[II]

Signs are taken for wonders. 'We would see a sign!'
 –   o – o o – o / o o   – o – /
The word within a word, unable to speak a word,
o – o – o –   o – o o –   o – /
Swaddled with darkness. In the juvescence of the year
– o   o – o /o o o – o o o – /
Came Christ the tiger
o   –   o – o /
In depraved May, dogwood and chestnut, flowering judas,
o o –   –   – o   o – o   – oo   – o /
To be eaten, to be divided, to be drunk
o o – o o o o – o o o –
Among whispers; by Mr Silvero
o o   –   o /o – o – o
With caressing hands, at Limoges
o   o – o   –   / o o –   /
Who walked all night in the next room;
o   –   – –   o o   –   – /

By Hakagawa, bowing among the Titians;
o – o – o /– o o –   o – o /
By Madame de Tornquist, in the dark room
o o –   o   –   –   /o o –   – /

Shifting the candles; Fräulein von Kulp
```
- o   o - o /- o  o  -
```
Who turned in the hall, one hand on the door.
```
o  -    o o - /-  -   o o - /
```
  Vacant shuttles
```
  - o   - o
```
Weave the wind. I have no ghosts,
```
 -    o  - / o o  - -     /
```
An old man in a draughty house
```
o  -  - o o -   o -
```
Under a windy knob.
```
-  o  o - o  - /
```

The second movement may be regarded as the most lyrical of the five. Musically, the quick two-stress rhythms are preponderant, numbering twenty-five by my count; and the range in the substance of these combinations is wide, so that sometimes we have trouble finding it, though at least we are always assured that it will be fresh and vivid. Do such properties not testify to the lyrical mode; and in the strictest sense, which means that the poem is like the song which the Greek poets sang to the rhythms of the plucked strings of the lyre?

Let us think of the poet in the act of composing such a movement. His head is full of many important ideas which have to find their images, and often the first image that comes is so bold that he refuses to change it, expecting us to grasp it if we can. Probably words came quickly and easily in this movement, and did not have to be so laboured as we imagine the first movement to have been.

The introduction to this movement requires four lines which come in the fourth to a climax of the first order: 'Came Christ the tiger'; the passage is left open without punctuation for immediate development in the second part and half of the third. And as to the three lines of preparation for it, Gerontion would have been well educated in religious as well as secular learning, and would have been acquainted with Bishop Launcelot Andrewes's sermon about the *infans*, the infant Christ who was a Word that could not speak a word. He employs Andrewes's phrases, and it is well. But Christ acquired at a prodigious rate the Word for his mission; that was well known everywhere in Gerontion's time, and to that faith Gerontion committed himself. Yet after some years, how many we do not know, Gerontion fell into a neglect of Christ. This Christ had appeared originally and officially on earth as the Lamb of God who by the sacrifice of his own body would take away the sins of the world. But now he appeared to come in the menacing image of Christ as tiger.

What is the significance of 'in the juvescence of the year'? The nearest analogue in Eliot's work is the opening passage of *Waste Land*, where 'April is the cruellest month' because it arouses us from the dull peace of the winter. But it suits the opening line of the second movement, where the trees appear sensuous – and even sexual, if we consider sexual function – as they come into luxuriant blossom. Its purport there is that Eliot is asking, Are we to conduct ourselves after the fashion of trees?

A small aside. Eliot in the 'Gerontion' has brought into the language three new though classical words. The first is the title word, straight from the Greek. The second is 'juvescence', supposedly from the Latin, but incorrect. The proper word was 'juvenescence'; and it may be that Eliot changed it because it would have given two stresses instead of the one he wanted. But if the Romans had wished to contract the long word, they would have made it *junescence*; for they really did contract the comparative adjective *juvenior* to *junior*. The third word is 'concitation' in Movement IV; it is as close to the Latin *concitatio* as our language permits. So much for the poet's versatility, which embraces so many kinds of linguistic device.

Coming now to line 5, we should know, perhaps, that the tree which we call dogwood was called by the Greeks 'dog's-tongue'; they would have meant the red-blossoming dogwood, thinking the petals were like the tongues of dogs in the chase. In that sense the blossom is menacing, and I cannot tell in what sense it is sensual. It is like the 'judas tree' which we associate with the unfortunate betrayer of Christ. But only the critics of this poem have made me think back upon my youth when we knew all the big chestnut trees as bearers of blossom and fruit, and never thought of the blossoms as other than specially handsome. We did not notice its spike as sensual association. But I cannot risk disagreeing with a symbolism which Eliot, like all his critics, may have observed.

We must admit anyway the 'depraved May' as a symbol of evil; and Fräulein von Kulp in line 12 bears a name related to *culpa*, guilt, and moves furtively in the hall as if up to mischief. My own conclusion would be that Gerontion had his degree of promiscuity, which may have contributed to his apostasy. But I cannot see in this movement, any more than in Movement I, any evidence that Gerontion has not now arrived at a point far beyond the possibility of dishonest representations, or that his great fault was not as he represents it in Movement I and in movements later than this one: to put the world before Christ.

The four persons recalled in the second and third parts of Movement II are offered as not being Christians. It must be Gerontion's understanding that Christ came 'to be eaten' and 'to be drunk', but that these persons either had not undertaken that in the first place, or had backslidden if they had. But they make a rich context of sad meaning.

In line 14 the conclusion approaches: 'Vacant shuttles/ Weave the wind. I have no ghosts.' The shuttles of the mind move busily, but they accomplish nothing; they have no threads to weave. Gerontion has known many people, including foreign people, but he shared no great friendship with them, nor thinks of them as faithful ghosts to be summoned up in his memory and held again in affection. The opposite of having no ghosts in this sense is the illusion of meeting again a wise and cherished ghost, as Eliot does in the second movement of the fourth *Quartet*; that ghost is W. B. Yeats, who had died three years before; and that passage has no superior even in Eliot's ripest verse.

Immediately after these rhythms we have, for conclusion,

the coda again, resembling that added to Movement I. I have
marked the seven stresses, but not divided them in any way.
They compose a perfect line in the ballad form. It is in the
Common Metre, as the hymn-books have it; the stresses are
not eight, nor six, as they might have been in Long Metre or
Short Metre, but seven. The instrumental music would have to
hold the final stress for another full bar, and the reader's voice
would have to make a full-stress pause after it.

[III]

After such knowledge, what forgiveness? Think now
o o —   — o   — o – o / —   — /
History has many cunning passages, contrived corridors
— o o / o   — o   — o   — o o o —   — o o
And issues, deceives with whispering ambitions,
o   — o   o –   o   —   o o o – o
Guides us by vanities. Think now
—   o o — o o / —   —
She gives when our attention is distracted
o —   o   — o– o   o o – o
And what she gives, gives with such supple confusions
o   —   o — / —   o   o   — o o – o
That the giving famishes the craving. Gives too late
o   o – o   — o o o — o / o   — —
What's not believed in, or is still believed,
o   — o —   o / o o –   o –
In memory only, reconsidered passion. Gives too soon
o — oo — o / — o – o   — o / o   — —
Into weak hands, what's thought can be dispensed with
o o — —   / o   —   o o o —   o /
Till the refusal propagates a fear. Think
o   o o – o– o– o– o o – / —
Neither fear nor courage saves us. Unnatural vices
o o —   o —   o —   o / o – o o – o
Are fathered by our heroism. Virtues.
o   — o   o o — o– / — o
Are forced upon us by our impudent crimes.
o —   o – o o o — o o —   /
These tears are shaken from the wrath-bearing tree.
—   — o – o o o o —   — o — /

In Movement III we may identify for the first time the silent auditor to whom the monologue is addressed. Line 1 puts a question; and then an imperative: 'Think now'/. The imperative is repeated twice more, and is made urgent by coming awkwardly at the end of the lines. The auditor is Christ, who in Movement IV will become the definitive 'you' and 'your'.

Four arguments are uttered in lines 2–11; they try to justify Gerontion's rejection of Christ. Fortunately they do not take an academic or intellectual form of expression. The deceitful temptress who causes Gerontion's apostasy is perhaps associated in his imagination with Fate, with Lachesis herself, the middle Fate, who was supposed by the Greeks to appoint the destiny of every mortal man; and to bring it to pass by circumstances which are wholly adventitious so far as he can tell, and not to be countered. But Gerontion is a modern, and he calls the woman 'History'. She arranges those 'cunning passages' which lead to doom. But suddenly the 'passages' cease to be generalized when they are translated into 'contrived corridors/ And issues', a physical image. Then she 'gives with such supple confusions/That the giving famishes the craving', which is marvellous; and we admire those 'supple confusions', which means that they are not confusions at all in those exact designs appointed by History. The third argument has her giving back his faith, but it comes too late. And finally he refers again to her first giving, but that came too soon; he had neglected it, and then been filled with fear. Beginning with the end of line 11 and continuing through line 14, he talks with great pith about courage and fear as producing each other, in alternation.

We must surely remark, I think, that 'what's thought can be dispensed with' contains a logical error. The 'what's' is wrong for 'what it's'. Possibly Gerontion preferred the wrong version because it would not require a stress on 'what' and spoil a five-stress line. At least half the lines can be counted as having nine stresses each. In this modern verse we may not exercise our old privilege of stressing in any line a weak word, or two or three, in order to fill up the blank verse; nor refuse to stress a strong word when it would make the line spill over with stresses. Eliot in his blank verse generally preferred to make his stresses sound loud and clear, and to let his weak syllables remain weak and manage for themselves. But I hold him in grateful memory because he hailed the ghost of Yeats, in that final *Quartet*, as both 'master' and friend; and because three years before he had presented himself in person in Ireland, at the tomb prepared for Yeats's body, and made a public speech in which he declared Yeats the greatest poet of his time and perhaps of all time. This last tribute I take from Joseph Hone's literary biography, *W. B. Yeats*; but it may have been on Eliot's part a little too generous, as according to the conventions of panegyric. Yet Yeats had used the old privileges of English prosody, and permitted himself to strengthen the weak words when necessary and slide over the strong words which could not keep their stresses in order to hold to the effect of a pure and prevailing form, a continuous bed of rhythm, such as ordinary language would never have worried into existence. Nevertheless, it does not appear even today that anybody has complained about this convention in Yeats. The voice of his great lines is that of an impassioned oracle. And doubtless we have observed that there has already been a partial return to the old metres, in reaction against the modern rhythms, among many of those fine poets who have established themselves in the generation now in middling age; they keep pretty well to their count of stresses and are rather indeterminate about the unstresses. A poet may still suit himself; but the better poets will keep some measure of control over their prosody.

After the four arguments we find three short sentences about fear and courage, virtues and crimes, alternatively producing each other. These observations are as accurate psychologically as they are untechnical and terse.

Line 15 concludes the movement with what we may call a coda: 'These tears are shaken from the wrath-bearing tree.' For Gerontion is of the seed of Adam, and was doomed to offend.

[IV]

The tiger springs in the new year. Us he devours. Think at last
We have not reached conclusion, when I
Stiffen in a rented house. Think at last
I have not made this show purposelessly
And it is not by any concitation
Of the backward devils.
I would meet you upon this honestly.
I that was near your heart was removed therefrom
To lose beauty in terror, terror in inquisition.
I have lost my passion: why should I need to keep it
Since what is kept must be adulterated?
I have lost my sight, smell, hearing, taste and touch:
How should I use them for your closer contact?

The Sewanee Review kindly permits me to insert the text of this movement and of the one following, for the reader's convenience; though I have not marked the prosodies.

There are only thirteen lines in this movement; which is not to say that it conforms to the rule of *The Waste Land* and *Four Quartets*, where the fourth movement in Eliot's five symphonic poems must be much shorter, and more lyrical, than the other movements. Here the fourth movement is only a little shorter.

'The tiger springs.' We know by now that the lamb who came to be devoured turns into the tiger when Gerontion has forgotten the lamb. And so with other people, such as the acquaintances he mentioned in Movement II; 'Us he devours.' The pronouns are inverted.

Gerontion uses language here which would fall a little short if he were a lesser poet. 'Reached conclusion' is a scholarly phrase, but how well he redeems himself at once by 'Stiffen in a rented house'; the scholar would never have thought of 'stiffen' as an image which would make words such as 'age' or 'grow old' seem stale; or may we say the phrase is 'jejeune'? The noun in that Latin family of words referred to a meagreness or poverty in one's vocabulary. 'Purposelessly' is a grammarian's cacophony, twice compounded of sibilants too difficult to pronounce briefly before the following l's. And it stands just over the word 'concitation' in the following line, a philologist's word, though novel to the English language. Does Gerontion propose not only to tell Christ of his final rejection, but to do it rather bookishly? But he concludes the sentence with some straight talk of the 'backward devils', who are probably the evil spirits prompting him to backslide. He takes care to profess his honesty, and considering his merciless self-exposure previously we like to believe him. All the same, we cannot but feel a satiric quality in his language now. We remember that Eliot, his author, was just coming out of a period of poems, some of them in savage satire against the religious institution, and others in which he was nostalgic for it. He had been one of those who blow hot and blow cold; one of the Laodiceans. He permitted the honest Gerontion to exhibit a trace of hostility to his auditor.

But the sentence of the last two lines is a crushing rejection. Its first line contains a top-grade hyperbole he has lost every bit of every one of his five physical senses. He lists them scrupulously as if he were preparing an official document showing all the specifications of his ground for asking to be relieved of a contractual obligation. But perhaps we would do better to call it a perfect litotes rather than a hyperbole. His senses have attenuated to zero; they have not increased to the point of maximum capacity.

We can do without the final coda we may have expected. We have at least the perfect phrase of conclusion.

[V]

These with a thousand small deliberations
Protract the profit of their chilled delirium,
Excite the membrane, when the sense has cooled,
With pungent sauces, multiply variety
In a wilderness of mirrors. What will the spider do,
Suspend its operations, will the weevil
Delay? De Bailhache, Fresca, Mrs Cammel, whirled

Beyond the circuit of the shuddering Bear
In fractured atoms. Gull against the wind, in the windy straits
Of Belle Isle, or running on the Horn.
White feathers in the snow, the Gulf claims,
And an old man driven by the Trades
To a sleepy corner.
                    Tenants of the house,
Thoughts of a dry brain in a dry season.

I think we must take this last movement, this grand finale, as the great one of the five. In its mastery of the vocabulary and the music of language, of course; and even in its high spirits, because Gerontion rejoices in having settled and dismissed an old uneasiness of conscience. It is like a little Ode on the Prospect of Death, exultant because he has brought to completion the best work of his whole lifetime, so that his going will be not with a whimper but a bang.

Gerontion is one of those men in whom we may say there has been a kind of displacement of their youthful and instructed faith by their increasing passion for an art. We are told nothing about his occupation. But seven of his acquaintances have been named, four in Movement II, and three more in this last movement. They all have foreign names, though Mr Silvero and Mrs Cammel had evidently come to live in England; and what is more significant, two of them, Mr Silvero and Hakagawa, were connoisseurs of porcelain and painting respectively; with Mr Silvero caressing his prizes and in his excitement walking all night in his room, and Hakagawa bowing before his Titians. Perhaps Gerontion, whatever his means of livelihood, had been an art-lover too, unable to make the grade as an artist himself; but late in life, when he could no longer travel, had found his true gift as a poet, just in time. Here I am trying to imagine the image which Eliot would have had of him; though Eliot characteristically had preferred to let the reader make his own image.

In the late twenties Eliot returned to the Church; and from that moment on he laboured diligently in the vineyard. It must have taken a monumental strength and patience to keep up at the same time his profession as poet and critic; and especially to protect the independence of his poetry as keeping to its aesthetic form. Now, to use Aristotle's valuable terms, the material cause (or medium) of poetry is the words, whether common or uncommon; the efficient cause is the poet (having both reason and imagination); the final cause is to give a unique pleasure, which may amount to ecstasy. But there is also a formal cause, without which a poetry is not formed; and that is the adaptation of the words to the rhythms of a music. Of course there are many excellent words and systems of words, as for example in theology and religious experience, which need not bother with this formal requirement and are content to remain other than poetry. But Eliot took care to hold all his religious verse strictly to the formal standard; his darting eye throughout the *Quartets* may have liked to hit upon moral and religious behaviours, as constituents of poetry especially dear to his heart; but they had to take a shape subordinated to the rhythmic form.

Eliot gave many examples of those special moments when something natural takes on a look of the supernatural; and many times defined these moments as the intersection of time with the timeless. But let us see something of the range they took in the *Quartets*. The best one is surely the first one, in the first movement of *Burnt Norton*, where the bird in the rose garden prompts the guests to look quickly before the vision is gone. On other occasions he would catalogue a whole set of moments in one passage. In the last movement of *The Dry Salvages*, for example:

> The distraction fit, lost in a shaft of sunlight,
> The wild thyme unseen, or the winter lightning
> Or the waterfall, or music heard so deeply
> That it is not heard at all, but you are the music
> While the music lasts.

All these, except the last, are natural images actually perceived by our senses, but supernatural too, as we feel in our moment of ecstasy. The shaft of sunlight perhaps comes sloping through a murky air and is apprehended by vision; the wild thyme is unseen but known by its fragrance; the winter lightning is like a light from heaven, totally unexpected and vanishing quickly; the waterfall is perhaps heard rather than seen, and imagination plays with it better than if it were seen. But finally there is music, made with instruments, and heard in our deepest being where we are not tempted to analyse it. Up to the point when this music occurs, all the presentations are actual, as the senses attest. But with the utterance of the formal music we are in the domain of artistic imagination, where the actual senses cannot testify to the fictions of art. That is an important distinction in the Kantian aesthetics. Perhaps I need to explain that I am taking the bare listing of the occasions for the special moments as being merely the poet's pointing, slightly in the didactic manner; as if saying, Watch out for occasions of that sort. But the heard music is more than recommendation; it is art itself, 'imitating reality'; not the presentation but the 'representation', as Kant put it.

The movement ends with this passage:

> We, content at the last
> If our temporal reversion nourish
> (Not too far from the yew-tree)
> The life of significant soil.

This means, we are obliged to think, that Eliot had no special fixation upon the resurrection of the body after death according to orthodox principle.

But in *Little Gidding*, the first movement, there is a passage about prayer; for in the offices of the Church there are many provisions made for the special moments of ecstasy:

> You are here to kneel
> Where prayer has been valid. . . .
> Here, the intersection of the timeless moment
> Is England and nowhere. Never and always.

And finally there is the conclusion of *Little Gidding* and of the whole book of *Quartets*:

> And all shall be well and
> All manner of thing shall be well
> When the tongues of flame are in-folded
> Into the crowned knot of fire
> And the fire and the rose are one.

Eliot was very well acquainted with Dante's visions, and they deserved it; but they were representations, not presentations. And may a later poet with another language use Dante's vision of the rose of Heaven? That would require a re-representation. I think one of Eliot's aims in *Little Gidding* was to harmonize within himself the poet and the churchman, and at the end he fell back too easily upon Dante. It is not in Eliot's own voice, and I wish it were.

And now, for my own conclusion, a few remarks upon the final movement. We must recognize exactly what Gerontion has been doing in the whole monologue. He lives with impoverished senses and pocketbook, but there is no poverty in his imagination or in his vocabulary. The first sentence (lines 1–5) has three beautiful predicates: 'Protract the profit...' and 'Excite the membrane...' and 'multiply variety/In a wilderness of mirrors'. The 'mirrors' are probably the most wonderful. Gerontion is not afraid of a few latinisms if they are choice, and in the image I have of him he started to say 'reflections', to pair with the 'deliberations' above. But imagination quickly got the better of reason, saying 'reflectors' would have more character, looking backward as they did; but why not 'mirrors'? How much better is the metaphor of the physical instruments, any number of them, searching into his past. And with that he has finished his confessions and turns to the future, which is now secure.

We could count all of lines 1–6 as being blank verses, if only Eliot had permitted him to stress a little *of* in line 2; and to bring the first word of line 7 back into its place in line 6, so that both 6 and 7 would be norms. But the modern prosodist is greatly prejudiced in favour of open-ended lines in this measure, and 'Delay?' would have brought line 6 to a full stop. As the text stands, there are two sentences, no line having a full stop.

It is when Gerontion asks the question about the spider and the weevil that he comes into his real theme; the first sentence is his repudiation of something that is finished. His author has not allowed him – but that is redundant and gratuitous; let us say he has not allowed himself to say in so many words what his theme is about. But we know now that he is his own man and is talking about death. The spider and the weevil are hateful creatures, but they work in their respective occupations till they collapse and are dead. But what of those men and women, people of distinction, who die by cataclysm and destruction, and have their bodies annihilated and scattered into fractured atoms? That is a heroic sort of death which Gerontion abhors, though the press will play loudly upon it. Then there is the gull's death, leaving his white feathers to be claimed by the Gulf; which is probably the Abyss, or Bottom of the World as the Greeks called it. These two sentences are the work of a master of his art, being so wildly beautiful.

But the second of these sentences is not quite finished; just here, in the most dramatic place possible, comes the old refrain or coda, about the humble old man in his corner. But there is a variation; it is a sleepy corner. He is thinking about that last sleep. Probably he will spend the last wakeful days reciting his own poem. Sometimes perhaps (but with his fingers crossed) he will cite the Scripture which follows the account of the six Days of Creation: 'And God saw every thing that he had made and, behold, it was very good.'

The two final lines, separated a little from the main text, do not repeat the coda; they recapitulate the theme of the whole poem; that is, they make a kind of epilogue to a dramatic work. They begin with a nice metaphor, 'Tenants of the house', which are translated back into reality in the concluding line. The two lines together form a full ballad line having four pairs of stresses making the rhythm, and it again is in Common Metre. It would have been read like this:

> Tenants of the house,
> Thoughts of a dry
> Brain in a dry
> Season.

He is playing with this irony again, as always. But after the one stress of the final rhythm the reader must make a full stop to fulfil the movement.

THE COMEDIES OF T. S. ELIOT[1]

By Helen Gardner

THE *Cocktail Party*, *The Confidential Clerk*, and *The Elder Statesman* are distinguished from Eliot's earlier plays by their author's obvious desire to accommodate himself to the conventions of the stage at their most conventional level. In the earlier plays, *Sweeney Agonistes*, *Murder in the Cathedral*, and *The Family Reunion*, Eliot was working in the experimental theatre of the thirties, using such devices as the chorus, the direct appeal to the audience, soliloquy, lyrical solos and duets, and ritual and symbolic acts. In these last plays he deliberately wrote within the limits of what has been contemptuously called the 'West End Play', or what Mr Terence Rattigan called 'Plays for Aunt Edna'. He used the picture-frame stage, with a conventional setting: the modern flat, the library, the consulting-room, the terraces of an expensive rest-home. He made no use of chorus, soliloquy, or aside, and employed for his machines the telephone and front-door bell. It has recently been said that Eliot was unfortunate in choosing to model his plays on a type of drama that was dying or dead by the time he came to imitate it, and that to the theatre-going public of the sixties (and, these critics assume, of the future) these plays are merely exercises in an effete tradition. I cannot take very seriously a criticism that assumes that what is temporarily unfashionable is permanently out-of-date. The tradition of social comedy which Eliot took up is a very tough tradition. It has broken out again and again in the course of the last two thousand and more years. At the moment these plays are dated, but as they recede into history their social verisimilitude will be as much a source of strength as is the

1. A lecture delivered to The Royal Society of Literature, 18 March 1965.

social truth of Restoration comedy. The fact that they belong so clearly to the early fifties makes them seem obsolescent in the sixties. They will look, I imagine, very different in the eighties and nineties. To catch the tone of an age is one of the merits of high comedy; and these plays catch the accents and the moral tone of what one may call 'polite society' in the post-war decade.

Eliot's desire to write plays that would be commercially successful was wholly in accord with his ideals as a writer. He always declared that a writer must use what lies to hand: that the poet's task is to make poetry out of the living speech of his day. Conditions may be unpropitious but they must be accepted. A poet cannot choose his linguistic environment; even more, a dramatist must use the theatre of his day. The poet, said Wordsworth, works under the single restriction of giving immediate pleasure to a human being. The dramatist works under a much severer restriction. He has to give immediate pleasure to an audience, a mass of individuals who must feel that pleasure simultaneously; for the presence in an audience of large numbers of persons who are not enjoying the play is fatal to the enjoyment of others. A dramatist's success is measured by his power to convert a heterogeneous collection of persons into an audience, stirred to a common hilarity, shocked by a common apprehension, or raised to a common sense of awe and wonder. The dramatist cannot give pleasure to the discerning few unless he is also giving pleasure to the less discerning many. Further he must give his audiences what they want, because otherwise he will have no audiences and so cannot discover what demands he can make of them. It is now, I think, clear that the experimental poetic theatre of the thirties struck no real roots. The great mass of the theatre-going public stayed away. Eliot was surely right to feel that plays acted to an audience of like-minded persons in small half-empty theatres or converted drill-halls were not really plays. If they could not draw an audience, and a mixed audience at that, they had failed artistically as well as socially. And Eliot was always deeply interested in the drama as the most socially relevant of the arts.

The three plays differ from Eliot's earlier plays not only in their acceptance of the banalities of the well-made commercial play of the first half of the twentieth century, but also in being, in some sense or other, comedies. *Sweeney Agonistes* was a fragment of an Aristophanic melodrama, *Murder in the Cathedral* a religious tragedy, and *The Family Reunion* a psychological tragedy. Eliot's first plays, like the greatest of his earlier poems, are informed by the tragic sense of human solitude. For his first full-length play he took a heroic subject, martyrdom; for his second, the story of Orestes the mother-murderer, the scapegoat hero, scourge and saviour of his family. The earlier plays, like the earlier poetry, communicate a sense that life is agonizingly trivial and meaningless, unless some power from without breaks in to create a gleam of meaning. It creates it within the individual heroic soul – in Thomas, the martyr, or Harry, the conscience of his unhappy family. But in the course of *Four Quartets* a change of mood is clearly apparent. There is a progress towards acceptance of the conditions of life in this world, the kind of acceptance that underlies the comic writer's realism, sympathy, human compassion, and moral concern. *East Coker* has the tragic sense of human loneliness, and of the irrelevance of human achievement. It is a poem about loneliness and suffering, ending with the tragic urge towards exploration: 'Old men ought to be explorers.' 'We must be still and still moving/Into another intensity.' But even in *East Coker*:

> There is a time for the evening under starlight,
> A time for the evening under lamplight
> (The evening with the photograph album).

And moving through *The Dry Salvages* to *Little Gidding* we pass beyond the tragic sense to a mood that transcends and includes both the tragic and the comic vision of life, the mood expressed by the saying of Julian of Norwich that Eliot put at the heart and at the close of his poem 'Sin is Behovely but all shall be well, and all manner of thing shall be well.' It is out of this mood that the last plays spring, and they may in one way be regarded as footnotes or *exempla* to *Four Quartets*. But in another sense their roots lie much further back. Tragedy deals with man in solitude, or forced into solitude. Comedy with man in society; not with man discovering his own fate, but with man discovering how to live with his fellows. Eliot's serious concern with the nature of the good society is apparent in his criticism and his prose writing long before it flowers in his poetry. In his last plays he attempted to embody in works of art problems he had revolved and conclusions he had arrived at in his editorship of *The Criterion*, and in his *The Idea of a Christian Society* and his *Notes towards the Definition of Culture*.

Comedy is often regarded as less serious than tragedy. Whether this is so or not, its proper seriousness is reached by the opposite route. Plot, which is the soul of all drama, must in tragedy have a rigid logic. The wild improbabilities of comedy, its coincidences and preposterous assumptions, are improper in tragedy, which must convince us of its essential truth to the course of human life as we know it. Abandoning fidelity to the audible and visible surfaces of life, dealing with those better than ourselves and with terrible and exceptional events, tragedy must not strain our credulity. But comedy, if it is to be serious in its own way, must turn to fantasy for its plot. Dealing as it does with men and women like ourselves, or worse in one thing, 'the ridiculous', which is a species of the ugly; showing us not archetypal characters but characters we can hardly think of apart from their setting in place and time; entertaining us by its mimicry of social habits, fashions, and our neighbours' follies, it must, if it is to reach beyond mimicry and give us a true *imago vitae*, reach from truth local and particular to truth general and universal, call on fantasy and fictions to shape its plot. This distinction, that the comic writer *invents* but the tragic writer *finds* his plot, is as old as the fourth century. Sentimental or domestic comedy is as much an offence against the nature of the comic kind as is sentimental or bourgeois tragedy against the nature of the tragic kind. Both are products of the destruction of the drama by the growth of the novel. Eliot saw this clearly, and with his sense of classic tradition did not attempt to give us dramatized novels, but to write comedies that would express through fictions and fables truths about man as a social being: not the discoveries that the tragic writer makes but the convictions out of which the comic writer writes. For if the tragic writer finds his story and discovers what pattern he can within it, the comic writer begins from assumptions already clarified in his mind and shapes his fable to express them. Comedy tends naturally towards the didactic, which is destructive of tragic feeling. Eliot's three comedies are naturally and unashamedly didactic, within plots artificially constructed to produce the maximum of comic surprise and comic encounter. The weakness of the third and last of the plays, *The Elder Statesman*, compared with *The Cocktail Party* and *The Confidential Clerk*, lies in its author's failure to invent sufficient complications of plot, and so incorporate his message in an artefact.

The plot of *The Cocktail Party* has a double origin. The central situation is taken from the *Alcestis*. In the Greek play a dead wife, who has died in place of her husband, is restored by the intervention of the semi-divine Heracles. Here a runaway wife is brought back, as if from the dead. In each case a marriage that had ended has to begin again. This, as Eliot said, was where he began from: 'the return of a dead wife'. But the *Alcestis* provided only the germ of the play, which in its final form owes very little to its primary source. Its only direct influence on the conduct of the plot is in the initial situation, where the husband disguises his domestic calamity in order to fulfil the duties of hospitality – and even here the motives of Edward are quite different from those of Admetus – and in the unconventional behaviour of the stranger at the party and after. Like Heracles, Reilly appears at first in the role of a badly behaved guest. There is a reminiscence of the return of Heracles leading the veiled stranger in Reilly's insistence that Lavinia, when she returns, will be a stranger and must be greeted as a stranger; and his condition – that Edward is to ask her no questions – reminds us of the three days' silence imposed on Alcestis by her consecration to the Gods below. But what in the *Alcestis* is a part of the machinery of the plot and a tribute to Greek religious sentiment becomes in *The Cocktail Party* a comment on human relationships: 'At every meeting we are meeting a stranger'; and a piece of good moral advice: 'Don't strangle each other with knotted memories.' At one moment in the last scene, there seems to be a reference to the sacrifice of Alcestis. Euripides' play suggests that there was a cult of Alcestis at Athens. The cult of the dead Celia, to whom the natives had 'erected a sort of shrine', seems a parallel to the prayer of the chorus in the Greek play: 'Let her grave not be accounted the resting-place of one of the departed dead, but let her be honoured as a god and receive the worship of the passers-by. Let the traveller turn aside from the road and say, "She gave her life for her husband and now she is a blessed spirit. Hail Lady, and be gracious to me."' The reminiscence, if it is one, underlines one difference between the two plays. Death is not cheated of his claim in *The Cocktail Party*. Edward's wife is restored to him; but another woman dies in his and her place. But although the *Alcestis* is only a remote source for *The Cocktail Party*, reference to it is of value. It helps us to get our focus right. *The Cocktail Party* began as a play about a marriage, and Edward and Lavinia are the central characters in its design. Also the memory of the Euripidean Heracles may help us not to take Eliot's saviour more portentously than we need to do.

The second source of the plot is no one work but the general tradition of high comedy. To the original triangle of husband, wife, and semi-divine saviour have been added the amorous entanglements that have been the stock-in-trade of social comedy since Dryden's *Marriage à la mode*. The central pair are flanked by two younger single persons, Celia, Edward's mistress, and Peter, who was once Lavinia's lover but is now in love with Celia. To balance this and preserve the symmetry of the plot, the original demi-god has been provided with two assistant doubtful deities: an elderly lady, a kind of fairy-godmother, and a young man who is a kind of modern Mercury. The re-interpretation of Greek myths in modern terms is very popular in this century, particularly on the French stage. But Eliot went further than a rendering of the *Alcestis* in terms of modern life. The world of drawing-room comedy engaged his imagination as much as the story of the *Alcestis*. *The Cocktail Party* has a double inspiration.

High comedy, like high tragedy, excludes all aspects of life irrelevant to its concern. Tragedy, in order to display the flaw in the universe that sets a man at odds with his environment and seems to suggest that this world is inimical to the nobility to which it gives birth, paints a world remote from ours. Its heroes are placed above daily annoyances and pains that they may suffer enormous griefs and be undistracted in their experience of them. High comedy, which like all comedy shows a world that is friendly to man if he will only learn how to live in it, is similarly exclusive. Its characters are relieved of the ordinary anxieties of life in order that they may give their whole attention to those anxieties that, for the mass of men, are mingled with the anxieties of earning a living, succeeding in a business or profession, preserving one's health, and fulfilling the duties of one's station. They inhabit a material paradise, free from want and fear of want. They are dowered with good looks and perfect health, and have ample leisure to devote themselves to the pursuit of personal satisfaction. They have no duty except the duty of being happy.

Restoration comedy took happiness to be success in love; and by success it meant the achievement of satisfaction in love without the forfeiting of other satisfactions. Love was shown as a dangerous game requiring high skill from its players, in which both man and woman ran the risk of social humiliation. The woman's stake was the higher; her triumph when she secured an accomplished gallant on her own terms – marriage – was consequently the higher. The man's task was to secure the lady without losing her own or his fortune. The butts of Restoration comedy are those who cannot play this game, who can neither win by skill, nor, when defeated, take their defeat with grace. The well-mannered hero and the witty heroine shine by contrast with the fops whom any woman of sense can put down, the rejected mistresses who cannot hide their wounds, and such ghastly figures as Lady Wishfort grotesquely refusing to acknowledge defeat at the hands of implacable Time. Its ruthlessness towards the old, the defeated, and the inept gives Restoration comedy a bitter flavour. If love is a game, then, as one of Congreve's heroines observes, 'consequently one of us must be a loser'[2]; and the dénouement of a Restoration comedy shows too many losers for us to feel much confidence in the permanence of the heroine's triumph. All we can be confident of is that she will preserve her dignity, good manners, and good temper. If her marriage turns out a failure, at least the world will not know it from her.

Comedy reflects the morality of its age. Restoration comedy is the product of a society in which the current serious philosophy did not rank sexual satisfaction very high in the scale of human values, and in which marriage was, in general, indissoluble in law. The comedy arises from the conflict between man's wayward passions and the stable structure of society. The satire is turned against social failures, not against society itself. Human inconstancy is taken for granted: 'Our love is frail as is our life and full as little in our power; and are you sure you shall outlive this day?'[3] Anything so unstable as human desire cannot be expected to give more than 'fun while it lasts'; the skilful can so manage their affairs that their 'fun' does not cost them the more enduring satisfactions represented

2. Cynthia in *The Double Dealer*, Act II, sc. i.
3. Emilia in *The Man of Mode*, Act II, sc. i.

by a settlement and social respectability. Our age gives sexual satisfaction a much higher place in the hierarchy of human values than the seventeenth century did; or indeed, I would say, than any previous age in Western Europe has. It also allows the unhappily married to obtain their freedom without loss of social standing. In our comedy love cannot be treated as a game, and marriage is not sufficiently stable to be mocked at. Social convention is not powerful enough to provide the context for a true comedy of manners. High comedy today must either be sentimental and satirical, exalting love and satirizing the frivolity of the wealthy, giving to its audience the pleasure of a romantic day-dream along with the pleasure of disapproving of those one envies; or it must be ethical, and use the limitations of the comedy of manners for a serious exploration of what personal happiness means. *The Cocktail Party* was born of a fusion between ancient myth and the assumption that underlies most modern social comedy: that the *summum bonum* for men and women in this world is the fulfilment of their personalities in love.

The *Alcestis* belongs to a world where the idea of duty reigns. In the world of modern comedy this conception has no place. Admetus lies to his guest to fulfil the duty of hospitality. Edward carries on with his party because to tell his guests that his wife has run away would be to expose himself to ridicule. Alcestis dies in obedience to a code by which a wife must put her husband's and children's welfare before her own. She dies that he may live and that their children may not be fatherless, the worst of fates in the ancient world. The childless Lavinia 'dies', or leaves her husband, in obedience to no such settled standards of behaviour; nor does she return to him from any sense of loyalty to her marriage vow. Celia's death, though a consequence of her remaining at her post, is not the result of any sense of duty to her fellow men. 'Fay ce que vouldras' is the motto of all the four main characters of *The Cocktail Party*. But the author confronts his characters with the necessity of discovering what it is then that they want. Accepting as a hypothesis the assumption that man's moral duty is the fulfilment of his personality, the play asks us to contemplate what this generalization means in terms of four individuals. The discovery of what one wants means discovering what one is. The play is concerned with choices; but in the end there is only one choice. Choose to be yourself or choose not to be. There are a lot of possible sub-choices under the heading 'Choose not to be'; but this is the main choice.

Edward and Lavinia have to learn they are not what they think they are. Edward is not a passionate man married to a cold wife; Lavinia is not an attractive woman whose husband does not appreciate her. Both are sentimentalists. Edward is an egoist hardly capable of loving at all. Lavinia, sharp-tongued and socially ambitious, is extremely unlovable. They are, as Reilly points out, admirably suited to each other. Edward needs to be loved; his weakness and vanity need support. Lavinia needs someone to love. Each has a root of virtue: Edward the knowledge of his own mediocrity; Lavinia the habit of taking responsibility for others. She may be bossy, but at least she is aware that her husband needs clean shirts. If Edward will accept being loved he may become loving, and if Lavinia will try to love she may become lovable.

Celia's lesson is different. She was not mistaken about herself. She is passionate. But she was mistaken in the object of her passion. What she has to give is a total gift, something Edward does not want. The offer terrifies him. It is perhaps something no human being wants or should be offered, unlimited devotion. She has to find a proper object for her passion. Whatever the pain, terror, and ignominy of her death, it is the consequence of her choice. Her offering is accepted. She is taken at her word. When she chose this life she chose death. For Peter who loved her, the 'naturally good man', who is to succeed by his own and the world's standards, and go far in his career as an artist, it is something he must come to terms with, something he has to learn to understand. The 'thought of Celia' is to be with him all his life, which will remain under

170

the judgement of her life and death. It will save him from pretence, reminding him that 'another race hath been and other palms are won'.

The element of fantasy which removes the play from drawing-room comedy is provided by the Guardians, the comic engineers of the plot, who are responsible for its surprises. At first they are apparently distinct and unconnected with each other, and resented for their interference, but at the close it is clear they have been in collusion all along and their interference is accepted. They are comic Furies who are in the end seen to be Kindly Ones. But although there would be no play without them and they seem to have worked things, fundamentally they do not. They bring the horses to the water; they do not make them drink, and at the end it is seen that the horses were asking to be brought to the water. The true Guardians are inner ones: Edward's 'stronger partner', who like Socrates' daemon says 'No'; Celia's 'sense of sin'; Lavinia's non-existent aunt, invented by Edward to explain what made her run away. Edward's own self-knowledge makes him reject Celia and want his wife back. Celia's knowledge that the ecstasy was real, even though she and Edward were not real to each other, is what makes her reject ordinary life and choose the road that leads to martyrdom. Lavinia, the least self-analytical, though extremely shrewd in analysis of the weakness of others, sets everything in motion. Something tells her she must break away and on Julia's advice she seeks out Reilly. Lavinia's aunt is therefore rightly the first and the last toast of the play. The Guardians are not at the centre of the action. At the true centre there is an unnamed Power who speaks within the heart and conscience of every man.

The underlying conception of the play as expressed in its plot is related to the conception of *The Family Reunion*, in which Harry has to discover his role in the drama of his family.[4] But here it is generalized. All four characters have to find their roles. Living is like acting in a play whose plot we

4. See my *The Art of T. S. Eliot*, pp. 142–51.

do not know, in parts we have not chosen. Our choice is whether we will play those parts or invent parts for ourselves. We are helped by an innate sense that tells us we are going wrong, which says: 'You are not cast for the leading lady; your part is the comic nurse.' There are some people we know who are able, like experienced actors acting with amateurs, to guide us, get us onto the right part of the stage at the right moment, and cover up our mistakes. They may even make us realize that we have a great role to play, that we must stop being charming, civilized, and popular and commit ourselves to the extreme. These persons have some detachment and seem to have some insight into the obscure intentions of the author of the play. But they cannot make us act well, or even act at all, and we can always decide that we will not act in this play but in another drama of our own making, in which we can hold the centre of the stage and act to ourselves to our own rapturous applause. All the same, we need not take these persons too seriously. If deities, they are comic deities; if angels, they are charged with folly: the one-eyed Reilly, the psychiatrist who has to lie down on his own couch, Julia, always losing her spectacles, and Alec, whose cooking 'is absolutely deadly'. They can be laughed at. There is only one thing that is beyond laughter: heroism. The heroic, von Hügel said, is the clear revelation of the supernatural.[5] Heroism is absolute: all wisdom is partial.

The distinction on which the play turns is between love, the exchange of tenderness, forgiveness, and loving-kindness between separate and ultimately solitary persons only partially understanding each other, and passion, which seeks to lose itself in its object, desiring ecstasy and a union that can only be perfectly attained in death, and which seeks to obliterate distinction of personalities in union. This conception may owe something to Denis de Rougemont's attack on the whole conception of romantic love in *L'Amour et l'Occident*, called in

5. *Essays and Addresses on the Philosophy of Religion*, 1951, pp. 198–201, and p. 280.

its English translation *Passion and Society*. De Rougemont saw romantic love, embodied in the Tristan story, as destructive of all social values and ultimately of life itself, a quest for death, something sterile and perverse; and he linked the origins of the concept of romantic love in Provence with the Catharist heresy, with its contempt for the created world. *The Cocktail Party* is built on the distinction between passion and love, *eros* and *agape*, and it is possible that de Rougemont's description of the organization of the Cathari, an invisible Church within society, may have suggested the handling of the Guardians. In Celia the romantic quest for union is directed to its true object and consummated in death. *Causa diligendi Deum Deus est; modus est sine modo.* It is a happy ending for her, for we see the alternative in her first savage reaction to Edward's cowardice and rejection of her. Too fastidious for a plunge into sexual experiments, she will become a devourer, destroying the unfortunate men who disappoint her. But we misinterpret the play if we find its meaning solely in Celia. Its concern is with a concept of society, where in different ways men and women can work out their salvation with diligence. A cocktail party is not one of the higher forms of hospitality. It is not a meal, but a prelude to a meal. The Symposium, the banquet of love, will come after. And at the Great Supper, in the house of many mansions, there will be places not only for 'the soldier saints, who row on row, burn upward each to his point of bliss', but also for those who have in various ways lived a 'good life', and learned while on earth to 'bear the beams of love' and exchange forgiveness.

The subject of any comedy of manners is always the relation between the sexes, since it is here that social conventions are most at war with human nature and manners are most required yet seem most remote from real feeling. A comedy of manners is always dominated by women and *The Cocktail Party* is a woman's play. Lavinia and Celia are 'better men' than Edward and Peter, and the apparently rattlepated Julia, not Reilly, is found to be the mastermind among the Guardians. *The Confidential Clerk* is not a comedy of manners and it is a man's play. Its subject is the relation of parents to children and of son to father rather than son to mother. Edward's profession as a barrister is irrelevant to the theme of *The Cocktail Party*. What Colby is to be, a financier or an organist, is the issue in *The Confidential Clerk*. The play has a complicated and highly entertaining plot in a very old tradition. Its source is the *Ion* of Euripides, the fountainhead of romantic comedy, the first play on the well-worn plot whose theme-song is 'Whose baby are you?' or 'Excuse me, sir, but have you by any chance a strawberry mark on your left shoulder?' As Shakespeare doubled his twins in *The Comedy of Errors* to make the fun faster, Eliot gave us two foundlings and an illegitimate daughter in place of the single foundling of the source. He used the fantastic mistakings of his plot to explore the problem of personal identity: Who am I? And for the first time he found a plot which gave him a natural dénouement in the discoveries of the third act. *The Confidential Clerk* differs from Eliot's earlier plays in having a weak and untheatrical opening but a strong third act, with a superb final curtain. Always before, the expositions raised expectations that the conclusion disappointed. Here the last act with revelation on revelation is a genuinely theatrical climax. On the other hand, the slow exposition is a price that has had to be paid for the complications of the plot and for the classic restriction of the cast.

The subject of *The Cocktail Party* was freedom and destiny, our narrow but real area of choice. *The Confidential Clerk* also turns on choice; but choice here is the recognition of choices made long ago, and not made by ourselves alone, which we have to live with. Mrs Guzzard, the mother of Colby Simpkins, the new confidential clerk to Sir Claude Mulhammer, chose long ago to be her son's aunt, not his mother, to pretend that her own child was her dead sister's illegitimate baby. She thought it would give him a better start in life to be under the patronage of that sister's wealthy lover, Sir Claude, than to be the orphan son of a poor organist. Lady Elizabeth also chose not to be a mother and let her lover farm out their illegitimate son. Then, after her lover's death, she conveniently forgot the name and address of the foster-mother and was able to grieve in perfect safety over the loss of her child. Sir Claude chose to be Colby's patron rather than his father, to keep a son as it were in cold storage or deep freeze until it was convenient to have him around, and to have a fiduciary relation with his illegitimate daughter, passing her off as the daughter of a dead friend. Sir Claude's passion in life is pottery. He was once tempted to be a potter; but he chose not to be. He decided that he would never be more than a second-rate potter and that he would follow his father's career, be a financier, and keep pottery as a hobby. Colby's passion is music. Sir Claude tries to persuade him that he will never be more than a second-rate musician and his music had better be, like Sir Claude's collection of pots, a hobby, an inner dream, a refuge.

Colby Simpkins holds the centre, a personable, intelligent, well-behaved young man whom everyone wants, the ideal son ready-made off the peg. At the beginning he is trying to adapt himself to what he conceives to be the true situation. In the second act he is claimed by both Sir Claude and Lady Elizabeth as a son. He asks for the truth and when in the last act his aunt is summoned, the Pallas Athene of the suburbs, and he is asked by her what he wants, he replies that what he wants is what he has had. The only true father he can ever have is a father who died before he was born, who did not reject him because he had no chance to do so, a father whom he may discover by report and within himself. His music is not like Sir Claude's passion for ceramics; it is something in his being, not a hobby or relaxation, but what he really likes doing. He is granted his wish and told the truth. His father was an unsuccessful organist, husband of the woman he has always known as Aunt Sarah. His mother must 'rest in peace'. She has become Aunt Sarah, whom he shows to her taxi. He will go to

see her, be grateful for what she did for him as a child, and no
doubt keep her photograph in a silver frame in his sitting-
room. (Living in the suburbs, he need not trouble himself with
Lady Elizabeth's standards of social propriety.) But she can
never be his mother though he was born from her womb. And
Sir Claude's fatherhood, which was always a spiritual fraud,
has now lost even its poor base in physical fact. Colby declares
that he will go the way of his true father and live with the old
clerk Eggerson in the suburb of Joshua Park, where the church
needs an organist. Like Colby, Eggerson gets his wish, though
he does not utter it. He is the only person in the play who has
had a true relationship, has really known a father's 'pains and
benefits'. He and Mrs E. had a son, born in lawful wedlock in
a bedroom, one imagines, with its walnut suite they had saved
up for, in Joshua Park; nursed through childish croup and
measles; taken to the panto at Christmas and to the sea for a
fortnight in the summer; seen through his school; and then –
'lost in action, his grave unknown'. 'To him that hath shall be
given, from him that hath not shall be taken away even that
which he thinketh he hath.' Sir Claude loses the son he thought
he had. To Eggerson, who truly had a son, a second son is
given, a son after the spirit. Mrs E. will be less low-spirited
around the 'season . . . getting near the anniversary' with Colby
in her dead son's bedroom to be fussed and petted as he works,
as Eggerson hints he will, for his ordination exams.

Sir Claude is left with the wife he married for her social
rank, with the daughter he has always regarded as a nuisance –
someone to be given an allowance and have her debts paid –
and with the extremely vulgar young man she is to marry, who
has turned out to be Lady Elizabeth's long-lost son. Lady
Elizabeth is left with the husband she has always regarded as
uninterested in 'higher thought', the son she abandoned as a
baby, a dreadfully common young man, and her husband's
much-disliked daughter, who is to be that son's wife. Comedy
always ends with the establishment of relationships, usually
with marriage. Here it ends with a family that has never

thought of itself as a family or tried to be a family before. Make-believe is over. They must make the best of what they are and of what is, and accept what cannot be undone.

The plot of *The Confidential Clerk* is preposterous and amusing. It is given *vraisemblance* by the lifelikeness of the characters: Lady Elizabeth, the 'seeker', at times shrewd, at times pathetic, at moments wise; Lucasta, with her pose of the tough blonde, a frightened, unhappy girl, embittered by the knowledge that her father is ashamed of her and that she is ashamed of her mother; B. Kaghan, whose brashness covers a similar need for reassurance; Sir Claude, a clever man who talks as if he were a wise one. His house of make-believe tumbles about his ears. In the first act he is sure he is right when he explains to Colby how he chose to follow his father as a successful financier. In the third act, waiting for Mrs Guzzard, he starts to talk for the first time to his wife and wonders if he has been wrong all the time. 'Could a man be said to have a vocation to be a second-rate potter?' he asks Colby ironically. The answer lies in another question: Can one have a vocation to be first-rate? What has vocation to do with success? The lay's theme is vocation and Sir Claude has persistently ignored 'callings' – the calling of his deepest nature, the calling of marriage, the calling of fatherhood. He has chosen to be a successful financier – he realizes at the end he was nothing more, and that he has not really followed his father, to whom finance was a passion; he has chosen to be the unloved and unloving husband of a wife he married for her title and connexions, and who he thought wanted an important husband; to give his daughter money without love; and to keep his son at a distance until he can, as it were, fit him in comfortably.

At the opposite pole from Sir Claude is the old clerk Eggerson, the Celia of *The Confidential Clerk*, who provides the test of values: good husband, good father, good servant, without ambition and without envy, whose inner and outer life are one

– and, one must say outright, a crashing bore. In *The Cocktail Party*, the divine broke into the pattern of ordinary relationships in the form of the heroic. Here, we are asked to feel its presence in a life of the utmost banality, and in a personality unenriched by our highest secular values. To Mr Eggerson, whose pleasure is in pottering about in his garden, who never opens his mouth without a cliché, and thinks everyone has a heart of gold, the marvels of the human spirit, the 'monuments of unageing intellect', are, I do not doubt, meaningless. His reading is the evening paper; the power of music, I imagine, means to him 'Abide with Me' and 'In a Monastery Garden'; and one hates to think of what pictures keep down the wallpaper, and what ornaments stand on the mantelpiece, in his home at Joshua Park. For a poet to place such a figure at the heart of his play is to declare that 'the poetry does not matter': that it is the whole conception of the play that is significant. That conception involves a more powerful reversal of worldly values than anything Eliot had written before. We bring what is within us to any work of art and we, like the characters in *The Confidential Clerk*, are shaped for life. I am a child of the London suburbs, not Joshua Park, which I locate on the Liverpool Street line,[6] and I know and knew as a child the kind of parish in which Mr Eggerson is vicar's warden and where Colby will be organist. The Christian faith first presented itself to my childish imagination not as inspiring great art and literature, nor as a great intellectual system, nor as a call to high adventures of the spirit; but as the informing grace of many obscurely faithful lives. When I came out of the theatre after seeing *The Confidential Clerk* I was haunted by memories of such 'Confidential Clerks', going about their master's business, and by some lines from a poem that Eliot once mentioned in a broadcast as one of the poems that came

6. Mrs Eliot tells me I was wrong here and that Joshua Park in fact is Muswell Hill in North London. Eggerson was a reminiscence of an old clerk in Lloyds Bank, where Eliot worked from 1917, who was always talking of his garden.

often to his mind: Johnson's lines on his humble and obscure friend Dr Robert Levet.

> Well tried through many a varying year,
>   See Levet to the grave descend;
> Officious, innocent, sincere,
>   Of ev'ry friendless name the friend.
>
> Yet still he fills affection's eye,
>   Obscurely wise and coarsely kind;
> Nor, letter'd arrogance, deny
>   Thy praise to merit unrefin'd. . . .
>
> His virtues walk'd their narrow round,
>   Nor made a pause, nor left a void;
> And sure th'Eternal Master found
>   The single talent well employ'd.

Spiritually Colby is to be Eggerson's son, to find happiness in doing his duty in that sphere of life to which it shall please God to call him; and by sphere of life is meant that whole complex of circumstances into which we are born, and grow up, and find ourselves. Colby is a natural solitary. His lonely childhood has shaped him for a special lot. 'When my father and my mother forsake me, the Lord taketh me up.' He is called to know more clearly than any of the others what Lady Elizabeth glimpses when she says, 'We are nearer to God than to anyone.'

I have left myself little time to speak of *The Elder Statesman*, the weakest of the three plays. Its plot is simplicity itself and I think one feels in it that Eliot's inventiveness and talent for comic surprise had failed him. Except that both are concerned with death, that Lord Claverton, like Oedipus, dies alone under a tree, that he has a devoted daughter, and that he quarrels with his son, the play bears no true relation to the *Oedipus at Colonus*. Its sources are in Eliot's own poetry: in the poem 'Difficulties of a Statesman', and particularly in the beautiful, sombre passage in *Little Gidding* on the gifts reserved for age'.

> Let me disclose the gifts reserved for age
> To set a crown upon your lifetime's effort.
> First, the cold friction of expiring sense
> Without enchantment, offering no promise
> But bitter tastelessness of shadow fruit
> As body and soul begin to fall asunder.
> Second, the conscious impotence of rage
> At human folly, and the laceration
> Of laughter at what ceases to amuse.
> And last, the rending pain of re-enactment
> Of all that you have done, and been; the shame
> Of motives late revealed, and the awareness
> Of things ill done and done to others' harm. . . .

Lord Claverton is one of those important persons – an 'eminent man' – who, in *East Coker*, 'all go into the dark'. He has had a stroke and retired from political life, where he has had an honourable and successful career, with a reputation for probity and ability. He has never quite reached the top – still by the world's standards he is a distinguished man, 'an elder statesman'. In fact his whole life has been a fraud, a pretence, an escape from himself. Dick Ferry has spent his life creating Lord Claverton, and in the face of death Lord Claverton is only a hollow man, an old guy, a public figure without a private existence. He will be forgotten in five years – perhaps at most mentioned in a footnote by historians as 'a member of So-and-So's Cabinet'.

Both Lord Claverton's loving daughter Monica, to whom he finally makes confession, and her lover are so shadowy as to be non-existent. The love-scenes between them are painfully unconvincing. But the central theme of the play is handled with the unsparing moral realism that is the strength of Eliot's other plays. The grim jest is that the blackmailers who come to harry the dying Lord Claverton, the ghosts of his youth, have not in one sense been ruined by him at all. They therefore cannot be bought off. And the things they know about him are not seriously discreditable. No scandal sheet would pay them for these 'secrets'. So it is impossible for him to say to them, 'Publish and be damned.' They have both done very well. Freddy Culverwell, having served his sentence for forgery, has become Gomez, a South American millionaire. Maisie Batterson, who was bought off by young Dick Ferry's father, is now Mrs Carghill, a wealthy widow. Both are apparently very well pleased with themselves. And yet, they are all the same lost souls; and they know it. They need not have been so. Freddie Culverwell, the grammar-school boy, might have got his first, and lived an honourable and useful life as a master at the kind of school from which he won his scholarship, if he hadn't been taken up by Dick Ferry and taught tastes and habits beyond his means. As for Maisie Batterson, she loved Dick Ferry and he loved her when they were both young and foolish. Though they were totally unsuited, and if they had married the marriage might have – probably would have – come to disaster, she might have been less wholly mercenary and sentimental in her middle age if he had not, like a coward, allowed his father to 'make it worth her while' to give up her lover. Why do they come back to haunt Lord Claverton on the verge of death? They are, of course, like the Tempters in *Murder in the Cathedral*, objectifications of the trouble in the dying man's mind: reminders of two occasions, symbolic of his whole life, when he was a coward and shirked his responsibilities, because to have faced them would have spoilt the picture of himself which he wanted to present to the world. But they are also themselves, persons he has ruined, and for all their apparent self-satisfaction they know it and want their revenge. In their first encounters they have the upper hand because they do know it and are not, as he is, frauds. Freddie Culverwell *is* Gomez; Maisie *is* Mrs Carghill. Lord Claverton is a stuffed dummy. They want revenge on the public figure because in their hearts they are still haunted by the young Freddie and the young Maisie whom he killed. Gomez is haunted by Freddie Culverwell, the simple, clever, but weak boy he was: Mrs Carghill by Maisie, the romantic chorus girl; and both of them by the young Dick Ferry whom they had loved and admired. In their final encounters they have lost the upper hand, for their victim has abandoned the weak defence of 'Am I my brother's keeper?' and knows that he has done what cannot be undone. He is free because he has owned the truth and is now ready to die. He has attained the only wisdom:

> Do not let me hear
> Of the wisdom of old men, but rather of their folly,
> Their fear of fear and frenzy, their fear of possession,
> Of belonging to another, or to others, or to God.
> The only wisdom we can hope to acquire
> Is the wisdom of humility: humility is endless.

The Elder Statesman is like an unfinished picture, a sketch drawn by a master's hand with only some portions worked up. I would not be without it; but I cannot believe that it will have a future on the stage. The central subject is powerfully handled and comes home strongly to the conscience. But the weakness of the love scenes and the facile satire on the expensive nursing-home that is not a nursing-home provide a bad frame for this sombre study of a life under the judgement of death. And, of course, the other two plays have serious weaknesses too. Eliot himself said that the last act of *The Cocktail Party* was too much of an epilogue to the play; and, apart from this, its substance is unsatisfactory. Celia's death has to be recounted as a piece of straight narrative, like a classical messenger's speech, which is stylistically inappropriate in a naturalistic comedy. It is also awkwardly introduced. Edward and Lavinia's 'good marriage' is inevitably rather tedious in representation. Just as happy nations have no history, so happy marriages lack drama. But Eliot need not have represented their domestic concord in such banal terms. We seem to have moved into the world of the women's magazines: 'Take an interest, dear, in what has happened in the office,' and 'Don't forget to tell her how nice she looks in her new dress.' There is an excessive use of conversation between two persons in *The*

Confidential Clerk; and the sheer weight of exposition in the first act is a heavy price to pay for the brilliance of the third. There is, perhaps, also a failure in the presentation of Eggerson, who is too much a 'character part', tempting the actor to give a plummy performance as a 'dear old man'.

But it is not the weaknesses of these plays that I would wish to dwell on. Their merits are to my mind far more conspicuous. I have left without comment one most striking merit: their 'speakability'. The unobtrusive vigour of their language modulates from chatter, gossip, or prattle to reflection and serious self-probing, without ever losing its rhythmic vitality. Eliot's desire to create a 'transpicuous language' as a vehicle for drama was fulfilled in what is best described as the 'heightened speech' of these plays. Their language would be a subject for an essay in itself. Here, I wished rather to concentrate on their reading of life. I cannot believe that *The Cocktail Party* and *The Confidential Clerk* will not find a place in the national repertory of the future. No other plays of our generation present with equal force, sympathy, wisdom, and wit the classic subject of comedy: our almost, but mercifully not wholly, unlimited powers of self-deception, and the shocks and surprises that life gives to our poses and pretences.

WITH BECKET IN
MURDER IN THE CATHEDRAL
By Robert Speaight

IT was in the early summer of 1935 that I received a letter from my friend Martin Browne inviting me to play the part of Becket in the first performance of *Murder in the Cathedral*. It was a sunny morning and I was due to leave for Rome the same afternoon to attend the ceremonies of canonization for John Fisher and Thomas More. The English do not often have their big moments in Rome, but this was one of them. My thoughts were with the second Thomas who had defied an English king, rather than with the first; and it was not until I was comfortably settled in the Rome express that I took out of my pocket the acting, and abridged, edition of *Murder in the Cathedral* which had accompanied Martin Browne's invitation. The play was to be performed at the Canterbury Festival of Music and Drama, and for some reason that I have never understood no play at Canterbury was allowed to last more than an hour and forty minutes. So the choruses and parts of the dialogue had been considerably shortened. I no longer possess the acting edition of the play; I imagine that by now it is something of a rarity.

I had not waited to read it before telegraphing my acceptance of the part. Eliot was an acquaintance, and an influence, of some years' standing. I used to meet him at Lady Ottoline Morrell's Thursday tea-parties, and he regularly attended the performances at the Old Vic, where I was then sharing the leading parts with Ralph Richardson. I remember that he liked my Malvolio a good deal more than I liked it myself. There was hardly any point of literary judgement or of religious belief on which I did not find myself in agreement with Eliot; or rather, perhaps I should say, upon which he did not influence my assent – for I am a natural disciple. Moreover, I liked and admired him personally. The slow voice and deliberate opinions, the brightness of the eagle eyes – and the eagle was not nearly so 'aged' as it would sometimes pretend – the rumbling, chuckling laugh, were in sharp contrast to the vaticinations of Yeats, who used to appear at the same tea-parties.

Eliot was still an untried dramatist, although Rupert Doone's production of *Sweeney Agonistes* had come off brilliantly, and the Choruses from *The Rock* had shown that this poet of recondite allusion could simplify his style for an average audience. The first performance of his first full-length play was bound to be an event in which any actor worth his ambition would wish to take part. Nevertheless, as I read the play in the train that thundered its way towards the Eternal City, I wondered at first where was the role of Becket and what were my qualifications for playing it. Becket was a man – if I remembered rightly – of fifty-six; I was only thirty-one, and middle age is not easily assumed. Becket was six feet four inches in height; I had no more than five feet eight and a half. Like most actors, I looked for theatrical opportunity, and of this there appeared to be very little. True, the Sermon was a skilful evasion of rhetoric, and its understatement was moving even at a first reading; but would an audience be prepared to listen to a sermon, and a rigorously theological sermon, even in the chapter house of Canterbury Cathedral? The most inspiring poetry was reserved for the Choruses; and I asked myself, further, how the positive character of Becket's personality could be reconciled with so passive a protagonist? Tempters, Priests, Chorus, and Knights all came at him in turns, and he reacted obediently. But where was his initiative?

I was, of course, crudely misreading the play. The initiatives were the initiatives of grace, and Becket's business was obedience. This became clear as we got into rehearsal on my return from Rome. Theatrically speaking, the auspices of that first production were modest. Only Martin Browne and I were fully professional actors. The Chorus was in the hands of students from the Central School of Speech Training and Dramatic Art, imperiously trained by Elsie Fogerty. They spoke beautifully, but they remained middle-class young women from South Kensington. Nothing more remote from the medieval poor could have been imagined. Sometimes they spoke as individuals; sometimes in groups of two or three; only occasionally in unison. They gave one Eliot's poetry without ever being able to give one Eliot's people. I believe that Eliot himself was best pleased with a chorus he heard at the National University in Dublin; here the soft brogue gave an unforced suggestion of the *folk* – of the wives and daughters of peasants and fishermen who must have composed the greater part of the faithful who welcomed Becket home from exile. Such a suggestion is easily conveyed by voices from the Celtic fringe of Britain; even the best drama schools of the metropolis would quickly stifle it.

The other male characters were played by Canterbury amateurs of varying competence, jealous of their rights in the Festival. The play was acted on a formal stage at the east end of the chapter house. There were no entrances at the side except from behind a screen, where the actors concerned had to take their place before the audience came in. Becket himself entered through the audience and was similarly carried out at the end, preceded by the Chorus with their lighted candles, singing the Litany of the Saints. It was a moving experience, when the night had fallen, to be carried thus into the Cloister and to pass within a few feet of the place where Becket is believed to have been murdered. The Tempters' costumes, designed by Stella Mary Pearce, were an ingenious blend of modern and medieval. The feudal bully brandished the suggestion of a golf-club and wore skirts that looked as if they would have liked to be plus-fours; the statesman carried a hint of decorations. The audience sat, not very comfortably, on rush-bottomed chairs – except for the Archbishop, who was more ceremoniously installed in the front row. The acoustics were difficult, the lighting rudimentary, and there was, of course, no curtain. Nevertheless the play gained from the historical and ecclesiastical associations of the place, and from the general disposition of the audience to accept the author's premises. In some ways it is easier to preach a sermon in a church or a chapter house where the acoustics are bad than in a theatre where they are good.

The play won immediate critical acclaim, but for all that not a single impresario came down from London to see it. No star performer even considered snatching the principal part from under my nose. The performing rights remained in the possession of Ashley Dukes, who presented the play six months later at the tiny Mercury Theatre at Notting Hill Gate. This was the headquarters – as it still is – of the Ballet Rambert. There were seats for only one hundred and thirty, and I have a lasting regret that they were too small to accommodate the bulk of G. K. Chesterton, for whom the play might have been written. Mrs Chesterton came to investigate and went sadly away. Even if we had used scenery, there was no space to fly it in; but the stage had a wide, curving apron, and although the theatre was so small it somehow did not inhibit the large-scale acting and speech which the play demanded. We kept the Canterbury Chorus, but all the other parts were in professional hands. Martin Browne's acute sensitivity to the spoken word secured that the poetry of the play should get the hearing it deserved, and that no directorial gimmickry should obscure its meaning. There have been more elaborate, and perhaps more inventive, productions of *Murder in the Cathedral,* but none more faithful.

An accident assisted our *première*. Charles Morgan, the drama critic of *The Times,* was on holiday. He had seen the play at Canterbury and admired it with reservations. His place was now taken by Dermot Morrah, who had no inhibitions about writing the kind of sentence which looks well on an advertisement; and when we were able to quote *The Times* as saying that this was 'the one play by a contemporary dramatist

187

now to be seen in London', our success was assured. We had expected to be acting the play for a month; we played it, with only brief intervals, at the Mercury Theatre and in the West End, from November 1935 to March 1937. Then we took it out on two long provincial tours, and early in 1938 presented it in Boston and New York. By that time *Murder in the Cathedral* had become part of theatrical history, and won for its author a popularity which he would never have gained by his poetry alone.

This success also brought its problems. The greatest pianist does not want to play the *Emperor* concerto every evening, and I soon found myself struggling against the monotony of the long-run system. It was easy to become mechanical in a part where many of the speeches were so long; to sleep upon the rhythm instead of seeming to dictate it. I had much else upon my mind at the time, and I was not able – nor always willing – to give my undivided attention to the play. Sometimes I discovered a fresh impulse to a conception which remained fundamentally the same; but I could not command these initiatives – they came and went. Whenever an actor is playing at his best, he should feel as if he is acting the part for the first time; then he will have the power to surprise his audience because in a sense he is surprising himself. All too often, I fear, my playing of Becket was predictable. And there were particular problems. What degree of emotion – if any – should Becket display at the end of the sermon? If he were to move his audience, how far dare he be moved himself? The sermon proved, theatrically speaking, the *pièce de résistance* of the play, and there was a consequent temptation to drag it out. Here I knew that nine minutes was the right length, and if I exceeded this the stage management would tell me so. Finally, there was the problem of giving concrete shape to a character which had been conceived, designedly, in the abstract. These bones were beautiful, but they needed the integument of flesh. I had to snatch at any clue which would suggest the man that Becket once had been, as well as the man he had become.

During the second of our provincial tours I complied with a publisher's request that I should write the biography of the man I was playing on the stage. In this I was helped by several friends who were also medievalists – notably by Christopher Dawson. I was at one with Dawson in not being able to make a great deal of Becket; how much more of subtlety there was in Gilbert Foliot, how much more of genius in Henry! It seemed to me, however, that Eliot's guess at Becket's principal weakness was a very plausible one. There was a self-dramatizing side to his character – as the chronicles record it for us – which might well have tempted him 'to do the right deed for the wrong reason'. *Murder in the Cathedral* is very far from being an historical chronicle, like Tennyson's play on the same subject; but it is all the better a play for sticking close to history, just as Anouilh's *Becket* is seriously weakened by departing from it. I must confess, however, that in spite of playing Becket more than a thousand times, I have never felt near to him as a man. He remains a figure in a tapestry or an effigy on a tomb – imposing, important, intransigent, undoubtedly heroic, but not very intelligent and with not very much to say to the modern world. Perhaps it was sensible to delete his feast day from the general calendar of the Church. How very differently I felt about Sir Thomas More, when I was playing the part in *A Man for All Seasons*! Here was a character whose company I looked forward to every evening of the week, although More is quite as exacting a part as Becket. It is only fair to remember, however, that no one would have invited me to play More in Australia, unless I had first been seen there as Becket. For *Murder in the Cathedral* not only gave me a reputation for which I should be churlish not to be grateful, but it stamped a pattern on my career from which I have sometimes wished to escape.

The American tour was not a success, and in this case accident worked against us. Although Ashley Dukes had the American rights of performance, Eliot – quite innocently forgetting this – told his New York publisher to arrange for a production if a suitable opportunity presented itself. So we were suddenly faced with a W. P. A. production in rehearsal. We should have been legally entitled to stop it, but this would have been rightly construed as a dirty blow against the New Deal and would have seriously prejudiced our reception in the United States when, as we still hoped, we brought our own production over there. We told the W. P. A., therefore, to go ahead but to limit their run in New York to eight weeks. Our plan was to open in Boston, where Eliot was a Harvard if not quite a household name, and then to take the play on an extended provincial tour. Bookings were made in Philadelphia, Washington, and Pittsburgh; and we hoped to include other cities as well. With the prestige of what was essentially the Canterbury production behind us, backed by an American success on the road, we thought that we could safely come into New York for a short season. That the plan did not work out as we expected illustrates the power of quite small things to upset a theatrical timetable and damage a theatrical investment.

We had an excellent opening at the Shubert Theatre in Boston, where the original production of *Our Town* was in competition at the Wilbur. The press was unanimous in its praise – these were still the days of the *Boston Evening Transcript* – but the advance booking, though good, was not quite what we had hoped for. Two days after the opening, Gilbert Miller, who was associated with Ashley Dukes in the American venture, decided that the provincial tour would be too risky an undertaking and that we had better come straight into New York. Our provincial bookings were cancelled, and it was arranged to bring us into the Ritz, a theatre long since demolished. Scarcely had this decision been taken when queues began forming up outside the Shubert box office, and for the rest of our two weeks' stay in Boston we played to near-capacity houses. We should have been less than human if we had not come down to New York with incautious anticipations of triumph.

Boston had spoilt us. A previous production of the play in

the courtyard of the Fogg Museum had merely whetted Cambridge appetites. Theodore Spencer, a close friend of Eliot, godfathered us with his peculiar grace and charm. But in New York it was different. Here we were no longer a novelty; the W. P. A. production had been generally praised, no doubt deservedly. It may well have been more theatrical – in the best sense – than ours. The stage of the Ritz was so shallow that we had to cut down our scenery, and the first-night audience, with its sprinkling of talent scouts, was cold to the point of hostility. After the performance I went out to a night-club, and bought the *New York Times* and *Herald Tribune* on my way home. One expected so dedicated a critic as Brooks Atkinson to treat the production as seriously as we treated it ourselves, and he did not disappoint us. Nor did his colleagues lag behind. It was a magnificent critical reception, but the public felt no temptation to emulate it. They had seen one production of *Murder in the Cathedral*; they had no desire to see another. We struggled on for three weeks, and I made desperate attempts to get further backing. Vincent Sheean was a tower of strength and encouragement and took me round to see 'Red' Lewis. We tried to mobilize the literary world, but it was no good. New York had said its devastating 'nay' and I had seen my name up in lights on Broadway for the first and last time. I have never played there since, and never really wanted to. I lingered on for a few weeks, moving to a hotel significantly lower downtown, and remembering the cautionary words of Brooks Atkinson when I had met him in London at a luncheon given by Charles Morgan at the Garrick Club. He had frankly predicted failure if we brought the play to New York in the wake of the W. P. A. We should have done well to heed his warning.

I did, as a matter of fact, play Becket in a production at the Catholic University at Washington in the spring of 1940; but apart from this, and radio and TV performances for the B.B.C., I had a rest from the play until we revived it for the first Edinburgh Festival in 1947, taking it back to the Mercury for a short season afterwards. The verbal and abstract convention of *Murder in the Cathedral* lends itself very well to radio treatment, giving at the same time visual opportunity to television. It was interesting to preach the Sermon as if I were talking to one person in a room instead of to several hundreds in a cathedral. By now the play was becoming internationally famous. In the summer of 1945 Jean Vilar invited me to attend a rehearsal at the Vieux Colombier, and shortly afterwards I saw his production, although he himself was then on holiday. He had a chorus of only five, brilliantly stylized; but I could not help feeling that this method of Gregorian incantation diminishes, if indeed it does not totally destroy, the human impact of the Chorus; and the pastoral relationship between Becket and his people is the most human aspect of the play. Henri Fluchère's translation was excellent, and I was able to judge this for myself when I presented Eliot before a Brussels audience for the Grandes Conférences Catholiques. After the presentation I read some passages from *Murder in the Cathedral* with actors from the Théâtre du Parc. This was in 1948, and two years later I was invited by Père Émile Legault to direct the play, acting my original part, at the Théâtre des Compagnons in Montreal. Here was the new impulse I needed.

Les Compagnons were at first a company of gifted amateurs, but they had now reached a semi-professional status. I had seen and admired their work at the Canadian Dominion Drama Festival in Anouilh's *Antigone*. I think their best days were over when I went out to produce them in *Murder in the Cathedral*, but they gave me ardent cooperation in a play that was quite foreign to the conventions within which they usually worked. We had only a limited success in Montreal, as we had had only a limited success in Dublin. I had supposed that a play so Catholic in its inspiration would have been welcomed in both cities, but people's playgoing habits – I have discovered – have little connexion with their churchgoing. The success of *Murder in the Cathedral* in Britain owed a great deal to the support of the Church of England. The play was, after all, an Anglican classic, and we were asking too much, perhaps, in expecting an equal support from the Church of Rome, although Eliot's thought was at no point at variance with Roman Catholic doctrine. I found it surprisingly easy to learn the part in French; Fluchère's translation had caught the rhythm, even when it could not catch the rhyme. I also found a new satisfaction in directing the play myself. With a Chorus of only five I could test the truth of Yeats's view that this was the ideal number; each individual stood out as a person, and when they spoke as a group they could still be heard and understood. In general, however, I did not consciously depart from Martin Browne's direction of the play. This was so clearly in tune with Eliot's own intentions that it could not lightly be disregarded. It is only fair to add that the play was far better understood and appreciated in Quebec than in Montreal.

I resumed the role of Becket ten years later under different conditions. In 1960 the first International Festival of Arts at Adelaide in South Australia decided to present *Murder in the Cathedral* in the Bonython Hall of the University, under the auspices of the Australian Elizabethan Theatre Trust. Hugh Hunt, then director of the Trust, invited me to play my original part and asked me if I would be willing to work under Robert Helpmann, who had directed the play in a production at the Old Vic with Robert Donat as Becket. Helpmann's long experience in ballet had resulted in some memorable effects with the Chorus. I met Helpmann in London, where we had preliminary discussions, but in the end he was not able to come to Australia, and Hugh Hunt himself took on the production. I arrived in Sydney, where rehearsals were to begin, after playing and producing *King Lear* in Los Angeles. It was my second visit to Australia and I frankly wished that I were coming out to appear in a part with which I was not already so familiar.

Hunt's production, however, soon rekindled my enthusiasm.

Neither from the men, nor – still less – from the Chorus of thirteen, was he able to secure the vocal refinement that Martin Browne had elicited from actors more experienced in this kind of work. But the visual and auditive effects that he contrived against the Tudor Gothic of the Bonython Hall were deeply impressive. An immense crucifix hung from the roof, and on the built-up stage a pair of heavy semicircular doors (on hinges that evidently felt the strain) closed or opened before the altar. These enabled Hunt to solve a problem which had always bothered me – of how to manage the murder itself. This takes place to the accompaniment of a long chorus, and in the English production it had been slowly mimed to reproduce the gestures and attitudes of the Knights as these are represented in the medieval iconography of St Thomas. But there was a hint of affectation in this which had always left me dissatisfied; the shock of sacrilege was missing. At Adelaide the Knights converged on Becket with a bestial roar, with their swords upraised as the doors closed in upon them. An effect of sudden violence was thus secured without any untidy realism. Hunt used the lateral stone galleries of the hall with great imagination, so that the voices of Becket's temptations literally filled the air. Once Becket had been killed he was not seen again, whereas in the English production his body had been revealed, laid out in full pontificals, on a catafalque. I had come to feel this a mistake, a premature anticipation of the *cultus*, with which the play is not directly concerned. The sense of final apotheosis is surely that the essential Becket is in heaven, not on earth. The long entrances of the Bonython Hall were used for Becket's arrival and, less successfully, for the Chorus's departure, declaiming the *Te Deum* as they went; the shorter ones for the Tempters and the ritual preliminaries of the Sermon. These were designed to emphasize the place of the sermon in the liturgy of the Midnight Mass.

The success of the play at Adelaide was quite phenomenal; I would return home after supper to find a queue already forming to besiege the box office on the morrow. The heat in the hall was overpowering, but the huge audience endured it without complaint. In Sydney we sorely missed the spaces of the Bonython Hall, although the Elizabethan Theatre where we played is very far from being a *théâtre intime*; and I came to the final conclusion that there is something in *Murder in the Cathedral* which quarrels with a conventional theatrical setting. Is it that a play designed for the Canterbury chapter house demands a similar hospitality of church or hall? My golden memories of the Adelaide Festival incline me to think so. Is it not significant that when Eliot began to write for a more conventional theatre he wrote a very different kind of play? Yet there seems to be a growing consensus of critical opinion that *Murder in the Cathedral* represents his most considerable achievement in this kind. It may be so. For my part, I am happy to reflect that although I have no letters of Eliot for the instruction of posterity, I have a first edition of *Murder in the Cathedral* inscribed with a dedication that modesty forbids me to reproduce.

AN ANATOMY OF MELANCHOLY[1]

By Conrad Aiken

PREFATORY NOTE

THE review of *The Waste Land*, with the above title, came out in *The New Republic* on 7 February 1923, in other words, four months after the poem's appearance in *The Criterion* of October 1922; and I suspect it was the first full-length favourable review the poem had then received – at any rate, I do not remember any predecessors. To be sure, I had the advantage of having known Eliot intimately for fifteen years – since my freshman year at Harvard – and had already, in 1917 and 1921, apropos of *Prufrock* and *The Sacred Wood*, heralded him as the fugleman of many things to come. Of *Prufrock* I said that in its wonderfully varied use of rhymed free verse there was a probable solution of the quarrel, at that time as violent as it is now, about the usefulness of rhyme or verse at all : the Imagists, and Others, including of course Williams and his eternal Object, were already hard at it. I think *Prufrock* still has its way.

As to *The Waste Land* and my review, it might be helpful for the general picture if I record here two episodes with Eliot, one before he had written the poem, and one after.

In the winter of 1921–22 I was in London, living in Bayswater, and Eliot and myself lunched together two or three times a week in the City, near his bank: thus resuming a habit we had formed many years before in Cambridge. He always had with him his pocket edition of Dante. And of course we discussed the literary scene, with some acerbity and hilarity,

1. Reprinted from *A Reviewer's ABC*, by Conrad Aiken, Greenwich Editions, published by Meridian Books, Inc., 1958; by permission of the author and the publisher. First publication, *The New Republic*, 7 February 1923.

and with the immense advantage of being outsiders (though both of us were already contributing to the English reviews); discussing also the then-just-beginning possibility of *The Criterion*, through the generosity of Lady Rothermere. And it was at one of these meetings, in midwinter, that he told me one day, and with visible concern, that although every evening he went home to his flat hoping that he could start writing again, and with every confidence that the material was *there* and waiting, night after night the hope proved illusory: the sharpened pencil lay unused by the untouched sheet of paper. What could be the matter? He didn't know. He asked me if *I* had ever experienced any such thing. And of course my reply that I hadn't wasn't calculated to make him feel any happier.

But it worried me, as it worried him. And so, not unnaturally, I mentioned it to a very good friend of mine, Dilston Radcliffe, who was at that time being analysed by the remarkable American lay analyst, Homer Lane. Radcliffe, himself something of a poet, was at once very much interested, and volunteered, at his next meeting with Lane, to ask him what he thought of it. And a few days later came the somewhat startling answer from Lane: 'Tell your friend Aiken to tell *his* friend Eliot that all that's stopping him is his fear of putting anything down that is short of perfection. He thinks he's God.'

The result was, I suppose, foreseeable, though I didn't foresee it. For when I told Eliot of Lane's opinion, he was literally speechless with rage, both at Lane and myself. The *intrusion*, quite simply, was one that was intolerable. But ever since I have been entirely convinced that it did the trick, it broke the log-jam. A month or two later he went to Switzerland, and there wrote *The Waste Land*.

Which in due course appeared in the first issue of *The Criterion*, by that time endowed by Lady Rothermere, and again in due course came to me from *The New Republic* for review. And once more it was as we proceeded from Lloyds Bank to our favourite pub, by the Cannon Street Station, for grilled rump steak and a pint of Bass, that another explosion occurred.

For I said, 'You know, I've called my long review of your poem "An Anatomy of Melancholy".'

He turned on me with that icy fury of which he alone was capable, and said fiercely: 'There is nothing melancholy about it!'

To which I in turn replied 'The reference, Tom, was to BURTON'S *Anatomy of Melancholy*, and the quite extraordinary amount of *quotation* it contains!'

The joke was acceptable, and we both roared with laughter.

To all of which I think I need add one small regret about that review. How could I mention that I had long been familiar with such passages as 'A woman drew her long black hair out tight', which I had seen as poems, or part-poems, in themselves? And now saw inserted into *The Waste Land* as into a mosaic. This would be to make use of private knowledge, a betrayal. Just the same, it should perhaps have been done, and the conclusion drawn: that they were not *organically* a part of the total meaning.

*

MR T. S. ELIOT is one of the most individual of contemporary poets, and at the same time, anomalously, one of the most 'traditional'. By individual I mean that he can be, and often is (distressingly, to some), aware in his own way; as when he observes of a woman (in 'Rhapsody on a Windy Night') that the door 'opens on her like a grin' and that the corner of her eye 'Twists like a crooked pin'. Everywhere, in the very small body of his work, is similar evidence of a delicate sensibility, somewhat shrinking, somewhat injured, and always sharply itself. But also, with this capacity or necessity for being aware in his own way, Mr Eliot has a haunting, a tyrannous awareness that there have been many other awarenesses before; and that the extent of his own awareness, and perhaps even the nature of it, is a consequence of these. He is,

more than most poets, conscious of his roots. If this consciousness had not become acute in 'Prufrock' or the 'Portrait of a
Lady', it was nevertheless probably there: and the roots were
quite conspicuously French, and dated, say, 1870–1900. A
little later, as his sense of the past had become more pressing,
it seemed that he was positively redirecting his roots – urging
them to draw a morbid dramatic sharpness from Webster and
Donne, a faded dry gilt of cynicism and formality from the
Restoration. This search of the tomb produced *Sweeney* and
'Whispers of Immortality'. And finally, in *The Waste Land*,
Mr Eliot's sense of the literary past has become so overmaster-
ing as almost to constitute the motive of the work. It is as if, in
conjunction with the Mr Pound of the *Cantos*, he wanted to
make a 'literature of literature' – a poetry actuated not more
by life itself than by poetry; as if he had concluded that the
characteristic awareness of a poet of the twentieth century
must inevitably, or ideally, be a very complex and very literary
awareness, able to speak only, or best, in terms of the literary
past, the terms which had moulded its tongue. This involves a
kind of idolatry of literature with which it is a little difficult
to sympathize. In positing, as it seems to, that there is nothing
left for literature to do but become a kind of parasitic growth
on literature, a sort of mistletoe, it involves, I think, a definite
astigmatism – a distortion. But the theory is interesting if only
because it has coloured an important and brilliant piece of
work.

The Waste Land is unquestionably important, unquestionably brilliant. It is important partly because its 433 lines
summarize Mr Eliot, for the moment, and demonstrate that he
is an even better poet than most had thought; and partly
because it embodies the theory just touched upon, the theory
of the 'allusive' method in poetry. *The Waste Land* is, indeed,
a poem of allusion all compact. It purports to be symbolical;
most of its symbols are drawn from literature or legend; and
Mr Eliot has thought it necessary to supply, in notes, a list of
the many quotations, references, and translations with which it

bristles. He observes candidly that the poem presents 'difficulties', and requires 'elucidation'. This serves to raise, at once, the question whether these difficulties, in which perhaps Mr Eliot takes a little pride, are so much the result of complexity, a fine elaborateness, as of confusion. The poem has been compared, by one reviewer, to a 'full-rigged ship built in a bottle', the suggestion being that it is a perfect piece of construction. But is it a perfect piece of construction? Is the complex material mastered, and made coherent? Or, if the poem is not successful in that way, in what way *is* it successful? Has it the formal and intellectual complex unity of a microscopic *Divine Comedy*; or is its unity – supposing it to have one – of another sort?

If we leave aside for the moment all other consideration, and read the poem solely with the intention of understanding, with the aid of notes, the symbolism; of making out what it is that is symbolized, and how these symbolized feelings are brought into relation with each other and with other matters in the poem; I think we must, with reservations, and with no invidiousness, conclude that the poem is not, in any formal sense, coherent. We cannot feel that all the symbolisms belong quite inevitably where they have been put; that the order of the parts is an inevitable order; that there is anything more than a rudimentary progress from one theme to another; nor that the relation between the more symbolic parts and the less is always as definite as it should be. What we feel is that Mr Eliot has not wholly annealed the allusive matter, has left it unabsorbed, lodged in gleaming fragments amid material alien to it. Again, there is a distinct weakness consequent on the use of allusions which may have both intellectual and emotional value for Mr Eliot, but (even with the notes) none for us. The 'Waste Land' of the Grail Legend might be a good symbol, if it were something with which we were sufficiently familiar. But it can never, even when explained, be a good symbol, simply because it has no immediate associations for us. It might, of course, be a good *theme*. In that case it would be given us. But Mr Eliot uses it for purposes of overtone; he refers to it; and as overtone it quite clearly fails. He gives us, superbly, *a* waste land – not *the* waste land. Why, then, refer to the latter at all – if he is not, in the poem, really going to use it? Hyacinth fails in the same way. So does the Fisher King. So does the Hanged Man, which Mr Eliot tells us he associates with Frazer's Hanged God – we take his word for it. But if the precise association is worth anything, it is worth putting into the poem; otherwise there can be no purpose in mentioning it. Why, again, Datta, Dayadhvam, Damyata? Or Shantih? Do they not say a good deal less for us than 'Give: sympathize: control' or 'Peace'? Of course; but Mr Eliot replies that he wants them not merely to mean those particular things, but also to mean them in a particular way – that is, to be remembered in connexion with a Upanishad. Unfortunately, we have none of us this memory, nor can he give it to us; and in the upshot he gives us only a series of agreeable sounds which might as well have been nonsense. What we get at, and I think it is important, is that in none of these particular cases does the reference, the allusion, justify itself intrinsically, make itself felt. When we are aware of these references at all (sometimes they are unidentifiable) we are aware of them simply as something unintelligible but suggestive. When they have been explained, we are aware of the material referred to, the fact (for instance, a vegetation ceremony), as something useless for our enjoyment or understanding of the poem, something distinctly 'dragged in', and only, perhaps, of interest as having suggested a pleasantly ambiguous line. For unless an allusion is made to live identifiably, to flower where transplanted, it is otiose. We admit the beauty of the implicational or allusive method; but the key to an implication should be in the implication itself, not outside of it. We admit the value of the esoteric pattern; but the pattern should disclose its secret, should not be dependent on a cypher. Mr Eliot assumes for his allusions, and for the fact that they actually allude to something, an importance which the allusions themselves do not, as expressed, aesthetically command, nor, as explained, logically comand; which is pretentious. He is a little pretentious, too, in his 'plan' – *qui pourtant n'existe pas*. If it is a plan, then its principle is oddly akin to planlessness. Here and there, in the wilderness, a broken finger-post.

I enumerate these objections not, I must emphasize, in derogation of the poem, but to dispel, if possible, an allusion as to its nature. It is perhaps important to note that Mr Eliot, with his comment on the 'plan', and several critics, with their admiration of the poem's woven complexity, minister to the idea that *The Waste Land* is, precisely, a kind of epic in a walnut shell: elaborate, ordered, unfolded with a logic at every joint discernible; but it is also important to note that this idea is false. With or without the notes the poem belongs rather to that symbolical order in which one may justly say that the 'meaning' is not explicitly, or exactly, worked out. Mr Eliot's net is wide, its meshes are small; and he catches a good deal more – thank heaven – than he pretends to. If space permitted one could pick out many lines and passages and parodies and quotations which do not demonstrably, in any 'logical' sense, carry forward the theme, passages which unjustifiably, but happily, 'expand' beyond its purpose. Thus the poem has an emotional value far clearer and richer than its arbitrary and rather unworkable logical value. One might assume that it originally consisted of a number of separate poems which have been telescoped – given a kind of forced unity. The Waste Land conception offered itself as a generous net which would, if not unify, at any rate contain these varied elements. We are aware of this superficial 'binding' – we observe the anticipation and repetition of themes, motifs; 'Fear death by water' anticipates the episode of Phlebas, the cry of the nightingale is repeated; but these are pretty flimsy links, and do not genuinely bind because they do not reappear naturally, but arbitrarily. This suggests, indeed, that Mr Eliot is perhaps attempting a kind of programme music in words, endeavouring to rule out 'emotional accidents' by supplying his readers, in notes, with only those associations which are correct. He himself hints at the musical analogy when he observes that 'In the first part of Part V three themes are employed'.

I think, therefore, that the poem must be taken – most invitingly offers itself – as a brilliant and kaleidoscopic confusion; as a series of sharp, discrete, slightly related perceptions and feelings, dramatically and lyrically presented, and violently juxtaposed (for effect of dissonance), so as to give us an impression of an intensely modern, intensely literary consciousness which perceives itself to be not a unit but a chance correlation or conglomerate of mutually discolorative fragments. We are invited into a mind, a world, which is a 'broken bundle of mirrors', a heap of broken images'. Isn't it that Mr Eliot, finding it 'impossible to say just what he means' – to recapitulate, to enumerate all the events and discoveries and memories that make a consciousness – has emulated the 'magic lantern' that throws 'the nerves in pattern on a screen'? If we perceive the poem in this light, as a series of brilliant, brief, unrelated or dimly related pictures by which a consciousness empties itself of its characteristic contents, then we also perceive that, anomalously, though the dropping out of any one picture would not in the least affect the logic or 'meaning' of the whole, it would seriously detract from the value of the portrait. The 'plan' of the poem would not greatly suffer, one makes bold to assert, by the elimination of 'April is the cruellest month' or Phlebas, or the Thames daughters, or Sosostris or 'You gave me hyacinths' or 'A woman drew her long black hair out tight'; nor would it matter if it did. These things are not important parts of an important or careful intellectual pattern; but they are important parts of an important emotional ensemble. The relations between Tiresias (who is said to unify the poem, in a sense, as spectator) and the Waste Land, or Mr Eugenides, or Hyacinth, or any other fragment, is a dim and tonal one, not exact. It will not bear analysis, it is not always operating, nor can one say with assurance, at any given point, how much it is operating. In this sense *The Waste Land* is a series of separate poems or passages, not perhaps all written at one time or with one aim, to which a spurious but happy sequence has been given. This spurious sequence has a value – it creates the necessary superficial formal unity; but it need not be stressed, as the notes stress it. Could one not wholly rely for one's unity – as Mr Eliot *has* largely relied – simply on the dim unity of 'personality' which would underlie the retailed contents of a single consciousness? Unless one is going to carry unification very far, weave and interweave very closely, it would perhaps be as well not to unify it at all; to dispense, for example, with arbitrary repetitions.

We reach thus the conclusion that the poem succeeds – as it brilliantly does – by virtue of its incoherence, not of its plan; by virtue of its ambiguities, not of its explanations. Its incoherence is a virtue because its *donnée* is incoherence. Its rich, vivid, crowded use of implication is a virtue, as implication is always a virtue – it shimmers, it suggests, it gives the desired strangeness. But when, as often, Mr Eliot uses an implication beautifully – conveys by means of a picture-symbol or action-symbol a feeling – we do not require to be told that he had in mind a passage in the *Encyclopedia*, or the colour of his nursery wall; the information is disquieting, has a sour air of pedantry. We 'accept' the poem as we would accept a powerful, melancholy tone-poem. We do not want to be told what occurs; nor is it more than mildly amusing to know what passages are, in the Straussian manner, echoes or parodies. We cannot believe that every syllable has an algebraic inevitability, nor would we wish it so. We could dispense with the French, Italian, Latin, and Hindu phrases – they are irritating. But when our reservations have all been made, we accept *The Waste Land* as one of the most moving and original poems of our time. It captures us. And we sigh, with a dubious eye on the 'notes' and 'plan', our bewilderment that after so fine a performance Mr Eliot should have thought it an occasion for calling 'Tullia's ape a marmosyte'. Tullia's ape is good enough.

T. S. ELIOT'S IMAGES OF AWARENESS

By Leonard Unger

IT is my intention to consider the poetry of T. S. Eliot according to a conventional mode of analysis, but with the hope of arriving at a fresh, or at least refreshed, awareness of the quality of the poetry. What I have in mind is the study of categories of images – by images meaning not only the visual but all the kinds of categories of reference. That certain images, themes, concepts, and so on prevail in Eliot's work is a fact that has long been familiar. In his critical prose Eliot gave emphasis to that kind of continuity and interrelatedness of a writer's work. This has been an increasingly conspicuous feature of his own work, and it is part of my task here to consider how details finally fit into a larger pattern.

My use of this familiar method will be limited. First, I will note what images prevail at the very opening of Eliot's career as a poet, and then I will examine some of these images as they appear in later stages of his work – meaning the plays as well as the poems. In offering a list of the images (or categories) which prevail in the poems of *Prufrock and Other Observations* I am admittedly influenced by the larger (meaning later) context of Eliot's work.

1. Flowers and gardens – eventually the rose and the rose-garden.

2. Water images of various kinds, especially under-water.

3. Months and seasons of the year, days of the week, periods of the day or night, the time of day.

4. Smoke and fog.

5. City streets.

6. Parts of the human body – especially arms, hands and fingers, legs and feet.

205

7. Human hair.
8. Stairs.
9. Images of music.
10. Images of smell.

The list is obviously not coordinate in an absolute and objective sense, but it is coordinate enough with respect to Eliot's poetry, and therefore enough for my purpose. Someone else might make a slightly different list, with alterations or extensions. For example, instead of stairs, or in addition, one might include houses and all their parts: rooms, doors, windows, floors, and so on. There may be other possibilities, but I believe that my list is essentially valid. There is one kind of image which I did not put in the list and which I mention separately because it is not coordinate with the others: this is the mind, or the awareness, for which all the other images exist.

Flowers and water are placed first on the list because I have discussed them in the past at some length.[1] In order to illustrate the merging of images, I have quoted the lines from *Marina* where these two kinds of images, as well as others, are merged.

Whispers and small laughter between leaves and hurrying feet
Under sleep, where all the waters meet.

Another example of such merging is to be seen in these lines from *The Waste Land*:

A woman drew her long black hair out tight
And fiddled whisper music on those strings. . . .

More common than such merging is the close association of several kinds of imagery. Any few lines from 'Preludes' provide an example, especially the following:

1. 'T. S. Eliot's Rose Garden', in *The Man in the Name*, and pamphlet 'T. S. Eliot' (especially pp. 35–7), both University of Minnesota Press, 1956 and 1961 respectively.

> The morning comes to consciousness
> Of faint stale smells of beer
> From the sawdust-trampled street
> With all its muddy feet that press
> To early coffee-stands.

Categories of the list present here are 3, 5, 6, and 10, as well as the image of awareness. As we turn to other purposes and other passages, we can observe, if we care to watch for them, how frequently the prevailing images occur in association with one another. The images which I shall examine in detail are the last three on the list: stairs, music, and smell – in that order. Each of these categories of imagery will serve in turn to guide us along certain directions and through certain realms of Eliot's work.

In the *Prufrock* group, the image of stairs occurs five times in as many poems.

> The October night comes down; returning as before
> Except for a slight sensation of being ill at ease
> I mount the stairs and turn the handle of the door
> And feel as if I had mounted on my hands and knees.
> > ('Portrait of a Lady')

> And indeed there will be time
> To wonder, 'Do I dare?' and, 'Do I dare?'
> Time to turn back and descend the stair,
> With a bald spot in the middle of my hair –
> > ('Prufrock')

> When evening quickens faintly in the street,
> Wakening the appetites of life in some
> And to others bringing the *Boston Evening Transcript*,
> I mount the steps and ring the bell, turning
> Wearily, as one would turn to nod good-bye to
>   La Rochefoucauld,
> If the street were time and he at the end of the street,
> And I say, 'Cousin Harriet, here is the *Boston Evening Transcript*.'
> > ('The *Boston Evening Transcript*')

Stand on the highest pavement of the stair –
Lean on a garden urn –
Weave, weave the sunlight in your hair –

('La Figlia che Piange')

The lamp said,
'Four o'clock,
Here is the number on the door.
Memory!
You have the key,
The little lamp spreads a ring on the stair.
Mount.
The bed is open; the tooth-brush hangs on the wall,
Put your shoes at the door, sleep, prepare for life.'

('Rhapsody on a Windy Night')

What are some significant features of these passages? In every case, the stairs are a literal reference. In addition to the stairs, there is always a person present in a position or in an activity relating to the stairs. In all the passages the stairs serve as the settings for arrivals and departures. I take it that Prufrock is contemplating a possible crisis of decision: having mounted the stair which leads to the entrance of a house, whether to enter and join his friends for 'the taking of a toast and tea', or whether 'to turn back and descend the stair'. In 'La Figlia' it is, of course, a man who has departed, leaving the girl to 'stand and grieve' at the top of the stair. Except for 'Rhapsody', each passage involves a troubled encounter between a man and a woman. This is emphatically so in 'Portrait' and 'La Figlia'. A troubled relation with women is intimated by the passage from 'Prufrock' just as it is intimated by the whole poem. In 'The *Boston Evening Transcript*' the relation between the speaker of the poem and his 'Cousin Harriet' is troubled only by ironic implication. Between the man and the woman there are no 'appetites of life' but only the *Boston Evening Transcript*. In the passage concluding 'Rhapsody' the man is returning to the solitude of his own quarters, but the quality of sexual anxiety is present here as it is in the complete poem and all the poems of the *Prufrock* group. Another point to be made about these images of the stairs is that in every case there is a character, the speaker, whose relation to the stairs includes what may be called a posture of awareness. There is some purpose here in comparing the phrase with its inversion, an awareness of posture. The speaker of 'Portrait' says that he feels '*as if* I had mounted on my hands and knees', thus giving the emphasis to a quality of awareness rather than to an actual posture. It should not be necessary to dwell on the passages from 'Prufrock', '*Boston Evening Transcript*', and 'Rhapsody' in order to claim that in each of these the stairs serve as the occasion or point of reference for a particular experience of awareness – which is in each case, including 'Portrait', a self-awareness. 'La Figlia' obviously differs from the others in the respect that it is the woman who is pictured on the stair, but she is so pictured by the speaker of the poem. The nature of some of the verbs in the poem, imperatives and conditionals, shows that the scenes of the poem are arrangements within the awareness of the speaker. The aspect of self-awareness derives, among other things, from the speaker's reference to 'my imagination' and 'these cogitations', and also from the identification, however indeterminate, between the 'I' and the 'he' of the poem.

Although, as noted, all these images of stairs are literal, when they are considered together and when it becomes evident that they have certain features in common, especially the quality of awareness, then the images, separately and collectively, acquire something which is beyond the literal. To the literalness of the image there has been added a measure of the symbolic.

In the rest of Eliot's poetry there are eleven occurrences of the imagery of stairs. These are of varying interest. The earliest, that of Princess Volupine preparing 'To climb the water-stair' ('Burbank with a Baedeker: Bleistein with a Cigar'), need be no more than noted. But there are two passages in *The Waste Land* which deserve closer attention. The first of these

comes in 'A Game of Chess', near the end of that opening
passage where there is the description of the woman seated
before her dressing-table, on which are her jewels and her perfumes.

> Footsteps shuffled on the stair.
> Under the firelight, under the brush, her hair
> Spread out in fiery points
> Glowed into words, then would be savagely still.
>
> 'My nerves are bad tonight. Yes, bad. Stay with me.
> 'Speak to me. Why do you never speak. Speak.'

And so on. A significant aspect of the image, the footsteps on
the stair, is the fact that it is the sole means by which the
man's arrival is reported, the only direct means by which his
presence is indicated. His presence is otherwise suggested by
the woman's form of address, and by the lines which are presumably his unspoken thoughts in the presence of the woman:
'I think we are in rats' alley. . . .'

The second image of stairs in *The Waste Land* comes in
'The Fire Sermon'. It is the last reference to the 'young man
carbuncular'.

> Bestows one final patronising kiss,
> And gropes his way, finding the stairs unlit . . .

The respects in which these two images relate to the *Prufrock*
set of images are obvious enough. They are both literal. One
image is of a man's arrival, and the other of a man's departure.
Each of the images involves a troubled encounter between a
man and a woman. The matter of awareness cannot be so
readily and so simply applied to these images as to those of the
early group. In the first image, however, it may be noted that
the man is, so to speak, kept out of sight except to the extent
of his awareness. As for the second image, the relevant awareness is that of Tiresias, who 'Perceived the scene, and foretold
the rest –' and whose voice narrates the encounter between the
typist and the young man. For these two, it is awareness which

is lacking. He is assured, vain, and patronizing, and she is indifferent. He gropes his way in the dark, and she is 'Hardly aware of her departed lover'. The groping and the stairs being unlit give this image a symbolic quality. But both stair images of *The Waste Land* have a symbolic inclination also because they have features which can be associated with the images of the *Prufrock* set. At this point there arises the consideration that if an image occurs frequently enough to become thematic, then it has in a respect also become symbolic.

At the opening of *Sweeney Agonistes*, when the telephone is ringing and Doris knows that it is Pereira calling, she asks Dusty to answer and to make any of several excuses for her, including this one: 'Say I broke my leg on the stairs.' In itself this image is of little interest, but it becomes more important when it is considered along with other images of the stairs as hazardous and unreliable. These appear in the plays *Murder in the Cathedral* and *The Cocktail Party*. In the earlier play there is the statement, 'A man may climb the stair in the day, and slip on a broken step', which we shall notice again in another connexion. In *The Cocktail Party* the image of stairs occurs in a passage of dialogue addressed to Edward Chamberlayne by the psychiatrist Sir Henry Harcourt-Reilly while he is still, in the early moments of the play, the Unidentified Guest:

> When you've dressed for a party
> And are going downstairs, with everything about you
> Arranged to support you in the role you have chosen,
> Then sometimes, when you come to the bottom step
> There is one step more than your feet expected
> And you come down with a jolt. Just for a moment
> You have the experience of being an object
> At the mercy of a malevolent staircase.

This imagery enriches the sub-category of stairs (as hazardous and unreliable) by relating it so dramatically to the conditions of awareness and of unawareness, and to the experience of a sudden shift in awareness.

The remaining images of stairs are to be found in *A Song for Simeon, Ash-Wednesday, Murder in the Cathedral,* and *Burnt Norton.* All of them are symbolic in one respect or another. Those requiring the briefest mention may be noted first. The 'saints' stair', in the final strophe of *A Song for Simeon,* and 'the figure of the ten stairs', in the final strophe of *Burnt Norton,* are both more effectively symbols than images – comparable to (and deriving from) the image of the ladder, which symbolizes some aspects of the spiritual discipline described by St John of the Cross in his *Dark Night of the Soul. Murder in the Cathedral* contains three references to stairs, which I shall consider in reverse order of their appearance. In the early moments of Part II, Thomas is addressed accusingly and contemptuously by the Four Knights speaking in unison, and their speech contains this statement:

> This is the man who was the tradesman's son:
> the backstairs brat who was born in Cheapside....

It is hardly an image. The Knights are berating Thomas with an account of his lowly origins and devious behaviour, and 'backstairs', by dictionary definition, conveys both these meanings. It need not convey both meanings at the same time, but it does as spoken here by the Knights. The second reference, more decidedly an image, comes in a stichomythic set of lines spoken by Chorus, Priests, and Tempters near the end of Part I.

> C: A man may walk with a lamp at night,
>   and yet be drowned in a ditch.
> P: A man climb the stair in the day, and
>   slip on a broken step.
> T: A man may sit at meat, and feel the cold
>   in his groin.

The image here has both literal and symbolic aspects. Climbing the stair by day, like walking with a lamp by night or sitting at meat, is a characteristic or typical activity, and as such also symbolic. The image is comparable to Eliot's earlier

212

usages, those in the *Prufrock* group, in that the detail of slipping on a broken step implies the ideas of awareness and of unawareness. The third image comes a few moments earlier and it is the most interesting. It is spoken by the Fourth Tempter, the only genuine tempter because he offers what Thomas himself has desired – martyrdom, sainthood, heavenly grandeur. In the passage containing the image the Tempter is revealing his knowledge of Thomas's own thoughts – that the shrine and the fame of sainthood will decay or be destroyed, and that the only part of sainthood worth desiring is the 'heavenly grandeur'. The Tempter says,

> Your thoughts have more power than kings to compel you.
> You have also thought, sometimes at your prayers,
> Sometimes hesitating at the angles of stairs,
> And between sleep and waking, early in the morning,
> When the bird cries, have thought of further scorning. . . .
> That the shrine shall be pillaged. . . .

The activities mentioned here, like those in the stichomythic set above, are meant to be characteristic and typical, and they are also much more highly specialized. While the others are things which any man may do, these activities have a special appropriateness for Thomas, the Archbishop. The detail of prayers has a specific relevance to the play and to the immediate context, but the other details have a more striking poetic quality and are otherwise of particular interest. The stairs, the time between sleep and waking, the early morning, the cry of the bird, all of these occur a number of times in Eliot's work and usually they signify a special moment of awareness. It may be noted that the last three details – sleep and waking, morning, bird-cry – are all descriptive elements of the same moment, so that the image of stairs is the central image of the series here, just as it is in the stichomythic set, and thus the stairs images receive in each case this same kind of emphasis. The clearest and most important fact about the stairs image here is that it is also an image of awareness:

'hesitating at the angles of stairs'. The Tempter has already said that these are occasions of 'thought', and the 'hesitating' – along with the detail of the 'angle' – gives dramatic emphasis to the nature of the occasion. The image here is, indeed, the posture of awareness, the symbol of awareness, and in so being it relates with marked significance to the images of the *Prufrock* poems. Each of those images is wholly circumstantial and literal in its own context, but when we observe that they share a common quality, then in their collective aspect they yield the paradigm of the posture of awareness. The image in the play is literal, but also general, and in its generality it is as a paradigm of the earlier set of images. The earlier images have a symbolic inclination, and the later image, by its generality and by its relation to the earlier, has an even sharper symbolic inclination.

We have already noted the image which appears in the opening lines of the last strophe of *Burnt Norton*:

> The detail of the pattern is movement,
> As in the figure of the ten stairs.

The stairs here are strictly a symbol of the order of paradigm, so acknowledged within the lines by the words 'pattern' and 'figure'. It is this paradigm of the stairs which is applied and elaborated to form the entire third section of *Ash-Wednesday*. All of Eliot's images of stairs, earlier and later, are consummated in this poem. As just stated, the activity of climbing stairs is the inclusive symbol. All the earlier images of stairs show an inclination toward the symbolic, and here the symbol is literalized, so to speak, in that the image is extended into a number of details. It is thus something like a metaphysical conceit. It is actually allegory, but allegory so vivid in its imagery that we may say that the meanings are not only signalized, but persuasively dramatized. As in the earlier instances, the climber of the stairs is also the speaker of the poem. If there is no troubled encounter between a man and a woman, there are the sexually 'distracting' images of the third strophe, from the 'slotted window bellied like the fig's fruit' through 'brown hair over the mouth blown, ... music of the flute, stops and steps of the mind over the third stair'. At the opening of each of the three main strophes of the poem, the speaker is at a 'turning of the ... stair', which is precisely the same posture of awareness as 'hesitating at the angles of stairs'. Just such 'hesitating' is stated in the words 'stops and steps of the mind over the third stair'. With the reference to the 'mind', the image might seem to be losing its dramatic vividness, becoming transparent, and revealing too obtrusively the allegorized meaning. But this consideration is made only to be rejected, so that emphasis may be given to the reverse idea, which is actually the truth – for this phrasing about the 'mind', with its 'stops and steps', produces the most vivid image of the poem, the one in which all the actions and situations of the poem are condensed and intensified. The image is, of course, the posture of awareness. Throughout Eliot's works, the experience of awareness is itself often a vividly realized image, as it is here in conjunction with the imagery of stairs.

*

While the analogy between music and poetry has always been obvious, it may be said that this analogy was a preoccupation for Eliot. The subject is explored and clarified in one of his finest lectures, 'The Music of Poetry'. Titles of poems which show the analogy are 'Preludes', 'Rhapsody on a Windy Night', the 'Five-finger Exercises' among the Minor Poems, and, of course, *Four Quartets*.

My remarks on images of music will not run parallel to those made on images of stairs. But I do wish to indicate that the two kinds of images have a common quality: they are both involved in what I have called Eliot's image of awareness. I shall not attempt to give an exhaustive account of images of music but will attend only to those which relate to the idea of awareness, and not even all of these will have an equal relevance. It so happens that these images appear in some of the

poems of the *Prufrock* group, the poem which is the third
section of *Ash-Wednesday*, and in *Four Quartets*. The earliest
of the *Prufrock* poems, 'Conversation galante', provides the
first instance:

> And I then: 'Someone frames upon the keys
> That exquisite nocturne, with which we explain
> The night and moonshine; music which we seize
> To body forth our own vacuity.'

The statement is derogatory with regard to the 'exquisite
nocturne' and those who listen to it – to paraphrase, the music
is a particularized representation of the mental emptiness of
the listeners. In still other words, the image of the music
serves also as an image of human awareness – such as it is in
this case.

In the poem 'Prufrock' there are only two images of music:

> I know the voices dying with a dying fall
> Beneath the music from a farther room.

> I have heard the mermaids singing, each to each.

It may be said of these passages that in each case the music is
overheard. This observation is relevant to the fact that Eliot
often indicates the degree of awareness and the kind of awareness with which the music is heard.

'Portrait of a Lady' is the one poem of which music is a
prevailing motif. The poem opens with the man and woman
having just arrived at the woman's room after attending a
concert of Chopin's *Preludes*.

> We have been, let us say, to hear the latest Pole ...

With the words 'let us say' the occasion is presented as typical
as well as specific. The phrase also serves to intimate that the
entire poem is recited within the memory of the man, who is
the speaker of the poem, rather than simply narrated according
to the indeterminate occasion of literary convention. So considered, the poem approaches the kind of 'interior monologue'

which is fully developed in 'Prufrock'. The perspective of memory and typicality and the mode of interior monologue are decidedly resumed in the final passage of the poem. Returning to the first section, we note that as 'the conversation slips', the sounds of violins and cornets echo in the mind of the man, thus indicating a diffusion of awareness and a quality of strain and distress in the man's relation with both music and woman. Since Chopin's *Preludes* are exclusively for piano, the shift in reference to violins and cornets contributes to the diffusion of awareness. Finally, to the mingled sounds of these instruments and the woman's conversation there is added an actual headache, which is represented in musical terms

> Inside my brain a dull tom-tom begins
> Absurdly hammering a prelude of its own,
> Capricious monotone
> That is at least one definite 'false note.'

The second section of the poem contains two images of music, both of which present music as unwelcome invasions of awareness. In the first of these the voice of the woman is again associated with the irritating sound of a musical instrument.

> The voice returns like the insistent out-of-tune
> Of a broken violin on an August afternoon. ...

The second image comes in the final lines of the section, at the end of a passage of interior monologue where the speaker describes himself as he might be found reading the newspaper 'any morning in the park';

> I keep my countenance,
> I remain self-possessed
> Except when a street-piano, mechanical and tired
> Reiterates some worn-out common song
> With the smell of hyacinths across the garden
> Recalling things that other people have desired.
> Are these ideas right or wrong?

217

In this passage the speaker tells of one kind of awareness being displaced by another. While reading the newspaper, he is self-possessed, a spectator standing aside from the commotions of the world, of other people – until the common song of the street-piano and the smell of hyacinths provoke an awareness of 'things ... desired', desired by the speaker himself as well as by 'other people'. The speaker loses his self-possession when he becomes aware of the desires which are common to mankind, including himself. This dichotomy between desire and the newspaper is the same as that between 'the appetites of life' and the *Boston Evening Transcript*.

The third section of the poem contains a single image of music. This comes in the very last lines of the poem, at the end of the passage already noted as being decidedly in the mode of an interior monologue. The passage opens with the speaker speculating on the possibility of the woman's death and on how that event might affect him, and then the poem ends:

> Would she not have the advantage, after all?
> This music is successful with a 'dying fall'
> Now that we talk of dying –
> And should I have the right to smile?

The words in quotation marks are so put, presumably, because Eliot intended an allusion to the opening lines of *Twelfth Night*, where Duke Orsino says, 'If music be the food of love, play on! ... That strain again! It had a dying fall. ...' But the music in Eliot's poem is not the food of love. I shall evade most of the complex multiple ironies and ambiguities with which the poem ends in order to consider a matter which is complex enough. With the speaker's reference to the poem as 'music' the identity of the speaker merges with that of the poet. 'Portrait of a Lady' is primarily a portrait of the man who speaks the poem, just as 'The Love Song of J. Alfred Prufrock' is a portrait of Prufrock, and both poems are in some respects portraits of the poet. Both poems are concerned with problems of love, including self-love. Each is a dramatic representation (especially in its conclusion) of an awareness which is contemplating itself, contemplating not only narcissistically, but also

> like one who smiles, and turning shall remark
> Suddenly, his expression in a glass.

The imagery of music in the *Prufrock* group is something less than lovely. In *Ash-Wednesday* the imagery is lovely, in itself and in its associations, but it is again an invasion of awareness. There is one main image of music, and this appears in that passage of the third section already noted:

At the first turning of the third stair
Was a slotted window bellied like the fig's fruit
And beyond the hawthorn blossom and a pasture scene
The broadbacked figure drest in blue and green
Enchanted the maytime with an antique flute.
Blown hair is sweet, brown hair over the mouth blown,
Lilac and brown hair;
Distraction, music of the flute, stops and steps of the mind over the third stair,
Fading, fading; strength beyond hope and despair
Climbing the third stair.

This sweet flute music, symbolizing the sweetness of the flesh, ✔ is a distraction, an alternate awareness, a 'stop' of the mind in its effort to climb the stair (which is the spiritual discipline of purgation). In the fourth section there is an imagery of the absence of music, for 'the fiddles and the flutes' are borne away, and while the Priapus-like figure appears again, his 'flute is breathless'.

All images of music in *Four Quartets* share a common quality: in no instance is the music both literally and normally heard. In *East Coker* 'the music/Of the weak pipe and the little drum' is part of the imagined scene in which the sixteenth-century men and women of the town dance 'around the bonfire'. Eliot relates the rhythm of this dancing to the complex rhythms of life and death in all of nature, but I am concerned here only with the pipe and drum as summoned by the imagination. A comparably simple image appears at the opening of the third section of *The Dry Salvages*, with 'the future is a faded song'. This is the familiar idea that all things are fleeting, moving into the past, including the times to come. The song is faded in the sense of being over-familiar, worn-out, and also in the sense of having faded from hearing.

The remaining images of music in *Four Quartets* are more complex. They are related to each other, and they are related also to some of Eliot's central poetic ideas and most compelling themes – essentially one idea and one theme, one and the same. We can briefly review this point by referring to a familiar passage at the end of the second section of *Burnt Norton*:

> Time past and time future
> Allow but a little consciousness.
> To be conscious is not to be in time
> But only in time can the moment in the rose-garden . . .
> Be remembered; involved with past and future.
> Only through time time is conquered.

Throughout *Four Quartets* the idea of the transcending of time and the theme of recapturing the childhood experience of the ecstatic moment in the rose-garden are expressed a number of times. In three such passages there are references to music. The first of these – 'unheard music hidden in the shrubbery' – appears in the rose-garden passage at the opening of *Burnt Norton*. The characteristics of the music here – 'unheard' and 'hidden' – occur in rose-garden passages throughout *Four Quartets* and are associated with an imagery of laughing children hidden among leaves or shrubbery. This occurs in the passage under consideration, with the words 'the leaves were full of children,/Hidden excitedly, containing laughter'. It occurs again in *Burnt Norton* at the very end: 'the hidden laughter/Of children in the foliage'. In the third section of *East Coker* it occurs within a catalogue of related images:

Whisper of running streams, and winter lightning.
The wild thyme unseen and the wild strawberry,
The laughter in the garden, echoed ecstasy
Not lost, but requiring, pointing to the agony
Of death and birth.

There is, finally, the imagery near the end of *Little Gidding*:

> At the source of the longest river
> The voice of the hidden waterfall
> And the children in the apple-tree
> Not known, because not looked for
> But heard, half-heard, in the stillness
> Between two waves of the sea.

A somewhat different image of music (because not contained in a rose-garden passage) comes at the opening of the final section of *Burnt Norton*:

> Words move, music moves
> Only in time; but that which is only living
> Can only die. Words, after speech, reach
> Into the silence. Only by the form, the pattern,
> Can words or music reach
> The stillness, as a Chinese jar still
> Moves perpetually in its stillness.
> Not the stillness of the violin, while the note lasts,
> Not that only, but the co-existence,
> Or say that the end precedes the beginning,
> And the end and the beginning were always there
> Before the beginning and after the end,
> And all is always now.

Here there is an analogy between poetry and music in the respect that these temporal arts may, by the completeness of form, achieve (or illustrate) the transcending of time. It should not be necessary to attempt an elaborate comment on this passage in order to indicate that there is a common element in the two images of music: the first is 'unheard', and the second is associated with 'silence' and 'stillness'. A final image, in the last section of *The Dry Salvages*, combines characteristics of the first two:

> For most of us, there is only the unattended
> Moment, the moment in and out of time,
> The distraction fit, lost in a shaft of sunlight,
> The wild thyme unseen, or the winter lightning
> Or the waterfall, or music heard so deeply
> That it is not heard at all, but you are the music
> While the music lasts.

This image of music is contained in a catalogue of images which are recurrent in Eliot's work and which provide the occasions for, and therefore the symbols of, 'the moment in and out of time'. But unlike the other images in the catalogue, it has its own logic for the transcending of time, which is in accordance with the idea of 'form' and 'pattern' set forth in the previous quotation. The image here is striking in still other respects. Like so many of the earlier images of music, this one too represents an invasion of awareness – except that this image is better described as an identification with awareness. Such too was the earliest image of music, that which bodies forth 'our own vacuity' in 'Conversation galante'. But this image is again striking in its contrast, because the music fills entirely our depths of awareness. Just as 'stops and steps of the mind over the third stair' is, in its context, a consummation of all of Eliot's imagery of stairs, so is this 'music heard so deeply' a consummation of all his imagery of music.

In Eliot's play *The Confidential Clerk* there is another kind of reverberation of the imagery of music. The difference here is that music is a subject which is central to the action of the play. At the opening of the play Colby Simpkins is the disappointed organist who has become the new confidential clerk to his quasi-father Sir Claude Mulhammer, and at the end of the play he has decided to leave this position in order to become the organist of an obscure parish church. Throughout the play there is much discussion of music, usually in its relation to special problems of awareness. But since there are so many references to the subject, we shall consider only those few points which are most closely related to the ideas we have been following.

The interchanges of dialogue which are about music are among the most revealing of the play. The first of these, near the end of Act I, is between Colby and Sir Claude. While Colby is a disappointed musician, it turns out that Sir Claude is a disappointed potter – and it is in their identities as disappointed artists, but still as artists, that the two commune with each other. Speaking of his pottery, Sir Claude says:

> To be among such things,
> If it is an escape, it is escape into living,
> Escape from a sordid world to a pure one. . . .
> I want a world where the form is the reality,
> Of which the substantial is only a shadow.
> . . . . Do you feel at all like that
> When you are alone with your music?

And Colby answers:

> Just the same.
> All the time you've been speaking, I've been translating
> Into terms of music.

This comparison between pottery and music reminds us inevitably of the comparison made in the last section of *Burnt Norton* between 'the form, the pattern' of words and music on the one hand and the 'Chinese jar' on the other.

Another revealing (and extensive) dialogue, at the opening of Act II, is that in which the communing is between Colby and Lucasta, Sir Claude's illegitimate daughter. In the earlier dialogue music is associated with the idea of pure form as represented by pottery, and in this dialogue it is associated with a quality of experience represented by the familiar and recurrent symbolic imagery of the garden – as in these words addressed to Colby by Lucasta:

223

And *your* garden is a garden
Where you hear a music that no one else could hear,
And the flowers have a scent that no one else could smell.

Finally, of course, Colby chooses, not the solitary experience of music and garden, but the position of organist in the parish church of Joshua Park – which is also a return to his music, but with a changed attitude, a new awareness.

*

A famous phrase in Eliot's early criticism is that of feeling one's thought 'as immediately as the odour of a rose'. Although the theoretical concept of the fusion of thought and feeling is no longer accepted as valid, the phrase remains an engaging one. This is so because the operation and effect of the phrase are actually poetic rather than theoretical. In this poetic phrase there is, in a sense, a fusion of thought and feeling. The phrase is one of Eliot's images of awareness. The image of the rose and the image of smell serve to produce an image of thought.

I have referred to this phrase by way of turning to the imagery of smell in Eliot's work. Such imagery is conspicuous among the early poems, involved in the effects of distress and dejection which prevail. For example, in 'Preludes' there are the 'smell of steaks in passageways' and 'faint stale smells of beer'. In 'Rhapsody on a Windy Night' there is a catalogue of such images – 'old nocturnal smells'. Of particular interest are 'a paper rose,/That smells of dust and eau de Cologne' and 'female smells in shuttered rooms'. The latter conveys the theme of sexual anxiety, already noted in connexion with other kinds of images. Eliot expressed the theme a number of times with further images of the order of 'female smells', such as the couplet in 'Prufrock':

> Is it perfume from a dress
> That makes me so digress?

In 'Whispers of Immortality' there is the 'rank ... feline smell' distilled by 'Grishkin in a drawing-room'. In *The*

Waste Land, in the opening passage of 'A Game of Chess', there is an elaborate imagery of the 'strange synthetic perfumes' of the woman whose 'nerves are bad tonight'.

I have delayed referring to 'the smell of hyacinths across the garden', in 'Portrait of a Lady', because that image requires special consideration. As noted earlier, the passage in which the image appears tells of an invasion of awareness, whereby the speaker of the poem is distracted from his newspaper by the street-piano and the hyacinths. These provoke him to recall 'things that other people have desired'. Indeed, the passage may be read so that it is simply the hyacinths which produce this effect. In any event, it is the evocative fragrance of the flowers which contributes intimations of poignancy to the occasion on which the street-piano is heard. In the larger context of Eliot's work, the hyacinths recall the 'hyacinth girl' of *The Waste Land* and thus the entire body of rose-garden imagery with all its familiar details and meanings. As an invasion of awareness, the 'smell of hyacinths' is also comparable to the distracting 'perfume from a dress' in 'Prufrock'. The two images also contrast with each other, thus representing the characteristic polarities of Eliot's female references: on the one hand the idealized figure ruefully lost and/or poignantly remote, and on the other hand a female presence which is repulsive in its physical immediacy.

Images of smell in Eliot's later poetry (excluding the plays) are for the most part references to the smell of growing things and of earth and sea. I will merely note some of these and dwell briefly on others. There are these in *Ariel Poems:* the 'valley ... smelling of vegetation' in *Journey of the Magi*, 'the fragrant brilliance of the Christmas tree' in *Animula*, and 'scent of pine' in *Marina*. More impressive images appear in the last section of *Ash-Wednesday*:

> And the lost heart stiffens and rejoices
> In the lost lilac and the lost sea voices
> And the weak spirit quickens to rebel
> For the bent golden-rod and the lost sea smell

Quickens to recover
The cry of quail and the whirling plover
And the blind eye creates
The empty forms between the ivory gates
And smell renews the salt savour of the sandy earth

In this statement of nostalgic recall of the delights of the senses, the sense of smell stands vividly in the foreground. In *Four Quartets* the few images of smell are of this kind – smells of nature. At the opening of *The Dry Salvages*, there are 'the rank ailanthus of the April dooryard' and 'the smell of grapes on the autumn table', both nostalgically associated with the rhythm of the river. At the opening of *Little Gidding*, in the description of 'Midwinter spring', it is the absence of smell which is noted: 'There is no earth smell/Or smell of living thing.'

Among Eliot's plays, it is chiefly the early ones – *Murder in the Cathedral* and *The Family Reunion* – which have images of smell. In these plays such imagery is more than incidental. The images are, in fact, of great importance, and they are all of the same kind. In both plays Eliot uses the sense of smell to represent the deepest and most intense kind of awareness. In *Murder in the Cathedral* Eliot has the Chorus use an imagery of all the senses, but especially smell, to express its sense (or awareness) of evil. This device is first used briefly in each of the last two speeches spoken by the Chorus toward the end of Part I:

There is no rest in the house. There is no rest in the street.
I hear restless movement of feet. And the air is heavy and thick.
Thick and heavy the sky. And the earth presses up beneath my feet.
What is the sickly smell, the vapour?

God is leaving us, God is leaving us, more pang, more pain, than birth or death.
Sweet and cloying through the dark air
Falls the stifling scent of despair. . . .

In Part II, following Thomas's first encounter with the threatening Knights, this thematic imagery is developed with elaborate detail in a long speech delivered by the Chorus. I shall quote selectively, including all of the figurative references to the senses:

> I have smelt them, the death-bringers, senses are
>   quickened
> By subtile forebodings; I have heard
> Fluting in the nighttime, . . . have seen at noon
> Scaly wings. . . . I have tasted
> The savour of putrid flesh in the spoon. I have felt
> The heaving of earth at nightfall. . . . I have heard
> Laughter in the noises of beasts. . . . I have seen
> Grey necks twisting, . . . I have eaten
> Smooth creatures still living, . . . I have tasted
> The living lobster, the crab, the oyster, . . . I have smelt
> Death in the rose, . . . I have seen
> Trunk and horn, tusk and hoof, in odd places. . . .
>   . . . I have felt
> The horn of the beetle, . . . I have smelt
> Corruption in the dish, incense in the latrine,
>   the sewer in the incense, the smell of sweet
>   soap in the woodpath, a hellish sweet scent
>   in the woodpath, while the ground heaved. I
>   have seen
> Rings of light coiling downwards, leading
> To the horror of the ape. . . .
> I have smelt them, the death-bringers. . . .

In this rhapsody of grotesque and nightmarish sensory images, it is the sense of smell, opening and closing the series, which is the dominant motif.

At some of the most crucial and most intense moments in the development of *The Family Reunion*, the imagery of smell appears as a vivid expression of awareness. Shortly after the opening of the play, Harry tells the members of his family that

he is alienated from them because they do not share his awareness of evil and guilt:

> I tell you, life would be unendurable
> If you were wide awake. You do not know
> The noxious smell untraceable in the drains,
> Inaccessible to the plumbers, that has its hour of the night; you
>   do not know
> The unspoken voice of sorrow in the ancient bedroom
> At three o'clock in the morning. I am not speaking
> Of my own experience, but trying to give you
> Comparisons in a more familiar medium. I am the old house
> With the noxious smell and the sorrow before morning,
> In which all past is present, all degradation
> Is unredeemable.

In *The Family Reunion* there are two other occasions when
comparisons are made in the familiar medium of smell. In
Part I, Scene II, after an extended dialogue with his cousin
Mary, Harry arrives at a moment of unexpected elation –
'Sunlight and singing' – which is almost immediately dispelled
by his sudden awareness of the presence of the ghosts. He
describes the awareness:

> That apprehension deeper than all sense,
> Deeper than the sense of smell, but like a smell
> In that it is indescribable, a sweet and bitter smell
> From another world.

The image of 'Sunlight and singing' is an intimation of the
rose-garden experience – which emerges fully in Part II,
Scene II, where Harry and his aunt Agatha speak with shared
knowledge of this experience, and of the prolonged suffering
which is in contrast to it. Each in turn refers to this suffering
with an image of smell – first Harry, with 'contagion of
putrescent embraces/On dissolving bone', and then Agatha,
with 'an immense and empty hospital/Pervaded by a smell of
disinfectant...'. After such references Harry and Agatha

speak again of the rose-garden, and then Harry is suddenly aware of the presence of the ghosts – the awareness, as before, compared to the sense of smell:

> Do you feel a kind of stirring underneath the air?
> Do you? don't you? a communication, a scent
> Direct to the brain ... but not just as before,
> Not quite like, not the same ...

'Not the same', since the restored moment of the rose-garden leads immediately into a scene of recognition and reversal, where Harry sees the ghosts whom he has been fleeing – the Eumenides – as 'bright angels' whom he now wishes to follow.

There is an image of smell in Eliot's latest poem, 'A Dedication to My Wife', which is on the last page of *Collected Poems 1909–1962*. An earlier version of this poem appeared at the front of the volume of Eliot's play *The Elder Statesman*, where it is called simply 'To My Wife':

To whom I owe the leaping delight
That quickens my senses in our wakingtime
And the rhythm that governs the repose of our sleepingtime,
    The breathing in unison

Of lovers ...
Who thinks the same thoughts without need of speech
And babble the same speech without need of meaning:

To you I dedicate this book, to return as best I can
With words a little part of what you have given me.
The words mean what they say, but some have a further meaning
    For you and me only.

In the later version the broken line is completed – 'Of lovers whose bodies smell of each other'. The colon after 'meaning' has been changed to a period. The entire last stanza has been dropped and these lines added:

No peevish winter wind shall chill
No sullen tropic sun shall wither
The roses in the rose-garden which is ours and ours only

But this dedication is for others to read:
These are private words addressed to you in public.

The punctuation after 'lovers', indicating a deletion, makes clear that Eliot considered the entire line an essential part of the poem. The sign of deletion tells us that the line belonged to the poem from the start, and that Eliot intended for it to be revealed eventually – and less conspicuously, as it is in the *Collected Poems*. The line is thus both inconspicuous and conspicuous – and I take this to be a typical example of Eliot's well-known serious wit. Another aspect of his familiar wittiness here is the fact that the line is shocking, for the witty and the shocking are sometimes closely related effects of the same occasion. The image of 'lovers whose bodies smell of each other' is not only an image of awareness, but of shared awareness, which is the subject of the entire passage and the entire poem. Such awareness, in being shared, differs significantly from so many of Eliot's images of awareness, which are images of isolation and of exclusively held intensities. The image of smell here also differs markedly from Eliot's earlier images of the human body, especially the female.

The revised ending of the poem is an improvement. In the earlier ending there is some ambiguity regarding the 'words' – are they the words of the play or the words of the dedication? My own first impression was that they are the words of the play. In any event the earlier ending speaks in effect of public words which have a private meaning, whereas the revised ending speaks of 'private words addressed ... in public' (the words, clearly, of the dedication) – and that is certainly more to the point. The private words about the smell of lovers' bodies are shocking because they are 'addressed ... in public' by T. S. Eliot, whereas they would not be shocking from another poet – Yeats, for example. In the later stages of his career – in the later plays and lectures – Eliot was concerned with changes of attitude and readjustments of position. With the private-public words of the dedication Eliot was, among other things, readjusting the image of himself. The shocking image of the smell of lovers' bodies finds its place in the larger pattern – and we become aware that the pattern, and the shock, are somewhat altered.

A BABYLONISH DIALECT[1]

By Frank Kermode

IN the middle thirties, emerging from my remote provincial background (but we wrote poems and asked whether Browning didn't sometimes go beyond bounds), I at last discovered Yeats and Eliot; and in that bewilderment one truth seemed worth steering by, which was that these men were *remaking* poetry. Although this recognition had very little to do with knowledge, and one waited years before being granted any real notion of the character of such poetry, it was nevertheless, as I still believe, a genuine insight. As one came to know the other great works of the wonderful years, one also came with increasing certainty to see that the imperative of modernism was 'make it new': a difficult but in the end satisfactory formula.

These were the years of Auden, of a poetry oscillating between an inaccessible private mythology and public exhortation, an in-group apocalypse and a call for commitment to 'the struggle'. It was going to be our war; we were committed whether or not we wanted to be; and there were many poems of Auden especially which have by now disappeared from the canon, but not from the memories of men in their forties. Meanwhile, as the war approached, the indisputably great, the men of the wonderful years, were still at work. What were they doing? Their commitment they consigned, mostly, to the cooler element of prose; but we could hardly suppose they were with any part of their minds on our side. 'Making it new' seemed to be a process which had disagreeable consequences in the political sphere. I forget how we explained this to ourselves, but somehow we preserved the certainty that the older poets who behaved so strangely, seemed so harshly to absent

1. A short version of this essay appeared in *The New Statesman*, London, in 1965.

themselves from our world – to hold opinions in the age of the Bristol Bomber which were appropriate to the penny-farthing – were nevertheless the men on whom all depended.

The death of Yeats in January 1939 therefore seemed to us an event of catastrophic importance. The news of Eliot's death immediately brought to mind, in surprising detail, the events and feelings of that dark, cold day nearly twenty-six years earlier. These were the men who had counted most, yet had seemed to have so little in common with us. Yet on the face of it the two events seemed to have little similarity beyond what is obvious. In the months preceding Yeats's death there had been an extraordinary outpouring of poetry – how impatiently one awaited the next issue of *The London Mercury*, and, later, the publication in the spring of 1940 of *Last Poems and Plays*! And that wasn't all: there was the poet himself, masked as a wild old man or a dangerous sage; there was the samurai posturing, the learned, more than half-fascist, shouting about eugenics and war, and this at a moment when we were beginning to understand that the enemy would soon be imposing both these disciplines on Europe. But one didn't hate the poet for what he thought he knew, remembering that he had always held strange opinions without damaging his verse. 'Man can embody truth but he cannot know it,' he said in his last letter; and years before, in a line which gives modern poetry its motto, 'In dreams begin responsibilities.' He made no order, but showed that our real lives begin when we have been shown that order ends: it is for the dreams, the intuitions of irregularity and chaos, of the tragic rag-and-bone shop, that we value him, and not for his 'system' or his 'thought'. The time of his death seemed appropriate to the dream; in a few months the towns lay beaten flat.

History did not collaborate in the same way to remind us of the responsibilities begun in Eliot's dream. His farewell to poetry was taken only a couple of years after Yeats's. It was no deathbed 'Cuchulain Comforted'; it was *Little Gidding*. Perhaps the Dantesque section of that poem grew in part from

Yeats's strange poem; certainly Yeats predominates over the others who make up the 'familiar compound ghost'. The famous lines tell us what we ought to make of our great poetry and of our great poets:

> ... I am not eager to rehearse
>   My thoughts and theory which you have forgotten.
>   These things have served their purpose: let them be.
> So with your own. ...

So much for the using-up of a poet's thought. As a man he continues to suffer and without reward:

> Let me disclose the gifts reserved for age
>   To set a crown upon your lifetime's effort.
>   First, the cold friction of expiring sense. ...
> Second, the conscious impotence of rage
>   At human folly. ...
> And last, the rending pain of re-enactment
>   Of all that you have done, and been. ...

So the ghost speaks of a Yeatsian guilt, remorse, and purgation. The man who suffers is now truly distinct from the mind that creates poems that have to be, as Picasso said of paintings, 'hordes of destructions'.

It is customary now to speak of a 'tradition of the new' in American painting, and it may even be possible to do the same of American poetry. There is no such tradition in English poetry. That our contemporaries on the whole avoid Eliot's influence is probably not important; perhaps it is the case, as Auden said in his obituary notice, that Eliot cannot be imitated, only parodied. But it *is* important, I think, that his insistence on making it new, on treating every attempt as a wholly new start, is now discounted. It may be true, as is sometimes said, that this wholly exhausting doctrine is on cultural grounds more likely to be successful in the United States than in England; certainly much of the evidence points that way. But that does not entitle us to ignore the doctrine.

After such knowledge, what forgiveness? The lesson was that the craft of poetry can no longer be a matter of perpetuating dialects and imitating what was well made; it lies in an act of radical analysis, a return to the brute elements, to the matter which may have a potentiality of form; but last year's words will not find it. In consequence, the writing of major poetry seems more than ever before a ruinous and exhausting undertaking, and no poet deserves blame for modestly refusing to take it on, or even for coming to think of Eliot and his peers as Chinese walls across their literature.

This, of course, is to apply to Eliot the damaging epigram he devised for Milton. Sir Herbert Read tells me that the English poet for whom Eliot felt a conscious affinity, and upon whom he perhaps in some degree modelled himself, was Johnson. All the same it seems to me that the more we see of the hidden side of Eliot the more he seems to resemble Milton, though he thought of Milton as a polar opposite. As we look at all the contraries reconciled in Eliot – his schismatic traditionalism, his romantic classicism, his highly personal impersonality – we are prepared for the surprise (which Eliot himself seems in some measure to have experienced) of finding in the dissenting Whig regicide a hazy mirror-image of the Anglo-Catholic royalist. Each, having prepared himself carefully for poetry, saw that he must also, living in such times, explore prose, the cooler element. From a consciously archaic standpoint each must characterize the activities of the sons of Belial. Each saw that fidelity to tradition is ensured by revolutionary action. (Eliot would hardly have dissented from the proposition that 'a man may be a heretic in the truth'.) Each knew the difficulty of finding 'answerable style' in an age too late. With the Commonwealth an evident failure, Milton wrote one last book to restore it, and as the élites crumbled and reformed Eliot wrote his *Notes*. If Milton killed a king, Eliot attacked vulgar democracy and shared with the 'men of 1914' and with Yeats some extreme authoritarian opinions.

Milton had his apocalyptic delusions, but settled down in

aristocratic patience to wait for the failure of the anti-Christian experiment, 'meanwhile', as Eliot said in the conclusion of *Thoughts after Lambeth*, 'redeeming the time: so that the Faith may be preserved alive through the dark ages before us'. In the end, they thought, the elect, however shorn of power, all bring down the Philistine temple; and the self-begotten bird will return. As poets, they wrote with voluptuousness of youth, and with unmatched force of the lacerations of age. And each of them lived on into a time when it seemed there was little for them to say to their compatriots, God's Englishmen. Eliot can scarcely have failed to see this left-handed image of himself in a poet who made a new language for his poetry and who transformed what he took from a venerable tradition:

Our effort is not only to explore the frontiers of the spirit, but as much to regain, under very different conditions, what was known to men writing at remote times and in alien languages.

This is truly Miltonic; but Eliot at first moved away and pretended to find his reflection in the strong and lucid Dryden, deceiving many into supposing that he resembled that poet more than the lonely, fiercer maker of the new, of whom he said that it was 'something of a problem' to decide in what his greatness consisted.

However, a great poet need not always understand another; there may be good reasons why he should not. And Eliot certainly has the marks of a modern kind of greatness, those beneficial intuitions of irregularity and chaos, the truth of the foul rag-and-bone shop. Yet we remember him as celebrating order. Over the years he explored the implications of his attitudes to order, and it is doubtful whether many people capable of understanding him now have much sympathy with his views. His greatness will rest on the fruitful recognition of disorder, though the theories will have their interest as theories held by a great man.

Many of the doctrines are the product of a seductive thesis and its stern antithesis. The objective correlative, a term probably developed from the 'object correlative' of Santayana,[2] is an attempt to depersonalize what remains essentially the image of romantic poetry, and to purge it of any taint of simple expressiveness or rational communication. Its propriety is limited to Eliot's own earlier verse, which is deeply personal but made inexplicably so by the arbitrariness of its logical relations, its elaborate remoteness from the personal, and its position within a context which provides a sort of model of an impersonal 'tradition' – the fragments shored against our ruin. It is neither a matter of 'the logic of concepts' nor something that welled up from an a-logical unconscious; in so far as it has 'meaning', it has it in order to keep the intellect happy while the poem does it work, and in so far as it has not, it has not in order to distinguish it from poems that 'make you conscious of having been written by somebody'.[3] The 'dissociation of sensibility' is an historical theory to explain the dearth of objective correlatives in a time when the artist, alienated from his environment, *l'immonde cité*, is working at the beginning of a dark age 'under conditions that seem unpropitious', in an ever-worsening climate of imagination.

Such theories, we now see, are highly personal versions of stock themes in the history of ideas of the period. They have been subtly developed and are now increasingly subject to criticism. The most persistent and influential of them, no doubt, is the theory of tradition. In a sense it is Cubist historiography, unlearning the trick of perspective and ordering history as a system of perpetually varying spatial alignments. Tradition is always unexpected, hard to find, easily confused with worthless custom; and it is emblematic that a father of

2. In a letter to Mr Nimai Chatterji in 1955, Eliot says he thought he 'coined' the expression, but discovered that it had been used by Washington Allston. Eliot adds characteristically that he is not 'quite sure of what I meant 35 years ago'. (Letter in *New Statesman*, 5 March 1965, p. 361.
3. This is from an early essay on Pound (*Athenaeum*, 24 October 1919) quoted by C. K. Stead in his interesting book *The New Poetic*, 1964, p. 132.

modernism should call himself Anglican, for the early Anglicans upset the whole idea of tradition in much this way.

He also called himself royalist, and this is an aspect of a larger and even more surprising traditionalism; for Eliot, in a weirdly pure sense, was an imperialist. This may seem at odds with certain aspects of his thought – his nostalgia for closed societies, his support for American agrarianism; but in the end, although he suppressed *After Strange Gods*, they grow from the same root. The essay on Dante, which is one of the true masterpieces of modern criticism, has been called a projection onto the medieval poet of Eliot's own theories of diction and imagery; but it has an undercurrent of imperialism, and can usefully be read with the studies of Virgil and Kipling.

This imperialistic Eliot is the poet of the *urbs aeterna*, of the transmitted but corrupted dignity of Rome. Hence his veneration not only for Baudelaire (where his Symbolist predecessors would have agreed) but for Virgil (where they would not). The other side of this city is the Babylon of *Apocalypse*, and when the *imperium* is threadbare and the end approaches of that which Virgil called endless, this is the city we see. It is the *Blick ins Chaos*.

The merchants of the earth are waxed rich through the abundance of her delicacies.... And the kings of the earth, who have committed fornication and live deliciously with her, shall bewail her, and lament for her, when they shall see the smoke of her burning.... And the merchants of the earth shall weep and mourn over her ... saying, Alas, alas that great city, that was clothed in fine linen, and purple, and scarlet, and decked with gold, and precious stones, and pearls! For in one hour so great riches is come to naught. And every shipmaster, and the company in ships, and sailors, and as many as trade by sea, stood afar off, and cried when they saw the smoke of her burning, saying What city is like unto this great city!

Here is the imagery of sea and imperial city, the city which is the whore and the mother of harlots, with Mystery on her forehead: Mme Sosostris and the bejewelled lady of the game of chess – diminished as the sailors and merchants have dwindled to Phlebas, the sea swallowing his concern for profit and loss, and to Mr Eugenides, his pocket full of currants (base Levantine trade) and his heart set on metropolitan whoring. This is the London of *The Waste Land*, the City by the sea with its remaining flashes of inexplicable imperial splendour: the Unreal City, the *urbs aeterna* declined into *l'immonde cité*.

In another mood, complementary to this of Babylon, Eliot still imagined the Empire as without end, and Virgil, its prophet, became the central classic, *l'altissimo poeta*, as Dante called him. In him originated the imperial tradition. To ignore the 'consciousness of Rome' as Virgil crystallized it is simply to be provincial. It is to be out of the historical current which bears the imperial dignity. In this way Eliot deepened for himself the Arnoldian meanings of the word *provincial*. The European destiny, as prophesied by Virgil, was imperial; the Empire became the secular body of the Church. The fact that it split is reflected in *The Waste Land*, where the hooded Eastern hordes swarm over their plains, and the towers of the city fall. And, as the dignity of empire was split among the nations, the task of the chosen, which is to defeat the proud and be merciful to the subject, was increasingly identified with Babylonian motives of profit – a situation in which Kipling's relevance is obvious. Eliot speaks of his 'imperial imagination'; and, given a view of history as having a kind of perspectiveless unity, Virgil, Dante, Baudelaire, and Kipling can exist within the same plane, like Babylon and the *urbs aeterna*, or like the interrelated motifs of *The Waste Land*. Thus does the poet-historian redeem the time. His is a period of waiting such as occurs before the apocalypse of collapsing cities. But behind the temporal disaster of Babylon he knows that the timeless pattern of the eternal city must survive.

Some such imagery of disaster and continuity – 'that the wheel may turn and still/Be forever still' – lies under *The*

Waste Land and is reflected also in Eliot's cults of continuity and renovation 'under conditions/That seem unpropitious'. Yet when we think of the great poem, we think of it as an image of imperial catastrophe, of the disaster and not of the pattern. For that pattern suggests a commitment, a religion; and the poet retreats to it. But the poem is a great poem because it will not force us to follow him. It makes us wiser without committing us. Here I play on the title of William Bartley's recent book, *Retreat to Commitment*; but one remembers that Eliot himself is aware of these distinctions. Art may lead one to a point where something else must take over, as Virgil led Dante; it 'may be affirmed to serve ends beyond itself', as Eliot himself remarked; but it 'is not required to be aware of these ends' – an objective correlative has enough to do existing out there without joining a church. It joins the mix of our own minds, but it does not tell us what to believe. Whereas Mr Bartley's theologians sometimes feel uneasily that they should defend the rationality of what they are saying, the poets in their rival fictions do not. One of the really distinctive features of the literature of the modernist *anni mirabiles* was that variously and subtly committed writers blocked the retreat to commitment in their poems. Eliot ridiculed the critics who found in *The Waste Land* an image of the age's despair, but he might equally have rejected the more recent Christian interpretations. The poem resists an imposed order; it is a part of its greatness and the greatness of its epoch, that it can do so. 'To find, Not to impose,' as Wallace Stevens said with a desperate wisdom, 'It is possible, possible, possible.' We must hope so.

No one has better stated the chief characteristics of that epoch than the late R. P. Blackmur in a little book of lectures, *Anni Mirabiles 1921–1925*; though it contains some of the best of his later work, it seems to be not much read. We live, wrote Blackmur, in the first age that has been 'fully self-conscious of its fictions' – in a way, Nietzsche has sunk in at last; and in these conditions we are more than ever dependent on what he calls, perhaps not quite satisfactorily, 'bourgeois humanism' – 'the residue of reason in relation to the madness of the senses'. Without it we cannot have 'creation in honesty', only 'assertion in desperation'. But in its operation this residual humanism can only deny the validity of our frames of reference and make 'an irregular metaphysic for the control of man's irrational powers'. So this kind art is a new kind of creation, harsh, medicinal, remaking reality 'in rivalry with our own wishes', denying us the consolations of predictable form but showing us the forces of our world, which we may have to control by other means. And the great works in this new and necessary manner were the product of the 'wonderful years' – in English two notable examples are *Ulysses* and *The Waste Land*.

The function of such a work, one has to see, is what Simone Weil called *decreation*; Stevens, whose profound contribution to the subject nobody seems to have noticed, picked the word out of *La Pesanteur et la grâce*. Simone Weil explains the difference from destruction: decreation is not a change from the created to nothingness, but from the created to the uncreated. 'Modern reality', commented Stevens, 'is a reality of decreation, in which our revelations are not the revelations of belief'; though he adds that he can say this 'without in any way asserting that they are the sole sources'.

This seems to me a useful instrument for the discrimination of modernisms. The form in which Simone Weil expresses it is rather obscure, though she is quite clear that 'destruction' is 'a blameworthy substitute for decreation'. The latter depends upon an act of renunciation, considered as a creative act like that of God. 'God could create only by hiding himself. Otherwise there would be nothing but himself.' She means that decreation, for men, implies the deliberate repudiation (not simply the destruction) of the naturally human and so naturally false 'set' of the world: 'we participate in the creation of the world by decreating ourselves.' Now the poets of the *anni mirabiles* also desired to create a world by decreating the self in suffering; to purge what, in being merely natural and human, was also false. It is a point often made, though in different language, by Eliot. This is what Stevens called clearing the world of 'its stiff and stubborn, man-locked set'. In another way it is what attracted Hulme and Eliot to Worringer, who related societies purged of the messily human to a radical abstract art.

Decreation, as practised by poets, has its disadvantages. In this very article I myself have, without much consideration for the hazards, provided a man-locked set for *The Waste Land*. But we can see that when Eliot pushed his objective correlative out into the neutral air – 'seeming a beast disgorged, unlike,/Warmed by a desperate milk' – he expected it, liberated from his own fictions, to be caught up in the fictions of others, those explanations we find for all the creations. In the world Blackmur is writing about, the elements of a true poem are precisely such nuclei, disgorged, unlike, purged of the suffering self; they become that around which a possible new world may accrete.

It would be too much to say that no one now practises this poetry of decreation; but much English poetry of these days is neither decreative nor destructive, expressing a modest selfishness which escapes both the purgative effort and the blame. America has, I think, its destructive poetry, which tends to be a poetry of manifesto; and in Lowell it seems to have a decreative poet. One way to tell them is by a certain ambiguity in your own response. *The Waste Land*, and also *Hugh Selwyn Mauberley*, can strike you in certain moments as emperors without clothes; discrete poems cobbled into a sequence which is always inviting the censure of pretentiousness. It is with your own proper fictive covering that you hide their nakedness and make them wise. Perhaps there is in *Life Studies* an ambivalence of the same sort. Certainly to have Eliot's great poem in one's life involves an irrevocable but repeated act of love. This is not called for by merely schismatic poetry, the poetry of destruction.

This is why our most lively sense of what it means to be alive in poetry continues to stem from the 'modern' of forty years ago. Deeply conditioned by the original experience of decreation, we may find it hard to understand that without it poetry had no future we can now seriously conceive of. It is true that the exhortations which accompanied Eliot's nuclear achievement are of only secondary interest. What survives is a habit of mind that looks for analysis, analysis by controlled unreason. This habit can be vulgarized: analysis of the most severe kind degenerates into chatter about breakdown and dissociation. *The Waste Land* has been used thus, as a myth of decadence, a facile evasion. Eliot is in his capacity as thinker partly to blame for this. Arnold complained that Carlyle 'led us out into the wilderness and left us there'. So did Eliot, despite his conviction that he knew the way; even before the 'conversion' he had a vision of a future dominated by Bradley, Frazer, and Henry James. We need not complain, so long as the response to the wilderness is authentic; but often it is a comfortable unfelt acceptance of tragedy. Not the least heartening aspect of Mr Bellow's recent book was his attack on his contemptible myth. *The Waste Land* is in one light an imperial epic; but such comforts as it can offer are not compatible with any illusions, past, present, or future.

This is not the way the poem is usually read nowadays; but most people who know about poetry will still admit that it is a very difficult poem, though it invites glib or simplified interpretation. As I said, one can think of it as a mere arbitrary sequence upon which we have been persuaded to impose an order. But the true order, I think, is there to be found, unique, unrepeated, resistant to synthesis. The *Four Quartets* seem by comparison isolated in their eminence, tragic, often crystalline in the presentation of the temporal agony, but personal; and closer sometimes to commentary than to the thing itself. When the *Quartets* speak of a pattern of timeless moments, of the point of intersection, they speak *about* that pattern and that point; the true image of them is *The Waste Land*. There the dreams cross, the dreams in which begin responsibilities.

THE DAY OF FIVE SIGNS

An Elegy for Eliot: 5 January 1965
(Georgetown & Estero Island)

By Robert Richman

It is dawn the eve of Twelfth Night;
The uncertain hour points your day of death.
And the colours are Homeric, the clouds
Sad written strokes of grey and rose.
Dawn points; in the end is your beginning.

This day of your death is your day of birth.
It is summer in winter – the sun shone halcyon
And semipiternal is Dumbarton Oaks, where once
We had walked speaking of Gardens. I said
It was St Basil that said Love was the Rose.

Nine roses bloom in this Garden where once
One May you'd said 'Signs are taken for wonders;
We would see a sign.' There were five signs;
For this day of birth, as a monk you'd awaited,
Dawned on the Eve of the Feast of Light.

O Light Invisible 'we give Thee thanks for Thy
Great glory' you said. On this Day of Light,
You proved by dying it was worth the living.
At Dumbarton Oaks and in Burnt Norton your
Shade echoes the Rose and the Fire are One.

This sea that is and was at the beginning tolls
San Carlos bell. You said 'I do not know much
About gods.' But God would say *Let this good*
Man come speak with Me on sea things and such;
Let his cry come unto Me. And all shall be well.

T. S. ELIOT: SOME LITERARY IMPRESSIONS

By G. Wilson Knight

1

DURING the years following the First World War London's more advanced literary thinking was dominated by John Middleton Murry and T. S. Eliot, editors of *The Adelphi* and *The Criterion*. Murry's approach was personal and emotional, Eliot's more objective and intellectual: they engaged once in a controversy regarding the respective rights of 'intuition' and 'intelligence'. Murry appeared to me the apostle of a new age; my own first articles were published in *The Adelphi*; and yet as my work developed his approval was withdrawn. This was a disappointment, since I had supposed our approaches to be similar.[1]

Meanwhile Eliot's *The Sacred Wood* and *For Lancelot Andrewes* had contained essays very different from Murry's. Cool and urbane in manner, they appeared to be objectifying, even distancing, the literatures discussed. I found his adverse judgements disturbing. I saw Eliot as primarily a 'critic', and Murry as an 'interpreter', of literary genius. The prophetic element in literature, all-important to Murry, seemed to be scanted by Eliot. This was my impression, and there was little doubt in my mind to which camp I belonged.

I had however an article on *Hamlet* submitted to *The Criterion* (which appeared in *The Wheel of Fire* before it could be published there), and when I called at Eliot's office he told me that he found its emphasis on death more illuminating

1. An account of my literary relations with Middleton Murry is presented among the essays presented to Bonamy Dobrée in *Of Books and Humankind*, edited by John Butt, Routledge & Kegan Paul, 1964.

than previous commentaries. I found him a man of a strange and disarming authority, very different from the withdrawn intensity of Murry. He invited me to dinner, to meet his wife, but owing to her ill-health the invitation was replaced by a lunch at his club. He was very kind.

Now, when my own investigations were beginning, as in my essay 'The Poet and Immortality' in *The Shakespeare Review* of October 1928, to assert the mystical properties of Shakespeare's last plays, I found Murry, who had himself had a powerful 'mystical experience'[2] which he was anxious to relate to poetry, unable to accept my formulations, while Eliot, whose critical writings had been, or at least to me appeared, in opposition to mystical interpretations, was strangely sympathetic. He received my 1929 brochure 'Myth and Miracle: on the Mystic Symbolism of Shakespeare' with a degree of approval, and offered to recommend, and even himself personally take, my other Shakespearian essays, which had been appearing in various religious periodicals, to the Oxford University Press, where they were published as *The Wheel of Fire*. On looking back I have two main impressions. One is of the extraordinary power Eliot had even then, for though I had earlier received a dubious reply from the Press regarding the prospect of their doing such a book, a word from Eliot and all went smoothly. Secondly, I am struck by his generosity in so putting himself out to forward a line of research diverging from his own critical tenets. When I told him that I had written a preliminary essay distinguishing between 'criticism' and 'interpretation', he replied, as though newly impressed by the thought: 'Ah. A necessary distinction.' On the publishers' suggestion, he agreed to write an introduction. It was not written from the standpoint of the essays themselves; it engaged in complications which I, rightly or wrongly, do not feel to be necessary; but the status which it gave, and still gives, my life's work has been invaluable.

2. Described in my essay, above, in which I refer to Murry's own account in his book *God* (1929).

That Eliot's response to 'Myth and Miracle' had been more than courtesy was witnessed during this same year, 1930, when he sent me his *Marina*, inscribed 'for' me as 'with, I hope, some appropriateness'. He had mentioned my 'papers' on Shakespeare's last plays in his introduction to *The Wheel of Fire*, referring perhaps mainly to the typescript of my 1928 (unpublished) book on them, *Thaisa*, which, since it had been submitted to Faber & Faber, he is likely to have read. This script Murry never saw. I had however solicited the interest of Mr John Masefield, visiting him on Boar's Hill at Oxford, but though he generously devoted time to it and wrote out an opinion for me, he remained dubious of so philosophical an interpretation.[3] How strange it all was. I have always regarded Masefield's 1924 Romanes Lecture 'Shakespeare and Spiritual Life' as a main influence behind my interpretations; and his own prose and poetry are saturated in spiritualistic apprehension. But neither Masefield nor Murry, who reviewed 'Myth and Miracle' adversely in *The Times Literary Supplement*, was now responsive; and it was Eliot who, despite his own critical caution stopping short, as he once (at the conclusion of 'Tradition and the Individual Talent') put it, 'at the frontier of metaphysics or mysticism', as a poet had seen so exactly what I was doing that he had composed in *Marina* a perfect poetical commentary on those Shakespearian meanings which I had unveiled. His full critical acceptance was witnessed further by his 1932 reference to them in his essay on John Ford.

Soon after the publication of *Marina* Eliot asked to see my commentary on *Coriolanus*, then in preparation, because, he said, he was engaged on a poem inspired by Beethoven's *Coriolan*. I must have first sent him some notes because on 30 December 1930 he wrote, after receiving my finished essay:

3. The inscribed copy of *Marina*, the typescript of *Thaisa*, and Mr Masefield's letter are together lodged among my other papers in the Reference Library at Birmingham. 'Myth and Miracle' is included in my volume, *The Crown of Life*.

You had already, so far as I am concerned, put the gist of it into the notes you sent me. That does not mean at all that you have not done quite right to expand it. What the complete essay adds for me is chiefly the detailed and convincing analysis of the type of imagery. That does increase my understanding and appreciation.

The allusion probably refers to my treatment of 'stone', 'metal', and 'city' imagery in Shakespeare's play, since 'stone', 'steel', and 'paving' occur in *Triumphal March*. Beyond that, my reading of *Coriolanus* as a dramatized balance of warrior values and love, rising to a powerful climax at love's victory, is reflected in, and perhaps lends point to, the repeated Shakespearian reminiscence of 'Mother' and 'O mother' in the second *Coriolan* poem, 'Difficulties of a Statesman'.

Shakespeare had dramatized a conflict of clearly separated values. Eliot was aiming at more than that, at a fusion of heroism and love, and six marvellous lines in *Triumphal March* glimpse the achievement within a figure of heroic repose, in close accord with the description of Nietzsche's 'Superhero' in *Thus Spake Zarathustra* (35; or II, 13):

There is no interrogation in his eyes
Or in the hands, quiet over the horse's neck,
And the eyes watchful, waiting, perceiving, indifferent.
O hidden under the dove's wing, hidden in the turtle's breast,
Under the palmtree at noon, under the running water
At the still point of the turning world. O hidden.

It is a vision of poetry incarnate, according to Keat's definition of poetry as 'might half slumb'ring on its own right arm', in 'Sleep and Poetry'.

The vision could only be glimpsed in static and imagistic terms. The super-hero envisaged may be beyond need of 'interrogation', but the secret of how war can be assimilated to the softer values remains 'hidden' within the resolving spirit, 'under the dove's wing.' In the second poem, 'Difficulties of a Statesman', the elements draw apart, divergent as they are in

Shakespeare's play. The difficulty of blending the Renaissance and the Christian ways, or war with love, is shown in these two poems as the harder for the multiplying logistics and committees attending state affairs as we today know them. Eliot is here at the very heart of our Renaissance conflict. That he should have attempted in two such brief pieces the task to which Byron's whole life was devoted and which forced Ibsen into the twin elephantine dramas of *Emperor and Galilean* was characteristic of his genius; and that he should have left the intended *Coriolan* sequence uncompleted is also characteristic. Nor did he engage this task again. *Murder in the Cathedral* shows little concern for any such balance of church and state as Tennyson gave us in *Becket*.

In *Marina* and *Triumphal March* Eliot was searching within a humanistic, or Renaissance, field for a positive direction to follow *The Waste Land* and 'The Hollow Men'. Christian orthodoxy had already been formally accepted, but as *Journey of the Magi* and *Ash-Wednesday* had shown, it was no easy acceptance. *Ash-Wednesday* opens by renouncing 'the infirm glory of the positive hour' called, by a brilliant paradox apt to Shakespeare's sonnets and *Troilus and Cressida* (both of which, one directly and one implicitly, are recalled on the first page, lines 4 and 18), 'the one veritable transitory power'; orthodoxy is being regarded, with a striking poetic honesty, as a *second-best* to the 'blessèd face' of some more immediately authoritative experience. If the first-best is recorded in the early 'La Figlia che Piange', we can relate the 'pose' of that poem to much of the later Eliot. He was renouncing a human wholeness through recognition of human inadequacy. This wholeness was momentarily recaptured in the lines on the Hyacinth Girl in *The Waste Land*. It is present, in mystical terms and with the help of Shakespeare's poetry under a modern interpretation, in *Marina*, Eliot's one uncompromisingly direct, happy, and assured statement; and in the six marvellous lines of *Triumphal March*. But the alignment was not to be prolonged and the Renaissance positive, though 'veritable', proved 'transitory'. The *Coriolan* sequence got only as far as its second part and was then dropped: heroism and love, state and church, remained apart. The world of *action* had proved intransigent.

Eliot's most whole-hearted devotion at this period was given to Dante, who both in his political thinking and in the *Paradiso*, so rich in the romantic essence, asserted the alignment at which he himself was aiming. When in 1930 or 31 I was at King's College, London, giving a lecture to the Shakespeare Association on Shakespeare's tempest symbolism (later published in *The Symposium*, New York, and afterwards expanded into *The Shakespearian Tempest*), I suggested to Eliot, who was there and had, if I recall aright, arranged the lecture, that he should crown his poetry with a new *Paradiso*. His reply was characteristically diffident; but this was, as the colourings of *Ash-Wednesday* suggest, his instinctive aim.

Such an aim was also reflected in the year 1933 in my book *The Christian Renaissance*, which was written from the romantic imagination in an attempt to harmonize Christian mythology and dogma with Renaissance poetry; and I added as an appendix (not included in the book's 1962 reissue, but to appear in a future collection) a brief commentary on Eliot, drawing particular attention to *Marina*, his poetry at this brief Renaissance period being obviously relevant to my purpose. When I next saw him he showed pleasure at my essay, wherein I had compared his poetry to Dante's and Shakespeare's. For many reasons I scarcely expected him to like the main book, though he expressed no adverse opinion. It was not a devotional work. In it I had no more committed myself to orthodoxy in a devotional sense than Eliot had been committed to Renaissance vision in *Marina* and *Triumphal March*. Neither would at any time have denied the authenticity of the statements made, but an imaginative adventure is not a personal commitment. It touches apprehensions beyond one's personal limitations and decisions.

2

My subsequent writings did not expect a continuance of Eliot's personal support. Nevertheless, our family was not destined to break the contact, for, while my own association with him was now less close – though he liked my *Chariot of Wrath* in 1942 – that of my brother, W. F. Jackson Knight, became strong, and probably stronger than mine had ever been, since the affinities went deep. He had already, in 1938, contributed a review to *The Criterion*, and had also written three books on Virgil, when in 1942 I suggested that he should show his recently completed *Roman Vergil* to Eliot with a view to publication by Faber & Faber. It was accepted, was published early in 1944, and won a considerable success.

My brother's literary temperament had much in common with Eliot's. The religious sympathies of both were Anglo-Catholic; both were cautious and self-critical, with a strong moral sense not only in life, which is natural, but in literary disquisition too, which is another matter. Both honoured the classics and set a primary value on the past, on tradition. 'Tradition' was a key-concept for Eliot, and my brother's view of great poetry, and in particular Virgil's, saw its greatness as the re-working, re-harmonizing, and culmination of vast stores from the mythology, folklore, and literature of the past. This was also Eliot's method. Both, too, were instinctively drawn to the Continent. Eliot's *Criterion* and much of his thought were continental in reach, and my brother's scholarly contacts and correspondence ranged widely among the French, German, Italian, Spanish, and Portuguese, as well as England and North and South America. The Cumaean Sibyl of *Aeneid VI*, germane to my brother's *Cumaean Gates*, had appeared in the epigraph to *The Waste Land*.[4]

4. An interrelation between *Cumaean Gates* (revised 1967, in *Virgil: Epic and Anthropology*) and Eliot's *The Waste Land* was noted by Grover Smith of Yale in 'T. S. Eliot's Lady of the Rocks', *Notes and Queries*, 19 March 1949, notes 6 and 8.

The cultural complex thus shared might be called 'Virgilian'. The word covers much of what we mean by such terms as 'classical', 'the European tradition', 'Western culture', and even Christianity too, since Virgil has for centuries been accepted by orthodox Christians as one of themselves, *'anima naturaliter Christiana'*. When at the foundation (on the initiative of Father Bruno Scott James) of the London Virgil Society at a dinner on 11 January 1943 my brother was offered the presidency, he accepted with the proviso that T. S. Eliot should be invited first. Eliot became president and he himself secretary; and they were in mutual correspondence on matters of policy. In 1945 he showed Eliot a book-script on Homer, composed before *Roman Vergil*, which Eliot greatly liked, but wanted amplified; and though the reading for the amplification went on year after year, Eliot's interest in the projected volume remained firm. On 12 August 1949 he answered a letter of mine, written in view of my brother's acute anxiety about the delay, assuring us of his understanding; and as late as 1964 we received a message from him saying that he was still thinking of, and hoping for, the book.

My brother's mental powers were nearer Eliot's than mine could ever have been. His natural insight and sympathy are evident in the essay 'T. S. Eliot as a Classical Scholar', which he contributed to Neville Braybrooke's *Symposium* for Eliot's seventieth birthday in 1958. His brilliant, darting, and comprehensive mind was at home with the complexities of modern poetry; he enjoyed all kinds of complexity; his conversation tended to be indirect and allusive, making the hearer's mind leap; and, above all, he liked complexities drawn from stores of racial history, as in Virgil, Eliot, or David Jones's *The Anathemata*, which he reviewed in *The Listener*. His own researches, in *Cumaean Gates* and elsewhere, had been largely concerned with anthropology and ritual; and with other origins within the subconscious, the link being Jung's concept of racial memory; and with the way centuries of twilight experience were caught up into the sophisticated poetry of a Homer or a Virgil, to be stamped with authority for subsequent ages.

While he was searching back into origins and bringing the story up to Virgil, I myself was on a different task: starting with the Renaissance, my field has been a later poetry, and this I have treated with scant regard to origins, but rather, inspecting its form and present contents, searched it for a future and prophetic pointing. The two lines of research were complementary. We were both exploring the mysterious reality behind and within poetry, he in terms of the past, I of the future, but both equally sensing its present otherness, its eternity, of which past and future are aspects. 'What is Poetry?' Byron once asked himself, and answered, 'The feeling of a Former world and Future' (Diary, 28 January 1821; *Letters and Journals*, V, 189); where, as so often in Byron's prose, an offhand simplicity conjures up vistas.

Eliot was as a writer more at ease with history in 'Gerontion', legend in *The Waste Land* and the ancestral places of the *Four Quartets*, and also with the psychological diagnoses of human causes in *The Family Reunion* and *The Cocktail Party*, than in attempts at teaching and prophecy, the best of which are to be found in the choruses of *The Rock* and certain passages in the *Four Quartets*, and the weakest in parts of his prose and the semi-prose of his last three dramas. He was in fact more moralist than prophet, drawing on, rather than reacting from, established authority. Therein lay from the start his divergence from Murry, on whom the prophetic mantle sat easily.

3

In the appendix to *The Christian Renaissance* I wrote that Eliot's was 'a small, but intense, poetic world of the same quality as Shakespeare's and Dante's'; and I was honoured when I next saw him by his evident pleasure at this brief essay by so unrenowned an expositor. I believe that, again like my brother, Eliot was in some deep way wanting in self-trust. When in 1948 or thereabouts he told me that he had deleted long passages from *The Waste Land* in deference to Ezra Pound's blue-pencilling, in particular an extended piece of sea-poetry near or in the section 'Death by Water',[5] I was shocked. It was now clear why *The Waste Land* was so *fragmentary*. That it is inartistically so may be seen from the relegation to a note of an organically needed statement regarding the function in the poem of the bisexual Tiresias. Without retracting my comparison of Eliot's poetry, at its best, with Dante and Shakespeare in point of 'quality', I should now say that his seems scarcely a *single* 'poetic world', being too fragmentary. 'These fragments I have shored against my ruins' applies widely to his work: *Sweeney Agonistes* was published as 'Fragments of an Aristophanic Melodrama', though I have heard that more exists and was used at the memorial performance in London; the *Coriolan* sequence was never finished; certain of his essays were deliberately – he seems to have *enjoyed* the emphasis – designated as part of an uncompleted book. Eliot's poetic world is not unified: Christian pieces are juxtaposed to those which are humanistic, and a relation is not – at least until *Little Gidding* and then only in meditative terms – established; his frequent use of successive noun-groups starting with 'the' is a symptom, on the level of syntax, of unrelatedness, of addition in place of multiplication. Pieces appear, big or little, in their own right, static and unrelated. There are good, if not finally satisfying, reasons for all this. The cause appears to be in what may be called 'diffidence': sometimes a fear of speaking out, of active commitment; perhaps more especially a fear of letting any poetry stand that fails of perfection, of the most perfect fusion; a desire for the purest verbal or imagistic gems, and those alone; together with a praiseworthy fear of pretending to a relation which has not been found. These are perhaps all characteristics of what is called 'imagistic' poetry. The image is supposed to speak without an active relation, as does 'Sunlight on a broken

5. In *The Waste Land* 'Death by Water' signifies an ultimate, static, sensual disaster to be contrasted with fertilizing rain and mastery of water in moving craft; and with fire, signifying purgation and spiritual advance.

column' in 'The Hollow Men'; and with Eliot the principle applies more widely, as perhaps with James Joyce too, than to images. In this connexion I would contrast the lucid style and the inexhaustible thought-riches, the organic mythology and vast interrelations, of Powys's *A Glastonbury Romance* with the obscurities, the verbal exhibitionism, the inorganic Homer-pattern, and crammed and elephantine unease of *Ulysses*; and yet there is a single, miraculous nature-transfiguration towards the close of Joyce's book, 'The heaventree of stars hung with humid nightblue fruit', that alone goes far to justify the rest. We find a similar gem-like transfiguring in some of the spiritualized phrase-solidities of Shakespeare's final period (discussed in *The Mutual Flame*, pp. 140–41).

Eliot did, however, perhaps relying on the achieved harmony of *Little Gidding*, attempt a more general relatedness in his last plays, though with doubtful success. What he could state in a poem was less easily realizable under the test of action. We shall do well to regard his 'critical' writings on dramatic language as masking the real problems of his dramatic involvement. He had concentrated on the Jacobean dramatists in the twenties. He was deeply aware of the sexual horrors lurking within human instinct,[6] and the Jacobeans presented these horrors raw. *The Waste Land* shows sexual revulsion; in *Sweeney Agonistes*, a key-statement, romance is equated with lust and lust with murder; and this sexual horror is submitted to the mechanics of psychological diagnosis in *The Family Reunion*. It is characteristic of Eliot's work that *The Rock* and *Murder in the Cathedral* were interposed, offering Christian solutions in morals and martyrdom. In 1948 or thereabouts Eliot told me that he rated higher his modern dramas than a costume-piece like *Murder in the Cathedral*; implying perhaps that they came nearer to facing the central sexual problem. *The Cocktail Party* handles both the marriage

6. This strain in Eliot's poetry I have discussed more fully in *Christ and Nietzsche*, London, 1948, pp. 92–3, and in *The Golden Labyrinth*, London, 1962, pp. 362–6.

sex-problem and the other consummation of martyrdom, thus covering in one design all earlier dramas, though with a loss in dramatic power. Eliot's early dramatic writing, in which I include *The Waste Land*, had jets of impressive force; but these were in the easier field of revulsion and horror which was to become so poetically powerful in *The Family Reunion*; and a vigorous *action* was never at any time engaged. *The Cocktail Party* has skill, teaching, and diagnosis but, despite its title, too little of blood or fire for the task in hand.

The complaint may be precisely formulated. The drama labours to fuse modern science with Christian sanctity by the creation of a psychiatrist who is also, in effect, a priest. The attempt to graft Church doctrine onto humanistic science is clear; and the attempt to twist what people today believe into a higher belief is praiseworthy. But though we have an ingenious mental pattern, it scarcely succeeds as drama. Sir Henry Harcourt-Reilly, and therefore the whole work of which he is the human pivot, is made from a factitious joining of scientific and religious externals. For the desired fusion a stronger element of the Dionysian, of spirit-blood, of that which is the basis equally of life and death, and therefore of science and religion, was needed. The arbitrary wine-libations, on the stage, do little: there is no soil for them, no atmosphere, to grow from. From ancient times until today drama of weight has been saturated in Dionysian properties; in what lies beyond the threshold of reason and daylight knowledge, beyond what is easy to accept; in ecstasy, in the occult, in ghosts, in spirit-lore of all kinds.[7] We find them in the Jacobeans and the Gothic plays of the Romantic period. The Faust tradition is made of them. The rise of modern spiritualism has given them vigour and impetus. Occultism is active in Shaw, in Masefield's *Melloney Holtspur*, in the dramas of W. B. Yeats. This story I have traced in *The Golden Labyrinth* and have

7. My reasons for attributing such wide powers to Dionysus are given in *The Golden Labyrinth*, London, 1962, I. See now also John Pollard, *Seers, Shrines and Sirens*, London, 1965, pp. 86, 89.

added to it in *Encounter* (December 1963; XXI, 6), enlisting, among others, *Huis Clos*, *Death of a Salesman*, *Waiting for Godot*, and the plays of Eugene Ionesco. Dionysus is part of the fabric of drama because he is part of the fabric of life and death, and the relation of the one to the other.

The Eumenides of *The Family Reunion* were superbly realized in poetry, but their stage realization was arbitrary and static; they failed to interlock with action and acting.

The Cocktail Party has its passing references to 'Guardians'. The gesture is to this extent made, but how many of the audience know that they are what Spiritualists call 'Spirit-guides' – like Masefield's King Cole? Dramatically they scarcely register. As for Sir Henry Harcourt-Reilly, on whom so much depends, there is no suggestion that he possesses occult powers until, briefly, in the last act. They form no part of his stage personality. He remains a puppet made of the will to force together science and sanctity.

And yet – how much more illuminating is Eliot's failure than the successes of lesser poets! For though they are not dramatically realized the needed spiritualistic elements are verbally present; and Eliot has here forced us to inquire whether, quite apart from drama, our two modern cultures, scientific and religious, can be harmonized, and action engaged, without such deeper contacts. More, we find ourselves asking whether the madhouse of incompatible disciplines that make of a modern university – to quote from Pope's *Essay on Criticism* – 'one glaring chaos and wild heap of wit' will ever become inter-communicative until each and all admit their spiritualistic basis. Eliot once wrote of the poet's mind as a 'finely perfected medium' in which various experiences 'enter into new combinations', and continued with his famous analogy of the catalyst. Well, Dionysus, god of nature, wine-fire, and the occult, of drama and of all deep poetry, is the supreme catalyst.

Both my brother, though he remained within the Anglican communion, and myself, he influenced by that fine Virgilian

Professor T. J. Haarhoff and I by him, became Spiritualists. Spiritualistic acceptance was for us natural. Both his researches in ancient folklore and death-ritual and my own in the more occult symbolisms of Renaissance poetry were by these new experiences ratified.

4

In more personal, meditative terms Eliot had, however, already achieved, or come near to achieving, success. The plays themselves if read as meditative patternings have their value, distinct from drama, in his progress. But only in the *Four Quartets* was the end properly attained. Here, in short space, though the state issues of *Coriolan* are not engaged, a universe is nevertheless subsumed. Elements of air, water, earth, and fire; paradisial gleams; purgatorial suffering; death; wisdom, Sanskrit and Christian; historic tradition and the metaphysics of space and time in mutual and living pattern – all cohere in a loose yet convincing organization, as Eliot reviews his own poetic world and brings it, as near as may be, toward peace.

It would be dangerous to read these as 'Christian' poems; they are quite as near, or nearer, the undoctrinal meditations of *Thus Spake Zarathustra*. Eliot has never, apart from *The Rock* and *Murder in the Cathedral*, been a whole-heartedly Christian poet in the sense that the seventeenth-century poets, or Hopkins, or Francis Thompson were Christian. His early balancing of Hippopotamus and True Church sends little echoes reverberating down his subsequent reservations. His most assured religious lines, those on 'light' in *The Rock*, are fruits of a general religious apprehension, independent of dogma; and much of the rest, as we have seen, views conversion as nearer agony than peace. Prayers are lifted to emblematic ladies, exquisitely pictured, in *Ash-Wednesday*, but Eliot's one memorable reference to Christ comes in the significantly explosive 'Christ the tiger' of 'Gerontion'.

The paradisial intimations of *Burnt Norton*, recalling 'La

Figlia che Piange', the Hyacinth Girl in *The Waste Land*, *Ash-Wednesday*, and *Marina*, are expressed through images of flowers, bird-song, and children without doctrinal implications; and the wonderful lyric in *East Coker* starting 'The wounded surgeon plies the steel', surely the grimmest statement on the Christian world-view ever penned by a devotee, offers a universe so riddled with negations and agonies that we must go to the anti-Christian polemics of Nietzsche – which its cutting phraseology recalls – for an analogy. *East Coker* opens out, at its conclusion, to 'the vast waters/Of the petrel and the porpoise'; and in these there is a release, to be expanded in the nature poetry of the river as 'a strong brown god' and the sea-descriptions of *The Dry Salvages*, where there is nevertheless also a lady-prayer of orthodox devotion, recalling *Ash-Wednesday*.

In the *Four Quartets* rival world-views, all honest and all tenable, are still left in the main mutually unrelated, except that they are all presented in autobiographical relation to the poet, and there is a recurring drive for sainthood, or something like it, and moments recording 'the impossible union of disparate spheres of existence'. There is comparatively little 'pure poetry' – in my judgement – that can compare with the pieces already praised in this essay; to which I should add 'The Hollow Men', my earliest delight. If we receive, as I think we do, a sense of final harmony, the credit for it goes mainly to the concluding piece, *Little Gidding*, Eliot's culminating achievement, which ends, convincingly, with an imagined weaving of spirit-flames into a 'crowned knot of fire', so that 'the fire and the rose are one'. The fire is that of agony and spiritual advance, as in 'O Lord Thou pluckest me out ... burning' in *The Waste Land* and 'the intolerable shirt of flame' woven by Love earlier in *Little Gidding*; and the rose covers all romantic flower-intimations from 'La Figlia che Piange' to *Burnt Norton*. The longed-for union, already hinted in *Ash-Wednesday*, of Eros and Christ, though Christ is not named, is convincingly stated.

If *Little Gidding* does indeed achieve this integration, it does so only through obedience to the principle we have already defined. For so ambitious an integration there must be present the catalyst, Dionysus, as god simultaneously of nature and the occult. The authority of the *Four Quartets* derives from the numinous atmosphere generated and pervading, helped by the presence of music in both structure and reference. Bird or spirit voices and unseen presences, like those in de la Mare's 'The Listeners', are awake in *Burnt Norton*. Death weighs as a dark portal to garden laughter in *East Coker*. Converse with 'spirits' is grouped with other occult practices, and 'daemonic' and 'chthonic' powers are touched on, not without respect, in *The Dry Salvages*. In *Little Gidding* the ancestral powers dominate:

> And what the dead had no speech for, when living,
> They can tell you, being dead: the communication
> Of the dead is tongued with fire beyond the
>   language of the living.

Than this there is surely no more potent spiritualistic statement in our literature. In *Little Gidding* 'We are born with the dead'; 'they return, and bring us with them'. But this is not all. The only dramatic personality in the *Quartets* is the 'familiar compound ghost' of 'some dead master', recalling the 'affable familiar ghost' of the passage on spirit-writing in Shakespeare's Sonnet 86 (and probably to be identified with W. B. Yeats) who speaks a long passage of authoritative counsel, ruling the poem. The ghost is spiritualistically conceived as living 'between two worlds become much like each other'; meaning, presumably, that he has found the planes less different than he expected. The delineation owes nothing to orthodoxy. The poet is writing from direct spiritualistic acceptance, like W. B. Yeats and John Masefield. The acceptance is common to a tradition of experience descending from the ancient world, active throughout the poetry of all times and all places, though today enjoying a more precise understanding and formulation than hitherto; and only through such an acceptance of the 'occult', meaning the 'hidden', which recalls the 'hidden' of *Triumphal March*, may the longed-for victory be won.

Eliot's contribution has been tremendous. Refusing easier expedients, he has concentrated on what in our time can make poetry of a high order; and in so doing has used poetry as a test for what is, and is not, valid. The complete canon, poetry and prose, may show a lack of harmony, of interlocking; neither state affairs nor dramatic action was artistically mastered. But Eliot's juxtapositions of disparate mind-adventures have had a clarity and a detonation that premature attempts at interrelation – the danger is clear in the last plays – might have reduced; the impacts would have been softened, and unity bought, as it was perhaps in *The Cocktail Party*, at too dear a cost. No poet has been more deeply honest. The results are simultaneously personal in substance and impersonal in technique. I write of Eliot as a poet, of his poetic self; and this self, I have argued, cannot be regarded as wholly, or even mainly, Christian: he has left no visionary statement so happily assured as *Marina*. As a man he was, we know, a Christian; his conversion existed in the order of decision and life-action, not of art. The two orders are distinct.

T. S. ELIOT AS A CRITIC

By Mario Praz

CARLO LINATI, who was among the earliest to write in Italy about T. S. Eliot, found his poetry 'irrational, incomprehensible ... a magnificent puzzle', but he added: 'The poet has chosen this form of poetry with a deliberate critical purpose. Because Eliot is first of all a critic, literary cricism is the field in which his personality has found its full expression.' For him the essays of *The Sacred Wood* were 'among the most perspicuous and vital of English literature of all times'. This Linati wrote in the late twenties. In *The Partisan Review* for February 1949, when Eliot's career was nearly concluded, Delmore Schwartz expressed this opinion: [1]

> When we think of the character of literary dictators in the past, it is easy to see that since 1922, at least, Eliot has occupied a position in the English-speaking world analogous to that occupied by Ben Jonson, Dryden, Pope, Samuel Johnson, Coleridge, and Matthew Arnold. It is noticeable that each of these dictators has been a critic as well as a poet, and we may infer from this fact that it is necessary for them to practice both poetry and criticism.

And the eminent historian of criticism René Wellek wrote in *The Sewanee Review* for July 1956: [2]

> T. S. Eliot is by far the most important critic of the twentieth century in the English-speaking world. His influence on contemporary taste in poetry is most conspicuous: he has done more than anybody else to promote the 'shift of sensibility' away from the taste of the 'Georgians' and to revaluate the major figures and periods in the history of English poetry. He reacted most strongly against Romanticism, he criticized Milton and the

1. 'The Literary Dictatorship of T. S. Eliot', p. 119.
2. 'The Criticism of T. S. Eliot', offprint, p. 3.

Miltonic tradition, he exalted Dante, the Jacobean dramatists, the metaphysical poets, Dryden, and the French symbolists as '*the* tradition' of great poetry. But Eliot is at least equally important for his theory of poetry which buttresses this new taste and which is much more coherent and systematic than most commentators have allowed. His concept of 'impersonal' poetry, his description of the creative process which demands a 'unified sensibility', and uses an 'objective correlative', his justification of 'tradition', his scheme of the history of English poetry as a process that led to the 'dissociation' of an originally unified sensibility, his emphasis on the 'perfection of common speech' as the language of poetry, his discussion of the relation between ideas and poetry under the term 'belief' – all these are important critical matters for which Eliot found memorable formulas, if not always convincing solutions.

Before closely examining these contributions of Eliot to criticism, it seems necessary to warn that he, with a typical Anglo-Saxon shyness, has waived any claim to systematic philosophical thought, in statements like the following:[3]

I have no general theory of my own. . . . The extreme of theorising about the nature of poetry, the essence of poetry if there is any, belongs to the study of aesthetics and is no concern of the poet or of a critic with my limited qualifications.

He does not want to indulge in 'speculations about aesthetics, for which [he has] neither the competence nor the interest'.[4]

There is a true foundation in these speciously modest disclaimers; if we survey Eliot's critical opinions throughout his career, we find that he is an empirical critic, that he has not scrupled to contradict himself, whenever he felt an urge to declare honestly what were his feelings in each case; and this habit can be easily traced to his Puritan education.[5] Although

3. *The Use of Poetry and the Use of Criticism*, London, 1933, pp. 143 and 149–50.
4. 'The Social Function of Poetry', in *Critiques and Essays in Criticism 1920–1948* (ed. R. W. Stallman), New York, 1949, p. 110.
5. See Edmund Wilson's chapter on Eliot in *Axel's Castle*.

he knows how to argue with extreme subtlety about his likings and dislikings, his real guide is not logic but intuition. In fact all his critical discoveries take the shape of a myth or an image. To begin with his earliest and most important one, his concept of the metaphysical tradition, it is interesting to see how Eliot hit on this discovery.

In 1894 a Scottish professor who later achieved eminence, John Clifford Grierson, appointed to the English chair in the University of Aberdeen, found that his predecessor had planned a course on John Donne. Turning thus to the study of the seventeenth century, he wrote in 1906 a volume on the early portion of it and prepared a critical edition of John Donne's poems with a full commentary, which appeared in 1912. It is difficult to assess what impact may have been made on Eliot's mind by a course of Professor Briggs on that poet which he had attended at Harvard University in 1906–7; there is however no doubt that Grierson's edition acted on him with the intensity of a shock of recognition: the poet's voice was for him like the voice of a brother. Eliot's culture at the time was not very extensive, but what there was of it was intensely experienced: Symons had revealed to him the French symbolists; Pound, the *stil nuovo* and Dante. In Eliot's mind the various elements of this little patrimony short-circuited into a poetical vision of genius which, according to Melville's phrase, 'all over the world, stands hand in hand, and one shock of recognition runs the whole circle round'. Struck by certain affinities between the English poet of the seventeenth century and Laforgue, Eliot developed the theory of the three 'metaphysical' moments in Western poetry, and the poetics of 'unified sensibility' or union of thought and sense ('sensuous apprehension of thought'), which he saw underlying both the poetry of Donne and that of Dante, Laforgue's and his own. So that when Frank Kermode maintained in 1956[6] that 'Donne was, astonishingly, transformed into a French poet,

6. 'A Myth of Catastrophe', *The Listener*, 15 November 1956, p. 792.

most like Laforgue', he was not very wide of the mark. The idea of unified sensibility was formulated by Eliot in an image which in a way appeared to him as convincing as an argument: 'A thought to Donne was an experience, it modified his sensibility ... he felt his thought as immediately as the odour of a rose.' Actually the idea of unified sensibility was not a new one; it can be traced to the editor of many seventeenth-century texts, the Rev. Alexander B. Grosart, who had hinted at the seventeenth-century peculiarity of feeling thought as sensation in his 1873 edition of the poems of Richard Crashaw. But Eliot brought this idea to its extreme consequences. It is relatively of little importance to ascertain how far the real state of things confirmed this theory of unified sensibility, which is supposed to have existed at least until the influence of Francis Bacon, which brought about a split between poetical imagination and positive thought, made itself felt in literature, causing the exclusion of certain elements (the prosaic, the unrefined, the obscure) from poetry. Historical accuracy is a requisite which needs no stressing, but on the other hand the vitality of a poem depends to a large extent on what the following generations see in it. Even if Eliot's interpretation of unified sensibility should turn out to be a myth, this interpretation offers a positive basis for appreciating the effect of the discovery of the metaphysicals on modern poetry and criticism. Eliot's interpretation of the history of English poetry has indeed been qualified by some scholars. Clay Hunt, for instance,[7] has remarked that Donne, far from being representative of a poetry of inclusion of the whole reality, suffers from paralysing limitations. Donne as an intellectual, an egotist devoid of social sense, is prevented by the analytical and scientific cast of his brain from conceiving the mysteries of religion otherwise than as intellectual puzzles. His very obsession with death serves only to emphasize his intense egotism and does not go together with a feeling of sympathy for the

7. *Donne's Poetry, Essays in Literary Analysis*, New Haven (Yale University Press), 1956 (second printing), pp. 147 ff.

common lot of men and things. Incapable of assimilating every kind of experience, as happens with the greatest geniuses, Donne's sensibility was therefore extremely limited, and it is precisely because his limitations are to a large extent those of the modern intellectual world, that he came so much to the limelight in the period between the two wars.

Anyhow Eliot, with his exaltation of Donne and of his type of inspiration, paved the way to the exploration of the origins of the metaphysical current in England and on the other hand contributed to give a different direction to research about Shakespeare, on whose images the critics focused now their attention.

The idea of a metaphysical brotherhood throughout the centuries is a poetical idea similar to Melville's one of genius standing hand in hand all over the world; no less poetical is the other idea of the objective correlative. Writers project their emotions into something external, into an object which becomes their symbol. 'The only way of expressing emotion in the form of art', Eliot wrote apropos of *Hamlet*, 'is by finding an "objective correlative", in other words, a set of objects, a situation, a chain of events which shall be the formula of that *particular* emotion; such that when the external facts, which terminate in sensory experience, are given, the emotion is immediately evoked.' Another idea of Eliot, that of the two planes on which a drama is played, is also due to a poetical intuition. He formulated it in his essay on Marston:

It is possible that what distinguishes poetic drama from prosaic drama is a kind of doubleness in the action, as if it took place on two planes at once.... In poetic drama a certain apparent irrelevance may be the symptom of this doubleness; or the drama has an under-pattern, less manifest than the theatrical one.... [In Marston's *Sophonisba*] in spite of the tumultuousness of the action, and the ferocity and horror of certain parts of the play, there is an underlying serenity; and as we familiarize ouselves with the play we perceive a pattern behind the pattern into which the characters deliberately involve themselves; the kind of pattern which we perceive in our own lives only at rare moments of inattention and detachment, drowsing in sunlight.

The poetical character of Eliot's critical ideas should not surprise us; in *The Sacred Wood* he had said that the only genuine criticism is that of the poet-critic who is 'criticizing poetry in order to create poetry': an assertion later modified into another, that 'the criticism employed by a trained and skilled writer on his own work is the most vital, the highest kind of criticism'. The creation of poetry being the ultimate aim of such a critic, it is only too natural that a poetical halo should hang about his concepts.

Also what Eliot sees in Dante – who is almost the sole poet for whom he has kept up a constant cult – is more the fruit of a poet's sensibility than of a critical evaluation. He sees in Dante clear visual images, a concise and luminous language: the impression left on him by the atmosphere of the *Purgatory* and the *Paradise* has spread itself over the whole poem, producing as a quintessence an ideal model which the poet was going to keep before his mind in his mature compositions, *Ash-Wednesday* and the *Quartets*. Dante provided Eliot also with the most conspicuous example of that impersonality of the poet which is the necessary premise of all classicism; and it is curious to note that sixteenth- and seventeenth-century Italian critics of Dante actually reproached him for the intrusion of his own personality into a serious poem, his speaking in the first person.

'The great poet, in writing himself, writes his time'; on the other hand, he is universal, places himself into a hierarchy which is timeless. In 'A Garland for John Donne' Eliot says:

We must assume ... that there is some absolute poetic hierarchy; we keep at the back of our minds the reminder of some end of the world, some final Judgment Day, on which the poets will be assembled in their ranks and orders. In the long run, there is an ultimate greater and less.

And in 'Tradition and the Individual Talent' (1919) he tried to define the interplay of forces which forms the vital current of literature:

[Tradition] involves, in the first place, the historical sense ... and the historical sense involves a perception, not only of the pastness of the past, but of its presence; the historical sense compels a man to write not merely with his own generation in his bones, but with a feeling that the whole of the literature of Europe from Homer and within it the whole of the literature of his own country has a simultaneous existence and composes a simultaneous order. This historical sense, which is the sense of the timeless as well as of the temporal and of the timeless and the temporal together, is what makes a writer traditional. And it is at the same time what makes a writer most acutely conscious of his place in time, of his own contemporaneity.

The critic's task should be to see literature '*not* as consecrated by time, but to see it beyond time; to see the best work of our time and the best work of twenty-five hundred years ago with the same eyes'. The figure of the past is subject to a continuous process of readjustment, to which Eliot himself has contributed by bringing into the limelight the poetic personality of John Donne, which before had been considered secondary, and by diminishing Milton's stature; but the order of the past, however we may reshuffle it, remains still simultaneous. In the fifth section of *Little Gidding* Eliot has said that 'history is a pattern/Of timeless moments'. And in his introduction to a selection of Ezra Pound's *Poems* he has said that 'true originality is merely a development'.

Tradition for Eliot coincides with what he calls classicism, and his idea of the essence of classicism is largely a polemical one, as it derives from writers who employed that term in order to contrast it with something against which they fought: from Matthew Arnold, who in order to integrate and counteract the northern qualities of the English proposed to them the example of the literatures of Greece and France; from Irving Babbitt, who had been among Eliot's masters at Harvard and exploded the Romantic idea of the world; from the French polemical writers who flourished at the time of Eliot's sojourn in Paris (1910–11), Lasserre, Seillière, and chiefly Charles Maurras, whose *Avenir de l'intelligence* (1905) made on Eliot a great impression: he even became a champion of Maurras when the Action Française was condemned. Maurras and Lasserre identified the classical with the Roman tradition; Eliot followed suit with his idea of an authoritarian tradition of order, of Latinity, of the heritage of Rome, opposed to an arbitrary interpretation of romanticism as equivalent to ethical and aesthetic anarchy. Eliot sees modern classicism as a 'tendency toward a higher and clearer conception of Reason, and a more severe and serene control of the emotions by Reason', and mentions Sorel, Maurras, Benda, Hulme, Maritain, and Babbitt as supporters of that tendency. In the preface to his essay *For Lancelot Andrewes* (1928) Eliot went so far as to declare himself 'classicist', 'royalist', and 'Anglican', a commitment which he later (in *After Strange Gods*, 1933) regretted as 'injudicious'.

Whereas at first Eliot stressed the autonomy of art, the 'integrity of poetry', he later inclined to recognize a double standard in criticism: artistic on the one hand, and moral–philosophical–theological on the other. In an essay (1935) on 'Religion and Literature' he wrote:

In ages like our own, in which there is no such common agreement [on ethical and theological matters], it is the more necessary for Christian readers to scrutinize their reading, especially of works of imagination, with explicit ethical and theological standards. The 'greatness' of literature cannot be determined solely by literary standards; though we must remember that whether it is literature or not can be determined only by literary standards.   *

As Wellek has remarked, 'this widely quoted passage assigns to literary criticism a mere preliminary sifting between art and non-art and leaves to moral and theological considerations the decision about "greatness" as if it were something merely added to minimal aesthetic value'. The passage about 'greatness' seems to leave a free hand to the evaluation of the various philosophies according to their truth, which for Eliot means their conformity to the Catholic tradition. Eliot reached this position through the influence of I. A. Richards, who had raised the question whether readers are expected to believe in the ideas of an author. At first Eliot answered that the reader was not called upon to believe in Dante's philosophical and theological beliefs, as there is a 'difference between philosophical *belief* and poetic assent'. In fact, Wellek remarks, 'the range of literature accessible to us would be extremely narrow if we had to agree with the beliefs of every poet we read'.

However in a note to the Dante essay Eliot admitted that in practice he could not wholly separate his poetic appreciation from his personal beliefs, and maintained that 'one probably has more pleasure in the poetry when one shares the beliefs of the poet'. In *The Use of Poetry and the Use of Criticism* (1933), apropos of Shelley, by whose ideas he felt 'affronted', and whose beliefs excited his 'abhorrence', he formulated this often quoted conclusion:

When the doctrine, theory, belief, or 'view of life' presented in the poem is one which the mind of the reader can accept as coherent, mature and founded on the facts of experience, it interposes no obstacle to the reader's enjoyment, whether it be one that he can accept or deny, approve or deprecate.

In fact, as Wellek has observed, Eliot offers no theoretical solution; it is just a question of personal reaction. Eliot deprecates and repudiates Lucretius's and Seneca's beliefs, but is able to enjoy them as literature because their beliefs are innocuous; on the contrary Shelley's revolutionary faith and what he thinks are Goethe's paganism and naturalism represent a challenge to Christian orthodoxy, and in consequence Eliot abhors them. The reproach of defective critical theory Wellek makes to Eliot has a foundation also in his idea about the sincerity of the poet. Speaking of George Herbert and of religious poetry in general, he says: [8] 'The greater the elevation, the finer becomes the difference between sincerity and insincerity, between the reality and the unattained aspiration.' But, says Wellek: 'Strength of belief has no relation to successful art, nor has truth of doctrine as such.' A well-known case in point is Ruskin, who found the reason for the excellence of Gothic architecture in the virtue and religious faith of the men who had created it, and despised the Renaissance as an artificial and irreligious product of an imitation of paganism.

One cannot truly say that Eliot's criticism is free of such Puritan prejudices. His attitude to Goethe is typical. In *What Is a Classic?* he denies that Goethe is a universal classic, finds him a 'little provincial'; in *The Use of Poetry and the Use of Criticism* he had already said that Goethe 'dabbled in both philosophy and poetry and made no great success of either; his true role was that of man of the world and sage – a La Rochefoucauld, a La Bruyère, a Vauvenargues'. His interpretation of Goethe as a pagan naturalist made the German poet an alien to the Christian tradition, and his devotion to the classical world was insufficient to redeem him in Eliot's eyes. However Goethe's case is also typical of another aspect of Eliot: his change of opinion as a consequence of an afterthought due to further information, or simply to a special occasion. On 5 May 1955 Eliot delivered in Hamburg a lecture on 'Goethe the Sage' (published in German in *Merkur* for August 1955). In this lecture he renounces his former opinion of Goethe, places him next to Dante and Shakespeare among the great European classics, and finds in him true wisdom, which is a different thing from the worldly wisdom of a La Rochefoucauld. Wellek has pointed out that this change of attitude seems the result of Eliot's reading of a German book, *Mensch und Materie*, by Ernst Lehrs (translated into English as *Man or Matter* in 1951), in which Goethe was interpreted as a forerunner of Rudolf Steiner's 'Anthroposophy'. As a consequence Eliot

8. In *The Spectator*, 2 March 1932, p. 360.

found Goethe less typical of his age than he had thought before, more universal, almost as much above his age as Blake. Unfortunately Lehrs's book seems to possess no more critical value than another book which modified Eliot's opinion of Shelley, whom Eliot had detested not only for his atheism and hatred of kings, but also for his confused imagery: if he later came 'to a new and more sympathetic appreciation of Shelley',[9] he was indebted for it to Leone Vivante's volume *La Poesia inglese ed il suo contributo alla conoscenza dello spirito* (1947), which he judged worthy of an English translation published in 1950 by Faber & Faber, the firm of which he was director. This capacity of finding nourishment in badly contrived works, or at best in works belonging to a sphere of vapid platitudes, is typical of a phenomenon analysed by Henri Peyre in a witty essay, 'The Criticism of Contemporary Writing':[10] that is, the frequency of errors in perspective and evaluation when one is called to judge contemporary works, such errors as those of which celebrated critics like Sainte-Beuve and Arnold were guilty.

Being an empirical critic, it is natural that Eliot should have been liable to waverings and recantations. The most clamorous ones of his career have been those relating to his opinions of Milton.

At a certain moment Eliot, in 'A Note on the Verse of John Milton' (1936), contrasted Donne's poetry with Milton's, whose early sensuousness would have been withered by book-learning: according to Eliot, his language is artificial and conventional. In fact he writes English like a dead language; all in him is sacrificed to a musical effect, with the occasional debasement of poetry into a solemn game. Antipathy to Milton had been communicated to him by Ezra Pound, who in *The Spirit of Romance* had said: '*Paradise Lost* is conventional melodrama, and later critics have decided that the devil is

9. Preface to Leone Vivante's *English Poetry*, London, 1950, p. x.
10. In *Lectures in Criticism*, Johns Hopkins University, 1949.

intended for the hero, which interpretation leaves the whole without significance.' In his essay on Dante in *The Sacred Wood* Eliot wrote: 'About none of Dante's characters is there that ambiguity which affects Milton's Lucifer.' And in his book on Dante he alludes to Milton's Satan as 'the curly-haired Byronic hero of Milton'. When later, in 'A Note on the Verse of John Milton', Eliot wanted to show that Milton lacked visual fantasy, and that sound was everything that mattered for him, we hear again the echo of what Pound had written: 'In Milton or Swinburne ... it is too often merely a high-sounding word, and not a swift symbol of vanished beauty.' Eliot writes, in fact: [11]

There is no interruption between the surface that these poets [Dante and Shakespeare] present to you and the core. While, therefore, I cannot pretend to have penetrated to any secret of these poets, I feel that such appreciation of their work as I am capable of points in the right direction; whereas I cannot feel that my appreciation of Milton leads anywhere outside of the mazes of sound.

About ten years later, in 1947, Eliot recanted about Milton, in a lecture delivered at the British Academy, saying that when he and his friends started to write, they found it necessary to return language to colloquial speech and thus, as poets, to oppose the dangerous influence of Milton. Now the revolution had been successfully accomplished, and the situation had changed: we were now in a period of elaboration of language, and poets could afford to pay attention to the experiment of Milton.

This episode throws considerable light on the empirical character of Eliot's criticism.

His type of criticism, in his own words, is meant to be an integration of scholarly criticism. In *The Music of Poetry* he

11. 'A Note on the Verse of John Milton', in *Essays and Studies*, by Members of the English Association, vol. XXI, Oxford, 1936, p. 38.

said that his method was that of a poet 'always trying to defend the kind of poetry he is writing'; in *Milton II*, that the scholar is chiefly 'concerned with the understanding of the masterpiece in the environment of its author', whereas the practitioner 'is concerned less with the author than with the poem; and with the poem in relation to his own age'.

He asks: Of what *use* is the poetry of this poet to poets writing to-day? Is it, or can it become, a living force in English poetry still unwritten? So we may say that the scholar's interest is in the permanent, the practitioner's in the immediate.
... No poet can teach another to write well, but some great poets can teach others some of the things to avoid. They teach us what to avoid, by showing us what great poetry can do without – how *bare* it can be.

Here is the foundation of Eliot's cult for Dante:

For the science or art of writing verse, one has learned from the *Inferno* that the greatest poetry can be written with the greatest economy of words, and with the greatest austerity in the use of metaphor, simile, verbal beauty, and elegance. When I affirm that more can be learned about how to write poetry from Dante than from any English poet, I do not at all mean that Dante's way is the only right way, or that Dante is thereby *greater* than Shakespeare, or, indeed, any other English poet. I put my meaning into other words by saying that Dante can do less *harm* to any one trying to learn to write verse, than can Shakespeare. Most great English poets are *inimitable* in a way in which Dante was not. If you try to imitate Shakespeare you will certainly produce a series of stilted, forced, and violent distortions of language. The language of each great English poet is his own language; the langauge of Dante is the perfection of a common language. In a sense, it is more pedestrian than that of Dryden or Pope. If you follow Dante without talent, you will at worst be pedestrian and flat; if you follow Shakespeare or Pope without talent, you will make an utter fool of yourself.

As I have said elsewhere,[12] this statement can be qualified so far as Italian literature is concerned. Whenever Italians

12. *The Flaming Heart*, Anchor Books, 1958, 350–51.

have tried to imitate Dante, they sometimes have produced flat and pedestrian verse, but more frequently have written precisely in that stilted and forced style which Eliot thinks proper to the worst imitators of Shakespeare. I gave instances from Monti and D'Annunzio and (I may add now) Belli, who found the perfect medium for his colloquial mood in the Roman dialect, but found in Dante only the model for forced academic compositions. On the other hand, Italians who read Shakespeare frequently find his language direct and possessing the very accent of life. In either case it could be easily shown that the illusion is caused by the ignorance in which one naturally is of the conventions of a foreign language. What matters in Eliot's case is not to ascertain to what extent Dante's style can be considered *simple* (in fact, Dante fits his language to the theme so that examples of all kinds of style may be found in him), but to know that to Eliot that style *seems* simple.

It is again this ideal of a simple style, of poetry created out of everyday language, which caused Eliot to oppose the subdued eloquence of Lancelot Andrewes's sermons to the solemn and turbid rhetoric of Donne's, and to praise Dryden for having restored English verse to the condition of speech; because 'literature must be judged by language, it is the duty of the poet to develop language', 'to preserve, and even to restore, the health of language'. This principle, which becomes identified with his own experience as a poet, guides his evaluation of English poets and prose writers; and among prose writers he places rather low Sir Thomas Browne and Jeremy Taylor, in whom he finds 'common sententiousness in reverberating language', a 'language dissociated from things, assuming an independent existence', he disapproves of the poetic prose of Ruskin and Pater, and, as we have seen, blames Milton for exploiting the musical resources of the language to the utmost. He even praises the verse of Goldsmith and Samuel Johnson: 'Their verse is poetry partly because it has the virtues of good prose.'

Eliot's criticism is the opposite of what he calls 'etiolated

275

creation' – that is, what is commonly known as 'creative critic-ism', the criticism of a Pater or a Ruskin, of all those who, imperfect artists as they are, practise criticism as a vicarious satisfaction for a suppressed creative wish. Eliot, on the con-trary, sees criticism as a means apt to improve his own crafts-manship as a poet. In his lecture *Edgar Poe et la France* he said: 'Notre succès en tant que poètes dépend de la con-science que nous avons de la tâche que notre position particu-lière dans le temps et dans l'histoire de notre langue nous impose.' The changes of perspective he introduced into the history of English literature have therefore a personal charac-ter, they had his own advantage in view, they were *ad usum poetae*. His idea of criticism, as Wladimir Weidle has no-ticed,[13] is close to Boileau's, whose *Art poétique* aimed at teaching the craft of writing poetry, and at pointing out models and criteria (*The Criterion* was in fact the name Eliot gave to his literary magazine). There is however in Eliot a very important difference from Boileau: the laws he tries to discover and apply have no absolute validity in his eyes; they are closely related to historical circumstances. Eliot is not an originator of systems; one may grant to Karl Shapiro[14] that Eliot's contribution to the history of criticism is, if not very slight, certainly less conspicuous than his reputation would lead one to think: he has been anyhow a leader of taste, a sower of fruitful seeds, of whom, within the limits of his self-imposed task of reformer, one must admire both the earnest-ness and uprightness which have won him a universal esteem, and also the fundamental coherence even in his apparent or actually substantial contradictions.

13. 'L'Œuvre critique d'un poète', in *Critique*, 43, December 1950.
14. 'T. S. Eliot: The Death of Literary Criticism', *The Saturday Review*, 27 February 1960.

ELIOT'S LITERARY CRITICISM

By Austin Warren

I⊤ is not possible for me to think of T. S. Eliot as dead. If this is for many reasons, it is chiefly because his transferable self has so entered mine that I no longer – for long – have needed to re-read him and because I can no longer quote, from his criticism, without dubiety whether I am paraphrasing him or expressing my own views.

The first part of this essay, not before printed (save recently, in Japan),[1] was written about 1940. Resuming the piece in 1965, to commemorate *On Poetry and Poets*, I still could not use the 'past' tense in writing of him, nor could I, revising the writing done in 1940. Happily, the present tense can express that which yet lives.

1

There would be general consent among serious readers of Anglo-American poetry and criticism, I suppose, that T. S. Eliot has already become a classic of poetry and criticism and that subsequent 'improvements' are unlikely to dislodge him from that position. His rank in contemporary poetry is with Yeats. In criticism, his status is quite as isolate.

In common practice critical reflection succeeds to creative exercise; but the poet and the critic in Eliot began almost concurrently (*Poems 1919*; *The Sacred Wood*, 1920) and have co-existed in close relation. In the poetry there has always been implicit a criticism of life; but, more, the poetry has been itself the fastidious product of a critical mind, impatient with the first thought and the loosely approximate phrase. The criticism, in turn, has been chiefly criticism of poetry, dramatic, epic, and meditative, most of this recognizable (like

1. In *The East-West Review*.

Coleridge's and unlike Arnold's) as the work of a poet analysing for the benefit of his own art the achievements of others and addressed to the general reader only through the form of a poet's counsel to poets – ultimately, to himself. Thus Eliot's long – and, for him, specialized – study of the Elizabethans was evidently sustained by his desire to revive poetic drama, a desire which much later found expression in *Murder in the Cathedral*, *The Family Reunion*, *The Cocktail Party*, and *The Confidential Clerk*.

This double resonance of poet and critic has given Eliot's name its authority, its place in the roll of English literary dictators which begins with Ben Jonson, follows with Dryden, Pope, and Samuel Johnson, and carries through the nineteenth century with the careers of those poet–critic–theologians, Coleridge and Arnold.

Eliot is not an easy critic to summarize. Trained in Oriental and Occidental philosophy, he has learned from his teachers rather caution than system-building. Prose like *The Idea of a Christian Society* is almost infuriating by virtue of the things which, amid a hundred implications and qualifications, it leaves unsaid and undone. Perhaps the chief of his 'teachers' in this cautious and elegant precision is the British neo-Hegelian, F. H. Bradley, on whom Eliot wrote a Harvard dissertation. *Selected Essays* commemorates Bradley in a brilliant piece written in 1927 upon the republication of the philosopher's *Ethical Studies*. Since Eliot's conversion to Anglo-Catholicism some time in the 1920s, readers have inquired and wondered concerning his grounds for faith in a time of which one might say, as the great eighteenth-century Anglican bishop, Joseph Butler, did of his own: 'It is come ... to be taken for granted by many persons that Christianity is not so much a subject of inquiry, but that it is now at length discovered to be fictitious.'

Yet Eliot has produced no apologia for his conversion; nor has he attempted to argue his political philosophy, which appears to be the Distributism of Chesterton and Belloc, best expressed in Belloc's *The Servile State*. He once described himself – in a statement which he has since regretted for its pontificality – as Anglo-Catholic in religion, royalist in politics, and classicist in literature; but he has long ago repented, not of his allegiances, but of his tone. His literary creed he is ready to defend; but, in spite of an increasing shift of interest from poetry and aesthetic analysis to sociology and theology, he has the full modern respect for specialized expertness and is unwilling to make the case for political or theological truth rest upon such arguments as a literary amateur can provide. In notes and appendices he will refer to his political and theological experts; but he shrinks, in dismay, from such frontal invasions as Arnold's *Literature and Dogma*.

He has repeatedly repudiated two positions characteristic of the nineteenth century and specifically of the criticism of Arnold: (1) that the poet possesses some special insight into the nature of reality, and (2) that poetry will more and more take the place of religion. He wrote in 1927

I can see no reason for believing that either Dante or Shakespeare did any thinking on his own.... The difference between Shakespeare and Dante is that Dante had one coherent system of thought behind him.... The poet who 'thinks' is merely the poet who can express the emotional equivalent of thought.

The business of the poet is to produce 'objective correlatives' for thought, the imaginative illusion of a view of life. Of the nineteenth century and the Arnoldian belief in 'salvation by poetry', Eliot declares:

The decay of religion, and the attrition of political institutions, left dubious frontiers upon which the poet encroached; and the annexations of the poet were legitimized by the critic. For a long time the poet is the priest; there are still, I believe, people who imagine that they draw religious aliment from Browning or Meredith.

Despite his pontifical style, of which he is aware, Eliot is not only a shy and self-distrustful but a spiritually humble man. Of the poet's work he says: 'We shall often find that not only the best, but the most individual parts of his work may be those in which the dead poets, his ancestors, assert their immortality most vigorously'; and, discussing the function of criticism, he writes: 'Those of us who find ourselves supporting . . . classicism believe that men cannot get on without giving allegiance to something outside themselves.' As in poetry, he has been unembarrassed by indicating his teachers – Dante, Webster, Donne, Dryden, Laforgue, Corbière, Pound – so in criticism, extrinsic and intrinsic, he has confessed his debts – confessions which must not be negated because they are often accompanied by that kind of detailed dissent which one come of age must always make from the tenets of his teacher. When the full chronicle of Eliot's tutelage comes to be written, the parts played in the formation of his mind by Arnold, by F. H. Bradley, by Rémy de Gourmont, by T. E. Hulme, by Ezra Pound, and by Irving Babbitt will be made clear.

His Harvard teacher he has called 'one of the most remarkable of our critics, one who is fundamentally on most questions in the right, and very often right alone . . .'; and, at the time of the humanist controversy, when Eliot, already convinced that only the Catholic Church could save civilization, was most remote from his affectionate allegiance, he could write: 'Having myself begun as a disciple of Mr Babbitt, I feel that I have rejected nothing that seems to me positive in his teaching. . . .' The influence of Babbitt has, in important respects, grown stronger in recent years.

One must remember that Eliot has a less dogmatic but a more subtle mind than that of his teacher and, further, that Eliot is and was a poet, while Babbitt was markedly insensitive to the arts except as the media of propaganda. Eliot, too, felt that Babbitt was – what perhaps followed from his insensitivity – inadequately aware of how, concretely, civilization is transmitted, through tradition, ritual, manners, and etiquette. In 'his interest in the messages of individuals – messages conveyed in books – he has tended', says Eliot, 'to neglect the conditions. The great men whom he holds up for our admiration and example are torn from their contexts of race, place, and time.' Eliot must make a twofold translation: as a man, he must find an 'objective correlative', an institution, an organism which shall supply the continuum and the incarnation for the sporadic abstraction, humanism; and, as a poet, he must discover the aesthetic equivalent of what was represented by Babbitt chiefly as a matter of sound ethical insight – classicism. The first of these needs led Eliot to England, where Henry James had found civilization still extant, and to the Anglican Church, and later to Agrarian Distributism, upon which, as represented by Southerners Ransom, Tate, and Davidson, he has bestowed his apostolic blessing. The second took earliest expression in the famous essay of 1919, 'Tradition and the Individual Talent', in many respects the germinal essay of Eliot's whole thought, specifically of his literary thought.

Babbitt had indoctrinated the young poet with his own anti-Romantic bias, and 'Tradition and the Individual Talent' can best be understood as an artists's version of *Rousseau and Romanticism*. Babbitt had derisively reiterated Rousseau's 'I may not be better than other men, but I am at least different'; and Eliot repudiates, with all the zeal of a convert, any ambition to 'difference'.

The artist's concern with originality ... may be considered as largely negative: he wishes only to avoid saying what has already been said as well as it can be.... To assert that a work is 'original' should be very modest praise: it should be no more than to say that the work is not patently negligible.

The quotations just made come from a work written in 1934; and *After Strange Gods* returns in a fashion to the essay of 1919, 'Tradition and the Individual Talent', to which the author, now older, prefatorily adverts:

I do not repudiate what I wrote in that essay any more fully than I should expect to do after such a lapse of time. The problem, naturally, does not seem to me so simple as it seemed then, nor could I treat it now as a purely literary one.

The 'purely literary' treatment of 1919 might be rehearsed somewhat as follows. Babbitt had talked of philosophical and moral tradition; Eliot, meditating the office of the poet, and concerned then neither to affirm nor to deny the transmission of ideology, translated what he apprehended into a parallel doctrine of aesthetic continuity. He was impressed by what Babbitt had to reiterate concerning the difference between the Renaissance conception of the poet as a man of learning and of aesthetic craft (a technical discipline) and the Romantic conception of the poet as a child, a dreamer, and a prophet, whose spontaneity was the badge of his office, who glorified not the 'we' but the 'I', whose poems were personal confessions, and whose production was unlikely to survive the adolescent years of eager curiosity concerning the self, eager contemplation of first love.

Like Newman, Eliot wanted to discover the 'second spring', the power of self-renewal. Why, in particular, was the history of American poetry so replete with unfulfilled promise? Was it not that, in too narrow and literal a sense, the poet 'looked into *his heart* and wrote'? Eliot was asking these questions for himself first of all, for he wrote the essay as he was nearing thirty – three years before the publication of *The Waste Land*, his first attempt at sustained poetry.

Answering his own questions in a 'purely literary' way, he had to reply that the poet can and must draw upon a strength outside himself, that of his ancestral poets, that of the communion of poets. The

historical sense ... we may call nearly indispensable to any one who would continue to be a poet beyond his twenty-fifth year; and the historical sense involves a perception, not only of the pastness of the past, but of its presence; the historical sense compels a man to write not merely with his own generation in his bones, but with a feeling that the whole of the literature of

Europe from Homer and within it the whole of the literature of his own country has a simultaneous existence and composes a simultaneous order.

This phrase 'simultaneous existence' supplies the needed corrective to the emphasis upon the 'historical sense'.

Like Babbitt, Eliot has always been concerned not with the historical scholar's or the Romanticist's 'pastness of the past' but with the classicist's and the critic's and the poet's 'awareness of the presence of the past'. Science improves, but art – except within specific modes – does not; and Eliot has never had the modernist's patronizing pity for the dead masters or Dr Johnson's regret for Milton, who wrote before Waller and Denham had refined our numbers.

As the poet's learning is a realization, not a discovery of new facts about the facts, so it is by no means necessarily a matter of courses and degrees. 'Some can absorb knowledge; the more tardy must sweat for it.' The neo-classical inquiry concerning Shakespeare's learning is essentially academic, for 'Shakespeare acquired more essential history from Plutarch than most men could from the whole British Museum'.

The corollary of this anti-romantic attachment to tradition and the 'presence of the past' is Eliot's attack on what C. S. Lewis has termed the 'Personal Heresy' and what may more obviously be described as the biographical approach to literature.

'Honest criticism and sensitive appreciation are directed not upon the poet but upon the poetry.' The test of a poet's achievement is that he has given self-subsistent life to a poem, that it can be understood and valued without referentially attaching it to the biography of its author. And this counsel applies to the poet as well as the reader, for the good poet is not concerned to perpetuate his private self. 'Poetry is not a turning loose of emotion, but an escape from emotion; it is not the expression of personality, but an escape from personality.'

All this sounds like a kind of classicism, and Eliot has several times named himself of that fold. But his classicism still less than Babbitt's is to be identified with 'Be Homer's works your study and delight'. Eliot has, to be sure, an affection for neo-classical artists like Ben Jonson (of whom he has written with penetration and justice), as for Dryden, Pope, Johnson, Racine; his 'classicism' includes Shakespeare and Dante; but includes, in some sense, Donne, Baudelaire, Corbière, Pound.

After Strange Gods does not succeed in making wholly clear what 'classicism' means to Eliot: The terms which stand for our basic concepts, the concepts *through which* we think, are exactly the terms we have most difficulty in defining;[2] but he offers two suggestive elucidations. Speaking as a poet who had produced poetry which seemed to Babbitt and Paul More (as well as Yvor Winters) anything but classical, Eliot makes the shrewd point that

romanticism and classicism are not matters with which *creative writers* can afford to bother overmuch; ... I doubt whether any poet has ever done himself anything but harm by attempting to write as a 'romanticist' or as a 'classicist'. No sensible author, in the midst of something that he is trying to write, can stop to consider whether it is going to be romantic or the opposite.

At the moment when one writes, one is what one is, and the damage of a lifetime, and of having been born into an unsettled society, cannot be repaired at the moment of composition.[3]

The second elucidation is offered by the word 'society'. 'Tradition' is not a purely literary term; it plays an important part in Catholic theology, and families and countries have their traditions. As he passes from the literary to the extra-literary, Eliot enlarges without substantially altering his sense

2. 'In defining criticism we are constantly using terms which we cannot define, and defining other things by them.' 'Experiment in Criticism', *Bookman*, New York, November 1929.
3. *After Strange Gods*, pp. 26–7. Italics mine. 'It shall hardly be necessary to add that "classical" is just as unpredictable as the romantic; and that most of us would not recognize a classical writer if he appeared ...', ibid., p. 31.

of tradition, associating it with 'orthodoxy', as the lack of tradition is to be associated with heterodoxy or heresy. Tradition 'is not solely or primarily the maintenance of dogmatic beliefs; ... it involves all those habitual actions, habits, and customs ... which represent the blood kinship of "the same people living in the same place"', the mores of a homogeneous population; it is 'a way of feeling and acting', largely unconscious, whereas its correlative, orthodoxy, is 'a matter which calls for the exercise of all our conscious intelligence'. Tradition 'has not the means to criticise itself'; and hence the need of a living orthodoxy, expressing itself in philosophy of religion as well as dogma, and maintained (Eliot has suggested, in language suggestive of Coleridge's) by a 'clerisy' of Christian intellectuals.

Unlike Babbitt, Eliot still makes a distinction between *literary* criticism and *moral*. Of *After Strange Gods*, he says, 'I ascended the platform ... only in the role of moralist', though to be sure he draws illustrations of morality and immorality from works of literature. Like Babbitt, Eliot knows that 'art' and 'prudence' belong together in life; but, like Aristotle and Maritain, Eliot believes that it promotes confusion not to allow for and to practise a preliminary distinction between Poetics, Ethics, and Politics. 'The "greatness" of literature cannot be determined solely by literary standards; though we must remember that whether it is literature or not can be determined only by literary standards.'[4]

To return to Eliot's literary criticism: After 'Tradition', his most famous and perhaps even more influential essay is that on the 'Metaphysical Poets', published in 1921, an essay which encouraged so ardent a cult for John Donne that Eliot himself, contributing the initial essay to an anniversary *Garland* (1931), felt called to chill it. This put into gradual operation a new hierarchic pattern for the history of English poetry.

4. cf. Eliot's stricture on Arnold: 'He was apt to think of the greatness of poetry rather than its genuineness.' *The Use of Poetry*, p. 110.

From time to time, every hundred years or so, it is desirable that some critic shall appear to review the past of our literature, and set the poets and the poems in a new order.... Dryden, Johnson, and Arnold have each performed the task as well as human frailty will allow. The majority of critics can be expected only to parrot the opinions of the last master of criticism; among more independent minds a period of destruction, of preposterous over-estimation, and of successive fashions takes place, until a new authority comes to introduce some order.

Eliot tactfully desists from naming himself as, in this important capacity, Arnold's successor; but the Harvard auditors of 1933 who listened to the first series of Norton Lectures, *quorum pars fui,* were ready to supply the name. This revaluation, which has been systematized and popularized by F. R. Leavis and Cleanth Brooks, extends through the range of Eliot's essays on English poetry and drama; but it is most concentratedly offered in his review of Grierson's *Metaphysical Lyrics.* Arnold, in his 'Study of Poetry', had rushed from the Elizabethans, whose quality we are supposed to know and esteem, to the ethical Wordsworth. There was the inadequately serious Chaucer; then Shakespeare, 'free' from the necessity of abiding our question; then, after a sad interregnum of neo-classical prose, calling itself verse, and of Gray, a frail classic, and of Burns, with his triple Scotch, 'At last, Wordsworth came.'

For Eliot, the height of English poetry comes earlier – in the late Elizabethans, the Jacobeans, and the Carolines.

The language went on and in some respects improved; the best verse of Collins, Gray, Johnson, and even Goldsmith satisfies some of our fastidious demands better than that of Donne or Marvell or King. But while the language became more refined, the feeling grew more crude.

Eliot's theory of poetry falls neither into didacticism nor into its opposite heresies, imagism and echolalia. The real 'purity' of poetry – to speak in terms at once paradoxical and generic – is to be constantly and richly impure: neither philosophy, nor psychology, nor imagery, nor music alone, but a significant tension between all of them.

Orthodoxy is always more difficult to state than heresy, which is the development of an isolated 'truth'; but Eliot excels at copious illustration and analysis of illustration; and his conception of poetic orthodoxy and the hierarchy of poets which he has arranged according to it may be said to have supplanted Arnold's.

This brilliantly sensitive analysis of illustrations cannot be exhibited by excerpts. And accurate as one hopes one's statements of Eliot's general position to be, one who places him, as I do, in the first rank of all critics past and present, must feel, as I do, that schematic outlines do him a special injustice. His characteristic virtue lies less in perspective than in that close study of the poetic text of which he was, in English, the inaugurator,[5] and in the extraordinary kind of critical wit by which he compares, by virtue of a special, shared quality or category, historically and sometimes stylistically disjunct poets – for example, Mallarmé and Dryden.

The critical instruments he once named as chief – analysis and comparison – he has used with exemplary skill. If his interest has gradually shifted from intrinsic criticism, it has been a shift of emphasis rather than a repudiation. The total effect of consecutively re-reading Eliot's remarkable criticism, written over a considerable time and chiefly 'occasional', is to be surprised far less by disjunction than by continuity and development.

5. 'The closeness of Mr Eliot in discussing a text may well be greater than anybody's before him, and he in turn now may be even exceeded in closeness by [the late R. P.] Blackmur, and perhaps others. These are close critics, and define our age as one of critical genius.' (Ransom, *The World's Body*, 1935, p. 173.) Eliot is not, I think, retracting his method when, in his 1956 'Frontiers of Criticism', he objects to the analysis of a single poem 'without reference to the author or to his other work' – what he calls 'the lemon-squeezer school of criticism'. (*On Poetry and Poets*, p. 125)

2

In 1957 Eliot published a collection of his critical essays, *On Poetry and Poets*, essays subsequent to *Selected Essays* (1932). Like its predecessor, this book represents the author's selection; and another critic may regret both omissions and conclusions. For my part, I certainly regret the omission of *From Poe to Valéry*, a study of Poe as seen by Baudelaire, Mallarmé, and Valéry, which was published in the *Hudson Review* in 1948 and privately printed by Harcourt, Brace; and I regret the inclusion of an address on 'Goethe as the Sage', in which Eliot, who does not like Goethe, though he knows one ought to admire him, is largely, and embarrassingly, reduced to an autobiographical account of his traffic with this world-figure, supplemented by quotations from modern German critics, Josef Pieper, Professor Heller of Cardiff, and Hans Holthusen.

But with this puzzlement over exclusions and inclusions on Eliot's part one is familiar. What was – and is – reassuring about the book is its testimony that with increased sense of social responsibility – as, say, Matthew Arnold's successor – Eliot was still capable of literary judgement.

The essay I would single out as most characteristic of Eliot's special gifts is 'What Is Minor Poetry?', which opens with the remark, 'I do not propose to offer, either at the beginning or at the end, a definition of "minor poetry".' The promise is kept; and, in consequence, the essay is scarcely more susceptible of summary than Eliot's best early essays. Like them, it abounds in remarks and insights, but the effect is to advance critical discrimination and critical sensibility, not to offer, or reject, principles which can be taken down in note-books and applied without sensibility or discrimination.

The take-off is undoubtedly the common, and even venerable and to be venerated, tradition that major poets are those who, like Virgil and Milton, have written, after their shorter, their 'minor' works, poems of sweep, scope, and amplitude, a view to which (in parenthetical passing) Eliot agrees as true of 'the *very* greatest poets'. But one gets closer to Eliot's position in his treatment of George Herbert, whose *Temple* gives the 'feeling of a unifying personality' and whose structured book of short poems gives one who knows it well not the recollection of 'a few favourite poems' but 'the whole work'.

Eliot ends this essay – if 'end' be the word – with a *caveat* (partly, like the whole essay, doubtless directed against Arnold's 'Study of Poetry', or what pedagogues have made of it): a word against premature concern, more particularly with poetry contemporary with us, as to whether it is 'major' or 'minor', when all we can hope to do is to pass judgement on whether it is '*genuine*' poetry or not.

The mere effort to summarize, after a fashion, this essay, which in 1957 gave me the happy feeling that – in becoming so many other things – Eliot had not lost the ability to be a *literary* critic, gives me anew, and probably better than in any other way, the judgement I expressed, twenty years ago, that 'schematic outlines do him a special injustice'.

I remember my first puzzlement at reading Eliot's essays, not wholly unlike that at first reading Emerson's essays. To say that neither could construct a discourse with exordium, pointed and numbered substance, and final summary is (as Emerson's early sermons show) absurd.

> Th' Eliotic touch, how exquisitely fine!
> Feels at each thread, and lives along the line.

The Eliotic essay says in a sentence what, sensibly, a teacher may expand by repetition in other words and by examples into a paragraph; but the essay is printed, or to be printed: if you don't understand the sentence the first time, re-read it, construct your own amplifying paragraph. It is as closely written as most poetry and as most philosophy, even though no one, in his own language at least, has been so sensitive to the distinctions among the three as has Eliot.

The earlier volume assembled essays chiefly written for

publication; the present, essays chiefly written (like *The Music of Poetry*) for reading before audiences. This distinction alters the essays less than one might fear. But the distinction is symptomatic. In the last fifteen or twenty years of his life, Eliot was an eminent man, eminent not merely among literary men and poets. But the distinction seems to hold that Eliot is weaker in his essays on relatively abstract topics like 'The Social Function of Poetry' or *What Is a Classic?*, stronger on essays on a specific poet. If I exempt 'What Is Minor Poetry?' it is for the same reason that I would certainly exempt 'The Metaphysical Poets' in the earlier volume : he is not attempting some *a priori* thinking about genres; he is testing tentative hypotheses against specific cases (e.g., Herbert, Herrick, Campion). But from the later volume I still miss that rapid (and almost unreproducible) collation not of names but of lines of verse from Latin, French, and English poets which appears, say, in the masterly essay on Marvell. And it is difficult not to connect that with the fact that the essays were the poet writing for himself primarily; the lectures, for an audience assembled to hear a topic discussed, and discussed with a certain weight and pontificality, by a man who, shy and proud, proud and shy, could find no more suitable *persona*.

In both volumes much attention is paid to verse drama. The earlier essays are those of a young man reading the Elizabethans to learn from them (that, of course, is a simplified account); the later essays, notably *Poetry and Drama*, are the accounts of a twentieth-century poet writing, at long last, his own verse dramas – the motifs out of Greek tragedy, the language relatively colloquial, though not that of Marie Lloyd and the British 'music hall', nor yet of *Sweeney Agonistes* (American vaudeville).

I think that Eliot didn't succeed at verse drama; and I think that his essays written while getting ready to write such have more to offer than his post-composition accounts – conscientious, certainly, however accurate – of where he thought he had blundered. But I am willing to believe that, like Henry

James's plays, they 'taught' their author much and were of all kinds of peripheral help. I wish that Eliot might have lived to demonstrate that life-renewing power.

Eliot has always put great stress upon the rhythm of verse: upon that, and upon the poet's imagery and his vocabulary. I want to say something about each.

So far as *rhythm* and *image* are concerned, the closest (even though vague) statement occurs in *The Music of Poetry*, when he declares that 'a poem, or a passage of a poem, may tend to realise itself first as a particular rhythm before it reaches expression in words', and 'this rhythm may bring to birth *the idea* and *the image*; and I do not believe that this is an experience peculiar to myself'; or again when, in his *Use of Poetry*, he defines the 'auditory imagination', which (primarily at least) is that of the poet, as 'the feeling for syllable and rhythm, *penetrating far below the conscious levels of thought and feeling,* invigorating every word; sinking to the most primitive and forgotten . . .' It 'fuses the old and obliterated and the trite, the current, and the new and surprising, the *most ancient and the most civilised mentality*'.

Behind this passage from *The Use of Poetry* is Eliot's view (tentative, perhaps, but so far as I know never abandoned) that 'the pre-logical mentality persists in civilized man, but becomes available only . . . through the poet'.

The later passage, from *The Music of Poetry*, less ambitiously offers some comment on the genesis of poems which can, I should think, be accepted without difficulty: i.e., sometimes a wordless 'tune' comes first, sometimes an 'image', sometimes 'the idea' – *image* and *idea* are both far from univocal words; as for 'the idea', the idea for a poem is very different from 'the idea' of pantheism, or of Nature, or of communism. If Eliot still felt daring in suggesting that rhythm might come first, it must have been the remainder of his New England conscience, remembering and reacting against the Boston Browning Society and remembering, and making far more subtle, the doctrine of that Southerner E. A. Poe.

Eliot thinks – and quite rightly, I believe – that the *meaning* of poetry is partly in its rhythm; that in some cases, the meaning as rhythm may come first; that in all cases, the rhythm is a substantive part of the meaning.

'The image,' says Eliot. One would think it more natural to say 'the imagery'. This very special use of 'the image' seems to go back to Ezra Pound's 1913 definition of an 'Image' as

that which presents an intellectual and emotional complex in an instant of time. It is the presentation of such a 'complex' instantaneously which gives the sense of sudden liberation; that sense of freedom from time limits and space limits . . . which we experience in the presence of the greatest works of art.

T. E. Hulme wrote to the same effect. Neither is concerned with what 'Imagism' suggests – namely, the limitation of poetry to the physical image. They seem nearest to meaning some Western equivalent of the Japanese *hokku* – and Pound expressly makes mention of these forms as he writes about his, the briefest and most famous Imagist poem, 'In a Station of the Metro'. But they seem also to mean what James Joyce later gave currency to by the theological word 'epiphany'. In his essay prefatory to *The Imagist Poem* (1963), William Pratt does not use Joyce's word; but he seems to be talking about the same thing:

What is the image of the Imagist poem? Essentially, it is a moment of revealed truth, rather than a structure of consecutive events or thoughts. The plot or argument of elder poetry is replaced by a single, dominant, image, or a quick succession of related images: its effect is meant to be instantaneous rather than cumulative.

In the concluding chapter to *The Use of Poetry* (1933), Eliot asks:

Why, for all of us, out of all that we have heard, seen, felt, in a lifetime, do certain images recur, charged with emotion, rather than others? The song of one bird, . . . an old woman on a German mountain path, six ruffians seen through an open window playing cards at night at a small French railway junction where there was a water-mill: *such memories may have symbolic value*, but of what we cannot tell, for they come to represent the depths of feeling into which we cannot peer.

The unstated implication is that these 'certain images' which have – or may have – 'symbolic value' are not purely personal: the poet certainly needs to think that in getting them written with precision he is saying something which an indefinite number of others will, at the wave of the poet's baton, perceive.

Now before I leave the 'auditory imagination' and 'the image' (partly, at least, visual), I must try to bring together – or at least into 'confrontation' – what seems the most patent self-contradiction in Eliot's theory of poetry.

It would seem, from Eliot's general remarks on the 'auditory imagination', that it is a boon and blessing to a poet. Yet the famous essay of 1936 seems to consider it damning. 'The most important fact about Milton, for my purpose, is his blindness.... At no period is the visual imagination conspicuous in Milton's poetry.' And both in the 1936 and the 1947 essays, Milton is grouped with Joyce – the later Joyce, especially the Joyce of *Finnegans Wake*.

The general answer appears to be that a poet should have *both* the auditory and the visual imaginations. It is but just to Eliot to say that, as a poet, he had both; and that he found both in Shakespeare and Dante. But the general answer doesn't wholly dispose of the matter. It is a particular kind of auditory imagination which Eliot objects to – what he sometimes calls (in the case of Milton) the *rhetorical*, sometimes the generalizing, sometimes (not quite naming it) the 'inhuman': the rhetoric of Milton and the second sequences and puns of *Finnegans Wake* are both the work of artists whose art was a mode of escape from the particularities of persons and personal relationships.

When, in 1943, Eliot lectured on 'The Social Function of Poetry', he was ready to dismiss most which most people would think of as the 'social function' of anything – such as moral edification. The 'duty of the poet, as poet, is only indirectly to his people: his direct duty is to his *language*, first to preserve, and second to extend and improve' – for the reasons that he makes his readers aware of what they feel already, but, still more, because he 'can make his readers share consciously in new feelings which they had not experienced before', but which are 'new variations of sensibility' which they can appropriate.

Language is bound up with thoughts, emotions, feelings. We can't think/feel without words to give them precision, so that 'unless we have those few men who combine an exceptional sensibility with an exceptional power over words, our own ability, *not merely to express*, but even *to feel* any but the crudest emotions, will degenerate'. The view here taken is plainly an aristocratic view: It is impossible to give precision to our feelings without naming them. This the poet knows, as the philosopher (Eliot by training) knows, that without such naming, concepts cannot be defined. That 'most men' should have read either philosopher or poet is unnecessary: his words descend, linger – becoming all the while more vague. Then, even to *preserve* the old meaning – whether concepts or emotions – new words have to be devised.

It used to seem to me strange that, of the *Four Quartets*, Eliot's most serious and, I dare say, lasting poem, three contain an express section on the 'problem' of language. Despite the first epigraph from Heraclitus ('But, though the Word is common, the "many" live as though they had a wisdom of their own'), these sections are not directly, still less exclusively, about the Christian Logos, prefigured though it may be by Heraclitus' Word. 'The Word made flesh' is, at a literary level, the Idea or the Wisdom given expression in human terms. Without ever ruling out this central theology, Eliot has, in the sections to which I refer, made a masterly series of modulations, transitions, implications. Being a poet, he naturally sees and says, in this centrally theological poem, something about the tiny ground which his profession entitled him to speak of as ground in common with the Great Poet. Eliot was never more successfully Dantesque than in these passages: on the one hand so remarkably personal, on the other so little personal. These passages can all be taken quite mundanely – or, at least, humanistically; yet imperceptibly, almost, they move from the 'words' to the 'Word', the shared Wisdom.

Words: we can't speak, think, or feel without them; yet neither can we speak, think, or feel relying on them: they are treacherous all. Words 'slip, slide, perish,/Decay with imprecision, . . ./Will not stay still.'

In *Little Gidding*, during an air-raid (a time when a poet may well ask him what the 'social function' of poetry may be) the poet meets a composite ghost of dead masters, of which Henry James seems chief. This 'ghost' says,

> 'Since our concern was speech, and speech impelled us
> To purify the dialect of the tribe. . . .'

And the second line I quote is a translation from Mallarmé's 'Le Tombeau d'Edgar Poe' – 'Donner un sens plus pur aux mots de la tribe.'

3

Thus far I have written of Eliot as a critic preparing himself to write. But I do not want to end without comment on Eliot as an historical critic (something quite other than an historical scholar), as he shows himself in 'Johnson as Critic and Poet' (1944), one of his sensitively best performances. I wish Eliot had written more such emphatic studies. 'I consider,' he says,

Johnson one of the three greatest critics of poetry in English literature: the other two being Dryden and Coleridge. All of these men were poets, and with all of them, a study of their poetry is highly relevant to the study of their criticism, because each of them was interested in a particular kind of poetry.

Eliot's comparably close studies of Dryden and Coleridge were never written; but the 'Johnson' gives one a notion of how they would have been conducted and even – for the ambitious, but not for ambitious novices – some notion of how to conduct them.

Most signal is the fact that Eliot set himself to read the poets who, at Johnson's instigation, were added to the poets whom the booksellers who got up the collection Johnson was to preface proposed adding: Sir Richard Blackmore, perhaps the chief. And then Eliot read carefully the writers of blank verse whom Johnson exempted from his general indictment of blank verse – notably Akenside. The attempt is to read closely Johnson's praise, together with its reserves, and apply *it* to a poem, or passage from a poem, by the poet closely criticized by Johnson. This is not so simple as it sounds: like studies in 'sources' and 'influences', it is work for the most sensitive and mature, not apprentice work for beginners.

In praising Akenside's *Pleasures of the Imagination*, Johnson said: 'With the philosophical or religious tenets of the author I have nothing to do; my business is with his poetry.' As a matter of fact, Johnson's hostile views of Milton, as of other poets, are to be found in the 'Lives', which are always separated from the critical analysis and appraisal of the 'Works'. But Johnson – and this is a part of the envy with which Eliot views him –

was in a position, as no critic of equal stature has been since, to write purely *literary* criticism, just because he was able to assume that there was [in his age] a general attitude towards life, and a common opinion as to the place of poetry in it.

4

There is no particular value in trying to read Eliot's criticism rapidly or trying to summarize it for examinations. For such purposes, many critics whom I respect, or at least consider competent – critics whose names I should not cite – will serve better.

But Eliot does himself an injustice by thinking of himself as offering 'Thoughts from a writer's workshop'. He wrote in a time of difficulty, when the general cultural assumptions he ascribes to Johnson no longer prevailed. He wrote (in his best work) for himself, but not merely about the 'problem' of his own reviving of verse drama or anyone's reviving it (a dubious attempt in my judgement).

He wrote with that courage which – strange name to link with Eliot's – Emerson had: that courage to suppose that one could help others think and write, creatively or critically, by addressing himself, contending with his own intellectual difficulties, by trying to be as precise as possible, by not simplifying, not supplying rhetorical beginnings and endings, by never generalizing without accompanying analysis of specificities, by never being analytic of the specificity without attempting to see what, in consequence, happened to one's necessary hypothetical generalization.

BAUDELAIRE AND ELIOT:
INTERPRETERS OF THEIR AGE

By Wallace Fowlie

THE poet T. S. Eliot, whom we are honouring today, did not wait for eternity in order to change into himself. His voice, the expression on his face, as well as his work, testified, during the last years of his life, to certain ways of thinking and feeling which are usually associated with a classical writer, with a man who already occupies his place in the history of letters and the history of civilization.

The slightly transformed line of Mallarmé serving as our initial sentence was first applied to the American Poe whom Eliot perhaps would not have read so attentively if Baudelaire had not revealed him to American readers of poetry. The poet is a wayfarer, an intercessor, an intermediary, because of whom we are able to feel related to forces that surpass our minds. Because of him, the universe perceived by our senses, seasons and cities, men and their wretchedness, are loved attentively and fervently and knowingly. Baudelaire and Eliot were poets, and for that reason they are today, when they are no longer among the living, our witnesses. They speak for us. We hardly know them. But they know us, and they know many things beyond us.

Toward the middle of the nineteenth century, Baudelaire was representative of a certain number of elements which the spiritual make-up of France did not possess at that time, and which, ever since Baudelaire's age, have been studied and explored with an ever-renewed critical acumen.

Toward the middle of the twentieth century, between 1930 and 1950, Eliot's position in England and America was comparable to Baudelaire's. Every page in the writings of Baudelaire, and every page in the writings of Eliot, celebrates the imagination as man's noblest faculty. A little more than half a century separates the two poets, but each, in his own age, gave evidence of the same gifts and the same plans for a poetic work: the analysis, the lucidity, and the affirmation of the self. Both nurtured the impassioned plan to rediscover authentic human values, and to oppose those forms of stagnation which in each generation man invents for his own misery.

Baudelaire and Eliot were never militant members of any group. Somewhat distant and somewhat secretive, but with an intellectual firmness which caused them to be respected and even a bit feared, they studied a certain number of matters which have dominated the critical conscience and poetic creativity in Europe and America during the last one hundred years.

Eliot's tradition was as French as it was English. He read Baudelaire for the first time in 1907 or 1908, and he himself said that this reading moved him deeply. The book of Arthur Symons on the French Symbolists, read in 1908, revealed Laforgue to him, and for some time after that, Laforgue's influence was stronger than Baudelaire's. Eliot was especially impressed by Baudelaire's feeling for his age. Baudelaire's art represented an awareness of man's situation in the modern world. Baudelaire's example taught Eliot that it was necessary to find a new language, a language adequate to transmit the feelings of modern man. The poet's first obligation is to create a language that is his, in order not to lose his identity as a poet.

In his essay 'Donne in Our Time', Eliot develops the thesis that a poet in the early part of his career should find a particular poet or a particular school of poetry for whom or for which he feels a close sympathy, and because of whom he can train his talent. To a large degree, Baudelaire was this poet for Eliot.

If we place side by side the two careers of Baudelaire and Eliot, the first beginning about 1845 and the second ending about 1955 or 1960, we have an extent of time which, roughly, is the modern era, a century of European and American civilization, of which the principal characteristic, according to Baudelaire and Eliot, is disorder. Disorder in every domain.

For Eliot, Baudelaire was much more than a poet. He was the inventor of a significant attitude, an outlook on the disorder he saw everywhere. He was also the inventor of a way of feeling, a way of understanding disorder. He was perhaps especially for Eliot the believer in moral values. For Baudelaire was the writer who, at the dawn of modern poetry, claimed that all first-rate poetry is preoccupied with morality. According to Eliot, Baudelaire's greatness was largely due to his awareness of the problem of good and evil. If Baudelaire discovered for himself certain religious values – humility, for example, the need for prayer, the notion of original sin – his obligation as a poet (Eliot said this many times) was not to practise Christianity as a religion, but to make its necessity felt in the modern world.

In his last essay on Baudelaire, that of 1930, Eliot repeated the thought of his important sentence: 'Man is man because he can recognize supernatural realities, not because he can invent them.' Villon's poetry, as well as Baudelaire's, was for Eliot an unconsciously Christian poetry. In answer to an interview in *La France Libre* in 1944 (15 June), Eliot, in explaining what France meant to him, said that if he had not discovered Baudelaire, and the lineage of Baudelairian poets, he believed that he would not have become a writer.

The new American poetry, that which derived from neither the tradition of Poe, a tradition emphasizing subjectivism and musical qualities, nor the tradition of Whitman, more rhetorical and popular, was born in London about 1915. The influence of the French Symbolists marked and enriched all of the new poetry. W. B. Yeats, in Chicago, on the evening of 1 March 1914, in the rooms of the Cliff-Dwellers, where he was being honoured at a dinner given by *Poetry Magazine*, said in a speech reported in the April 1914 issue of the magazine: 'It is from Paris that nearly all the great influences in art and literature have come, from the time of Chaucer until now. . . .' Yeats spoke bluntly about 'the sentimentality, the rhetoric, the moral uplift' he found in American periodicals, and claimed that those traits existed, not because Americans were too far from England, but because they were too far from Paris. He related a Paris incident when he met Paul Verlaine. He asked Verlaine why the French poet did not translate Tennyson, and Verlaine replied to Yeats that Tennyson was 'too *anglais*, too noble' to be translated into French. Yeats added to his praise of French literature his belief that 'the best English writing is dominated by French criticism; in France is the great critical mind'.

René Taupin, in his remarkable thesis on French and American poetry, was the first to call attention to Yeats's Chicago speech of 1914, and the first pioneer critic to study the subject of this present essay, Baudelaire and Eliot.

In a poem written directly in French, 'Mélange adultère de tout', Eliot has given us a self-portrait. He is the sophisticated cosmopolite who plays a different role in each country he visits:

> *En Amérique, professeur. . . .*
> *En Angleterre, journaliste. . . .*
> *En Yorkshire, conférencier. . . .*
> *A Londres, un peu banquier. . . .*
> *À Paris, jemenfoutiste. . . .*
> *En Allemagne, philosophe. . . .*

The tone of this short poem where Eliot tells of his wanderings,

> *J'erre toujours de-ci de-là. . . .*
> *De Damas jusqu'à Omaha. . . .*

has the ironic ring of Laforgue, but the isolation of the nomadic dilettante recalls Baudelaire's dandyism. Contrary to the spirit of his poem, Eliot will sink his roots into old England. And we remember that Baudelaire hardly ever left Paris.

What today are commonplaces in Baudelairian criticism: the author of *Les Fleurs du mal* became the voice of his century; he created a literary form capable of expressing a moment of civilization; by translating himself, he translated his time – all of this will soon be said, has already been said, of T. S. Eliot.

The initial impulse of poetry is the emotion a poet feels in his relationship with himself, in his relationship with others, with the world around him, and also with his past, with childhood, with the dead. This theme is central in Baudelaire and Eliot.

At the beginning of the first quartet, *Burnt Norton*, Eliot speaks of time which is eternally present, of the rose garden of his childhood:

> Go, said the bird, for the leaves were full of children. . . .

And at the end of the fourth quartet, *Little Gidding*, he tells us that

> We are born with the dead . . .
> The moment of the rose and the moment of the yew-tree
> Are of equal duration.

The poet's work is truly the quest and exploration of the past. In examining certain works of art, Baudelaire wrote that he often experienced a vision of the childhood of the artists. In one sentence in particular, he announces a principle associated today with Proust, concerning a child's sorrow, which, when enlarged, may become in the adult of a marked sensitivity the foundation of a work of art. '*Tel petit chagrin, telle petite jouissance de l'enfant, démesurément grossis par une exquise sensibilité, deviennent plus tard dans l'homme adulte, même à son insu, le principe d'une œuvre d'art.*' This passage, of great importance for Baudelaire's aesthetics, ends with the celebrated formula: 'Genius is childhood distinctly formulated.' ('*Le génie n'est que l'enfance nettement formulé.*')

It is defensible to say that in Baudelaire and Eliot the poetic imagery derives less from their readings than from the sensations and memories of their youth. Love of the sea, for example, occupies a large place in their writings. The one sea voyage in Baudelaire's life inspired some of the most striking passages in his verse. In 'La Vie antérieure':

> Les houles, en roulant les images des cieux. . . .

In 'L'Homme et la mer', where the sea is the protector of secrets:

> O mer, nul ne connaît tes richesses intimes,
> Tant vous êtes jaloux de garder vos secrets!

In 'La Chevelure', where Jeanne's hair is an ebony sea:

> Tu contiens, mer d'ébène, un éblouissant rêve
> De voiles, de rameurs, de flammes et de mâts . . .

In 'Je te donne ces vers', where the poem offered to the mistress is called a vessel:

> Vaisseau favorisé par un grand aquilon . . .

In 'Le Beau Navire', where the beauty of a woman walking is compared to a boat sailing in the open sea:

> Tu fais l'effet d'un beau vaisseau qui prend le large. . . .

In 'Le Voyage', the metaphor for the soul seeking the ideal is a three-masted schooner:

> Notre âme est un trois-mâts cherchant son Icarie . . .

Eliot, in the third quartet, *Dry Salvages*, evokes a small group of rocks, with a beacon, off the New England coast of Cape Ann, in Massachusetts, and develops the major themes of time, history, and human destiny, by means of sea metaphors: beaches, algae, sea anemone, lobsterpot, oar, seagull, fog bell, drifting wreckage, ragged rock, waves, fogs, seamark . . .

> The river is within us, the sea is all about us . . .
> The starfish, the horseshoe crab, the whale's backbone . . .

In telling us that the sea contains many gods and many voices, Eliot sings of the alliance between the sea and the land:

> The salt is on the briar rose,
> The fog is in the fir trees.
> The Sea howl
> And the sea yelp, are different voices
> Often together heard....

In 1910 Eliot lived in France and in Paris, where he took courses at the Sorbonne, and private French lessons from Alain-Fournier, who was to publish *Le Grand Meaulnes* in 1913. The Paris which Eliot observed in 1910 was the past and the future of the city: the *Cahiers de la Quinzaine* were appearing at that time in Péguy's shop, enthusiasm for Henri Bergson filled to capacity every week an auditorium in the Collège de France, *La Nouvelle Revue Française* was really new. Many years later, in speaking of the year 1910, in an article of homage to Jacques Rivière, Eliot said that 'France represented poetry' for him at that time. There he was attracted to the work of Laforgue, Corbière, Verlaine, Baudelaire, Rimbaud, and Gautier. He was also reading at that time certain French prose writers: Stendhal, Flaubert, the Goncourt brothers, Benda, and Maritain.

Of all these French writers, Baudelaire had the deepest influence on Eliot. With Baudelaire he felt the closest affinities. Affinities even in temperament and reserve of character, in the liking for self-discipline and for the challenge of a difficult art, in the desire to create a different art. Baudelairian dandyism, visible in Eliot's personality, was first an isolation, but it was especially the heroism of concentration, the spiritual struggle for inner perfection.

Almost at the same time in their careers, when they were still quite young, Baudelaire and Eliot realized that the poet and the critic are one. At its highest degree of lucidity, the critical mind is transformed into poetic inspiration. Both poets felt the reciprocal dependence of their critical and creative faculties.

Baudelaire's example and influence are especially apparent in the early poems of Eliot and in those that preceded *The Waste Land* of 1922. The first poems are fragmentary pictures of a civilization in a state of disintegration. The poet's vision is intense in these first exercises in which he is learning how to fashion an instrument suitable to reveal what he has seen.

Baudelaire taught him ways by which to renew the poetic art by drawing from the daily life of a large metropolis. He taught the American poet especially the way to translate ideas into sensations. 'Prufrock', as a 'love song', is reminiscent of the *Complaintes* of Laforgue, or even of *La Chanson du mal-aimé* of Apollinaire. But Prufrock has also a Baudelairian temperament: he sees around him concupiscence, turpitude, evil. He is sickened by the vulgarity of a large city. Eliot's word tends to fill the void between poetry, or what was traditionally understood by poetry, and the modern world. And this is exactly what Apollinaire and Max Jacob have done in France in the twentieth century.

Baudelaire's greatness is in the degree of intensity to which he elevated poetic imagery. His renovation of poetic language was accompanied by a renovation of his attitude toward life. In Baudelaire's aesthetics, illustrated by *Les Fleurs du mal*, the slightest object may be magnified by the poet. He taught that there is poetry and beauty in the most trivial aspects of modern life: a swan escaping from its cage and dragging its white plumage through all the dust of the street, an old man walking down a city street, a multitude of people deadened by pleasure....

One day a long study will be written on the close relationship between the prolonged metaphor of Baudelaire, in which the idea and the image are magically fused ('La Chevelure', for example) and the 'objective correlative' of Eliot, or the image capable of translating and supporting a significant human experience, and the 'memory-sensation' of Proust, that sensorial experience which permits a man to recover a feeling by which he was once animated. Eliot, in *Ash-Wednesday* and *Four Quartets*, and Proust listening to Vinteuil's music, or tasting a madeleine cake dipped in tea, rediscover places and privileged moments. They are non-temporal moments. A half-century earlier, Baudelaire, in a poem such as 'Le Balcon', had announced the principle of that mnemonic art.

> *Je sais l'art d'évoquer les minutes heureuses,*
> *Et revis mon passé blotti dans tes genoux.*

Time recalled is not time for Eliot:

> Time past and time future
> What might have been and what has been
> Point to one end, which is always present.

The happiness which invades Marcel, as he drinks the cup of linden tea, makes of him a being freed from contingencies: he ceases being accidental and even mediocre. This is exactly what Baudelaire had said in the last stanza of 'Le Balcon', in the form of an interrogation:

> *Ces serments, ces parfums, ces baisers infinis,*
> *Renaîtront-ils d'un gouffre interdit à nos sondes ... ?*

Proust in Paris, and Eliot in London, discovered almost at the same time a Baudelairian principle concerning time and the way in which a poet interprets time (because Proust, in countless passages of his book, is notably a poet). Baudelaire, in translating the feeling of spleen, had said:

> *J'ai plus de souvenirs que si j'avais mille ans.*

And Proust, in *Le Temps retrouvé*, says in one of his most profound sentences:

> *Une heure n'est pas qu'une heure, c'est un vase rempli de parfums, de sons, de projets et de climats!*

And Eliot, in his fervent meditation on time, says at the end of *Burnt Norton*:

306

Even while the dust moves
There rises the hidden laughter
Of children in the foliage
Quick now, here, now, always –
Ridiculous the waste sad time
Stretching before and after.

Baudelaire and Eliot bring the same understanding to the artist's role and duty. (And this definition is easily applicable to Proust.) The artist is the man who narrates himself and at the same time narrates the customs of his contemporaries and his fellow-men. When this writer, as both Baudelaire and Eliot did, tells his dreams, his fantasies, his loves, he is telling the dreams, fantasies, and loves of other men. To be the interpreter of his age is a first duty for the poet, but it is not a comfortable duty when the poet is embittered by the ugliness of contemporary life. Before writing *The Waste Land*, Eliot had seen in *Les Fleurs du mal* that vast dusty plain without vegetation, where unfolds the life of inert stone and mineral.

Eliot makes a distinction between young poets and those who continue to be poets after their twenty-fifth year. He says that the meaning of history is indispensable for the man who wants to remain a poet. In this way the artist develops a sharper consciousness of his place in time. The meaning of history is also the meaning of myths, the meaning of Antiquity. Eliot, in *The Waste Land*, will underscore the parallelism between the contemporary event and the myths of Antiquity. It is the principal procedure used by Joyce in *Ulysses*. It is also visible, but in a less striking way, in *A la recherche du temps perdu*. And Baudelaire, in his major poem on Paris, the city where everything changes, when he sees a swan escaped from its cage, thinks of the great exiled figures of history, and especially of

Andromaque, des bras d'un grand époux tombée, . . .
Auprès d'un tombeau vide en extase courbée . . .

The Waste Land is composed in accordance with one theme for which Eliot found a series of variations. And this theme is first heard in the prologue poem of *Les Fleurs du mal*, the poem entitled 'Au Lecteur'. Men, having lost the notion of good and evil, cease living in the usual sense. At times the waste land is the desert in the vision of Ezekiel, and at times it is today's metropolis. When it is the present, the vision of today's waste land, cursed by sterility, this present is ceaselessly broken in upon by the intrusions of the past. Words spoken by the great sages of the past, their cries, their revindications return so often into the picture of the present that all demarcation between the centuries is effaced. The past becomes present in the phrase of Saint Augustine:

> To Carthage then I came

in an evocation of a circle in Dante's hell:

> I see the crowds of people, walking round in a ring

in an alexandrine of Verlaine where the poet recalls a Holy Grail ceremony:

> *Et O ces voix d'enfants chantant dans la coupole!*

The overture section of *The Waste Land*, 'Burial of the Dead', has four verses which evoke London today:

> Unreal City,
> Under the brown fog of a winter dawn,
> A crowd flowed over London Bridge, so many,
> I had not thought death had undone so many.

Eliot himself in his notes gives us the two sources of this passage: the third canto of Dante's *Inferno*:

> *si lunga tratta di gente*

and the Baudelaire poem, 'Les Sept Vieillards', which begins:

> *Fourmillante cité, cité pleine de rêves,*
> *Où le spectre en plein jour raccroche le passant!*

Baudelaire's poem is a walk through the streets of Paris, and during this walk the city becomes the setting for an eruption of demonic forces. The city takes on a human form. Baudelaire calls it a colossus ('*colossée puissant*'). At the beginning of the poem, where the narrow canals ('*les canaux étroits*'), become arteries, the circulatory system of the giant, the reality of exterior Paris is destroyed. The city loses its shape and the old man coming into the vision of the poet is hostile to the universe. This '*sinistre vieillard*' is doubled and multiplied. The one real action in this part of the city, shaken by the noise of tumbril carts, is an inner Satanic action taking place in the poet's imagination.

In the composition of *The Waste Land*, the poet incorporates this expansion of reality of which Dante and Baudelaire had been, according to Eliot, the principal artisans. Eliot presents a vision of contemporary life, but so strange that it contains all centuries and all ages. In his first essay on the French poet, which he called 'The Lesson of Baudelaire,' he said: 'All first-rate poetry is occupied with morality: this is the lesson of Baudelaire.' Eliot had resumed his study of *Les Fleurs du mal* in 1919 or 1920, during his work on *The Waste Land*. In 'Burial of the Dead', the first movement of the long poem, he shows us the inhabitants of the stricken earth, the waste land, as fearful of being awakened to life, as having lost all sense of reality.

The phantom city, 'Unreal City', is first the city that Baudelaire had sung of in 'Les Sept Vieillards', the '*cité pleine de rêves*', and then Dante's limbo, where we see those dead who had a perfectly neutral life. The judgement of the world in 'Burial of the Dead' is very harsh, and the poet does not exclude himself from his judgement. The passage ends with a line of Baudelaire:

'... *hypocrite lecteur! – mon semblable, – mon frère!*'

The verse, quoted in French in Eliot's text, evokes more clearly than a translation could have done the theme of modern *ennui*, which is the central subject of the poem 'Au Lecteur'. *Ennui*, called by Baudelaire the ugliest of our vices, explains the atmosphere of *The Waste Land*, the mournful, neutralized atmosphere which comes from a universe of evil and even from the diabolical universe of 'Les Sept Vieillards'.

Eliot's arid earth, the hardened calcined region from which all life has withdrawn:

> And the dry stone no sound of water

was called by Baudelaire in 'Un Voyage à Cythère'

> *Un désert rocailleux troublé par des cris aigres.*

Whether it is Baudelaire's Paris of the swan escaped from its cage or the sinister old man, or the London of Eliot and the crowd on London Bridge:

> And each man fixed his eyes before his feet –

whether it is the *'désert rocailleux'* of Cythère or 'this stony rubbish' of *The Waste Land*, the poet's art is the use of the sensible world. The two poets speak of the death inherent in each life, but especially of the spiritual death of modern man. The poet renders present this sterility thanks to the poetic process which Baudelaire called *'sortilège'* or *'sorcellerie évocatoire'*.

Alone among the French poets – romantics, symbolists, decadents – Baudelaire revealed an understanding of Christianity which Eliot was to continue. The French poet of the nineteenth century, like Villon in the century of Jeanne d'Arc, had a very personal sense of religious values. He was also obsessed by vice and sin, an obsession which Eliot will not have. But Eliot studied in the writings of Baudelaire the Christian meaning of the real which is concealed beneath the appearances of the real. Baudelaire speaks of that very imprecise restlessness of men which comes with evening:

> *Aux uns portant la paix, aux autres le souci.*

And Eliot recasts the image:

> When evening quickens faintly in the street,
> Wakening the appetites of life in some. . . .

There is an even more striking example in the same sonnet of 'Recueillement', where the clouds, coloured by the setting sun, appear as balconies in the sky, and the poet's past appears in the form of women in old-fashioned dresses on the balconies:

> *Vois se pencher les défuntes Années,*
> *Sur les balcons du ciel, en robes surannées . . .*

And the opening of the 'Love Song', where evening is compared to a sick person on an operating table, is reminiscent of 'Recueillement':

> When the evening is spread out against the sky
> Like a patient etherised upon a table. . . .

The affinity is not only in the images designating the tranquillity of evening. It is especially in the feelings and thoughts of the two poets.

Eliot saw in Baudelaire the example of a writer for whom criticism and poetry are converging aspects of the same literary process. The books of each one represent the search for a form of analysis capable of translating the consciousness of an age, when it is a question of poetic creation, or a form of analysis capable of translating the consciousness of an objective work, when it is a question of criticism. Whether it is a poem or a critical essay, the definitive result recapitulates a personal reaction in which the intelligence of the writer and his sensibility are similarly engaged.

'Le Voyage' of Baudelaire and 'Gerontion' of Eliot are two poems which can be explained in terms of a cultural context. For Baudelaire, the world has become so small that it is reduced to what a single man sees, to the image of the inner life of a man:

Amer savoir, celui qu'on tire du voyage!
Le monde, monotone et petit, aujourd'hui,
Hier, demain, toujours, nous fait voir notre image. . . .

The same motifs of time, of consciousness of evil, and of spatial and chronological ambiguities are to be found in 'Gerontion':

After such knowledge, what forgiveness? Think now
History has many cunning passages. . . .

It is futile to try to analyse the meaning of these two poems, because they are so deeply rooted in the meaning of an historical period. Baudelaire's voyager is the man who sets out for the pure joy of leaving his familiar world, and he is also the child who does not leave, who is in love with maps and pictures:

l'enfant, amoureux de cartes et d'estampes. . . .

The character in Eliot's poem,

An old man in a draughty house. . . .

finds it difficult to return to former experiences and to comprehend them. But the minds of Eliot's old man and of Baudelaire's voyager contain the universe. There is a moment at the end of each poem when the protagonist experiences the intoxication and the exaltation of the infinite:

Gull against the wind, in the windy straits
Of Belle Isle. . . .
Nos cœurs que tu connais sont remplis de rayons!

Each of these poets has sung of the aridity of contemporary life, and each one also has sung of the same aspiration toward purity, the same search for humility. Baudelaire's influence was double, as Eliot's is double today. Each offers us the example of the creative and the critical intelligence. In reading the measured verses of these two poets we become accomplices of extreme sentiments. This poetry does not reassure us. It does not engulf us with illusions.

In one of his earliest essays, 'Tradition and the Individual Talent', Eliot taught two generations that it is impossible to evaluate a poet by himself. In order to understand him in a true sense, for the purposes of comparison and contrast, he has to be situated in relationship with the dead. This is an entire programme an elaborate principle of literary criticism in which Eliot affirms the solidarity of the centuries. Baudelaire, who possessed far less culture than Eliot, emphasized his belief that all great poetry must have a moral basis, that all great poetry must reflect the problem of good and evil.

Many scholars have pointed out themes common to Baudelaire and Eliot: the strong attraction to the sea, an obsession with the city and its populous quarters, spleen, a tone of derision, and especially perhaps the theme of anguish, comparable to the anguish studied by Jean-Paul Sartre in *La Nausée*. But no one has yet studied an art, specifically Baudelairian, which Eliot learned from the French poet and perfected in accordance with his own aptitude and talent. It is the art of evoking a memory, and often a distant memory, deliberately and wilfully, the art of associating the sensation of this memory with the spirit and the intellect, and at the same time excluding all sentimentality.

Bergson used to say that poets understood and felt the concept of time better than philosophers. This preoccupation with time, common to Baudelaire and Eliot, designates more lucidly than other preoccupations the close bonds existing between the poetic work and the spirituality of the writers. The nostalgic resurrections of the past, apparent throughout all of Eliot's work, but especially in *Four Quartets*, are related to Baudelaire's *Correspondances*:

Comme de longs échos qui de loin se confondent
Dans une ténébreuse et profonde unité....

More fervently than any other poet of the twentieth century, Eliot has sung of the permanence of time, the experience of one time which is all time. He sings of it when he speaks of the flower that fades, of the sea that seems eternal, of the rock in the sea, and of the prayer of the Annunciation:

There is no end of it, the voiceless wailing,
No end to the withering of withered flowers,
To the movement of pain that is painless and motionless,
To the drift of the sea and the drifting wreckage,
The bone's prayer to Death its God. Only the hardly, barely prayable
Prayer to the one Annunciation.

In such a passage, as in the best passages of Baudelaire, the poet reveals his true mission, that of transmuting his intimate emotions, his personal anguish, into a strange and impersonal work. In this way the poet becomes aware of his presence in the world, where his major victory is the imposing of his presence as a man by means of his lucidity and his creative power.

T. S. ELIOT: THINKER AND ARTIST[1]

By Cleanth Brooks

ELIOT'S career is no loose bundle of unrelated activities but possesses an essential unity. Indeed, once discovered, this unity of purpose becomes increasingly evident. Few literary men in our history have so consistently related all their activities to a coherent set of principles. And the consistency of his various writings reflects the quality of the man. In a time of disorder, Eliot moved toward a restoration of order – toward the restoration of order that poetry alone, perhaps, can give.

Thus Eliot's fundamental reassessment of the twentieth-century literary and cultural situation was *not* expressed in his poetry alone. The poetry arose out of a mental and spiritual activity that necessarily showed itself in literary and social criticism, not only in his brilliant essays on the Elizabethan dramatists, for example, but also in a work like *Notes towards the Definition of Culture*.

When one discusses literature, few things are so deadly as the recital of abstract statements and wide generalizations. Moreover, it seems impertinent to treat a poet in this fashion, especially a poet who succeeded so brilliantly in giving his ideas concrete embodiment and who devoted so much of his discursive prose to this very split in the modern mind, this dissociation of sensibility, in which Eliot saw not only the distemper of literature but a symptom of a more general disease. Let me try to illustrate the essential unity of Eliot's work from a single topic, his treatment of the urban scene. In an essay written near the end of his life he has told us how he discovered that the urban scene was proper material for poetry, and specifically the special material for his own poetry. The

1. A lecture given at Eliot College, University of Kent at Canterbury, 10 December 1965.

passage I mean to quote begins with some observations on literary influences and what a poet can learn from earlier poets.

Then, among influences, there are the poets from whom one has learned some one thing, perhaps of capital importance to oneself, though not necessarily the greatest contribution these poets have made. I think that from Baudelaire I learned first, a precedent for the poetical possibilities, never developed by any poet writing in my own language, the more sordid aspects of the modern metropolis, of the possibility of fusion between the sordidly realistic and the phantasmagoric, the possibility of the juxtaposition of the matter-of-fact and the fantastic. From him, as from Laforgue, I learned that the sort of material that I had, the sort of experience that an adolescent had had, in an industrial city in America, could be the material for poetry; and that the source of new poetry might be found in what had been regarded hitherto as the impossible, the sterile, the intractably unpoetic. That, in fact, the business of the poet was to make poetry out of the unexplored resources of the unpoetical; that the poet, in fact, was committed by his profession to turn the unpoetical into poetry. A great poet can give a younger poet everything that he has to give him in a very few lines. It may be that I am indebted to Baudelaire chiefly for half a dozen lines out of the whole of *Fleurs du Mal*; and that his significance for me is summed up in the lines:

> *Fourmillante cité, cité pleine de rêves,*
> *Où le spectre en plein jour raccroche le passant!*

I knew what *that* meant, because I had lived it before I knew that I wanted to turn it into verse on my own account.

I want to consider further both Eliot's notion that the poet, by his very profession, is committed 'to turn the unpoetical into poetry', and his idea that poetry is a fusion of opposites – in this instance, a fusion of 'the sordidly realistic and the phantasmagoric', of 'the matter-of-fact and the fantastic'.

Poetry is evidently not to be thought of as a bouquet of 'poetic' objects. The implication is that the materials the poet uses are not in themselves poetic. To be agreeable or pleasant or charming is not the same thing as being poetic. Poetic value is a quality of a different order. It is not a *property* of objects but a relationship among them, a relationship discovered and established by the poet. Moreover, the relationship may be one of tension in which the materials pull against each other and resist any easy reconciliation. In this instance it is the realistic and the phantasmagoric that may seem intractable, or the matter-of-fact and the fantastic.

All of this Eliot had said before, and, because he had said it before, in this rather late essay he could afford to touch upon it lightly. But when he first enunciated this view of tension in poetry, it very much needed saying – or at least needed re-saying. And his statement of this conception, together with the poems that embodied it, inspired the literary revolution that is sometimes given Eliot's name.

It is useful to refer to another passage in which Eliot discusses the poet's use of what the Victorians sometimes regarded as hopelessly unpromising materials for poetry. The Victorian in this instance is Matthew Arnold commenting upon the ugliness of the world of Robert Burns. After quoting Arnold's rather prim observation to the effect that 'no one can deny that it is of advantage to a poet to deal with a beautiful world', Eliot suddenly rounds on the nineteenth-century critic and quite flatly denies his basic assumption. The essential advantage for a poet, Eliot remarks, is *not* that of having a beautiful world with which to deal, but rather 'to be able to see beneath both beauty and ugliness; to see the boredom, and the horror, and the glory'. 'The vision of the horror and the glory', he rather acidly concludes, 'was denied to Arnold, but he knew something of the boredom.'

This is excellent polemics: the hard backhand drive that rifles across the court and just dusts the opponent's back line. Yet the reader may wonder at the energy with which Eliot rejects Arnold. He may wonder too at what may seem an almost gratuitous reference to 'boredom', not, surely, an

obvious member of a cluster that would include 'horror' and
'glory'. But references to boredom often come into Eliot's
account of urban life, and we have in this passage mention of
concerns central to his poetry.

They are indeed central to his experience of the modern
metropolis where so many people find themselves caught in a
world of monotonous repetition, an aimless circling without
end or purpose. Eliot's early poetry is full of it:

> The morning comes to consciousness
> Of faint stale smells of beer
> From the sawdust-trampled street
> With all its muddy feet that press
> To early coffee-stands.

> With the other masquerades
> That time resumes,
> One thinks of all the hands
> That are raising dingy shades
> In a thousand furnished rooms.

*

> They are rattling breakfast plates in basement kitchens,
> And along the trampled edges of the street
> I am aware of the damp souls of housemaids
> Sprouting despondently at area gates.

*

> At the violet hour, the evening hour that strives
> Homeward, and brings the sailor home from sea,
> The typist home at teatime, clears her breakfast, lights
> Her stove, and lays out food in tins.

> Let us go, through certain half-deserted streets,
> The muttering retreats
> Of restless nights in one-night cheap hotels
> And sawdust restaurants with oyster-shells:
> Streets that follow like a tedious argument
> Of insidious intent. . . .

The wanderer moving through the deserted city streets long past midnight walks through a genuine nightmare in which

>   the floors of memory
> And all its clear relations,
> Its divisions and precisions

are dissolved, a fantastic world in which every street lamp that one passes

> Beats like a fatalistic drum . . .

Yet when the wanderer turns to his own door, he steps out of one horror into a worse horror:

> The lamp said,
> 'Four o'clock,
> Here is the number on the door.
> Memory!
> You have the key,
> The little lamp spreads a ring on the stair.
> Mount.
> The bed is open; the tooth-brush hangs on the wall,
> Put your shoes at the door, sleep, prepare for life.'

> The last twist of the knife.

The wound in which this knife is twisted is modern man's loss of meaning and purpose. When life to which one expects to rise after sleep – a daylight world of clear plans and purposes – turns out to be simply a kind of automatism, as absurd as the bizarre world of the nightmare streets, the knife in the wound is given a final agonizing twist.

It may be useful to remind the reader, especially the reader who finds that Eliot's Anglo-Catholicism sticks in his craw and prevents his swallowing the poetry, that in passages of the sort that I have been quoting, we are not getting sermonizing but drama, not generalizations about facts but responses to situations, not statements about what ought to be but renditions of what is.

Eliot once remarked that prose has to do with ideals; poetry, with reality. The statement has proved puzzling to many a reader who has been brought up on just the opposite set of notions, but Eliot's observation seems to me profoundly true. Discursive prose is the medium for carrying on arguments, drawing conclusions, offering solutions. Poetry is the medium *par excellence* for rendering a total situation – for letting us know what it feels like to take a particular action or hold a particular belief or simply to look at something with imaginative sympathy.

Here are some presentations of reality – an urban vignette, a winter evening in the city:

> The winter evening settles down
> With smell of steaks in passageways.
> Six o'clock.
> The burnt-out ends of smoky days.
> And now a gusty shower wraps
> The grimy scraps
> Of withered leaves about your feet
> And newspapers from vacant lots;
> The showers beat
> On broken blinds and chimney-pots,
> And at the corner of the street
> A lonely cab-horse steams and stamps.
>
> And then the lighting of the lamps.

The Song of the third Thames-daughter:

> 'Trams and dusty trees.
> Highbury bore me. Richmond and Kew
> Undid me. By Richmond I raised my knees
> Supine on the floor of a narrow canoe.'
>
> 'My feet are at Moorgate, and my heart
> Under my feet. After the event
> He wept. He promised "a new start."
> I made no comment. What should I resent?'

'On Margate Sands.
I can connect
Nothing with nothing.
The broken fingernails of dirty hands.
My people humble people who expect
Nothing.'

la la

Even the raffish Sweeney's recital of his philosophy – a view of life held, incidentally, by many of Sweeney's betters – is a bit of reality too; for it is a dramatic projection of a man, not an abstract formulation. Its very rhythms testify to a personality and an attitude.

Birth, and copulation, and death.
That's all the facts when you come to brass tacks:
Birth, and copulation, and death.
I've been born, and once is enough.

Readers have responded powerfully to such passages, even readers who hold very different conceptions of what the world ought to be. What is primarily at stake in all these passages is not the reader's approval or rejection of a statement, but his response to authentic reality. The only compulsion to respond is that exerted by the authority of the imagination. Perhaps the poet can never do more than exert such authority; but in any case he cannot afford to do less.

This matter of the reader's response has another and more special aspect. Eliot suggests that many of those who live in the modern world have been drugged and numbed by it. One task of the poet is to penetrate their torpor, to awaken them to full consciousness of their condition, to let them see where they are. The theme recurs throughout Eliot's poetry from the earliest poems to the latest.

The people who inhabit *The Waste Land* cling to their partial oblivion. They say:

Winter kept us warm, covering
Earth in forgetful snow, feeding
A little life with dried tubers.

Or like the old women of Canterbury, they may say:

> We do not wish anything to happen.
> Seven years we have lived quietly,
> Succeeded in avoiding notice,
> Living and partly living.

The trivial daily actions, they point out, at least marked

> a limit to our suffering.
> Every horror had its definition,
> Every sorrow had a kind of end. . . .

What they dread now is the 'disturbance' of the seasons, the decisive break in the numbing routine that will wake them out of their half-life.

But the partially numbed creatures may be, and usually are, people of the contemporary world. They may, for example, be like the characters in *The Family Reunion* who do not want anything to rumple their rather carefully arranged lives – who want things to be 'normal' – and who cannot see that – to use their nephew's words – the event that they call normal 'is merely the unreal and the unimportant'.

They may be like certain well-bred inhabitants of Boston, Massachusetts:

> . . . evening quickens faintly in the street
> Wakening the appetite of life in some
> And to others bringing the *Boston Evening Transcript* . . .

Or they may be the bored drawing-room characters in 'The Love Song of J. Alfred Prufrock' whom Prufrock would like to confront with the truth about themselves. He would like to say to them:

> 'I am Lazarus, come from the dead,
> Come back to tell you all, I shall tell you all' . . .

But he well knows that these overcivilized and desiccated people would not be impressed by the Lazarus of the New

Testament, much less by a self-conscious man 'with a bald spot in the middle of [his] hair', a man aware of the fact that he wears a 'necktie rich and modest, but asserted by a simple pin'. In any case, these people would not understand the talk of a man who had experienced real death or real life.

The themes that run through so much of Eliot's poetry – life that is only a half-life because it cannot come to terms with death, the liberation into true living that comes from the acceptance of death, the ecstatic moment that partakes of both life and death:

> ... I could not
> Speak, and my eyes failed, I was neither
> Living nor dead, and I knew nothing,
> Looking into the heart of light, the silence.

These and the other themes that recur in Eliot's poetry bear the closest relation to his concern with the boredom and the horror and the glory that he finds in our contemporary metropolitan life. They also bear the closest relationship to the sense of unreality that pervades a world that has lost the rhythm of the seasons, has lost any sense of community, and, most of all, has lost a sense of purpose. Such a world *is* unreal: the sordid and the matter-of-fact do not erase the phantasmagoric but accentuate it. The spectre does indeed in broad daylight reach out to grasp the passer-by. London, 'under the brown fog of a winter noon' as well as 'under the brown fog of a winter dawn', is seen as an 'Unreal City', and the crowds flowing across London Bridge might be in Dante's Hell:

> I had not thought death had undone so many.
> Sighs, short and infrequent, were exhaled,
> And each man fixed his eyes before his feet.

The echo of *The Divine Comedy* is not merely a flourish or an attempt to touch up the modern scene by giving it literary overtones. What connects the modern scene with Dante's

'Inferno' is the poet's insight into the nature of hell. The man who sees the crowds flowing over London Bridge as damned souls, if challenged for putting them thus into hell, might justify his observation by paraphrasing a line from Christopher Marlowe: 'Why, this is hell, nor are they out of it.'

In view of the complaint that Eliot sighs after vanished glories, sentimentalizes the past, and hates the present, one must insist on Eliot's ability to dramatize the urban reality with honesty and sensitivity. If the world about which we must write has lost the rhythm of the seasons, then the poet must be open to the new rhythms so that he can relate them to the old. Eliot once wrote that the poet must be able to use the rhythms of the gasoline engine:

> At the violet hour, when the eyes and back
> Turn upward from the desk, when the human engine waits
> Like a taxi throbbing waiting ...

If the modern world has lost its sense of community, the poet must present that loss not as a generalization but as a dramatic rendition, not as observed from the outside but as felt from the inside. He has done so not only in the nightmare passages of *The Waste Land* –

> There is not even solitude in the mountains
> But red sullen faces sneer and snarl
> From doors of mudcracked houses –

but also in the realistic passages:

> 'My nerves are bad to-night. Yes, bad. Stay with me.
> 'Speak to me. Why do you never speak. Speak.
>   'What are you thinking of? What thinking? What?
> 'I never know what you are thinking. Think.'

But he has also on occasion rendered the sense of community in positive terms – not as something lost but as a present reality:

O City city, I can sometimes hear
Beside a public bar in Lower Thames Street,
The pleasant whining of a mandoline
And a clatter and a chatter from within
Where fishermen lounge at noon....

As for the sense of loss of purpose, that loss is never merely asserted but always rendered concretely. It occurs so frequently in Eliot's poetry that it hardly needs illustration. Indeed, it may be best in this instance to take the illustration from Joseph Conrad's *Heart of Darkness*, a story that lies behind so much of Eliot's early poetry. Marlow, the character who relates the story, finds many of his experiences tinged with unreality. As he makes his way to the African coast and then on up the Congo to try to locate Kurtz, his sense of unreality is magnified – not merely because the jungle seems fantastic, but because the civilized characters he meets are disoriented, obsessed, and thus absurd. One object stands out sharply from this miasma of unreality. Marlow finds in an abandoned hut

an old tattered book, entitled *An Inquiry into Some Points of Seamanship,* by a man Tower, Towson – some such name.... Not a very enthralling book; but at the first glance you could see there a singleness of intention ... which made these humble pages ... luminous with another than a professional light.... [The book] made me forget the jungle and the [ivory-seeking] pilgrims in a delicious sensation of having come upon something unmistakeably real.

It seems so because it is instinct with purpose – because, to use Marlow's words, you could see in it 'an honest concern for the right way of going to work'. This is why the book shines with the light of reality.

The sense of unreality is also associated with the vision of a world that is disintegrating. In *The Waste Land* the cities of a disintegrating civilization seem unreal as if they were part of a mirage. The parched traveller asks:

> What is the city over the mountains
> Cracks and reforms and bursts in the violet air
> Falling towers –

but these cities are also like a mirage in that they are inverted, are seen as upside-down; and the passage that follows shows everything turned topsy-turvy:

> . . . bats with baby faces in the violet light
> Whistled, and beat their wings
> And crawled head downward down a blackened wall
> And upside down in air were towers
> Tolling reminiscent bells, that kept the hours
> And voices singing out of empty cisterns and exhausted wells.

Eliot also uses the empty whirl in order to suggest the break-up of civilization. Toward the end of 'Gerontion' we have such a vision, people whose surnames suggest that the disintegration is international and worldwide: De Bailhache, Fresca, and Mrs Cammel are whirled

> Beyond the circuit of the shuddering Bear
> In fractured atoms.

Though 'Gerontion' was written long before the explosion of the first atomic bomb, I suppose there is some temptation nowadays to read into the passage our present unease and to regard the fractured atoms into which humankind has been vaporized as the debris of an atomic war. But I doubt that Mr Eliot ever changed his opinion about the way the world ends.

'The Hollow Men', who know in their hollow hearts that they are not really 'lost/Violent souls', but only 'stuffed men', sing

> This is the way the world ends
> This is the way the world ends
> This is the way the world ends
> Not with a bang but a whimper.

The vortex in which De Bailhache, Fresca, and Mrs Cammel are caught is essentially described in *Burnt Norton*:

> Men and bits of paper, whirled by the cold wind
> That blows before and after time....

With the empty whirl, the purposeless moving in a circle, we are back once more to the theme of boredom, and there is a good deal of evidence that Eliot did indeed see in such torpor and apathy the real dying out of a civilization. In 1934, for example, he wrote: 'Without religion the whole human race would die, as according to W. H. R. Rivers, some Melanesian tribes have died, solely of boredom.' This is a polemical passage out of a polemical essay, but we need not discount the idea merely for that reason. It is an integral part of Eliot's thinking. It is to be found everywhere in his prose and poetry – even in a poem like *Sweeney Agonistes*, where we have the following spoof on the cinematic stereotype of the golden age, life on a South Sea island:

> Where the Gauguin maids
> In the banyan shades
> Wear palmleaf drapery
> Under the bam
> Under the boo
> Under the bamboo tree.
>
> Tell me in what part of the wood
> Do you want to flirt with me?
> Under the breadfruit, banyan, palmleaf
> Or under the bamboo tree?
> Any old tree will do for me
> Any old wood is just as good
> Any old isle is just my style
> Any fresh egg
> Any fresh egg
> And the sound of the coral sea.

Doris protests that she doesn't like eggs and doesn't like life on 'your crocodile isle'. And when the singers renew their account of the delights of such a life, Doris replies:

> That's not life, that's no life
> Why I'd just as soon be dead.

Doris is a young woman who is clearly no better than she should be, but in this essential matter, she shows a great deal more discernment than J. Alfred Prufrock's companions, the ladies who 'come and go/Talking of Michelangelo'.

I have tried to suggest how the themes and images of Eliot's poetry are related to his convictions about the nature of our present-day civilization. But I shall have badly confused matters if in doing so I have seemed to reduce his poetry to a kind of thin and brittle propaganda for a particular world view. The primary role of poetry is to give us an account of reality, not to argue means for reshaping it. To be more specific: if a culture is sick, the poet's primary task is to provide us with a diagnosis, not to prescribe a specific remedy. For all of his intense interest in the problems of our culture, and in spite of the fact that he himself was deeply committed to a doctrinal religion, Eliot was careful never to confuse poetry with politics or with religion. The loss of a sense of purpose, the conviction that one is simply going round in a circle, is an experience that many of the readers of Eliot's poetry have recognized as their own; but in their decisions as to what to do about it, such readers have differed as much as the Christian differs from the atheistic existentialist. To get out of the circle, to find one's proper end and begin to walk toward it – this is a matter of the highest importance, work for the statesman, the sage, and the saint; but Eliot was too modest ever to claim any of these roles for himself, and he was as well aware as anyone of the confusion of tongues that makes it difficult for men of our century to agree on what the proper goal is. At any rate, he argued the case for what he took to be the true goal, not in his poetry, but in his prose.

In a time of grave disorder, Eliot has moved toward a restoration of order. Not the least important part of this work of restoration has been to clarify the role of poetry, not claiming so much for it that it is transformed into prophecy, or Promethean politics, or an *ersatz* religion; but at the same time pointing out its unique and irreplaceable function and defending its proper autonomy.

Genuine poetry, seen in its proper role, performing for us what only it can perform, does contribute to the health of a culture. A first step toward the recovery of the health of our culture may well be the writing of a poetry that tells us the truth about ourselves in our present situation, that is capable of dealing with the present world, that does not have to leave out the boredom and the horror of our world in order to discern its true glory. More modestly still, a poetry that can deal with the clutter of language in an age of advertising and propaganda restores to that degree the health of language.

Eliot was well aware of this problem. Advertising and propaganda were for him instruments for 'influencing ... masses of men' by means other than 'their intelligence'. And he once went so far as to say: 'You have only to examine the mass of newspaper leading articles, the mass of political exhortation, to appreciate the fact that good prose cannot be written by a people without convictions.'

The difficulty of writing good prose in our era extends to other kinds of writing, including poetry. Of this too, Eliot was aware. In *The Rock*, he has the chorus assert that 'The soul of Man must quicken to creation' – not only to create new forms, colours, and music but so that

Out of the slimy mud of words, out of the sleet and hail of verbal imprecisions,
Approximate thoughts and feelings, words that have taken the place of thoughts and feelings,
... [may] spring the perfect order of speech, and the beauty of incantation.

329

In a later and finer poem he puts this ideal of style more precisely and more memorably still, and he makes this ideal structure of the language a model of that thing which men must try to accomplish in their lives. It is Eliot's description of the relation that obtains among the words that make up a passage luminous with meaning. In it

> ... every word is at home,
> Taking its place to support the others,
> The word neither diffident nor ostentatious,
> An easy commerce of the old and the new,
> The common word exact without vulgarity,
> The formal word precise but not pedantic,
> The complete consort dancing together....

These beautiful lines celebrate the poet's victory over disorder, the peculiar triumph possible to a master of language. They describe what Eliot actually achieved many times in his own poetry. They provide an emblem of the kind of harmony that ought to obtain in wider realms – in the just society and in the true community.

T. S. ELIOT AND *THE LISTENER*[1]

By *Janet Adam Smith*

IN the summer of 1933, when I was assistant editor of *The Listener* (the weekly published by the British Broadcasting Corporation) and responsible for choosing the poetry, we published (on 12 July) a four-page supplement of poetry and woodcuts. The woodcuts were by Gwen Raverat, and on the first and fourth pages were poems by C. Day Lewis, Bernard Spencer, John Hewitt, Herbert Read, John Lehmann, Charles Madge, T. H. White, and Arthur Ball. On the second and third was a spread of W. H. Auden's 'The Witnesses', in a different and longer version from that which appears in his *Collected Shorter Poems* – twenty-nine six-line stanzas enclosed by Gwen Raverat's menacing, elongated 'Guardians of the gate in the rock/The Two'. There was also a leading article on modern poetry which reads rather quaintly today, but reminds one that in 1933, when Eliot and Pound were still objects of alarm and suspicion to established academic opinion, it was necessary to make such pleas 'for open and unprejudiced and informed reading of poetry'.

It was plain, from this article, that there had been many complaints from readers about poems published in *The Listener*; there were rumblings within the Corporation too, and a few days after the supplement appeared, Jove thundered. I was summoned to Sir John Reith, the Director-General, and catechized on the poems we published in general, on this supplement in particular, and especially on 'The Witnesses'. The D.-G. wanted to know why there was so much that seemed odd, uncouth, 'modernist', about our poems. He was not choleric, like the outraged pundits who wrote to us from

1. Reprinted from *The Listener*, London, 21 January 1965, by permission of the author.

the Athenaeum, but puzzled. He made it plain that he wasn't objecting to modern poetry as such any more than to the modern music broadcast by the B.B.C., but I think he was anxious that poems which appeared in *The Listener* – those in the supplement may have struck him as the choice of an individual of eccentric tastes – should be recognized as having merit by responsible and informed persons beyond the paper. We talked for some time on modern poetry, and I mentioned T. S. Eliot's name; Sir John then suggested that it would be interesting to have *his* opinion of the poems we published. Possibly he had in mind Mr Eliot the critic, the director of Fabers, indeed, the member of the Athenaeum, rather than the poet of *The Waste Land*.

I did not then know Mr Eliot, so I asked Herbert Read if he would find out, on Mr Eliot's return from America that summer, whether he would be willing to give an opinion on our poems. Mr Eliot was willing, so I sent him the supplement, and cuttings of all the poems published in the last two years. This collection included poems by Conrad Aiken, George Barker, Julian Bell, J. N. Cameron, Gavin Ewart, David Gascoyne, Louis MacNeice, Edwin Muir, William Plomer, Kathleen Raine, Michael Roberts, Stephen Spender, A. S. J. Tessimond, and R. E. Warner.

After a few weeks Mr Eliot sent in his report, which at first glance disappointed me. I suppose that, ardent in the defence of the poets I admired and longing to rout the Philistines, I had hoped for a glowing testimonial from one whom I regarded as an ally in the fight. Mr Eliot did not supply that at all. There was no glow of enthusiasm in his grave and measured sentences. But he supplied something much more valuable, both in its immediate effect on Sir John Reith and in its stimulus to me to think more rigorously about the business of choosing poems for the paper.

Mr Eliot began by considering 'upon what grounds a weekly periodical is justified in publishing specimens of contemporary verse, and with what frequency, and on what principles it should choose verse to publish'. The money to be earned in this way was derisible; the one strong motive was advertisement.

It is only the younger poets to whom a weekly can appeal on this ground; when the best older poets give you contributions, you may regard it as an act of charity on their part. For the first ten years of his working life a poet has something to gain by having his verse seen occasionally in weeklies; later, he has nothing to gain and indeed something to lose. On both moral and practical grounds therefore a weekly, if it publishes poetry at all, should look to the younger writers.

He went on to discuss the kind of poem that an editor should look for. It could be the 'anthology piece', the occasional *trouvaille* of authors the bulk of whose work might be worthless. Far more sensible would be to 'take up the young poets who seem to have any *promise*, and give each of them a number of chances, over a period of several years, until we are forced to the conclusion that his promise has not been fulfilled'. By thus nursing young writers a periodical could justify its publication of verse; but 'even the most gifted poetry editor must be content to have a great many more failures than successes'.

The Listener, to judge from its other contents, struck him as aiming at a public

which is curious and avid of information about the latest facts, ideas and discoveries in contemporary art and thought; its readers, so far as they are interested in poetry, must want to know what sorts of verse are being written. From this point of view, whether the verse is of the highest quality does not matter much: what you want to be able to say confidently to your readers is that this is representative of the best that is being written by men and women of a certain generation. At least, it will serve as a document upon the time, and if the time should not produce any poetry worth preserving, that would be an interesting fact in itself.

In the second part of the report, Mr Eliot considered the collection of poems which I had sent him, remarking that he knew many of the poets as contributors, or would-be contributors, to his quarterly *The Criterion*, and that Fabers had published books by Auden and Spender on his recommendation. Except for the virtual absence of American poets (next year when we produced a supplement on American literature he gave me some excellent advice on topics and writers) he found the collection 'for good or bad' representative of the verse of its time. 'As one must expect of any time, the great majority is mediocre and conventional; it reveals the occasional influence of myself, Mr Yeats, Mr Pound and Gerard Hopkins, and some other more discredited originals.' His conclusion was that 'while not encouraging for poetry, the selection is on the whole very creditable to *The Listener*', which was one of the very few weeklies in which he would not dissuade any promising young poet from seeking to appear.

For the rest of the time that I was at *The Listener* there was still abuse from the Athenaeum, still muttering within the Corporation, and I had to be ready with a glib paraphrase of every poem in case it were challenged by someone in the hierarchy. (I remember trying to explain Dylan Thomas's 'Light breaks where no sun shines' to the retired soldier who was a controller of programmes.) But from Jove there was no more thunder. I don't think that Sir John Reith ever liked the poems we published, but Mr Eliot had convinced him that we were not likely to get any that were much better, and that we did well to publish poetry at all.

A PERSONAL MEMOIR

By Robert Giroux

To me he was a great human being, quite aside from being a great artist – and they are not always, I need hardly add, the same thing.

In retrospect, the most striking single aspect of the years (nearly twenty) during which I was privileged to know him as a friend is the contrast between the rather sad and lonely aura that seemed to hover about him in the earlier period, and the happiness he radiated in the later one. 'Radiant' may seem an odd word to apply to T. S. Eliot, yet it is an accurate description of the last eight or so years of his life, and this was due of course to his marriage in 1957 to Valerie Fletcher. More than once in those years I heard him utter the words, 'I'm the luckiest man in the world.'

There was a performance of the Yeats version of *Oedipus Rex* to which we went in 1946, during the first post-war appearance of the Old Vic company in New York. The play was so superbly done, and Laurence Olivier was so magnificent as Oedipus, that we were numb and silent as we left the theatre, with the final words of the Chorus in our ears: 'Call no man fortunate until he is dead.' I remember that we walked from The Century Theatre north to Fifty-ninth Street, and then east along the dark and gloomy southern boundary of Central Park. Perhaps I would not have felt so depressed if I could have imagined that my friend's future would turn out to be 'the summer, the unimaginable zero summer'.

It was still midwinter, and for me the typical image of the period was Eliot playing solitaire. Whenever he was staying at my apartment I would invariably find him, when I came home from my office, stooped over the card-table and dealing out the deck to himself. Of course he would always push the cards

335

aside and pour the drinks, becoming his lively, amusing self and raising mischievous questions such as the one he put to me about the *Oedipus Rex* we had seen: 'I can't help wondering, Bob, since Yeats knew no Greek, what did he translate *from*?'

As for the later period, I think of the scene at the pier, when I met the Eliots on their first visit here together. As they came down the gangplank, they were holding hands and beaming. It was wonderful to see that he had found such happiness at last, and those who loved him are grateful for those blessed final years.

*

I first met T. S. Eliot in 1946, when I was an editor at Harcourt, Brace under Frank Morley. I was just past thirty, and Eliot was in his late fifties. As I remember it he had come into the office to have lunch with Morley, who had been his close editorial colleague at Faber & Faber, and Morley discovered that he had forgotten a previous luncheon appointment for that day. Since I did not know this when Morley introduced us, I was dumbfounded when Eliot said, 'Mr Giroux, may I take you to lunch?' It was like being invited to eat with a public monument, and almost as frightening as shaking hands with the statue in *Don Giovanni*. I wondered what I could find to say to him.

We went across the street to the old Ritz-Carlton. It was a lovely spring day and the courtyard restaurant – I think it was called the Japanese Garden – had just been opened for the season. For some reason I was astonished at the sight of newly hatched ducklings swimming in the centre pond, perhaps because they seemed to embody the odd and improbable quality the occasion had for me.

Eliot could not have found a kinder, or more effective, way of putting me at ease. As we sat down, he said, 'Tell me, as one editor to another, do you have much author trouble?' I could not help laughing, he laughed in return – he had a *booming* laugh – and that was the beginning of our friendship. His most memorable remark of the day occurred when I asked him if he agreed with the definition that most editors are failed writers, and he replied: 'Perhaps, but so are most writers.'

It was at least a year before I could bring myself to call him Tom, and that was only because his old friends, Ted and Marian Kauffer, insisted it would be unfriendly of me not to. He liked good food and drink as well as good talk, and he told marvellous stories. One had to do with his early years in London, at a garden party at Buckingham Palace, when he found himself next to a very old man with white whiskers who said to him: 'What! Your name is Eliot and you're a writing chap? Don't tell me you're related to that horse-faced woman I knew years ago who wrote those interminable novels!'

*

Then there was the famous encounter with Carl Sandburg that everyone tried to prevent. I liked Sandburg, and we sometimes discussed Eliot's poetry, about which Carl had violent opinions. When he once complained that Eliot was always using 'foreign' words, I pointed out that in this respect Eliot resembled Walt Whitman, one of Carl's heroes. Inevitably the day came that we all dreaded: Eliot and Sandburg arrived in the office on the same morning. We worked out a plan to keep them from meeting; Eliot was to stay in my office with the door closed, while Sandburg was put in an office at the other end of the building. At one point I went out to the drinking-fountain and when I returned, Sandburg had already drawn up a chair and was moodily gazing across my desk into Eliot's eyes. 'Just look at him!' Sandburg said to me, pointing at Eliot. 'Look at that man's face – the suffering, and the pain.' By this time Eliot was wearing a great big grin. Sandburg continued, 'You can't hold *him* responsible for the poets and critics who ride on his coat-tails!' With that, he walked out of the office and I realized that one of the great literary encounters of our time had occurred, and as far as I knew Eliot had not uttered a single word.

Late that spring, Eliot asked me to accompany him to the American Academy of Art and Letters, where his friend Marianne Moore was to be honoured and Sandburg was to speak. Though Eliot was invited to sit on the stage as an honorary member, he waited until the lights were dimmed and slipped into the auditorium. He thought Sandburg's speech a good one, and he particularly enjoyed the introductory exchange between Sandburg and Douglas Freeman, somewhat in the manner of interlocutors at an old-time minstrel show.

*

Eliot's sense of fun turned up at unexpected moments. In 1948, when news of the Nobel Prize came (he was then at Princeton), he told me that he knew only two things about it – first that he would wear formal clothes at the presentation ceremony in Stockholm, and second that he would be asked to crown the Swedish Snow Queen at the Winter Festival during his visit. 'I hope they'll combine the two events in a skating rink,' he said. 'Then I'll be able to wear ice-skates with my tails.'

When he left for Stockholm, the Kauffers and I took him to the airport where a reporter asked, 'Mr Eliot, what book did they give you the Nobel Prize for?' 'I believe it's given for the entire corpus,' he replied. 'When did you publish *that*?' the man wanted to know. When he had gone, Eliot said to us, 'It really might make a good title for a mystery – *The Entire Corpus*.'

Soon after the musical *New Faces* opened on Broadway, I told Eliot that the hit song, Eartha Kitt's rendition of 'Monotonous', contained the line, 'T. S. Eliot writes pomes to me.' He immediately took out his card, inscribed it to Miss Kitt, and asked me to have the florist send her roses. I happily did so, and the only indication that the flowers reached her was an item in a newspaper column to the effect that 'Eartha Kitt *claims* that T. S. Eliot sent her a bouquet' – a line Eliot enjoyed almost as much as the one in her song.

Of his several statements on the issue of racial prejudice, with which he was unfairly and repeatedly charged at different periods of his career, I prefer his immediate reply to the reporter in Chicago who caught him coming off a plane with the question, 'Are you anti-Semitic, Mr Eliot?' He replied: 'I am a Christian, and therefore I am not an anti-Semite.'

In 1959 the opera of *Murder in the Cathedral*, set to the music of the Italian composer, Pizzetti, was performed at the Vatican before John XXIII. Eliot was delighted when Pope John, through the Apostolic Delegate in England, sent him a formal letter of thanks, commending his 'services to the Christian faith' in writing his play. This little-known statement by Eliot was made when he accepted the Campion Award *in absentia*: 'The gladness with which Christian churches of every description recognized the activities [for ecumenicity] of your great Pope John testifies to a universal longing for unity.'

He told me he admired Joe Louis, not only for his boxing style, but for his succinct style of speech. He cited two splendid examples, Louis's comment on a fast stepper he was about to meet in the ring – 'He can run, but he can't hide' – and Louis's answer to the criticism that he should not have enlisted in a segregated Army – 'There's nothing wrong with the U.S. that Hitler can cure.'

When Meyer Berger succeeded in getting Joe Louis to talk, and his series was running in *The New York Times*, Eliot was delighted that so much of Louis's style had been caught on paper and asked me to inquire about the possibilities of doing the series as a book. Unfortunately it did not work out, for the odd reason that an earlier ghosted 'autobiography' by Joe Louis involved a contractual agreement that no other *book* by Louis could be published.

Eliot regretted that he never encountered Joe Louis in person. He was once cornered at a cocktail party by a woman who screamed at him: 'All my life I've wanted to meet T. S. Eliot, and here you are! I can hardly believe it!' He replied: 'If that's how you feel, then you're luckier than I am. All my life

I've wanted to meet Joe Louis and I haven't.' I doubt if she believed him but he was merely doing what he so often did, stating the truth.

*

The only practical help I can remember being able to give him had to do with his public readings of his poems. He took the readings seriously, and gave much thought and time to them. (I was always amazed to observe, incidentally, that as the zero hour approached he would be as nervous as a cat, showing his agitation by eating little, and on one occasion by breaking out in a sweat. Yet once the reading started, a great calm would descend and he would do a superb job.) My advice had to do with his habit, in the early period, of reading the last line of a poem and going ahead, almost without pause, to the next poem. I convinced him that listeners were sometimes not aware that the previous poem was finished. He was grateful for this tiny contribution, and thereafter figuratively counted ten before going on.

The only writing of his to which I believe I made an indirect contribution was *The Confidential Clerk*. In 1950, when I was taking music lessons under the G.I. education bill, Eliot asked me on several occasions to play some Chopin for him. Whenever I did so, I always wondered aloud why I played so much better when I was alone. Not long after, when Eliot was in London, I had the pleasure of escorting Marianne Moore to the New York première of the play, and I recognized that the beginning of the second act, with Colby at the piano, reflected this experience. When Eliot sent me a copy of the play, inscribed 'Gratefully', I knew I had not imagined the connexion.

Though I shared his passion for the theatre, he did not share mine for the movies. When I asked him why he did not go more often, he said, 'They interfere with my daydreams.' In the year of its first American showing, I persuaded him to see Akira Kurosawa's *Rashomon*, and he agreed it was a work of art, one of the best films ever made. Much later he saw the same director's *Throne of Blood*, a Japanese version of *Macbeth*, and liked it; the Lady Macbeth, he said, was the best he had ever seen. Olivier's *Henry V* was also one of his favourites and, of course, the Chaplin films – though he was rather disappointed in the last film, *The King of New York*.

In a particularly festive mood one evening, Eliot was inspired by the sight of a plaque to the memory of George M. Cohan in the Oak Room of the Plaza to recite and sing the verses of more Cohan songs than I knew existed. He even remembered the verses of a song – was it Cohan's or Ethel Levy's, another favourite of his – called 'What Did Robinson Crusoe Do with Friday on Saturday Night?'. On leaving the hotel, the sight of a hansom cab lined up with the open hacks for hire made him reminisce about his first visit to New York, in the company of his older brother, Henry, when he was in his teens. They rode down Fifth Avenue in a hansom, he said, and went to a musical – a Cohan show, if I remember correctly. His love of musicals and music halls was incurable and his comment on *My Fair Lady*, when Roger and Dorothea Straus and I took him to the original production, was characteristic: 'Shaw has been greatly improved by music.'

Some of these anecdotes are trivial, to be sure, but to me they revealed that Eliot had a liveliness of spirit, a humour, and an attitude wholly unlike the solemn pontifical manner that was generally ascribed to him, to the exclusion of any other. I also had reason to know what a wonderful and loyal friend he could be. In 1955, when I faced a difficult decision about my own career, his support and encouragement saw me through a crisis. In fact, when I joined the publishing firm with which I am now associated, it was Tom who, unasked, sent me his next book, *On Poetry and Poets*, and the books that followed as well. It was a rare act of generosity and of friendship.

*

He was always happy near the sea. Whenever he talked of his boyhood at Cape Ann, his joy in remembering those days seemed to me to bring out the look of the boy he must have been, wide-eyed, intense, and very bright. And when he and Valerie spent their winters in the Caribbean, he revelled in the swimming and it was a joy when I visited them to see him and Valerie walking along the beach, hand in hand. The waters of Nassau, Bermuda, Barbados, and Jamaica seemed to assuage his final illness as nothing else could – except, of course, his domestic happiness, for London was home, and no matter how pleasant the sunny shores might be, he always looked forward to returning to their home in England.

The last time I heard his voice was three days before his death. Valerie wrote during the Christmas holidays in 1964 that the bad weather there had caused him a setback. I called London on the first day of January to wish them a happy New Year. Valerie told me, to my delight, that Tom was in his chair beside the fireplace, and in the background I could hear his cheerful tones of greeting. When he died on January fourth, the world became a lesser place, and it was not until I found these words of Izaak Walton, written on the death of Donne, that I began to feel consoled:

The melancholy and pleasant humour were in him so con-tempered that each gave advantage to the other, and made his company one of the delights of mankind. . . . His vigorous soul is now satisfied, and employed in a continual praise of that God that first breathed it into his active body; that body which once was a temple of the Holy Ghost and is now become a small quantity of Christian dust: but I shall see it reanimated.

MR ELIOT'S SUNDAY MORNING *SATURA*:
PETRONIUS AND *THE WASTE LAND*

By Francis Noel Lees

> ... and we think more highly of Petronius
> than our grandfathers did. (*The Sacred Wood*)

THAT the main sources of the principal imaginative material used by Eliot in *The Waste Land* were Frazer's *Golden Bough* and Jessie L. Weston's *From Ritual to Romance* is, of course, certified by Eliot himself in the notes he appended to the poem. He also indicated his indebtedness, sometimes obvious, sometimes not, and of varying degrees of importance, to many other works. Students of the poem have greatly added to his list of sources and allusions, and as well have pointed out significant influences on his technique. Arthur Symons, Rémy de Gourmont, T. E. Hulme, and the Imagists are now familiar names in respect of this last; and that an important part was played by Ezra Pound in producing the final version of the poem is an established fact, though the exact degree of his responsibility has never been revealed. It might seem that there is reason to associate Pound's name in the authorship: it is certain that any attempt to trace the genesis of a poem completed in this way is up against an exceptionally difficult problem.

As there is prefixed to the poem a passage from Petronius's *Satyricon*, it is surprising that that work should have received so little attention in this connexion; the more so since the quotation prefixed to the collection of essays *The Sacred Wood*, published two years earlier, in 1920, is also taken from the *Satyricon*. Yet there are in that fragmentary work enough reminders of *The Waste Land* to suggest that it may have contributed to the propulsive mixture of the poem or at least to the process of ignition. In a number of instances, of course, *The Waste Land*'s reflection of earlier works is only the latest of a succession of reflections; as, to take a relevant example, *The Divine Comedy* reflects from the *Aeneid* what the *Aeneid* itself has reflected from the *Odyssey*. As this makes the discerning of critical influences difficult and their exact isolation probably impossible, it is fortunate that absolute exactness of determination can be forgone with no especially calamitous results. That something may be gained from the identification of sources will, none the less, be generally agreed.

Eliot certainly made use of the Loeb editions of Latin authors, and the Loeb Petronius, with an English translation by Michael Heseltine, was published in 1913. I shall therefore use that edition, but without prejudice to the question of Eliot's particular textual source (and without question of the virtues of the translation).

The theme of drowning is a very important one in *The Waste Land*, where the destructive power of the sea is sardonically juxtaposed with the life-giving power of rain. The latter is a necessary implication of the primary metaphor of the poem, the waste land, and it therefore comes straight from Frazer and Jessie Weston; but the former cannot be traced back to Frazer or Weston, and it is not easy to attribute its emergence in the poem solely to the fact that, on the very page of the Mermaid edition of Webster's *White Devil* on which occur the lines openly adapted by Eliot from the dirge in that play, there is reproduced in a footnote the remark of Charles Lamb: 'I never saw anything like this dirge, except the ditty which reminds Ferdinand of his drowned father in *The Tempest*. ...' Now the death-by-drowning theme takes its start from the scene with the businesslike, commonplace Madame Sosostris, 'famous clairvoyante', who tells her client to 'fear death by water' and in laying out his fortune allots him the card 'the drowned Phoenician Sailor'; and this scene leads straight back with ironic bathos to the gloomy legendary Sibyl of the lines which precede the poem proper: '*Nam Sibyllam quidem Cumis ego ipse oculis meis vidi.* . . .' – 'Yes, and I myself with my own eyes saw the Sibyl hanging in a cage; and when the boys cried at her: "Sibyl, Sibyl, what do you want?" "I would that I were dead," she used to answer.' (§ 48, pp. 84–6). The theme, that is, has a visible connexion with the *Satyricon*, from which the epigraph is taken; and in the *Satyricon* is to be found a very vivid evocation of the death-by-water idea (in a Mediterranean setting, as is Eliot's) when (§§ 114–15, pp. 238ff.) there occurs the episode of the wreck of Lichas's ship and cargo. This is charged with the idea of the sea as a treacherous and untimely destroyer (as also are the poems attributed to Petronius which have survived outside the text of the *Satyricon* but which seem likely to belong to the original whole work, of which only a relatively small portion is extant); and some particulars distinctly bring to mind Eliot's 'Death by Water' section. Encolpius, the narrator hero (or perhaps we should say 'anti-hero'), who with his friends has safely reached shore, tells the story thus:

. . . the sea rose. . . . But the wind did not drive the waves in any one direction, and the helmsman was at a loss which way to steer. . . . Then . . . Lichas trembled and stretched out his hands imploringly . . . , and said, 'Help us in our peril. . . .' But even as he shouted the wind blew him into the water, a squall whirled him round and round repeatedly in a fierce whirlpool, and sucked him down. . . . Next morning I suddenly saw a man's body caught in a gentle eddy and carried ashore. I . . . began to reflect upon the treachery of the sea. 'Maybe,' I cried, 'there is a wife . . . or a son or a father, maybe, who knows nothing of this storm; he is sure to have left some one behind whom he kissed before he went. . . . Look how the man floats.' I was still crying . . . when a wave turned his face towards the shore . . . and I recognized Lichas. . . . Then I could restrain my tears no longer . . . and cried, 'Where is your temper and your hot head now? Behold you are a prey for fish and savage beasts. . . . Lo! this man but yesterday looked into the accounts of his family property. . . .

You tell me that for those the waters whelm there is no burial.
As if it mattered, how our perishable flesh comes to its end, by
fire or water or the lapse of time. . . .' So Lichas was burned on
a pyre. . . .

Eliot's Phlebas the Phoenician 'Forgot the cry of gulls, and the
deep sea swell/And the profit and loss'; 'A current under
sea/Picked his bones in whispers. As he rose and fell/He
passed the stages of his age and youth/Entering the whirlpool.'
There is also to note the reminder of Eliot's use of Shakespeare's Ferdinand ('musing upon the king my father's death')
in developing the drowning theme from the start ('Those are
pearls that were his eyes. Look!'); and the collocation of fire
and water which recalls that the 'Death by Water' section immediately follows the 'Burning burning burning burning' lines
from the Buddha's Fire Sermon – so closely indeed that over
very many years one of Eliot's explanatory notes to them was
erroneously given under the heading of the 'Death by Water'
section.

There is also an earlier reference to loss at sea in Petronius,
where (§ 75, pp. 150ff.) Trimalchio tells his guests that his
first fleet was wrecked: *'omnes naves naufragarunt, factum,
non fabula.'* He tells how having come as a slave from Asia he
had then built ships and become a merchant, and that a Greek
astrologer, Serapa, had told his fortune and correctly predicted
this disaster. In the execution of Eliot's poem Mr Eugenides,
'the Smyrna merchant', as Eliot himself notes, 'melts into the
Phoenician Sailor, and the latter is not wholly distinct from
Ferdinand Prince of Naples': a similar melting of Trimalchio
into Lichas and Encolpius, *prior* to the making of the poem, is
not inconceivable. Trimalchio earlier (§ 39, pp. 62–3) has a
further link with common fortune-telling when he discourses
on zodiacal influence and speaks of his own zodiacal sign, the
Crab. (Another fortune-telling, by the witch Oenothea to Encolpius, is satirically presented later in the *Satyricon* (§ 137,
pp. 310–12).)

The helmsman of Lichas's vessel, also, has a counterpart in the Phlebas[1] piece, in the remaining lines of the section; and it is at this point of the examination that we can best take notice of other strains in Eliot's harmony of echoes. The problems then presented, arising from the multiple reflection already spoken of, are as difficult as they are interesting. The conclusion of 'Death by Water' is: 'Gentile or Jew/O you who turn the wheel and look to windward,/Consider Phlebas, who was once handsome and tall as you'; lines which cannot fail to activate recollections of Palinurus, Aeneas's '*gubernator*', dragged overboard to his death by the god of Sleep in the guise of his former companion Phorbas, and encountered by Aeneas in the underworld among those spirits denied passage across the Styx until their bodies shall receive burial. It is by virtue of possessing the 'golden bough' that Aeneas can enter the underworld (and Frazer's book); he has also just previously lost another companion, Misenus, by drowning (and Misenus as well as Palinurus could well 'melt' into a 'Phoenician Sailor'); and the death of Misenus has been foretold by the Sibyl of Cumae, whose aid Aeneas has sought immediately upon arrival in Italy. The body of Misenus must be given its due burial rites, which it receives after cremation on a funeral-pyre. Here, then, in Virgil we have perilous voyaging, deaths by water, burials of the dead, all related in a setting distinctly associated with Phoenicia; and with the Sibyl of Cumae present and at work – for she tells Aeneas his fortune as well as directing him to the golden bough. She speaks of the dangers of the sea overcome as she predicts that there still lie ahead those of war ('*Bella, horrida bella*') and of another foreign woman ('*coniunx hospita*') – in which latter case, at any rate, she is at one with Madame Sosostris in her warning against 'Belladonna, the Lady of the Rocks/The lady of situations' in the first section of *The Waste Land*, 'The Burial of the Dead'. Furthermore, behind Virgil lies Homer, whose imperilled voy-

---

1. Could 'Phlebas' come from 'Phorbas' crossed with *flebas*, imperfect tense of *flere*?

ager, Ulysses, also visits the underworld and meets the spirit
of a former companion, Elpenor, awaiting the due burning and
burial of his dead body – and also the seer Tiresias, who in
The Waste Land is 'the most important personage', Eliot
notes. (But the roots of Eliot's Tiresias include at least Sophocles, Tennyson, Swinburne, and Apollinaire, as well as the
Ovid Eliot himself cites.) Dante is the acknowledged source of
the atmosphere of the 'Unreal City' paragraph of Eliot's
'Burial of the Dead'; but as Virgil recalls Homer, so Dante
Virgil, and that paragraph moves us into the 'underworld' of
modern London immediately after the fortune-telling of
Madame Sosostris, just as Aeneas enters the underworld immediately after the Sibyl's pronouncements. The 'brown fog'
of London's 'winter dawn' may remind us too that Ulysses
found the underworld in 'the city of the Cimmerian people,
wrapt in mist and cloud'.

The matter is evidently complex; but by now Petronius may
look to have been pretty vigorously edged out of the genetic
picture. And it may seem only to diminish his claim to having
participated when it is pointed out that in the *Satyricon* also
there is plain reference to the *Aeneid*, and that the adventures
of Ulysses are explicitly used there as an ironic thematic
parallel to the misfortunes of Encolpius – as, perhaps in imitation, they were later to be used by Joyce for Leopold Bloom.
Yet Eliot's epigraph is there to prove that Petronius was in, or
near to, his mind and, the other references show, a good deal
earlier than when *The Waste Land* was completed[2]: and a
short poem thought to have originally belonged in *The Waste
Land* appeared in *The Tyro*, 1921,[3] over a pseudonym, 'Gus
Krutzsch', remarkably reminiscent of the English of 'Encolpius', namely 'the Crutch, or Crotch'. In fact, there are so far
two points at which a resemblance in Petronius seems not to

2. Since this article was written, Eliot's close undergraduate reading of Petronius has been revealed by Herbert Howarth in his *Notes
on Some Figures behind T. S. Eliot.*
3. Misdated 1922 in Donald Gallup's Bibliography of Eliot's work.

be duplicated by the other several or combined currents of ideas; and these are, first, the vulgarizing of the practice of divination, and, secondly, the feeling and certain of the details of the drowning of Lichas, a trader – which incident itself echoes earlier talk of an Asian merchant's losses at sea. From action by these elements on the Virgilian/Homeric ones could well have come Eliot's own sardonic result; indeed from them could have emerged a hint towards the whole mode of incorporating and developing Jessie Weston's remarks on the Tarot pack of divinatory cards. If this were so, we might connect also the fact that Mr Eugenides, 'the Smyrna merchant', is 'unshaven'; for (§ 104–5, p. 212) when Encolpius and his friends are shaved on Lichas's ship, the ill-omened occurrence alarms a fellow-passenger and arouses the master's fury: 'What, has anyone cut his hair on board my ship, and at dead of night too? Quick, bring the villain out here. . . .'

In the *Satyricon* (§ 83, pp. 164–6), Encolpius remarks on a painting of the myth of Hyacinth (Frazer material which leaves its mark on *The Waste Land*), and then Eumolpus, the old poet, comes in. What then follows is the passage used as epigraph to *The Sacred Wood*:

. . . a white-haired old man came into the gallery. His face was troubled, but there seemed to be the promise of some great thing about him, though he was shabby in appearance; so that it was quite plain by this characteristic that he was a man of letters, of the kind that rich men hate. . . . 'I am a poet,' he said, 'and one, I hope, of no mean imagination, if one can reckon at all by crowns of honour, which gratitude can set even on unworthy heads.' 'Why are you so badly dressed, then?' you ask. 'For that very reason. The worship of genius never made a man rich.' (§ 83, pp. 166–7)

It is not perhaps merely fanciful to remember that the phrase from *The Spanish Tragedy* introduced near the end of *The Waste Land* – 'Why then Ile fit you' – continues thus in Kyd: '. . . say no more./When I was young, I gave my mind

/And plied myself to fruitless poetry;/Which though it profit the professor naught,/Yet is it passing pleasing to the world.' And when Lichas's ship is wrecked (§ 115, p. 240) Eumolpus has to be dragged off the ship at the last moment, furious at the interruption of his verse-writing:

> We were surprised at his having time to write poetry with death close at hand, and we pulled him out.... But he was furious ... and cried 'Let me complete my design; the poem halts at the close.' I laid hands on the maniac. ...

(In the Eliot, 'Hieronymo's mad againe': the poet Eliot writes on, shoring fragments against his ruins.) There would be a humour very characteristic of Eliot in such a submerged association.

There remain other items of particular resemblance to be remarked. As Encolpius with his companions enters Trimalchio's house (§ 29, p. 40), he is startled by a wall-painting of a big dog on a chain; 'and over him was written in large letters "BEWARE OF THE DOG".' Eliot's 'O keep the Dog far hence, that's friend to men,/Or with his nails he'll dig it [the corpse] up again' at once comes to mind; and if we can extend that acknowledged borrowing from the dirge in *The White Devil* into *The Duchess of Malfi*, to Ferdinand's 'The wolf shall find her grave, and scrape it up,/Not to devour the corpse, but to discover/The horrid murder', and thence to the Doctor's diagnosis that Ferdinand's disease is 'lycanthropia' ('they .../Steal forth to churchyards in the dead of night/And dig dead bodies up'), then there may be point in mentioning Niceros's story of a werewolf (§ 61–2, pp. 112–16). Also one notices at Trimalchio's vulgar dinner-party that a servant-boy beginning to imitate a nightingale is at once shut up by the host (§ 68, p. 130); that there is a lyrical reference to the nightingales singing as Encolpius embraces Circe by the river (and fails sexually with her again) (§ 131, p. 292); and that an ironically named matron, Philomela, appears (§ 140, p. 316). In *The Waste Land* the painful story of Philomela makes several appearances. Lastly, Eumolpus's serious and powerful poem, the *Bellum Civile* (§§ 119–24, pp. 252–75), describes the decadence and succeeding calamities of Rome in a manner which reminds us of Eliot's own severe vision.

The present exposition of an argument that the *Satyricon* may have played more part in the birth and growth of *The Waste Land* than merely to have furnished an epigraph for it, contains nothing which plainly establishes a fresh understanding of difficult parts of the poem, but if the relationship suggested truly exists, further thought may yield more than is at the moment apparent. Certain broader implications do, however, present themselves immediately. As suggested earlier in this article, the *Satyricon* could have helped to switch in the 'Death by Water' theme and with it the particular treatment of a modern sibyl and the rendering of the Phoenician Sailor/ Smyrna merchant figure; it could certainly have strengthened that theme in its combination with those taken from Frazer and Weston and with the idea of Tiresias. In connexion with this latter, it should not be forgotten that Apollinaire's *Les Mamelles de Tirésias* (1917) is a proclaimed attack on voluntary human sterility; but neither should it be overlooked that the *Satyricon* is essentially concerned with the *involuntary* sexual impotence of its hero (the result of some offence against Priapus): 'I tell you, brother, I do not realize that I am a man, I do not feel it. That part of my body where I was once an Achilles is dead and buried.' And, further, there is a strong element of bisexuality in the work, as there is in Eliot's Tiresias.

More important, perhaps, an impulse to Eliot's medley of styles might have come from what is technically a 'medley' (*satura*), which is described by its recent translator, William Arrowsmith, as 'one great continuous mélange of genres and styles ..., setting high speech against low speech in endless profusion of parody and mockery ... the condition of its ironies is the criss-crossing of crucial perspectives and incongruous styles' – and this in reaction against a decadence of rhetoric as well as of other values which has something in common with Eliot's literary position. A further hint for Eliot is his Imagist attempt to give 'dramatic monologue' a range which Browning attained in *The Ring and the Book* only at the cost of intolerable length could even have come from the accidental *lacunae* in the extant fragment of the *Satyricon* or from the casual but curiously arresting juxtaposition of the poems which are given following that text.

Finally, whatever degree of agreement there may be with the view of Professor Arrowsmith (affirmed in a recent address as yet unpublished[4]) that Petronius in his immoralist fashion is seriously and pointedly following out the traditional sequence of topics of the Roman moral satirists (best briefly suggested by the heading *Luxuria*), it seems evident that the acid rendering of a debauched and vulgar world would assist in focusing Eliot's own moral observation; and that *The Waste Land*, with its tones of the pulpit, its echoes of Ezekiel and The Preacher, is, as *satura* and (so to say) *satira*, a counterpart of the *Satyricon* in its own way. And perhaps, therefore, in some measure a consequence of it.

4. Delivered at the Bread Loaf School of English, July 1964.

MISTAH KURTZ: HE DEAD[1]

By H. S. Davies

MANY of the obituary notices of T. S. Eliot remarked on his kindness, his active helpfulness to young writers, and even to mere would-be writers, but there was hardly room in them for concrete and personal description of the means by which this kindness and helpfulness were exerted. As one of those who benefited from these qualities, at a time when they meant very much to me, I am trying to describe them a little more fully. I should, of course, have expressed my gratitude to Eliot himself, and often thought of doing so, but funked it, partly because of his eminence, and even more because it could hardly have seemed that my gratitude was much worth having. For that failure, this attempt is an appropriate penance, since I must in the course of it claim almost publicly what I hesitated to presume upon in a private letter to him – an acquaintance with him. But it is perhaps fair to add at once that at the time when he was so good to me, his eminence was very different indeed from what it became in recent years. It was no whit less in itself, but it was apparent to but a small circle of readers, of which my own generation made up the outer enthusiastic fringe.

My first acquaintance with Eliot was of course through his poetry, which I first read in the mid twenties, under those stimulating difficulties which lent such poignant attraction to extra-curricular reading at a boarding school. The days were full – or rather filled for us by ingenious and distrustful masters who believed that 'Mischief still the tempter finds,/ For idle hands and idle minds.' They kept him captive in his lair by leaving no more than a few quarters of an hour un-

1. This essay appeared in *The Eagle*, Cambridge, vol. LX, no. 264, May 1965.

accounted for in our daily lives. The nights closed round us early in the dormitories, long before my capacity for reading was exhausted. In the junior school, much of my reading was done by flashlight under the bedclothes, but it was terribly expensive in batteries, and in other ways unrewarding – I remember reading *Dracula* thus, and put down its lack of effect on me to the dulling of my perceptions by the suffocating fug within this tent of bedclothes. By the time I had covered the gap between *Dracula* and Eliot I was senior enough to have more room for manoeuvre, and my more private reading was done in the only place where a light, however dim, shone all night, and where one could, however incommodiously, sit down. But although conditions were much improved by this change, my own perceptions were still very limited, and the effect of Eliot's poetry on me was in some ways oddly like what I had been assured I should get from *Dracula*, and had failed to find in it. The main structure of its comment on the age, the suggestive drift of its remedies, were almost wholly lost on me, but from the imagery of deserts and waste places I got the kind of direct thrill which had failed to emerge from werewolves, ruined abbeys, and the rituals of necrophily. The language, too, struck me with that tang which, in the last analysis, can perhaps only be tasted fully from writing which is deeply and even violently contemporary. It was a shock wholly delightful to find that poetry could use 'a selection of the language really used by men'. The words were common, everyday, but what of that? They had behind them, to my mind, the terrific suggestiveness of words heard in dreams, of phrases spoken in nightmares. And my delight in this poetry was enhanced when my English master picked the book up from my desk one day, glanced at it for a few minutes, and handed it back with the advice that I should not waste my time on such 'Bolshevik' stuff. My own unspeakable and unreadable verses were, of course, full of desert scenery, red rocks, and rats' feet slithering over broken glass. Eliot's images for the barren waste of English culture lent themselves very readily to an indulgence in the facile melancholies of adolescence which was, in those days, a very long-drawn-out affair – some of us can only hope to attain maturity in the wood. I came up to Cambridge with a fair stock of verses in this manner, and here, of course, I met many other young men from other schools with similar portfolios.

It was a year or two later when I first met Eliot himself, through Herbert Read, another notable patron of young writers, at a *Criterion* party above The Poetry Bookshop which Harold Munro kept gallantly in being, opposite the British Museum. It was there, indeed, that I had bought my copy of Eliot's poems four or five years earlier, and many other books of the same kind, but not of quite the same quality, including the *Chapbooks* in which Harold Munro combined the last flings of Georgian poetry with what was left of the Imagists. In those last years at school, and in my early years at Cambridge, I was provincial enough to believe that there must be a metropolis somewhere, some kind of centre for the world of letters and culture. London as a whole being obviously too vastly amorphous and too grossly provincial to fill this bill, I was forced to create this centre for myself. Its eastern boundaries were the Bloomsbury squares, in one of which Eliot worked as a publisher and editor of *The Criterion*; to the west, it ended in Fitzrovia, so named after The Fitzroy Tavern in Charlotte Street, a pub with much character in those days, not all of it good; the northern boundary was vague, but the southern was beyond any question The Poetry Bookshop, and I went to that party fully convinced that at last I was going to see something of this real metropolis. And so, in a sense, I did; enough at least, to set in motion the process by which I was, not too long afterwards, liberated from that particular provincial illusion. Of the party itself, I remember little but drink and noise: Harold Munro's rather lugubrious elegance – 'I've seen you downstairs, haven't I?' – his first recognition of my long series of pilgrimages to his shop: an Imagist poet called Frank Flint who produced for my benefit some fearful images

– one about a red gash in a black cat haunted me on and off for years afterwards (the trouble with experience is that one can only have it, never un-have it). But Eliot was there, composed, gently sardonic, and quite evidently the most forceful though also much the quietest, person in the room. He asked me whether I had been writing anything that might do for *The Criterion*, and I gave him an over-optimistic reply.

I hope that his biographers and critics will, in their summing-up of his achievements, do no less than justice to his editorship of *The Criterion*, and to its relevance to his large design of preserving some kind of coherence and some standards worth having in English culture. It was, I suppose, the last example of a practice which had grown up in the nineteenth century among publishers, of running a periodical in double harness with book-publishing, and using it partly as a trial and recruiting ground for their authors; partly as a way of giving their work preliminary or partial publication. At its best, it was a very lively kind of symbiosis, and its liveliness coincided with what may well turn out to have been the golden age of serious publishing, with *The Criterion* its last astonishing survival into another age of inferior metal. And Eliot should certainly be remembered, not only as one of the first great poets of the twentieth century, but also as the last great periodical editor of the nineteenth. None of his predecessors could have shown more diligence, courtesy, and personal concern for the recruiting of young writers, for exploring the temper of their generation, and encouraging them to put as good a face as possible on being themselves. His usual method of doing all these things was the luncheon *à deux*. I still remember very vividly my own first experience of this institution, not long after that meeting in The Poetry Bookshop. We met at his office high up above Russell Square, where the atmosphere was of a hard morning's work just being completed, and walked through the heart of my imagined metropolis to a French restaurant in Charlotte Street, where the food, carefully chosen by Eliot, was as admirable as it was beyond my own means. The conversation was even better, and quite beyond my means. Eliot was ready to elicit young theories and tender ambitions, and to listen to them with an attentive kindliness beyond praise. He would give advice, too, especially if he had been burdened with some of the writing for which he had asked, and to which he had evidently given the sort of care which made one feel that he ought to be spending his time better than that. One injunction of his I remember particularly, because I have never been able to follow it, and because he often had some difficulty in following it himself. It was to the effect that, in writing a piece for *The Criterion*, one should record opinions simply and forcibly, omitting all the qualifications and cautions which scholarly diffidence would wish to drape round them. 'People like just to be told what to think,' he said. He would talk too, though more warily, about his own concerns. Because I was then reading Classics, and because he insisted on exaggerating the extent to which I was doing so, he liked to talk about Aeschylus, and I had some glimpses of his long preoccupation with the *Oresteia*, from *Sweeney Agonistes*, which of course I knew, to *The Family Reunion*, which was not yet there to be known. He also spoke about other literary apprentices who had recently lunched with him, reported their views on one thing or another, tested them out seriously and respectfully. He really did all that could have been done to make us interested in one another, and to feel that there was promise of some kind lying about among us. Looking back at it now, from the other end of the gun as it were, it is impossible to imagine that the young could have been encouraged more generously and effectively. To feel that we mattered – and above all to him – was no small thing.

Among ourselves, of course, these luncheons were a matter for tactful boasting. 'I had lunch with Eliot the other day' was a phrase which I remember hearing, and I am sure I must have uttered it too, though I remember that less clearly. The tone of voice appropriate to such an utterance was very level, unemphatic, almost a throw-away, such was the inherent force of the fact itself. Only one of us, much the most resourceful in the management of English idiom, found a way of improving on it, to 'I was lunching with Eliot the other day', and we were left to wonder whether this subtle modal meddling with the verb might not indicate a frequency of meetings denied to most of us.

When I became, through a curious series of improbable accidents, a fellow of my College, it came within my power to return a little of the handsome hospitality of those lunches. I remember, for example, having Eliot as a guest to a feast in about 1934. After a dinner of which I was not ashamed, and one of those desserts in the Combination Room of which one could feel proud, we went up to the rooms of another fellow whose guest was a very intelligent and civilized Italian Marxist. Most of the conversation was between him and Eliot, and they both seemed to enjoy it. As we walked back through the empty courts in the small hours, Eliot made one comment which I always found very helpful in understanding his religious position. There was, he quietly observed, a great difference between the Marxists and himself, not only or merely in the content of their beliefs, but even more in the way in which they were held. 'They seem so certain of what they believe. My own beliefs are held with a scepticism which I never even hope to be quite rid of.' This helped me to appreciate, among other things, his natural affinity with the Anglican establishment of the seventeenth century, for the religious verse of Donne and Herbert turns almost as much on doubt as on faith, and even more on the constant interplay between the two. The doubt or difficulty which begets one poem, and seems to be triumphantly resolved by the end of it, is there again to initiate the next audible moments of the unending inner argument. We often used to wonder, in those days, whether Eliot would not go on to complete the classic syndrome and pass through Anglo-Catholicism to Rome – a speculation not unreasonable after his pamphlet *Thoughts after Lambeth*. But when I recalled that utterance of his in Second Court, I thought it more likely that he would stay where he was.

That feast well illustrates another aspect of Eliot's career, and of his relation with my generation. The seating-plan was, then as now, circulated in advance, as a kind of human counterpart to the menu: it gave the social bill of fare, so that one could welcome one's friends, even if guests of another fellow, and without unhospitable impoliteness avoid dishes one disliked. Only one fellow, out of sixty or so, commented on the name of my guest. And this absence of remark was, I think, entirely typical of the early phase of Eliot's eminence. He had spoken to the condition of a very small minority, but to them with enormous force, giving a new perspective to the world of eye and ear, and inner contemplation. His poetry was, indeed, a weighty and discernible part of that internal duologue which is the ultimate reality of mental and spiritual life; many of my generation, when we thought, or felt, or thought that we felt, would find its phrases there already, in our own heads, before we could find words of our own. But to the majority, to the general public, he was not even caviare; they never tasted him, and his name was unknown to them.

The turn towards the later, larger, and more public eminence came with *The Rock*, a 'pageant' performed at Sadler's Wells in aid of a fund for the London churches. It was a strange experience to attend a performance, to sit among the crowded audience, many of whom had come from their parishes in charabancs and busloads; stranger still to hear the appeals during the interval, by Bishops, Cabinet Ministers, and so forth. It was like being part of a diagram, illustrating past and future – though the future was still only dimly visible. Scattered thinly through the auditorium were a few of those to whom Eliot was already as eminent as he could be; surrounding us, quite swamping us, were those with whom it clearly lay in his power to be eminent in a slightly different fashion. He can hardly have been unconscious of the possible change, the possible choice – I never remembered him missing much subtler points than that. What must have made the choice specially hard for him was that, if it went one way, there would be some rewards of a kind which he did not want, but could hardly avoid – fame, public recognition, titles, decorations. It has often occurred to me that the central problem in his next, and I suppose his best, play, *Murder in the Cathedral*, the difficulty of 'doing the right deed for the wrong reason', may have gained force from his own experience in those crucial years.

As this new eminence settled upon him, I saw much less of him, but we met occasionally until the unsettlements of the war. In one of the Choruses of *Murder in the Cathedral* I had observed the cunning interweaving of some lines from one of the Sherlock Holmes stories, and told him of my observation. He was pleased, and noted that not as many of his readers as should be were familiar with those stories. He added that, since he had given up writing notes to his poems, many people supposed that he had given up incorporating in them fragments from other authors, and said that he would be obliged if I would draw attention to this particular insertion as opportunity offered. I gladly do so: and for the benefit of those who know the play better than they know Sherlock Holmes, add that the lines are to be found in the Musgrave Ritual, in the story of that name.

Just one more memory of our acquaintance is worth recording, partly because I doubt if it will be recorded anywhere else, but even more because it illustrates a quality in him which marked him as a writer not merely good, but probably great. Though his concern for literature and for writing was close and professional, of life itself, even in forms not specially natural to his range of experience, he was avid and explorative. I had, on one occasion, illustrated some remark – I think it was on Machiavelli – with a reference to the game of Rugby football. He said that he had never seen the game, but would like to do so. After some very anxious consideration, I decided that the best prospect was at the Oxford and Cambridge match at Twickenham – for I wanted him to get a proper specimen in case it was the only one he ever got. It was, as things turned out, a very lucky decision, for the game which we saw was, I believe, later recognized as one of the classics of its kind. The Cambridge fly-half was perhaps the wittiest player to appear on the field in my time. By constant changes of pace and direction, dramatic passes after which the ball was still in his hands, earnest appeals just behind his immediate opponent to players who did not in fact exist – by these, and such-like devices, he not only avoided the clutches of those who would lay hands on him, but made them fall down on either side of him, leaving the swathe of his best runs strewn with these ridiculous casualties. Eliot enjoyed, to the best of my hopes, this demonstration of the superiority of intelligence, imagination, and dramatic insight over mere brute strength. At the end of the display, he noted the fact that the game seemed much more suitable to be played by university men than American football. And he was kind enough to allow, having seen the thing for himself, the justness of my remark on Machiavelli.

THE OVERWHELMING QUESTION

By B. Rajan

To read 'Tradition and the Individual Talent' today is to become aware of its distinguished obsolescence. The essay takes its place among those monuments, the ideal order of which it once sought to alter by the injection of the radically new. Literary judgement moves onward though not necessarily forward; and the expanding worlds of the collective and the anonymous, the growth of mass communications and the increasing difficulty of communicating the authentic, have given to words like 'personality' and 'identity' a rallying power they once did not possess. The struggle to achieve definition without exterior compromise is now a condition of the creative conscience. In such circumstances, it becomes almost necessary to remind ourselves that the famous words which follow were the clarion call of criticism forty years ago.

Poetry is not a turning loose of emotion, but an escape from emotion; it is not the expression of personality, but an escape from personality. But, of course, only those who have personality and emotions know what it means to want to escape from these things.

One test of a critic is his power to repent. As the times changed, Mr Eliot changed cautiously with them. Fifteen years later he had carried his flight from personality sufficiently far to look detachedly over his shoulder at whatever was pursuing him.

The whole of Shakespeare's work is *one* poem; and it is the poetry of it in this sense, not the poetry of isolated lines and passages or the poetry of the single figures which he created, that matters most. A man might, hypothetically, compose any number of fine passages or even of whole poems which would each give satisfaction, and yet not be a great poet, unless we felt them to be united by one significant, consistent, and developing personality.

The juxtaposition is not offered as a lesson in historical irony. To change one's mind, as has been suggested, is an indication that one's mind is alive, though with some critics there is, unfortunately, no other evidence of life. With Mr Eliot the change is important not only because it is not unreasonable, but because of the weight it assumes in his later critical doctrine. A year prior to the essay on John Ford from which the passage above is quoted, Mr Eliot had expressed a similar view on Herbert: 'Throughout there is brain work, and a very high level of intensity: his poetry is definitely an œuvre to be studied entire.' In 1939, in considering Yeats's growth as a poet, Eliot found the merit of the later poetry to lie in the fuller expression of personality within it. In 1944 the test of wholeness was applied to Milton:

The important difference is whether a knowledge of the whole, or at least of a very large part, of a poet's work, makes one enjoy more, because it makes one understand better, any one of his poems. That implies a significant unity in his whole work. One can't put this increased understanding altogether into words: I could not say just why I think I understand *Comus* better for having read *Paradise Lost*, or *Paradise Lost* better for having read *Samson Agonistes*, but I am convinced that this is so.

Finally, in his last critical essay, Mr Eliot reiterates, in a more specific context of judgement, the earlier view he had expressed on Herbert:

To understand Shakespeare we must acquaint ourselves with all of his plays; to understand Herbert we must acquaint ourselves with all of *The Temple*. Herbert is, of course, a much slighter poet than Shakespeare; nevertheless he may justly be called a major poet.

Mr Eliot has described his criticism as a by-product of his poetic workshop. The self-deprecation in the phrase has tended to obscure the element of truth in it, which is that Mr Eliot's criticism has always been enmeshed in a given literary situation and has found its strength because it has usually been charged with the forces needed to make that situation creative. Since part of the milieu which the criticism illuminates and moves forward is formed by Mr Eliot's own poetry, it is reasonable that motifs predominant in the criticism should find their substantiation in the creative work. Those who regard 'Tradition and the Individual Talent' as the best of commentaries on *The Waste Land*, 'Dante' as the best commentary on *Ash Wednesday*, and *The Music of Poetry* as the best commentary on *Four Quartets* will not think it rash to sense in the passages quoted a clue to the understanding of Mr Eliot's poetry as a whole. The implicit criterion is one of continuity, sometimes expressed in, but not necessarily identified with, the presence of a literary 'personality'. The important thing is that the continuity should possess the power of development, that it should be capable of creating and sustaining a significant process or a meaningful world.

Continuity is a concept which one tends to resist, partly because modern criticism has educated us so successfully in the self-sufficiency of the individual poem. It becomes desirable to tell ourselves that one critical hypothesis does not exclude the other and that because a work of art stands by itself it does not necessarily have to stand alone. Literature stripped of all contexts is unusual, if only because the language which enters literature is wrought from a context of both history and experience. Given the nearly unavoidable presence of a context, that of the *œuvre* can be as instructive and at least as fully designed as the context of genre or of milieu.

The problem for each poet is to find the right metaphor of wholeness, one that will grasp but not deform the poetry. One must also remember, though the warning may seem naïve, that poets write poems which are sometimes sheerly themselves and which decline to belong to anything larger. These eddies do not prove the absence of a mainstream; they merely add to it the richness of occasional dissent. Yet even the word 'mainstream' can be misleading, since the basic metaphor (or the figure, as Rosemond Tuve might call it) can be one of pattern as well as of movement or process. With Milton, for example, one thinks of five different literary forms reaching into a common centre of recognition; and the centre, if one may label it with the blatant crudeness demanded on these occasions, is that of man's responsibility for what he makes of himself. Each form conducts its exploration of this centre, according to its inheritance and resources. Each, so to speak, creates its own individual strategy of insight. The resultant literature is in a sense generic, but the collective design adds richness to the specific vistas opened by each form; and a powerful sense of inevitability is created as all roads end in the controlling truth. That this should happen is an aesthetic consequence of that massive and inclusive vision of order which Milton was perhaps the last man to feel in its entirety; wherever one begins and however one proceeds, one must in the end uncover the same pattern.

With Yeats, more than one metaphor may be necessary, but one of the metaphors would be quasi-biological. The poetry is written out of a series of lived positions fitted into the trajectory of an individual life; and the whole truth is given by a series of lives fitted into the wheel of possibilities. Truth can only be experienced and not known; it cannot be talked about, but only presented and embodied. To live the truth is to live only part of it, because to live is to make choices, to accept exclusions, to be both the child and the victim of natural necessities. Man achieves his particular fragment and maximizes the size and validity of the fragment by moving through the possibilities that are permitted and by ensuring that each possibility is both completely and intensely lived.

With Eliot, the curve of accomplishment is not based on the natural trajectory of life; its outline is rather that of an achieved and consolidated advance into knowledge. Each poem represents a step forward, or upward, building on the position won in the previous poem. The stairway is thus the vertebral metaphor; but the garden into which the stairway leads, the 'time of the tension between birth and dying', is such that the perilous balance of understanding requires the quest to be entered again and its conclusions renewed. The movement of *Four Quartets* is essentially cyclic:

> We shall not cease from exploration
> And the end of all our exploring
> Will be to arrive where we started
> And to know the place for the first time.

The shape of Mr Eliot's poetry is thus composed by two forces: the spiral of process and the circle of design. Each necessitates the other and both stipulate the search for reality as a condition of man's being. It is not a search which can end in decisive findings: humankind cannot bear very much reality, and the enchainment of past and future protects mankind from heaven as well as from damnation. The sea of doubt is man's natural element, and the hints and guesses at the truth which illuminate that sea are designed not so much to end doubt as to save it from the whirlpool of despair. Eliot's poetry as an *œuvre* is thus given a unique and, as it were, double honesty, by its sense of a pattern won out of experience and by the manner in which the nature of the pattern entails a further commitment to experience through which the pattern is once again validated.

If these circumnavigations are not irrelevant, 'Prufrock' must take its place not simply as a beginning, but as a beginning which looks forward to an end, and which defines the terms of the unending inquiry. It has been remarked more than once that Prufrock's love song is never sung; what should be added is that his inability to sing it is not simply ironic, but part of the specifications of failure. To sing is to achieve a definition and Prufrock's fate is to fall short of definition, to bring momentous news only to thresholds. At the outset we are told that we will be taken through certain half-deserted streets

> that follow like a tedious argument
> Of insidious intent
> To lead you to an overwhelming question. . . .

The slumming tour is also a return to underground life, and it is plain even at this stage that the overwhelming question is more than the proposal of marriage to a lady, that the love song must eventually be sung to Beatrice. In these circumstances Prufrock's 'Oh, do not ask, "What is it?"' is also more than a suggestion that the question will reveal itself as one strolls along. Much is in character here: the exaggeration that does not really exaggerate, the turning away from definition, and the implication that further inquiry would not be in good taste. We are in fact moving on two levels, and Prufrock's gestures, volubly in excess of the occasion, correlate fully to another order of reality which Prufrock unfortunately cannot confront and make explicit. He is too much the child of his milieu to achieve the outrageousness of proper definition; and since the ambience of 'Prufrock' is comic, the framing of the question must be an exercise in outrage, not, as in 'Gerontion', a diagnosis of guilt. Eliot's favourite life-death ambiguity is potent here as nearly everywhere else. What seems to be life is death and to die into the true life one must die away from the salon. The paradox is sharpened at the climax of the poem when Prufrock drowns because he is awakened by human voices. But submarine or underground existence is not the answer and Prufrock does not undergo true death by drowning; the staircase he climbs is also, for the same reason, not a purgatorial stair. The reader is aware, through Prufrock, of the shocking nature of knowledge:

> Do I dare
> Disturb the universe?

But the scandal of recognition is beyond Prufrock himself. It is Lazarus and John the Baptist who are the proper ambassadors of reality to the salon, who can convey to it the angry, clawing truth. Prufrock still lives (and fails to live) by a minor and less taxing scale of values. Visions and decisions shade off into revisions. An eternal footman holds a coat, and the confession 'in short, I was afraid' reduces the deeper terror to everyday nervousness. 'Would it have been worth it, after all...?' Prufrock asks reassuringly, and the size of the exaggeration dismisses the enterprise:

> To have squeezed the universe into a ball
> To roll it towards some overwhelming question. . . .

At a deeper level, however, the responsibility continues. The echo from Marvell reminds us that Marvell's suitor was more daring. As the poem develops, Prufrock's initial 'do not ask, "What is it?"' takes its proper place in the outline of failure. The overwhelming question has to be asked. It cannot be left to define or uncover itself. It must be forced into being in that passion for definition which can seize the moment and drive it to its crisis. The cost of definition will be more than ridicule. One is entitled to fear the cost. But not to meet it means the death of the man. The gesture of comic and yet of cosmic defiance – 'Do I dare/Disturb the universe?' – collapses now into mere sartorial rebellion:

Shall I part my hair behind? Do I dare to eat a peach?
I shall wear white flannel trousers, and walk upon the beach.

If the ambience of 'Prufrock' is comic, the Jacobean corridors of 'Gerontion' are slippery with images of evasion and betrayal. Gerontion, an old man arithmetically, has known neither natural youth nor natural age. He is in fact that typical Eliot character who cannot die because he has not lived. The thought is mentioned in the second line and does not recur until the last line links the dry brain to the dry season. Cut off from the organic world, Gerontion is cut off also from the living truth, the sustaining sense of relatedness. He knows that Christ the tiger is also the helpless child of Lancelot Andrewes's sermon; but his mind cannot keep the paradox in balance, and as guilt drives him mercilessly against the wall it is the tiger that stalks through his unnatural year. The confrontation of reality cannot be endured; the images twist away into rites of expiation and anxiety, surrogates for the truth that will not be faced. It is this falling short, this failure of metaphysical nerve, that makes the difference between dying and dying into life. So the tree of life becomes the tree of wrath, and neither fear nor courage can save us, because both fear and courage acquire their full nature only when they are morally rooted.

> The tiger springs in the new year. Us he devours.

This is the death of annihilation that looks forward to, yet is completely different from, another devouring in the desert by three white leopards. Gerontion's vehement declarations of design ('We have not reached conclusion. . . . I have not made this show purposelessly'), with the repeated 'Think now' and the final 'Think at last' forcing the moment to its intellectual crisis, do seem to result in a last-minute facing of reality:

> I would meet you upon this honestly.

But it is the honesty of the man against the wall, not that deeper confrontation which Eliot describes as 'that peculiar honesty, which, in a world too frightened to be honest, is peculiarly terrifying'. Gerontion's response is that of fear, not courage, in the metaphysical sense, and both its content and emptiness are pitilessly exposed in what is perhaps the most moving passage of the poem, as the imagery of old age blends into the sense of withering away from God:

> I that was near your heart was removed therefrom
> To lose beauty in terror, terror in inquisition.
> I have lost my passion: why should I need to keep it
> Since what is kept must be adulterated?
> I have lost my sight, smell, hearing, taste and touch:
> How should I use them for your closer contact?

In terms which are closer to the nerves of pity and terror, Gerontion's predicament is that of Prufrock. He has moved forward in the act of definition, but he cannot cross the threshold, cannot make that surrender to reality which involves the death of the illusion which is his life. When the question is not asked the collapse into triviality must follow:

> These with a thousand small deliberations
> Protract the profit of their chilled delirium,
> Excite the membrane, when the sense has cooled,
> With pungent sauces, multiply variety
> In a wilderness of mirrors.

Gerontion's frivolity may be more opulent than that of Prufrock, but the terms of failure are not dissimilar; the darker colouring is the result of a more sombre ambience, with the sense of guilt blocking the tentative effort at definition, just as the fear of ridicule did in the earlier poem. The death of the self follows the failure to achieve relationship, notwithstanding the multiplying of the self in mirrors; the poem's threatening rhetoric here calls for a grimmer extinction than Prufrock's elegant drowning. Gerontion's identity is disintegrated and even pulverized. His mind may have its fragments, but it is permitted no ruins against which to shore them, and the vestigial white feathers in the snow of oblivion, drawn into a gulf that is more than geographical, express vividly the sense of sheer obliteration, even down to the collapsing cadence.

When Pound dissuaded Eliot from making 'Gerontion' a part of *The Waste Land*, he could not have been aware of the evolving logic of the *œuvre*. Nevertheless, his action contributed to that logic. 'Gerontion' looks forward to *The Waste Land* if only because there must be a world at the bottom of Dover cliff. Gerontion himself is unable to enter that world. His monologue, made up of the thoughts 'of a dry brain in a dry season', is carefully distanced from experience, and even the encounter to which he reaches imaginatively cannot be totally faced. To go forward from this point is to enter the abyss and to be prepared to prove nothingness on one's pulses.

When one accepts the risk one also discovers that the risk is the only possibility of survival.

Seen in the symbolic continuum, the waste land is Prufrock's world more fully realized, a world where prophecy has fallen to fortune-telling, where love has hardened into the expertise of lust, where April is the cruellest month, and where the dead are no longer buried but planted in gardens. The fifth section is a break-out from this world, the dimensions of which are carefully controlled to fall short of a break-through. Because survival cannot be preached, but only endured, the mythologizing structure is crucially important in ensuring that whatever progress is achieved is not simply talked about, but lived through imaginatively. What the thunder says is the result of what the poem becomes, though, for reasons which will be apparent, the thunder speaks as a voice sought for by the poem but remaining outside it.

The Waste Land does not end where it begins. It may return to where it started with deeper understanding, but the mytho-dramatic progress is not depicted as circular. A journey to Chapel Perilous is undertaken, delirium and near-death evoke an ancient experience, a damp gust brings rain from which the leaves are limp, the thunder speaks, proclaiming oracularly the conditions for deliverance, and the protagonist ends, fishing on the shore with the arid plain behind him. These are small gains but their very narrowness suggests their authenticity. As for the thunder, its pronouncements are designed to leave one in what Eliot once called a state of enlightened mystification. Oracles achieve validity rather than clarity, and what they mean is decided by how experience reads them. One strong note in the voice of this oracle is a call to commitment – the awful daring of a moment's surrender, the recognition of the self as a prison, and the sea that would have been calm if one had chosen to venture on it, all seem to point straightforwardly in the same direction. When the protagonist decides to set his lands in order, as the bridges of the unreal city fall about him, we are witnessing the recovery of a traditional understanding. The collapse of civilization which a superficial reading (abetted by Eliot's notes) invites us to see here is also the death of an illusion, and reality can be born only from inward renewal.

The thunder speaks from the horizon of *The Waste Land* because what it has to say is discerned rather than experienced. The break-out from sterility is no more than that; it is not a movement into fruitfulness. The poem is an advance from 'Gerontion', building on that poem's terrified recognitions and taking the vital step forward from a condition in which neither fear nor courage can save us. Its conclusion sets the arid plain behind and moves us to the fringe of a world which the poem can formulate but cannot enter. To make that entrance is the function of *Ash-Wednesday*.

In *Ash-Wednesday* the protagonist endures a death unlike those suffered by Prufrock, Gerontion, and Phlebas and climbs a stair, decisively unlike that climbed by Prufrock, to the threshold of the overwhelming question. He reaches a garden, a precarious state of enlightenment, only to realize that the place of understanding must be held in constant struggle against the persistent downward pull of the flesh. He looks out finally on that sea of doubt and renewal where all that he has learned must be revalidated. It is repetition with a difference, the difference marking, with such precision as is possible, the movement forward in the life of the whole work. The death by devouring in *Ash-Wednesday* has a special place in this infra-structure. Unlike all previous dyings it is a dying into life; and its differences from Phlebas's death, which precedes it in the sequence, invite and respond to critical attention.

Phlebas too owes his place in the *œuvre* to Pound, and Pound, whether he knew it or not, was once again marking a turning-point. Phlebas's is the last of a series of old-style deaths, a warning of man's mortality, the inexorable reminder of the skull beneath the skin. Fear in a handful of dust is a step forward from the rather more animal fear of Gerontion, and the collocation of two mysticisms, as well as the play between purgatorial fire and the destructive fires of the flesh, points to the direction in which this fear can lead. It leads in fact to Chapel Perilous, but Phlebas's remains do not lie along this route. As a representative of that mercantile mentality for which the early poems preserve a special contempt, he is not permitted the consolation of any remains. De Bailhache, Fresca, and Mrs Cammel are despatched into outer space and disintegrated into 'fractured atoms' in what seems a reasonably thorough process of destruction. But Phlebas has his bones picked for fourteen days by the mocking whispers of a current under sea and then enters a whirlpool, where he is presumably churned into a further refinement of non-being. In *Ash-Wednesday* the death-rites may be superficially as gruesome, but the total effect is of a curious, limpid happiness. Despite its relevance, one would hesitate to use the word 'gaiety' if the voice of the thunder had not legitimized it. It is, in fact, something akin to Yeats's 'gaiety transfiguring all that dread' that lies on the other side of radical commitment, though to reach that other side one must pass through an experience, translatable only by the metaphor of death. The verse, by the manner in which its singing sweetness lives through and overrides the macabre narrative, embodies fully the elusive sense of metamorphosis into a higher reality. In what is later to be described as 'A condition of complete simplicity/Costing not less than everything' there is a kind of lucid, tranquil givenness, symbolized in the creative destitution of the landscape. To be aware of this it is not necessary to assign specific functions to the leopards; the number three is sufficiently evocative. As for the indigestible portions which the leopards reject, those may, as Unger indicates, represent a residue of the self which survives destruction, but they also surely stand for the difference between mere dying and dying into life. Two significant links in the chain remain to be added. First, the prison of the self is broken – the bones are united by their forgetfulness of themselves and each other. Second, the protagonist's cry in *The Waste Land* – 'Shall I at least set my lands in order?' – is answered by: 'This is the land. We have our inheritance.' As understanding passes into experience the ruined tower becomes the tradition redeemed.

Man's mind was not born for peace. It inhabits a time of tension and a place of twilight. To die into life, it renounces everything, including renunciation. Then, reborn, it must climb a stairway, along which the process of struggle and rejection is once again enacted. The higher reality may be given to us eventually, but it is not given for settlement. The desert is in the garden and the garden in the desert. The withered apple-seed of our failing may be spat out but there is every possibility that the seed will flourish again. In the story of the quest, the chapter called *Ash-Wednesday* has a certain stubborn honesty because of its quiet demonstration that the only end to the quest is its renewal.

The very title of *Four Quartets* implies repetition, and the epigraph from Heraclitus, the Yin and Yang of the inverted mottoes that enclose *East Coker*, the images of circular and spiral movement, the persistent metaphors of journeying, not only take up and consummate a literary past already familiar and achieved, but also make real the involvement of pattern in process. 'In my beginning is my end' speaks from the biological as well as the unchanging world. The detail of the pattern is movement, and even that love which is beyond all movement is caught in limitation between unbeing and being. The moment of enlightenment is in and out of time, half-heard in the stillness between two waves of the sea.

Since it is only through time that time is conquered, there can be no alternative or end to exploration. We begin in a house with a settled order and a formal garden, with meditations precise and tentative. Innocence inhabits the garden and enlightenment may return to it; but to live in a house is to learn that one must leave it, to make the discovery that 'houses live and die'. The sense of design must reassert itself in a circle of experience, slowly widening and increasingly corrosive. The houses of *East Coker* face the sea, and the protagonist, middle-aged like Prufrock, looks out over the vast waters, hearing not the fluting voices of mermaids, but the 'wave cry' and the 'wind cry', through the empty desolation. Whatever understanding one achieves has been lived through and must therefore be left behind; the future is always a new beginning and a different failure. *The Dry Salvages* accepts the inevitable journey, committing the protagonist to that perilous ocean on which the houses of *East Coker* and the rocks of *Ash-Wednesday* look. Both the river within us and the sea around us are made to live as forces of chaos, attacking and eroding the boundaries of order. As the second section of the poem tolls in the accumulated rhythm of the meaningless, we are brought again to the landscape of destitution, the world of bleached bones and sand, and the overwhelming question, where the sense of form becomes the will to survive.

At the margin, small movements are decisively significant. They mark the difference between life and death, between despair and indestructible meaning. On this beach, as in the desert of *Ash-Wednesday*, the poetry centres its weight of realization and its power to resist defeat on minute gains, defined with the precision of the authentic. The 'unprayable/Prayer' becomes the 'hardly barely prayable/Prayer'. The 'calamitous annunciation' becomes the 'one annunciation'. The protagonist who in *East Coker* felt the world become 'stranger' and the pattern 'more complicated' is now reassured because a pattern exists which is not a mere sequence or a development. There is a meaning not given *by* but given *to* experience.

> We had the experience but missed the meaning,
> And approach to the meaning restores the experience
> In a different form, beyond any meaning
> We can assign to happiness.

At the edge of nothingness, the birth of meaning (or the refusal of the indigestible portions to die) takes place in a manner both creative and ancient. Poetry cannot report the event; it must *be* the event, lived through in a form that can speak about itself while remaining wholly itself. This is a feat at least as difficult as it sounds, and if the poem succeeds in it, it is because, however much it remembers previous deaths by drowning, it creates its own life against its own thrust of questioning. The careful separation of enlightenment from any possible 'meaning' of happiness is typical of the specificity achieved. At the same time the reader is conscious of a momentum which gained force before the poem and will endure beyond it. What is said here acquires additional power, because the literary past, the life of the *œuvre*, has a pattern that is not a mere sequence and cannot be called development.

The Dry Salvages represents the maximum horizon of *Four Quartets*. When the sea of nihilism (only Arnold saw it as a sea of faith) has been denied its total victory, elemental time, older than the time of chronometers, civilizes itself into historic time, and past, present, and future are found again in an organic relationship. This is one man's way of knowing that

> If you came this way,
> Taking any route, starting from anywhere,
> At any time, or at any season
> It would always be the same. . . .

The circle completes itself or, to put it differently, contracts to the point which is its centre. We end as we begin, entering the unknown, remembered gate to the garden. But we also end, knowing the unity, between the fire of energy and the rose of perfect form.

A critical metaphor sufficient to compass Eliot's poetry has its betrayals as well as its excitements. If it is not kept in its place, it may impose upon the work an obsessive logic and an intolerable tidiness. To lay down such Procrustean definitions is no part of the business of this article. All that is suggested is that such metaphors are possible and that they have their role in shaping critical perceptions. The interpretations of 'Gerontion' and 'Prufrock' offered here, for example, differ from customary readings; but they fit the facts as well as any alternatives and enable the facts themselves to be fitted into a larger pattern. *The Waste Land* and *Ash-Wednesday* also gain in richness and in solidity when we are aware of the total life from which they issue and against which they are set. Whether such increments are aesthetic in nature (or indeed whether they are increments at all) is, of course, for the reader to judge. At any rate this article pays Eliot the courtesy of taking him at his word on the difference between major and minor achievement.

In a tentative exploration, not every fact can be decisively located, and some facts, as has already been suggested, are part of the poet's right to forget his own patterns, whether known or instinctive. Certain other poems have not been considered, not because they are in conflict with the metaphor studied here, but because they do not contribute to it as characteristically as the poems chosen. The plays are a different problem and perhaps require a metaphor of their own. This is not to suggest that Mr Eliot's dramatic and poetic concerns are dissimilar; the point is that the force of continuity in the drama calls for a different specification. What should have emerged with some firmness from this essay is Eliot's remarkable power of wholeness. His work is not simply a series of individual excellences but a totality fully experienced and almost painfully lived through. The movement suggested here, the carefully built trajectory of understanding, the attainment of enlightenment under conditions that compel the quest to be re-enacted, the circle closed and yet forever open, all point to a design too subtle and too organic to be planned. What we are facing is what, in another context, has been interestingly called the artifice of reality.

Eliot's essay on Pascal has an unmistakable eloquence of involvement. Reading it, we are always aware that what he says applies to more than his subject. Nowhere is this clearer than in the following remarks:

... every man who thinks and lives by thought must have his own scepticism, that which stops at the question, that which ends in denial, or that which leads to faith and which is somehow integrated into the faith which transcends it. And Pascal, as the type of one kind of religious believer, which is highly passionate and ardent, but passionate only through a powerful and regulated intellect, is in the first sections of his unfinished Apology for Christianity facing unflinchingly the demon of doubt which is inseparable from the spirit of belief.

The parallels are evident and revealing. Eliot's poetry is a process of living by thought, of seeking to find peace 'through a satisfaction of the whole being'. It is singular in its realization of passion through intelligence. It is driven by a scepticism which resolutely asks the question but refuses to stop short at it, by a sensibility sharply aware of 'the disorder, the futility, the meaninglessness, the mystery of life and suffering'. If it attains a world of belief or a conviction of order, that conviction is won against the attacking strength of doubt and remains always subject to its corrosive power. Not all of us can share Eliot's faith. But all of us can accept the poetry because nearly every line of it was written while looking into the eyes of the demon.

T. S. ELIOT IN THE SOUTH SEAS

A look at the poems and short stories that he wrote when he was sixteen in St Louis[1]

By Neville Braybrooke

IN the British Museum catalogue there are over a thousand references to books about aspects of T. S. Eliot's life and work. But there is one aspect that is completely ignored. This concerns his juvenilia, especially the short stories that he wrote at school in St Louis. Moreover this neglect becomes doubly strange when it is remembered how much store has been placed on other details of his childhood: the fact, for instance, that some parts of *Ash-Wednesday* can be linked with an engraving of Murillo's 'Immaculate Conception' which hung in his parents' bedroom at 2,635 Locust Street.

In a centenary address given in 1953 at Washington University, Eliot declared that he had received the most important part of his education at Smith Academy, and in three numbers of the school magazine dated 1905 there is to be found a selection of his first published prose and verse. Most of it is simply initialled T. E., although there is one item signed in full – namely, 'A Lyric'. This is written in the Ben Jonson manner – and begins:

> If time and space, as sages say,
> Are things which cannot be,
> The sun which does not feel decay,
> No greater is than we....

Two years later it was reprinted under the title of 'Song' in the *Harvard Advocate*, with several slight changes. There have been fewer than a score of references to either version by critics.

1. Part of a 'book in progress

379

To Eliot's first poem there have been even fewer references. This is called 'A Fable for Feasters', a rather Byronic set of twelve verses about medieval England which he published two months before 'A Lyric'. Much of it is little better than doggerel, with an occasional lively phrase thrown in: 'They made a raid/On every bird and beast in Aesop's fable'; 'His eye became the size of any dollar.' Yet such interest as it possesses today comes primarily from curiosity: 'the beginning shall remind us of the end', as he wrote in his last Ariel poem of 1954.

In the fable a band of merry friars are given to heavy feasting, and at Christmas-time their refectory tables groan. But they are haunted by a ghost who steals their fatter cows, plays tricks with the bells in their belfry, and who once sat their prior

> on the steeple
> To the astonishment of all the people.

So, the abbot vows that once and for all at Christmas they shall be free of these pranks. He purchases the relics of a Spanish saint, sprinkles his gown liberally with holy water, and douses also the turkeys, capons, and boars that they are going to eat. The doors are then bolted and barred. But ghosts prove 'fellows whom you *can't* keep out'. The abbot is pulled from his chair and whisked up the chimney 'before anyone can say "O jiminy" '. There follows the moral:

> . . . after this the monks grew most devout,
>   And lived on milk and breakfast food entirely;
> Each morn from four to five one took a knout
>   And flogged his mates 'till they grew good and friarly.
> Spirits from that time forth they did without,
>   And lived the admiration of the shire. We
> Got the veracious record of these doings
> From an old manuscript found in the ruins.

This is boisterous stuff, and many schoolboys in their time have written in a similar vein. The dissolution of the monasteries at which in rather an indirect way the fable hints, was expressed much more forcibly thirty years later in *Murder in the Cathedral*. Indeed, if his St Louis poems have a merit, it is as 'class exercises' – which is how his English master at the time rated them.

Far more original and far more exciting are his short stories of this period. These first appeared in the *Smith Academy Record* and, unlike 'A Lyric' (which was resurrected by Tambimuttu in a symposium honouring the poet's sixtieth birthday in 1948), they have never been reprinted. Their titles are 'A Tale of a Whale' and 'The Man Who Was King'.

The author was sixteen at the time, and neither runs to more than a thousand words; in fact economy and precision are two of their hallmarks. 'A Tale of a Whale' opens:

It was in '71, I remember, that I was on a whaling ship 'Parallel Opipedon', in the South Pacific. One day after a prolonged spell of bad luck we happened to be becalmed off Tanzatatapoo Island. We lay motionless for several days, and although the mizzen top-gallant shrouds had been repeatedly belayed to the fore staysail, and the flying jib-boom cleared, and lashed to the monkey-rail, we made no progress whatever. It was a very hot and sultry day, and the captain was pacing the quarter-deck, fanning himself. The watch were amusing themselves holystoning the deck, while the rest of the crew were eating ice-cream in the fore chains.

This has something about it of the dash of Robert Louis Stevenson in his stories of the South Seas. The pace is fast and furious, and there is exhibited a youthful writer's delight in displaying his knowledge of ships. The year before, Mrs Eliot had hired a retired mariner to teach her two sons sailing; later in life, her younger son named yachting as one of the sports that he loved most. To holystone means to scour, and 'monkey-rail', I suspect, is a misprint for 'monkey-tail', a sailor's slang for a short hand-spike. Captain Marryat's sailors in his books use it as rhyming slang for nail.

Tanzatatapoo, like the island of Kinkanja in *The Cocktail*

Party, is a made-up place. Eliot's genius for choosing significant names showed early. Nor in the whaler records of the 1870s does any ship feature called 'Parallel Opipedon'. This is not so surprising when the name is examined, since it is probably either a play on the word 'parallelepiped', or on 'O pipe do(w)n' – a pun which should put the over-zealous researcher well and truly in his place. After all, a good while passed before Eliot revealed publicly that the notes to *The Waste Land* were something of a leg-pull. Nor did the years lessen Eliot's love of punning. In *The Confidential Clerk* there is Lucasta Angel, who is described by another character in the same play as being 'rather flighty'. Yet what distinguishes 'A Tale of a Whale' is its packed brevity. In the remaining five paragraphs there is enough action to fill fifty pages.

A whale is sighted, they give chase to it, and the narrator (who is the harpooner) jumps into a gig. The harpoon is shot, and in fury the beast hurls the gig 'seventy-three feet into the air'. From the beginning, these touches of exactitude characterized Eliot's work. Yet though the gig is dashed to pieces, fortunately the narrator and two of the crew manage to land on the beast's back. And there they stay, 'rather worse off than Jonah', since what they fear is that at any moment the monster may decide to dive into the deep.

Their food consists of flying fish – 'we merely had to stand and let them hit against us'; jelly-fish (a rather childish pun); and spongecake made out of the sponges which grow on the bottom of the great animal. The oil needed for frying they extract by burning large chunks of the beast's back. On the fourth day it dies. The cause is put down to either indigestion brought about by having swallowed a boat whole, or loss of flesh brought about by the frying. 'At any rate we were free from the danger of sinking.'

In the two closing paragraphs everything is brought to a swift conclusion. The narrator decides to have a swim and spies some wreckage floating by (presumably from 'Parallel Opipedon'). With the help of the other two, he hauls it aboard their floating island. They then dig a hole in the whale's back and set up a mast as a sail. Three months later they arrive in Honolulu after 'an uneventful voyage'. No phrase could be more vintage Eliot; it has the same final quality about it which is to be found at the reaching of the stable in the *Journey of the Magi*: the place 'was (you may say) satisfactory'.

'The Man Who Was King' was published two months after 'A Tale of a Whale' and is also set in the South Pacific. It concerns Captain Jimmy Magruder, a retired mariner, who is reputed to be famous for telling sea-stories. As a boy Eliot revelled in listening to the stories of the sailors in Gloucester Harbour, New England, and in 1928 he recalls this in a preface that he wrote for James B. Connolly's *Fishermen of the Banks*, published by his own firm in London. Further in his *Smith Academy Record* second story, he begins by telling his readers that there is one tale of which Magruder is particularly fond, but adds that each time this old salt relates it, it is embellished with more and more 'wonderful incidents'. The author, acting as a kind of editor, then says that in every edition certain facts remain constant and that it is these which he is going to pass on.

These facts begin with a shipwreck. Magruder's vessel is a sealer of the last century and, 'about latitude 22 degrees south', it is smashed to pieces in a storm. He finds himself clinging to a spar. Later (for he cannot remember what happened in between), he finds himself washed up on the long sandy beach of an island. This proves to be in the Paumotu group, although the island's actual name of Matahiva is not listed in the world gazetteer. Magruder is the first white man to land here, and since the local king has just died, the natives take both his whiteness and sudden arrival as signs from the gods that he is to be their new ruler. He is given a harem, a royal fishing boat, and a palace which is 'about the size of a large woodshed'. Life consists of bathing, feasting, and getting drunk.

The previous king had been in the habit at feasts of breathing fire or performing the rope trick, but Magruder can do none of these feats. Nor is his repeated drunkenness 'remarkable enough ... to excite applause'. So his deposition becomes imminent, and a trusty slave warns him to fly before rebellion breaks out. Without delay, therefore, he stocks the royal boat with provisions and sets course. His object is Tahiti, which lies 'three hundred miles' away, and after an uneventful voyage he reaches it two weeks later.

In the sixty years that passed after the publication of these two adventure stories, Eliot travelled far. In the landscapes of his poems islands frequently occurred. Often too he linked them with the theme of drowning – though drowning for Eliot did not necessarily mean the sea. In his poem 'Morning at the Window', which came out in his *Prufrock* volume, the street was also seen as a sea in which people drowned: 'brown waves of fog toss up ... Twisted faces from the bottom of the street...' For the point about all Eliot's poems is that in some sense or other they were all voyages: those who went on them were not the same people when they arrived at their destination, since in the course of them they underwent what in oriental religions is known as a metempsychosis, or in the Christian religion as a change of heart. His boyhood descriptions of voyages to Honolulu and Tahiti may have been imaginary, but they set a pattern. The question that remains to be asked is – Why at sixteen did he choose to set them in the South Seas?

Two years before, when he was fourteen, and at a time when the contemporary poetry of the period meant nothing to him, he read the *Rubáiyát* of Omar Khayyám. The effect of Fitzgerald's translation on him was overwhelming, he later recalled: 'the world appeared anew, painted with bright, delicious and painful colours'. Yet it was a distant, Eastern world, and by comparison with it the islands of Hawaii and Paumota in the Pacific seemed much less remote and closer to his St Louis and New England background. So the exoticism of Omar's world, it would seem, he replaced with an exoticism of his own in which the natives of Matahiva drink *madu-nut* wine, an imaginary nut wine, and in which they beat *bhghons*, a made-up name for a musical instrument that is a 'cross between [a] tin pan and [a] gong'.

This was the range of his invention then, and the significance of this early prose and verse in the light of his later work was the use to which he put and adapted his boyhood fictions and observations: the leviathan of his first story – and 'the whale's backbone' remembered in *The Dry Salvages*; the thicket of tari-bushes under which Magruder is awakened by the islanders – and the juniper-tree of *Ash-Wednesday*, under which the Lady sits with three white leopards; or the moral for feasters in his first Christmas fable – and his warning ten years before his death, in *The Cultivation of Christmas Trees*, to distinguish between what is 'childish' and 'the vision of the child'.

These are some of the links that a look at his juvenilia in the *Smith Academy Record* suggest. How much longer will it be before this aspect of his work is given the serious and detailed treatment that it deserves?[2]

2. Since I wrote this article, I have read Herbert Howarth's *Notes on Some Figures behind T. S. Eliot*, Chatto & Windus, 1965. This is one of the most rewarding books on Eliot that has come my way. It includes an invaluable reconstruction of the poet's childhood and his St Louis background.

POSTSCRIPT BY THE GUEST EDITOR

A FEW days after January fourth of last year I knew that I needed to do something about the loss I was becoming more and more aware of in the death of T. S. Eliot. On the afternoon of the fourth a reporter at *The New York Times* had telephoned me in Minneapolis and asked me for an 'estimate of Mr Eliot's place in modern literature' – and had I known him and could I think of any interesting anecdotes? This crass incident delayed the shock of realization; and it was several days later that I understood that T. S. Eliot was dead. One dies every day one's own death, but one cannot imagine the death of the man who was *il maestro di color che sanno* – or, since he was an artist and not, after his young manhood, a philosopher: *il maestro di color che scrivonno*. To see his *maestro*, Dante had to 'lift his eyelids a little higher', and that was what I knew, after January fourth, I had been doing in the thirty-six years of an acquaintance that almost imperceptibly became friendship. *I looked up to him*, and in doing so I could not feel myself in any sense diminished. What he thought of 'us' – by us, I mean his old but slightly younger literary friends – we never quite knew because he never quite said. The un-Eliot or anti-Eliot people thought that his literary reticence was 'cagey' and ungenerous. It was the highest form of civility. If he didn't know whether we were good writers it was because he didn't know, in spite of his immense fame, whether he himself would last. Somewhere, in print, he put himself with Yeats. But would Yeats last? I am sure he didn't know. He was simply aware – and he would have been obtuse had he not been aware – that he and Yeats dominated poetry in English in this century; but that, to a deeply empirical mind, meant little in the long run of posterity.

What, then, could I do? On the death of a friend one may meditate the Thankless Muse, even if the friend was not a poet. The meditation becomes more difficult, and one almost gives it up, if the friend is not only a poet but perhaps a great poet. The Poet-as-Greatness is not, as our friend might have said in his Harvard dissertation on F. H. Bradley, an object of knowledge: it is only a point of view. Private meditation at best must land one in the midst of The Last Things, beyond the common reality; but poetry begins with the common reality, and ends with it, as our friend's friend, Charles Williams, said of Dante. It could be equally said of Tom Eliot; and that is why it is not inappropriate, on this occasion, to see him first as a man, and to speak plainly of him as Tom; for he was the uncommon man committed to the common reality of the human condition. Only men so committed, and so deeply committed that there is no one moment in their lives when they are aware of an act of commitment, express the perfect simplicity of manners that was Tom Eliot's. There were times when he was silent: I remember a luncheon at a London club, at which Bonamy Dobrée and Herbert Read were also present, when he was *withdrawn*; but he was not withdrawn from us; he was withdrawn into himself. This, too, I take to be a form of civility. Among friends one has the privilege of saying nothing; the civility consists in the assumption that one's silence will be civilly understood. I can imagine a small gathering of friends who say nothing all evening: they recoil from saying anything that the others don't want to hear; and their silence would be the subtlest courtesy.

What – I repeat the question – what, then, could I do? What could I do about the loss I felt in the death not of Tom Eliot but of T. S. Eliot? I almost distinguish the two persons because my friendship with Tom Eliot was a private matter to which the public might have indirect access only if I were capable of writing a formal pastoral elegy like 'Lycidas'; but then Tom Eliot would become T. S. Eliot the public figure, a figure considerably larger than his elegist. Is it not customary for the greater man to appropriate the elegiac mode to celebrate the hitherto unknown talents of the lesser? Had Milton's friend King been a great poet Milton could not have *somewhat* loudly swept the strings: he might have been tempted to indulge in hyperbole instead of what he did, which was to forget King, as posterity was to forget him, and give us Milton. Whatever I might do about Tom Eliot or T. S. Eliot, I could not forget him and exhibit the dubious poetic virtuosity of Tate.

What I could do is what I have done, for what one does reveals the limit of what one can do. I have brought together, at the invitation of the editor of *The Sewanee Review*, some twenty essays in reminiscence and appreciation by T. S. Eliot's old friends; by some persons who knew him slightly; and by others who didn't know him at all, but who seemed to me to add to our knowledge of the work. There may be some literary criticism in the essays, but with two or three exceptions criticism is merely implicit in the assumption of the great distinction of the subject. Here and there are brilliant illuminations of the work through personal knowledge of the poet which goes back forty to fifty years; but there is no invasion of the severe privacy which Tom Eliot the man and T. S. Eliot the poet maintained throughout his seventy-six years. His poems came out of the fiery crucible of his interior life; yet all of the interior life that we know is in the poems; and that is as it should be; for his theory of the impersonality of poetry met no contradiction in the intensely personal origins of the poems. When I asked his old friends to write essays I hoped that they would bear witness to the part that his character and mind had played in their lives and works.

My own fragmentary writings, I think, bear this sort of witness; yet I surmise that we became friends because I never tried to imitate him or become a disciple. He abhorred disciples and his imitators bored him. My other master in literature, John Crowe Ransom, who is within a few months of Eliot's age, different as the two men are, has always treated his younger friends as if we were his equals; we had to accept equality even though we knew we did not deserve it. We must be friends or nothing. The high civility of Eliot and Ransom has almost disappeared from the republic of letters. Its disappearance means the reduction of the republic to a raw democracy of competition and aggression, or of 'vanity and impudence'. (I borrow the phrase from I. A. Richards's moving tribute to his old friend.)

This postscript – or let me call it a meditation after all – has been difficult to write. I have not been consistent in my attempt to distinguish Tom Eliot from T. S. Eliot; perhaps I should not have tried. As I look back upon the thirty-six years of our friendship I see that Tom gradually emerged from T. S., forming a double image of a unified mind and sensibility. I first met him in London in 1928, at one of the *Criterion* luncheons, to which Herbert Read had invited me and to which Frank Morley took me. There had been some formal correspondence as early as 1923 concerning some of my early poems which he had declined to publish in *The Criterion*. Years later, in 1956, when he was my guest in Minneapolis, I showed him his first letter to me in which he said that I ought to try to 'simplify' myself – advice I was never able to take, try as I would. When he had finished reading the letter, with that sober attention that he always gave to the most trivial request of a friend, looking over his spectacles, he said: 'It seems awfully pompous and condescending'; and then he laughed. His laugh was never hearty; it was something between a chuckle and a giggle; and now he was laughing both at himself and at me – at me for what he evidently considered the absurdity of keeping a letter of his all those years.

In the autumn of 1958 I was at tea with him and his wife Valerie at their flat in Kensington Court Gardens. I arrived a little late and mumbling an apology said that I had had a late lunch with The Honorable —. He was a member of a millionaire American family that had migrated to England in the seventies or eighties and had been ennobled. Tom (not T. S.) smiled and glanced at his wife. He said: '*We* had not heard of *them* before the War between the States.' I suppose I must explain this sectional joke. Tom Eliot, as everybody knows, was of New England origin, and would not have called that war the War between the States had I not been present. He was telling his wife and me that he thought those people 'newcomers', but he was slyly attributing the prejudice to me as a Southerner who might be supposed to take an unfavourable view of New York millionaires. I cannot think of a better example of the complex simplicity of his humour; and British as he became in many ways, his humour was unmistakably American.

ALLEN TATE

THE WORKS OF T. S. ELIOT

POETRY

Prufrock and Other Observations
The Waste Land
Poems, 1909–1925
Journey of the Magi
A Song for Simeon
Animula
Ash-Wednesday
Marina
Triumphal March
Collected Poems, 1909–1935
Old Possum's Book of Practical Cats
East Coker
Burnt Norton
The Dry Salvages
Little Gidding
Later Poems, 1925–1935
Four Quartets
The Cultivation of Christmas Trees
Collected Poems, 1909–1962

DRAMA

Sweeney Agonistes
The Rock
Murder in the Cathedral
The Family Reunion
The Cocktail Party
The Confidential Clerk
The Elder Statesman
Collected Plays

ESSAYS AND BELLES–LETTRES

Knowledge and Experience in the Philosophy
of F. H. Bradley

THE WORKS OF T. S. ELIOT

The Sacred Wood
Homage to John Dryden
For Lancelot Andrewes
Dante
Selected Essays, 1917–1932
The Use of Poetry and the Use of Criticism
Elizabethan Essays
Notes toward a Definition of Culture
On Poetry and Poets
Elizabethan Dramatists
To Criticize the Critic

ADDRESSES AND OTHER BRIEF PIECES

Ezra Pound, His Metric and Poetry
Shakespeare and the Stoicism of Seneca
Thoughts after Lambeth
Charles Whibley: A Memoir
After Strange Gods
The Idea of a Christian Society
The Classics and the Man of Letters
The Music of Poetry
Reunion and Destruction
What Is a Classic?
From Poe to Valéry
Milton
Poetry and Drama
American Literature and the American Language
Religious Drama
Frontiers of Criticism
The Literature of Politics
The Value and Use of Cathedrals in England Today
Address at the Memorial Service of
William Collin Brooks
Geoffrey Faber, 1889–1961
George Herbert

NOTES ON CONTRIBUTORS

I. A. Richards British linguist, poet, critic. University Professor Emeritus at Harvard University.

Sir Herbert Read British art historian, poet, man of letters.

Stephen Spender British poet, former consultant in poetry at Library of Congress. Professor at Northwestern University.

Bonamy Dobrée British author and critic. Professor Emeritus of English Literature at University of Leeds.

Ezra Pound American poet. Awarded the Bollingen Prize in Poetry.

Frank Morley American author, editor, publisher. One of the founding directors of Faber & Faber, London.

Cecil Day Lewis British poet and novelist. Has been Professor of Poetry at Oxford University and Charles Eliot Norton Professor of Poetry at Harvard University.

E. Martin Browne Producer in London and New York of all the plays of T. S. Eliot.

John Crowe Ransom American poet and critic. Editor of *The Kenyon Review* 1939–59.

Helen Gardner British critic. Merton Professor at Oxford University.

Robert Speaight British actor, director, and man of letters. Fellow of the Royal Society of Literature.

Conrad Aiken American poet and critic. Awarded the Bollingen Prize, Pulitzer Prize, National Book Award for his poetry. Member of the American Academy of Arts and Letters.

Leonard Unger American critic and poet. Professor Emeritus at University of Minnesota.

Frank Kermode British critic. Co-editor of *Encounter*. Professor of American Literature at University of Bristol.

Robert Richman American poet and critic. President of the Institute of Contemporary Arts. Former editor of *The New Republic*.

G. Wilson Knight British author and critic. Professor Emeritus of the University of Leeds.

NOTES ON CONTRIBUTORS

Mario Praz Italian critic. Professor Emeritus of American Literature at University of Rome.

Austin Warren American critic. Professor of English at University of Michigan.

Wallace Fowlie American critic. Professor of French Literature at Duke University.

Cleanth Brooks American critic and scholar. Professor of English at Yale University.

Janet Adam Smith British critic and biographer. Has been Literary Editor of *The New Statesman* and Visiting Professor at Barnard College.

Robert Giroux Editor-in-chief and vice-president of the publishing house of Farrar, Straus and Giroux.

Francis Noel Lees British critic. Senior Lecturer in English Literature at University of Manchester.

H. S. Davies Fellow at St John's College, Cambridge.

B. Rajan Indian critic, editor, and novelist. Professor of English, University of Windsor, Windsor, Ontario, Canada.

Neville Braybrooke British critic, editor, man of letters.

Allen Tate American poet, critic, and editor. Professor of English at University of Minnesota. Member of the American Academy of Arts and Letters.

ACKNOWLEDGEMENTS

The publishers wish to express their appreciation to *The Sewanee Review* in whose pages all of this material orginally appeared.

All references to and quotations from Mr Eliot's letters are with the kind permission of Valerie Eliot.

The quotations from the works of T. S. Eliot are reprinted by permission of Faber & Faber Ltd. (London); Farrar, Straus and Giroux Inc. (New York), especially for *The Elder Statesman*; and Harcourt, Brace and World Inc. (New York), especially for *Collected Poems: 1909–1962, Four Quartets, Murder in the Cathedral, The Family Reunion, The Cocktail Party* and *The Confidential Clerk*. 'Gerontion' from *Collected Poems: 1909–1962* by T. S. Eliot, copyright, 1936, by Harcourt, Brace and World, Inc; copyright © 1963, 1964, by T. S. Eliot.

The seven lines of *Sweeney's Round* in the essay by Bonamy Dobrée are quoted by permission of Dr Orlo Williams, whose copyright it is.

MORE ABOUT PENGUINS
AND PELICANS

Penguinews, which appears every month, contains details of all the new books issued by Penguins as they are published. From time to time it is supplemented by *Penguins in Print*, which is a complete list of all books published by Penguins which are in print. (There are well over three thousand of these.)

A specimen copy of *Penguinews* will be sent to you free on request, and you can become a subscriber for the price of the postage. For a year's issues (including the complete lists) please send 25p if you live in the United Kingdom, or 50p if you live elsewhere. Just write to Dept EP, Penguin Books Ltd, Harmondsworth, Middlesex, enclosing a cheque or postal order, and your name will be added to the mailing list.

Some other books published by Penguins are described on the following pages.

Note: *Penguinews* and *Penguins in Print* are not available in the U.S.A. or Canada

Penguin Modern Classics

THE FATHERS

Allen Tate

'A work of great formal beauty, the product of a most distinguished mind' – Walter Allen

Lacy Buchan, an old man obsessed by events in his boyhood, recalls the vividly contrasting characters of his father and brother-in-law; a contrast which symbolizes the break-up of the Buchans' feudal way of life caused by the American Civil War.

Major Buchan is a 'great gentleman', a South Virginian landowner governed by the outworn traditions of intricate courtliness; an anti-secessionist whose Negroes are part of his family. While George Posey is impulsive and violent, ready to sell his servants to raise a fast buck; a man without a code, an agent of destruction . . .

Not for sale in the U.S.A. or Canada

FOUR MODERN
VERSE PLAYS

In 1935 E. Martin Browne, the editor of this volume, produced T. S. Eliot's *Murder in the Cathedral* and so gave the
impetus to modern verse drama. In this book he has
selected four more examples so that the reader may come to
his own assessment of this particular genre. *The Family
Reunion*, thought by many critics to be Eliot's best play,
sets out to interpret in a modern setting the scheme of
retribution of an Aeschylean tragedy. *A Phoenix Too
Frequent*, the first of Christopher Fry's plays to win acclaim,
retells in charming verse Petronius' story of the swiftly
consoled widow. Charles Williams portrays *Thomas Cranmer
of Canterbury* as a lovable, pitiable human being crushed by
spiritual conflict and historical circumstance. Donagh
MacDonagh's *Happy as Larry* is a comic fantasy of Irish
rural life – its style and rhythm are derived from the popular
street-ballads of Dublin.

*For copyright reasons this edition is not for sale in the U.S.A.
or Canada*